SmartSuite® 97

fast & easy

How to Order:

For information on quantity discounts contact the publisher: Prima Publishing, P.O. Box 1260BK, Rocklin, CA 95677-1260; (916) 632-4400. On your letterhead include information concerning the intended use of the books and the number of books you wish to purchase. For individual orders, turn to the back of this book for more information.

SmartSuite® 97

fast & easy

Sharon Podlin

PRIMA PUBLISHING

P is a registered trademark of Prima Publishing, a division of Prima Communications, Inc. Prima Publishing is a registered trademark of Prima Communications, Inc. Visual Learning Guides is a trademark of Prima Communications, Inc. Prima Publishing, Rocklin, California 95677.

Publisher: Matthew H. Carleson
Managing Editor: Dan J. Foster
Acquisitions Editor: Debbie Abshier
Development Editor: Kelli Crump
Project Editor: Geneil Breeze
Technical Reviewer: Jay Gillund
Interior Layout: Marian Hartsough
Cover Design: Prima Design Team
Indexer: Katherine Stimson

IMPORTANT: If you have problems installing or running SmartSuite 97, notify Lotus Development Corporation at (800) 553-4270 or on the Web at www.lotus.com. Prima Publishing cannot provide software support.

ISBN: 0-7615-1192-X

Library of Congress Catalog Card Number: 97-67392

Printed in the United States of America

98 99 HH 10 9 8 7 6 5 4 3 2

This book is dedicated to my husband, Mark,
who supports me in everything I do,
and my son, Hunter,
who is the joy of my life.

Acknowledgments

I would like to thank Debbie Abshier for giving me the chance to write this book. It was an opportunity that I had been looking forward to for a long time. I would also like to acknowledge Kelli Crump for her enthusiasm for this project. And last but not least, thanks to the unsung heroes of any book, the editors. As any writer knows, a book is only as good as the editors who reviewed it.

About the Author

Sharon Podlin is a graduate of the University of Texas and president of PTSI, a consulting firm specializing in the development and presentation of computer training courses. Sharon has more than 15 years in the industry and has worked primarily with Fortune 100 companies including J. C. Penney, Hyatt International Hotels, and United Airlines. She has worked with Lotus products since the ancient days of 1-2-3 back in the early 1980s. She can be reached via CompuServe at podlin@compuserve.com.

Contents at a Glance

Contents at a Glance

PART VIII APPENDIXES 281

Introduction

This new Visual Learning Guide from Prima Publishing will help you use the many and varied features of Lotus's popular SmartSuite product. SmartSuite is designed to answer most of your personal and professional computing needs. It provides you with a word processor, worksheet program, database manager, personal calendar/contact management system, and presentation graphics program.

The problem with a program that provides you with a suite of products is that so many features are available you may feel overwhelmed. Visual Learning Guides teach you with a step-by-step approach, clear language, and color illustrations of exactly what you will see on your screen. The *SmartSuite 97 Visual Learning Guide* provides the tools you need to successfully tackle the potentially overwhelming challenge of learning to use SmartSuite 97. You will be able to quickly tap into the program's user-friendly integrated design and feature-rich environment.

WHO SHOULD READ THIS BOOK?

The easy-to-follow, highly visual nature of this book makes it the perfect learning tool for a beginning computer user. However, it is also ideal for those who are new to this version of SmartSuite, or those who feel comfortable with computers and software, but have never used these types of programs before.

In addition, anyone using a software application always needs an occasional reminder about the steps required to perform a particular task. By using the *SmartSuite 97 Visual Learning Guide*, any level of user can look up steps for a task quickly without having to plow through pages of descriptions.

In short, this book can be used by the beginning-to-intermediate computer user as a learning tool or as a step-by-step task reference.

ADDED ADVICE TO MAKE YOU A PRO

You'll notice that this book uses steps and keeps explanations to a minimum to help you learn faster. Included in the book are a few elements that provide some additional comments to help you master the program, without encumbering your progress through the steps:

- Tips often offer shortcuts when performing an action, or a hint about a feature that might make your work in SmartSuite quicker and easier.
- Notes give you a bit of background or additional information about a feature, or advice about how to use the feature in your day-to-day activities.

In addition, three helpful appendixes will show you how to use SmartSuite to create a professional letter, complete a budget, and create a meeting presentation.

Read and enjoy this Visual Learning Guide. It is certainly the fastest and easiest way to learn Lotus SmartSuite 97.

PART I

Learning Lotus SmartSuite 97

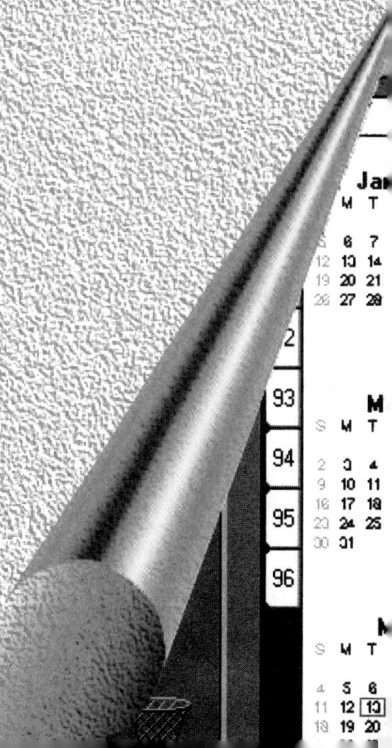

1 Getting Started with SmartSuite 97

SmartSuite 97 is designed to meet the majority of your everyday software needs. Using SmartSuite, you can perform a multitude of tasks including creating letters, generating reports, tracking your budget, producing a slide show presentation, and designing a database to track your videotape collection. SmartSuite is versatile yet powerful enough to be useful to both the office professional and the home user. Before you start, you'll want to familiarize yourself with the components that make up SmartSuite. In this chapter, you'll learn how to:

- Understand the parts of SmartSuite
- Use the SmartCenter
- Get help on SmartSuite functions and features

UNDERSTANDING THE PARTS OF SMARTSUITE

SmartSuite is not just one application. It is a group of several different applications. Each application in SmartSuite is designed to have a specific function. The following sections explain what these roles are.

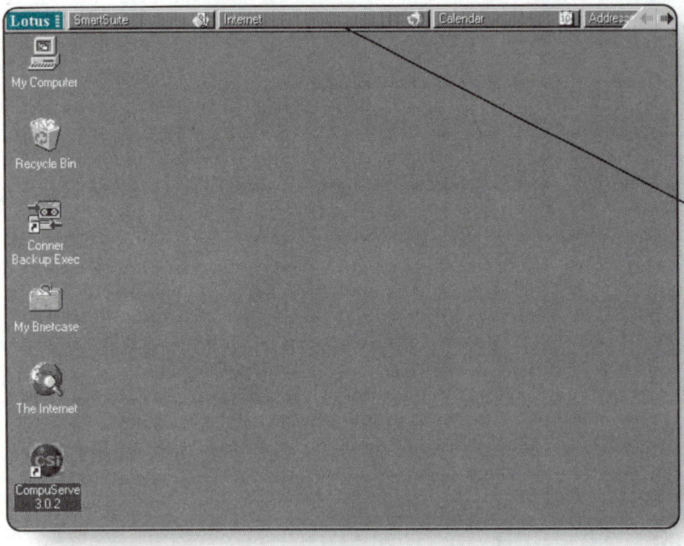

SmartCenter

SmartCenter acts as a hub for the SmartSuite applications. Using SmartCenter's drawers and folders you can organize your work.

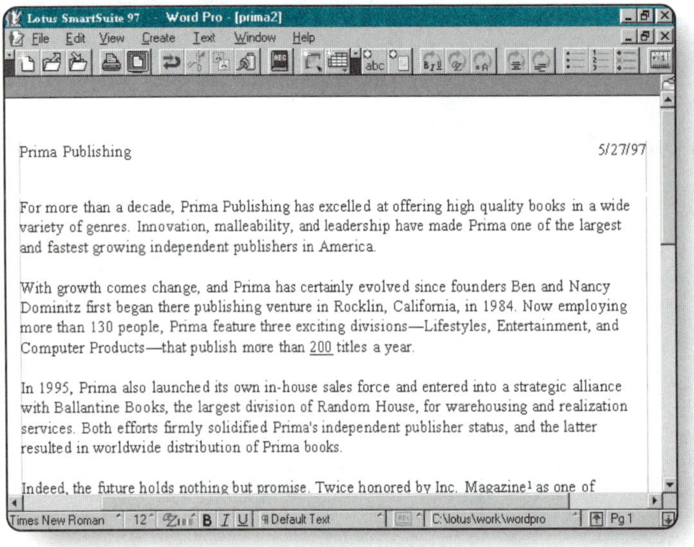

Word Pro

Word Pro is SmartSuite's word processor. This is the tool you'll use when you need to work with text. Word Pro can create a wide range of documents including letters, memos, faxes, reports, newsletters, and calendars.

Word Pro is a WYSIWYG (What You See Is What You Get) word processor. This means that the document on the screen looks like the printed document.

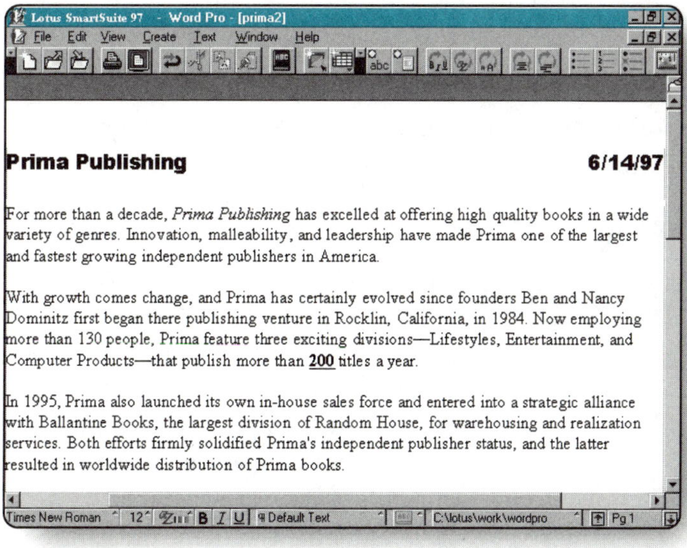

You can see immediately the impact, for example, of making text bold or changing its font on the screen. This makes Word Pro great for working with any kind of document. You can see what adding a large font title would do to the appearance of your document. Or you might want to experiment with various locations for the placement of a graphic. Word Pro makes this easy for you to do.

1-2-3

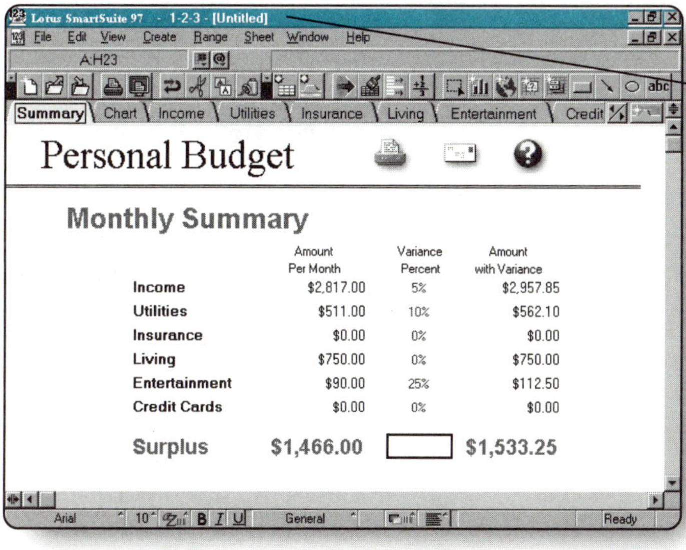

Lotus 1-2-3 is an easy to use, powerful spreadsheet application. Whenever you need to work with numbers, 1-2-3 is the application to use. Some of the uses for 1-2-3 include creating budgets, proposals, financial statements, and charts.

Using 1-2-3, you can enter the numbers you want to work with, perform calculations with them, and then create a chart from them if you want. And all these tasks are easy to do using 1-2-3.

Freelance Graphics

In today's visual world, how you present something is almost as important as the information itself. When you are giving a formal presentation, your audience expects professional-looking graphics and text that is not only informative but visually stimulating. This is where Freelance Graphics comes into play. Freelance Graphics makes creating quality presentations a matter of simply using your mouse to select format options and using your keyboard to enter the text of the presentation. If you have never created a presentation using a computer before, you are going to love using Freelance Graphics!

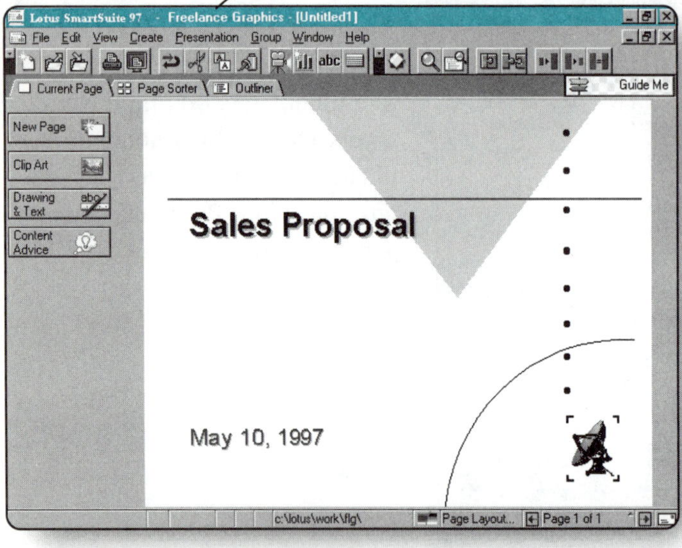

Approach

Approach is SmartSuite's database application. A database application is used to store and organize information. Examples of database uses include keeping a home inventory; managing a collection such as videos, baseball cards, or books; and tracking employee information.

This short list gives you an idea of the many uses for Approach. Not only can you use Approach to store this kind of information, but Approach also helps you sort and organize the information.

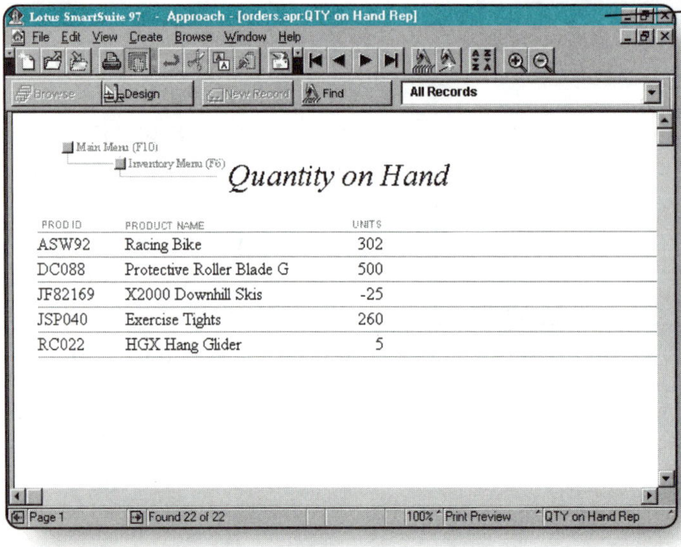

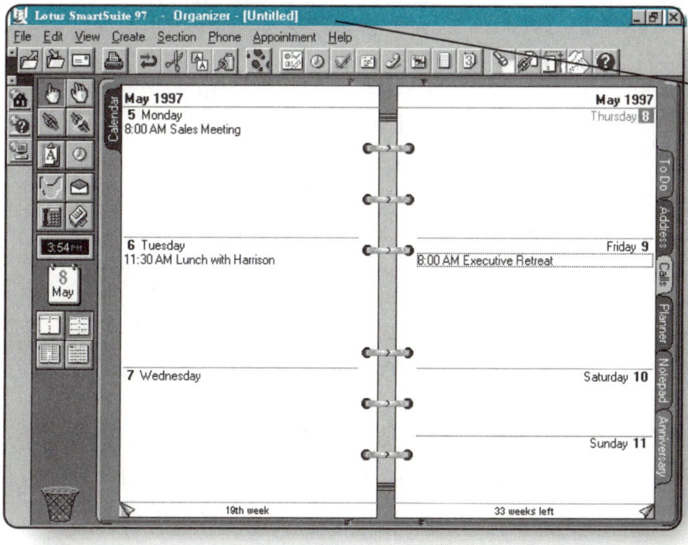

Organizer

To keep yourself organized, you may have one book to track your appointments and another to track names, addresses, and phone numbers. You may have a to do list as well. Organizer lets you manage all this information in one location on your computer. Using Organizer, you can track appointments, contact information, to do tasks, and phone calls.

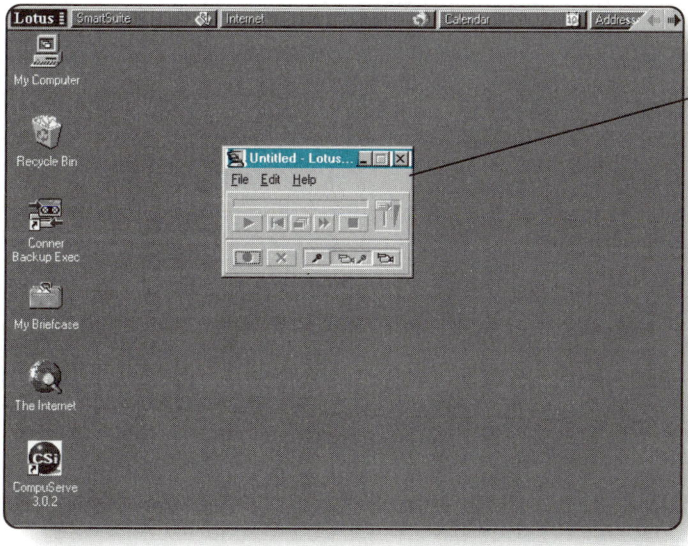

ScreenCam

ScreenCam is a tool that allows you to record your screen actions such as mouse movements and dialog box selections. Using ScreenCam, you can record a procedure, and a fellow coworker can play the procedure back on his or her computer. This is a great training tool.

USING SMARTCENTER

SmartCenter automatically starts when you turn on your computer after you have installed SmartSuite. SmartCenter allows you to do a variety of tasks including starting SmartSuite applications, opening files created with SmartSuite applications, accessing the Internet, opening and using your calendar and address book, as well as working with reminder lists.

Working with Drawers

SmartCenter is organized like a file cabinet. The first level of organization is the drawer. Just like drawers in a real file cabinet, SmartCenter drawers hold folders. SmartCenter has several drawers already set up for you: SmartSuite, Internet (this drawer only installs if you have Internet software already installed on your system), Calendar, Addresses, Reminders, Reference, Business Productivity, and Suite Help.

Using Drawers

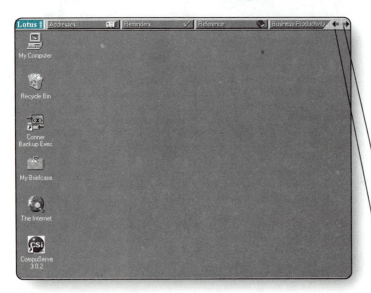

You may not see all the drawers found in the preceding list. This is because they can't all fit on your screen at the same time. To view the other drawers, use the scroll buttons found on the right end of the SmartCenter bar.

1. **Click** on the **right scroll button**. Additional drawers will be listed in SmartCenter.

2. **Click** on the **left scroll button**. The drawer listing will be scrolled back to the left.

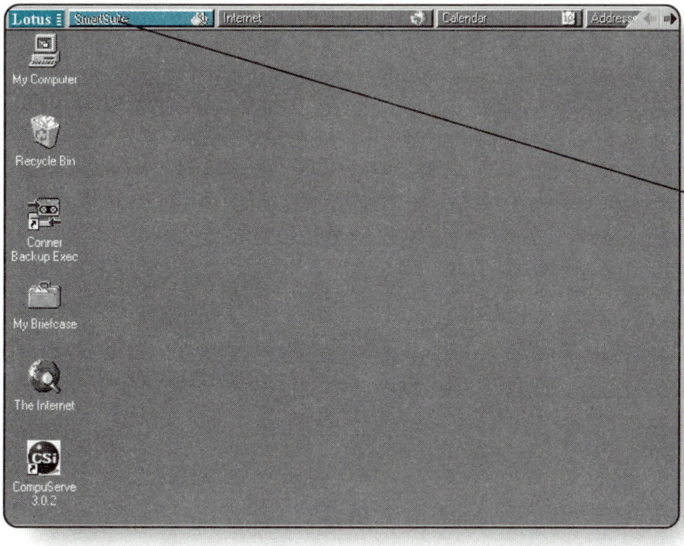

Each of these drawers contains folders. To view the folders in a drawer, you must open the drawer.

3. Click on the **drawer handle**. The folders in this drawer will appear. Folders come in different colors, and each folder has its name listed on its tab.

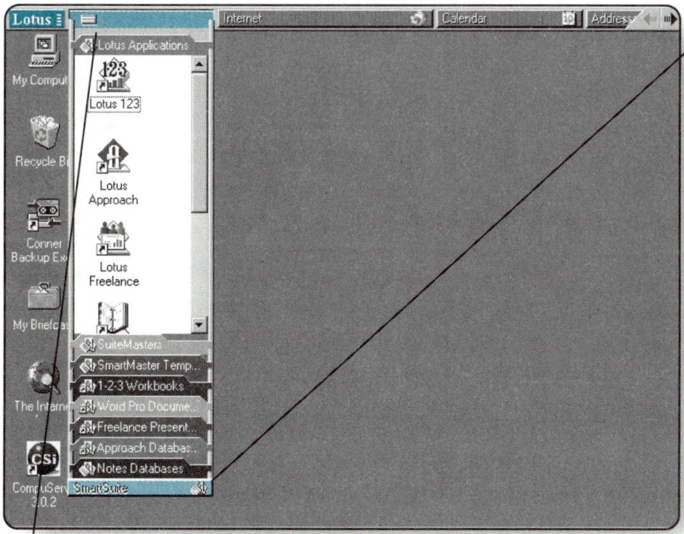

4. Click on the **drawer handle**. The drawer will close.

TIP

You can also click the gray bar located at the top of the opened drawer to close the drawer.

Working with Folders

Each SmartCenter drawer has several folders in it. Some of the folders act like those found in real file cabinets in that they store documents. Others have specialized designs so that they act as calendars or address books. And some of the folders are actually tools that allow you to work with the Internet and use the Thesaurus. The steps for accessing all these types of folders are identical.

1. **Click** on the **drawer handle** of the drawer where the folder is located. The folders located in that drawer will appear.

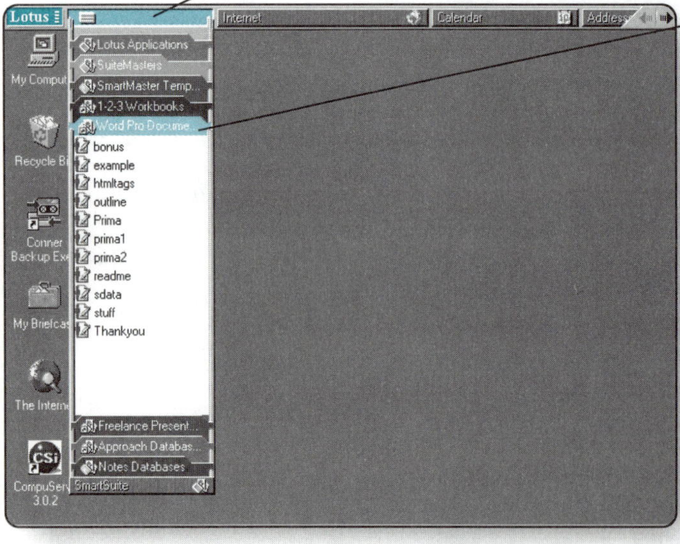

2. **Click** on the **folder tab** of the folder you want to work with. The folder will open.

After you open the folder, the folder type will determine your action. For example, if the folder contains documents, you can double-click the icon representing the document to open the document. If the folder is a calendar folder, you can click on a time slot to enter an appointment. After you are finished working with the contents of a drawer, it is a good habit to close the drawer so that your desktop will not be too cluttered.

GETTING HELP

SmartSuite provides you with a variety of ways to get help on using the many features available to you. All the applications in SmartSuite including the SmartCenter have online help. This help provides you with step-by-step instructions for performing a variety of tasks.

Online Help can be accessed from the SmartCenter or from any of the SmartSuite Applications.

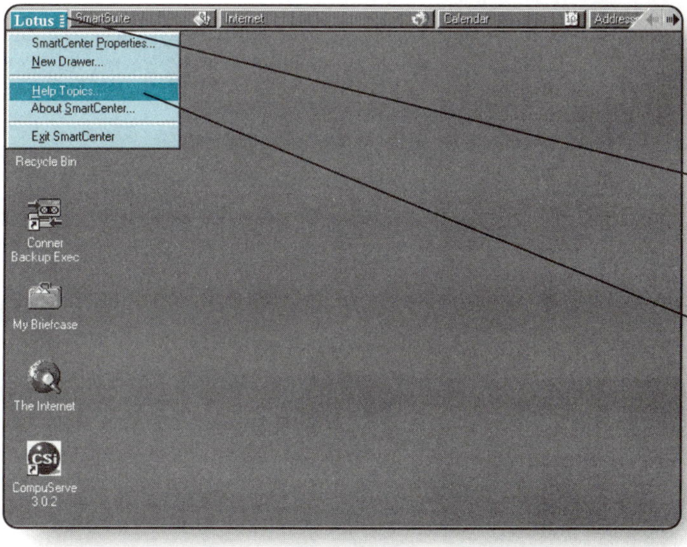

Accessing Help Topics from the SmartCenter

1. Click on the **SmartCenter menu button**. The SmartCenter menu will appear.

2. Click on **Help Topics**. The Help Topics dialog box will open.

Accessing Help Topics from a SmartSuite Application

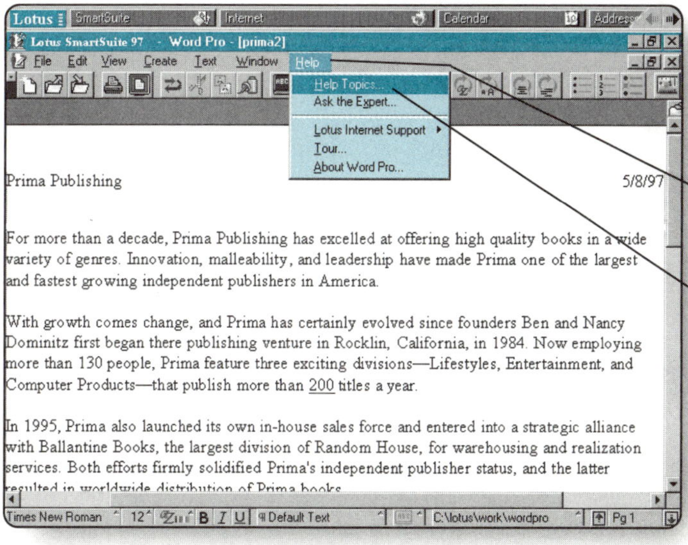

When you are working with any of the SmartSuite applications, you can access help through the Help menu.

1. Click on **Help**. The Help menu will appear.

2. Click on **Help Topics**. The Help Topics dialog box will open.

Using Help Contents

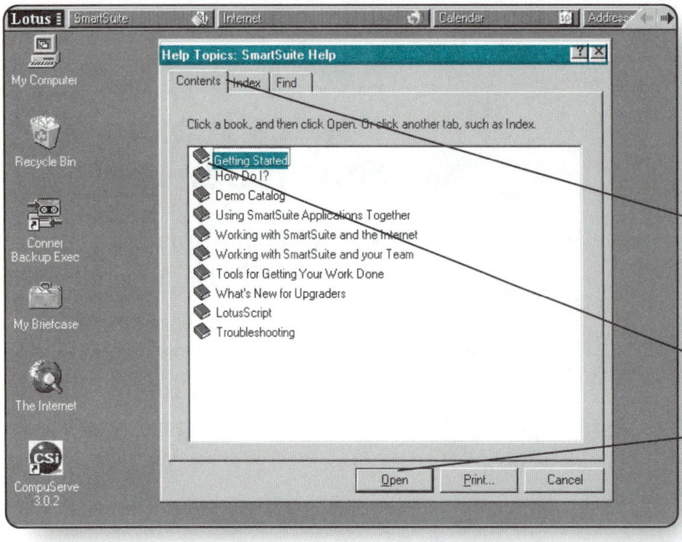

The Help Contents page of the Help Topics dialog box presents help information in a book-like format so that you can browse available topics.

1. **Click** on the **Contents tab** of the Help Topics dialog box. The tab will come to the front.
2. **Click** on a **book icon**.
3. **Click** on **Open**. Additional topics and, in some cases, books will appear.

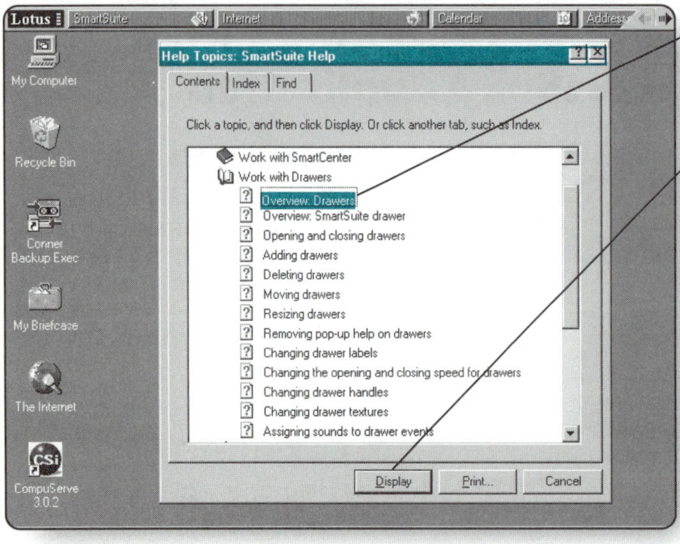

4. **Click** on the **topic** you want to view.
5. **Click** on **Display**. The SmartSuite Help window will appear.

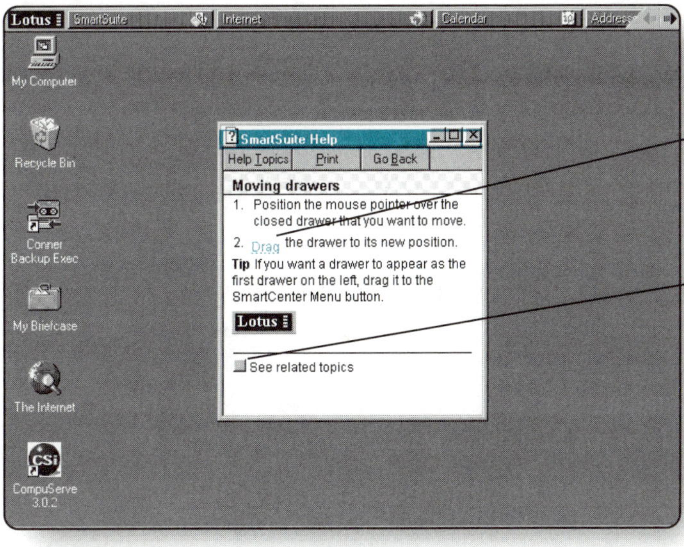

6. **Read** the **information** presented.

7. **Click** on **green underlined text** to display additional information.

8. **Click** on the **See related topics button**. The Topics Found dialog box will open.

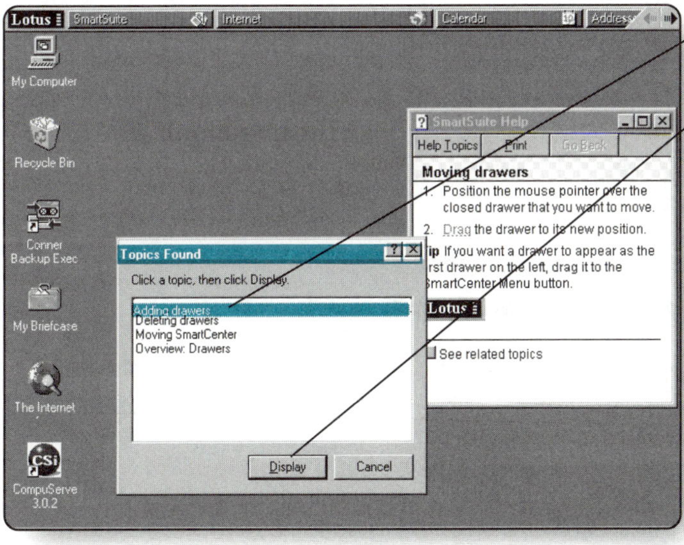

9. **Click** on a **topic**.

10. **Click** on **Display**. The SmartSuite Help window for that topic will appear.

PART I REVIEW QUESTIONS

1. **Is SmartSuite just one application?** *See "Understanding the Parts of SmartSuite" in Chapter 1*
2. **Which SmartSuite application should be used to create a presentation?** *See "Understanding the Parts of SmartSuite" in Chapter 1*
3. **Which SmartSuite application is best suited for managing your addresses?** *See "Understanding the Parts of SmartSuite" in Chapter 1*
4. **Which SmartSuite application would be the best choice for creating a report?** *See "Understanding the Parts of SmartSuite" in Chapter 1*
5. **How would you open the SmartSuite drawer?** *See "Working with Drawers" in Chapter 1*
6. **What is the difference between a drawer and a folder?** *See "Using SmartCenter" in Chapter 1*
7. **How do you get help in a SmartSuite application?** *See "Accessing Help Topics from a SmartSuite Application" in Chapter 1*
8. **What part of SmartSuite can be used to launch applications?** *See "Using SmartCenter" in Chapter 1*
9. **What would you do if you had a question about using SmartCenter?** *See "Accessing Help Topics from the SmartCenter" in Chapter 1*
10. **How would you find out about the type of help available?** *See "Using Help Contents" in Chapter 1*

PART II

Using Word Pro

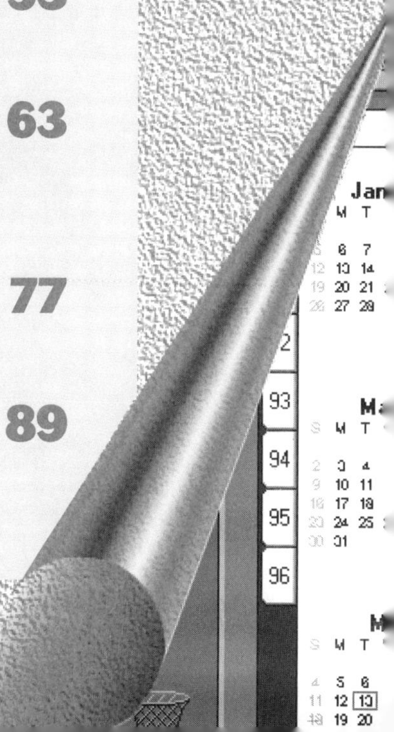

2 Creating a Simple Document

Word Pro may be able to trace its roots to the typewriter, but you'll find the typewriter is a distant relative to this word processor. When you need to create a document, you will use Word Pro. Word Pro is great for everything text based from the simplest letter to a professional-looking newsletter. You'll quickly become comfortable using its text editing capabilities. In no time you'll be adding text formatting such as bold, italic, and a variety of fonts to your documents. You'll love using features such as tables, styles, and the spell-checker to save you time and add polish to your documents. In this chapter, you'll learn how to:

- Start Word Pro
- Create a simple document
- Edit a document

STARTING WORD PRO USING THE SMARTCENTER

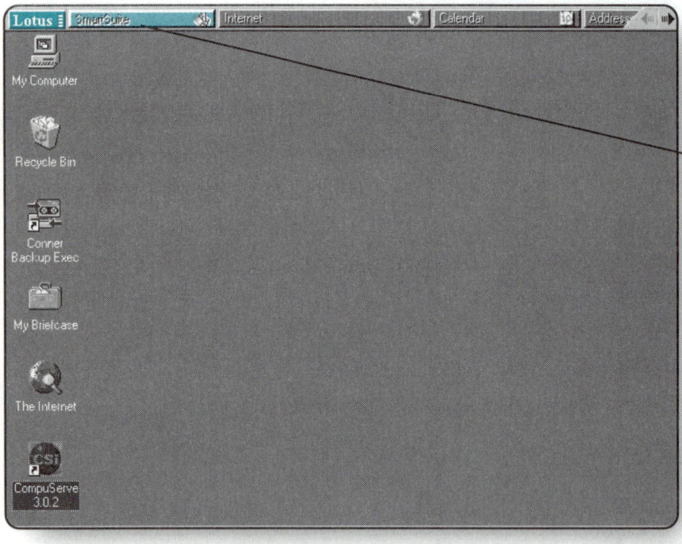

The SmartCenter makes it easy to start Word Pro and all the SmartSuite applications.

1. **Click** on the **SmartSuite drawer handle**. The drawer will open.

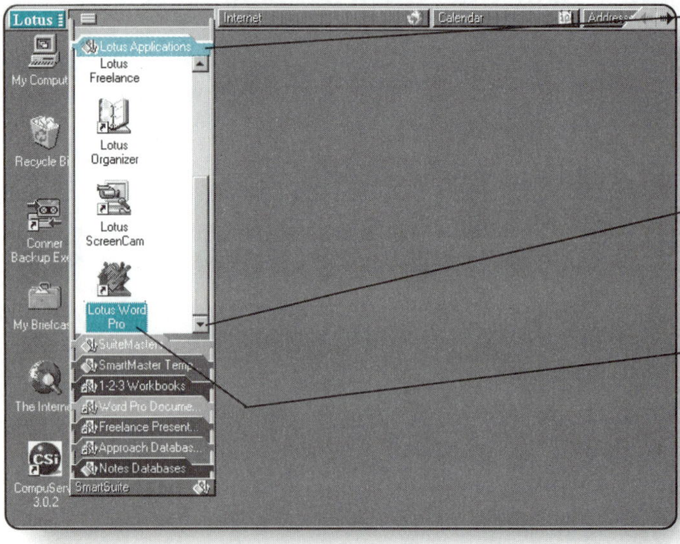

2. **Click** on the **Lotus Applications folder tab**. The contents of this folder will be displayed.

3. **Click** on the **down scroll bar arrow** until you see the Lotus Word Pro icon.

4. **Double-click** on the **Lotus Word Pro icon**. Word Pro will start, and the Welcome to Lotus Word Pro dialog box will open.

ENTERING A SIMPLE DOCUMENT

When you start the Word Pro application, the Welcome to Lotus Word Pro dialog box opens. This dialog box prompts you to select a SmartMaster to create the new document with.

Working with SmartMasters

A SmartMaster is a preformatted template that you use to create a document. Word Pro has several SmartMasters already designed and ready for you to use.

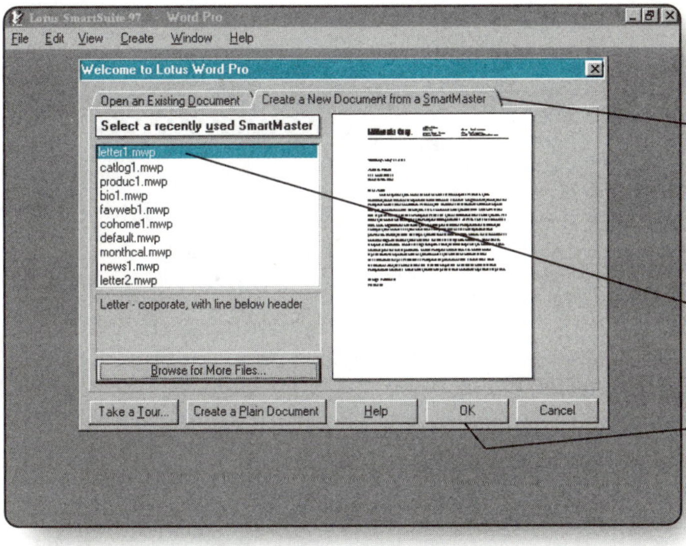

Using a SmartMaster

1. **Click** on the **Create a New Document from a SmartMaster tab**. A list of the SmartMasters will appear.

2. **Click** on the **SmartMaster** you want to use.

3. **Click** on **OK**. The new document will appear with the selected SmartMaster applied.

Entering Text in Click Here Blocks

Most SmartMasters have Click Here blocks included as part of the template. These areas are green in color and begin with the words "Click here." These blocks guide you to where to place certain types of text.

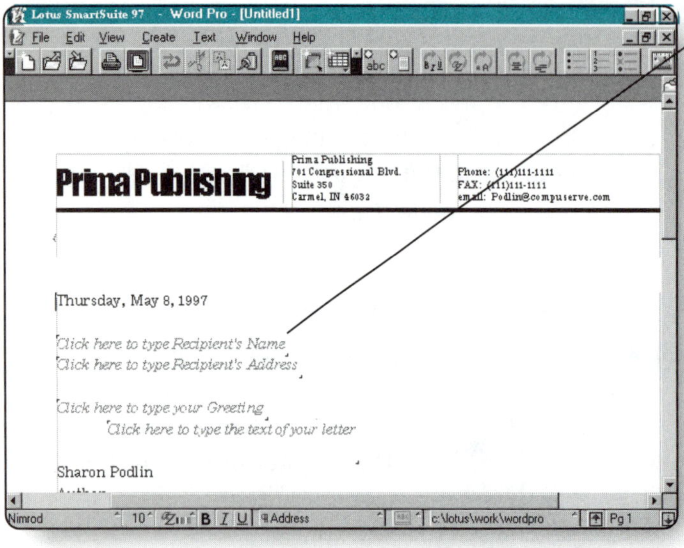

1. **Click** on the first **Click Here block** in the document. Bubble help will appear to let you know what type of information to enter for that block.
2. **Type** the **appropriate text** for the Click Here block.
3. **Press** the **Tab key**. You will be moved to the next Click Here block.
4. **Type** the **appropriate text** for the Click Here block.
5. **Repeat** the process of **typing** and **pressing** the **Tab key** until all the Click Here blocks have text typed into them.

EDITING THE DOCUMENT

Gone are the days when if you wanted to make a change to a document you had to retype it. Editing a document is simple with Word Pro.

Making Changes to Text

The greatest feature of a word processor like Word Pro is the capability to quickly and easily make changes to the text of a document.

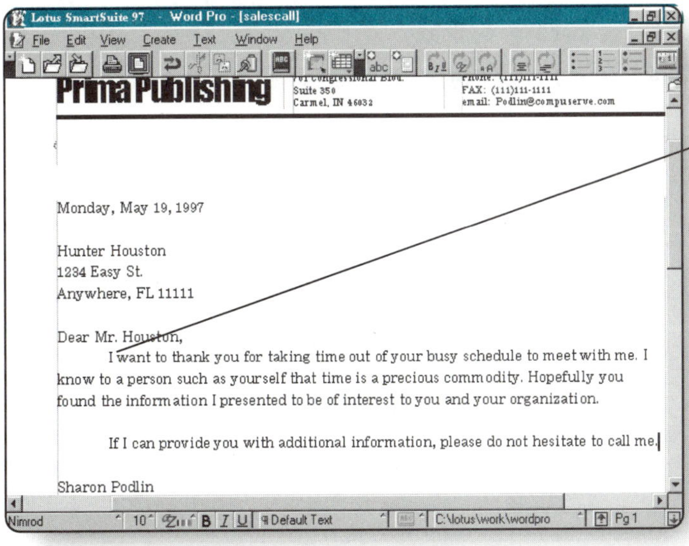

Inserting Text into a Document

1a. Click on the location where you want to insert additional text.

OR

1b. Press the **arrow keys** until the insertion point is correctly positioned.

2. Type some **text**.

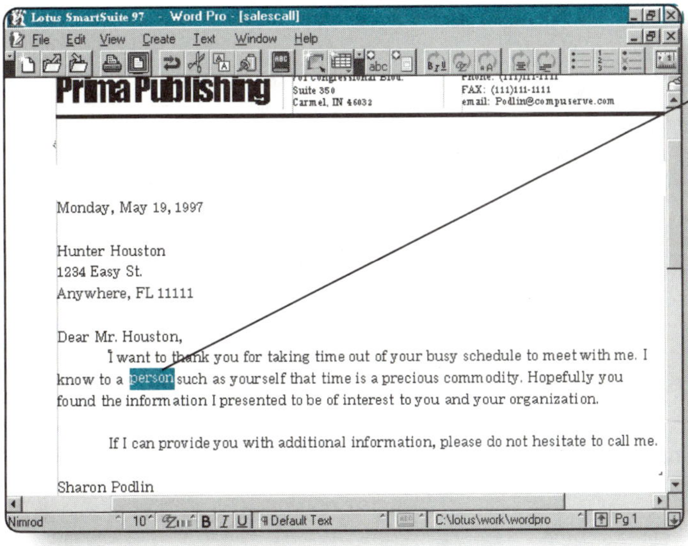

Replacing Text

1a. Click and **drag** the **mouse pointer** across the text you want to replace. The text will be highlighted.

OR

1b. Press and **hold** the **Shift key** while **pressing** an **arrow key** until the text you want to replace is highlighted.

2. Type new **text**.

TIP

To quickly highlight a single word, double-click on the word.

Navigating in a Word Pro Document

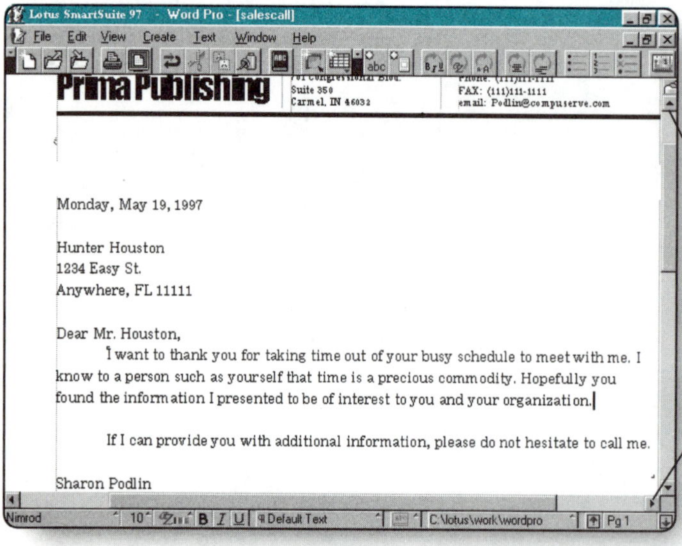

Word Pro provides several ways to move around a document quickly.

Using the Scroll Bar

1. **Click repeatedly** on the **arrow** at either end of the vertical scroll bar to move the document up and down in the window.

2. **Click repeatedly** on the **arrow** at either end of the horizontal scroll bar to move the document left or right in the window.

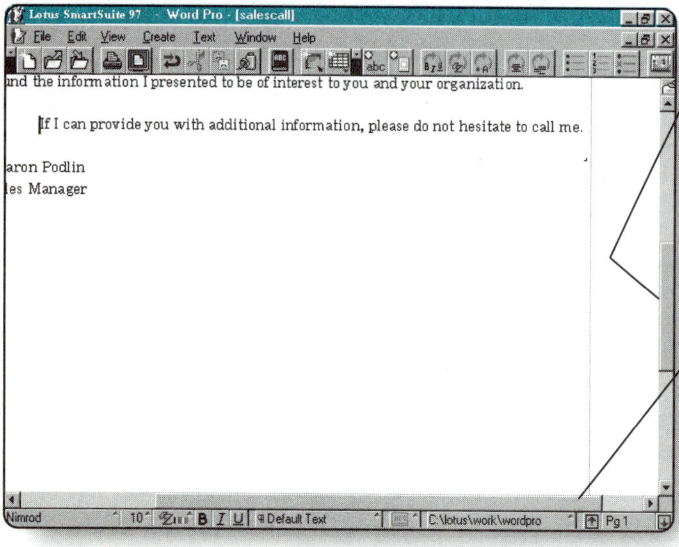

3. **Click** on the **vertical scroll box** and **hold** the **mouse button** while you **drag** box up or down. Notice that when you move the scroll box, an indicator box will appear telling you which page you're scrolling over.

4. **Click** on the **horizontal scroll box** and **hold** the **mouse button** while you **drag** box left or right.

NOTE

When you move through a document using the scroll bar, the display changes, but the insertion point does not move. You must click in the document to move the insertion point to a new location when using the scroll bar.

Using Navigation Keys

You may prefer to use your keyboard to move around in your document.

Press This Key	To Move
Ctrl+Right Arrow	Right one word
Ctrl+Left Arrow	Left one word
Home	To the beginning of a line
End	To the end of a line
Ctrl+Up Arrow	To the beginning of the paragraph
Ctrl+Down Arrow	To the beginning of the next paragraph
Page Down	Down one screen
Page Up	Up one screen
Ctrl+Home	To the beginning of the document
Ctrl+End	To the end of the document

Cutting, Copying, and Pasting Text

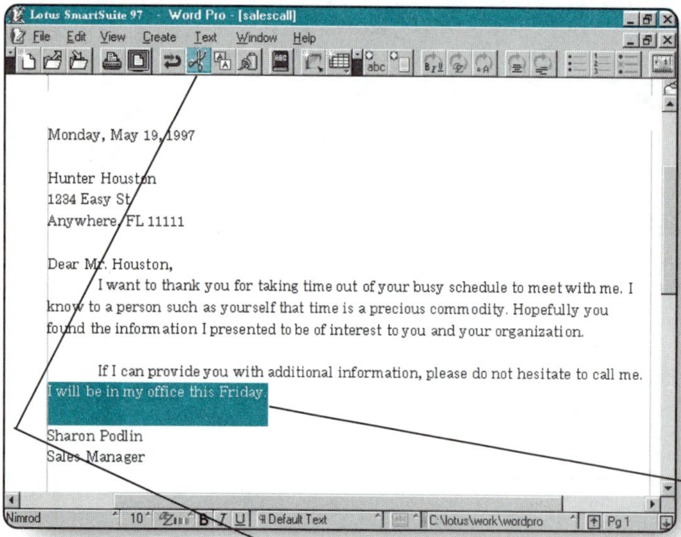

One of the advantages of a Windows-based word processor like Word Pro is its capability to let you easily move and duplicate text.

Cutting and Pasting Text

By cutting and pasting text, you can move text around in your document.

1. **Select** some **text**. The text will be highlighted.

2. **Click** on the **Cut button**. The text will be removed from the document and placed on the Clipboard.

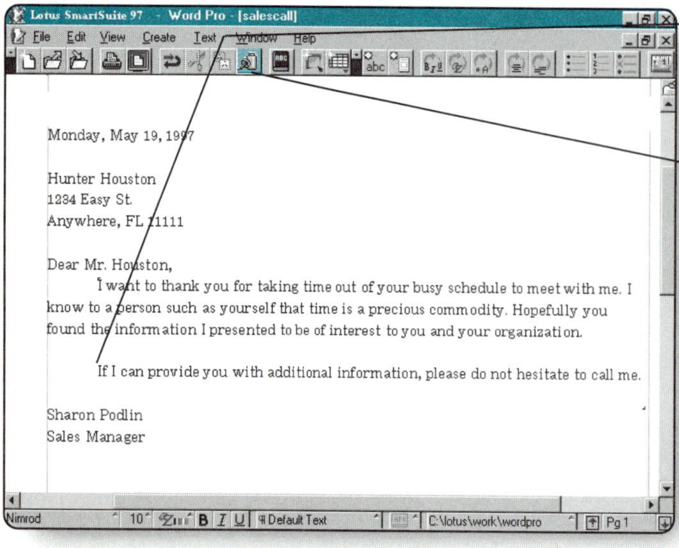

3. **Click** in the **document** where you want to move the text. The insertion point will move.

4. **Click** on the **Paste button**. The text will be copied from the Clipboard to the selected location.

Using Drag-and-Drop

A quick way to move text, if you are comfortable with your mouse, is by using Word Pro's Drag-and-Drop feature.

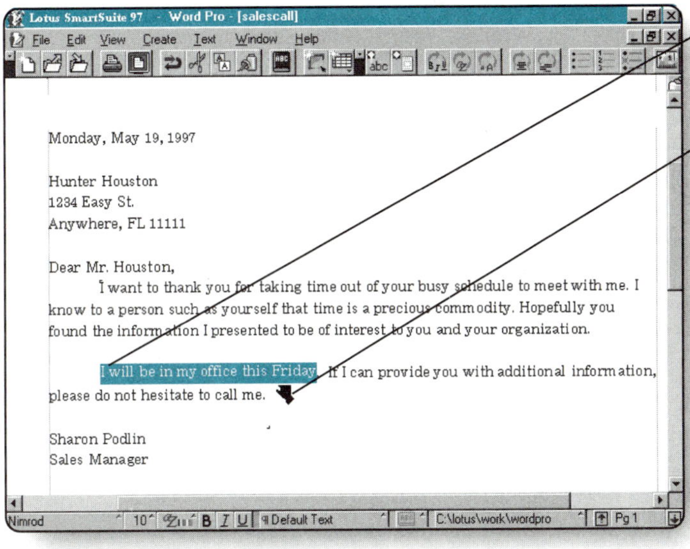

1. **Select** some **text** to move. The text will be highlighted.
2. **Position** your **mouse pointer** over the highlighted text.

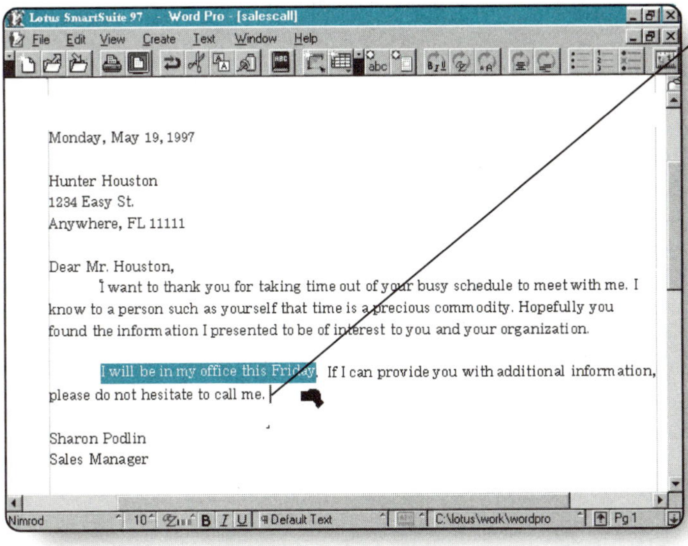

3. **Press** and **hold** the **mouse button** as you **drag** the **text** to a new location. The mouse pointer will look like a hand holding a small rectangle. The current insertion location will appear as a red vertical line.
4. **Release** the **mouse button** when you have reached the correct insertion point. The text will be inserted into the document.

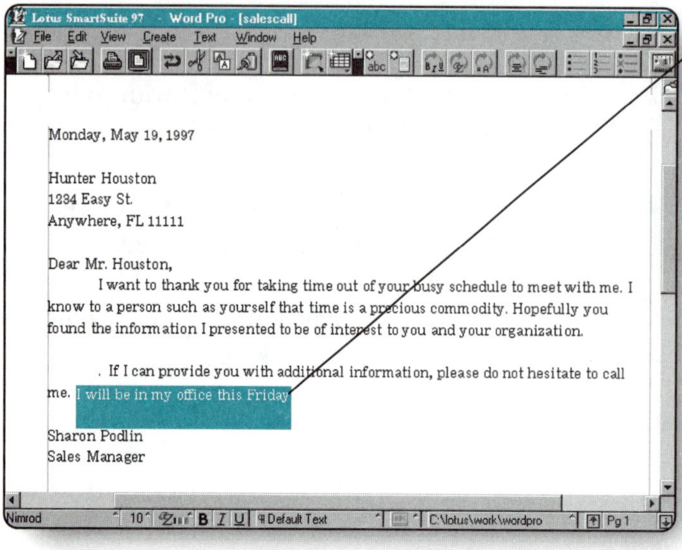

The text that is dropped into a new location in the document remains highlighted until you move the insertion point by clicking on the document or using your keyboard.

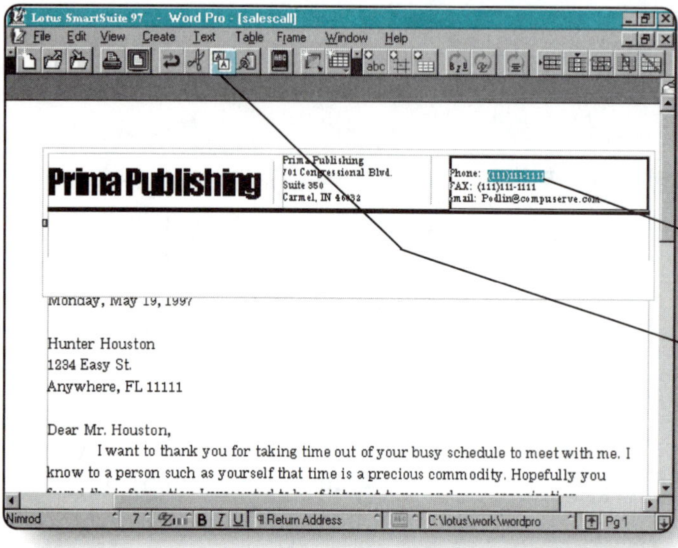

Copying and Pasting Text

If you want to reuse text you can copy it.

1. **Select** some **text**. The text will be highlighted.

2. **Click** on the **Copy button**. The highlighted text will be copied to the Clipboard.

3. **Click** in the **document** where you want to place the text. The insertion point will move.

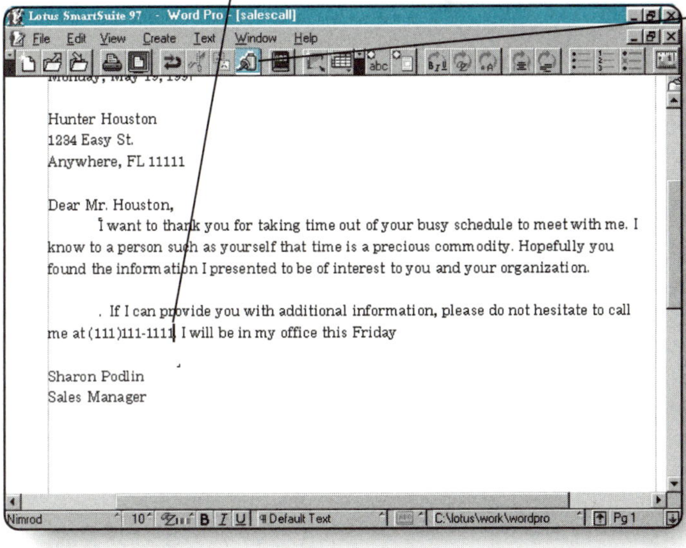

4. **Click** on the **Paste button**. The text will be copied from the Clipboard and inserted at the selected location.

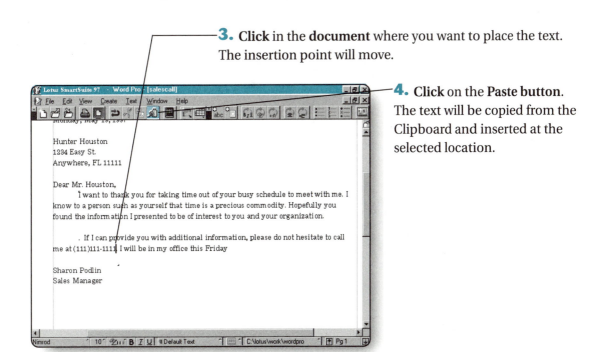

3 Saving and Printing Your Work

One of the most important things you learn to do with any application is save your work. Who wants to spend hours on a document only to lose it because it wasn't saved? Saving a document also allows you to exit from Word Pro and return to your document later so that you can work on it further. You'll also need to know how to print your work. Using Word Pro, you can create a variety of printed documents including letters, memos, faxes, and newsletters. In this chapter, you'll learn how to:

- Save a document
- Print a document
- Exit Word Pro

SAVING YOUR DOCUMENT

Let's face it. Computers are equipment, and equipment fails. Computers need electricity, and electricity goes out. This means that you should save your work often. Saving your document not only retains your work but also files it electronically for you so that your can find it and use it again at a later time.

1. Click on the **Save button**. If this is the first time you've saved the document, the Save As dialog box will open.

The Save in: drop-down list box lists the folder where the file will be saved. The default folder that appears is wordpro. If you don't want to save to this folder or you want to save your document to another disk, you can select another one. Click on the down arrow (▼) to browse.

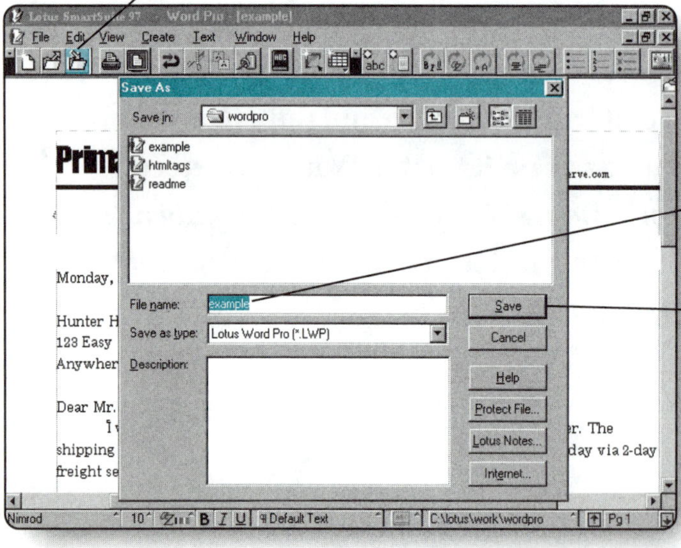

2. Type a **name** for your file in the File name: text box.

3. Click on **Save**. Your document will be saved. Word Pro automatically adds an .LWP extension to the filename. The .LWP extension indicates that this is the default file format used to save Word Pro files.

4. Click on the **Save button** regularly to continue to save your document as you work on it to ensure that you do not lose any changes you have made. The Save As dialog box will not open for this document again.

VIEWING AND PRINTING YOUR DOCUMENT

Word Pro is a WYSIWYG ("What You See Is What You Get") word processor, meaning that text and other elements such as graphics appear on the screen the same way they will look when the print out. There are viewing options you may want to use such as viewing your document full screen. You'll also need to know how to print your document.

Viewing a Document Full Screen

Viewing a Document full screen allows you to size the document so that an entire page is visible. That way, you can get an idea of how document layout settings such as margins will look on the printed document.

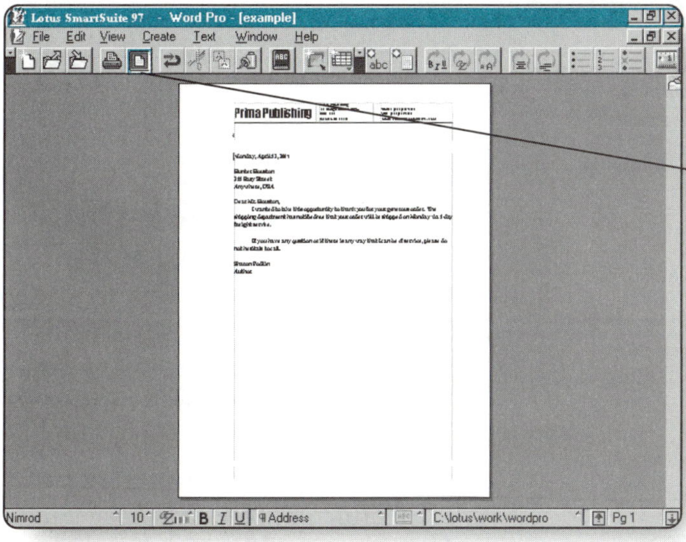

1. Click on the **Zoom to Full Page button.** The document will be sized so that an entire page is visible on the screen.

2. Click on the **Zoom to Full Page button** again. The document will be sized to display at 100% magnification.

TIP

If you want to view more text on a screen, you can change the display in a variety of ways. Click on View and then click on Zoom To. A list of available zoom options will display. These options include Margin Width, Page Width, 75%, 150%, 200%, and Custom Level.

Printing Your Document

Typically, the end result of entering a document into Word Pro is to get text onto paper.

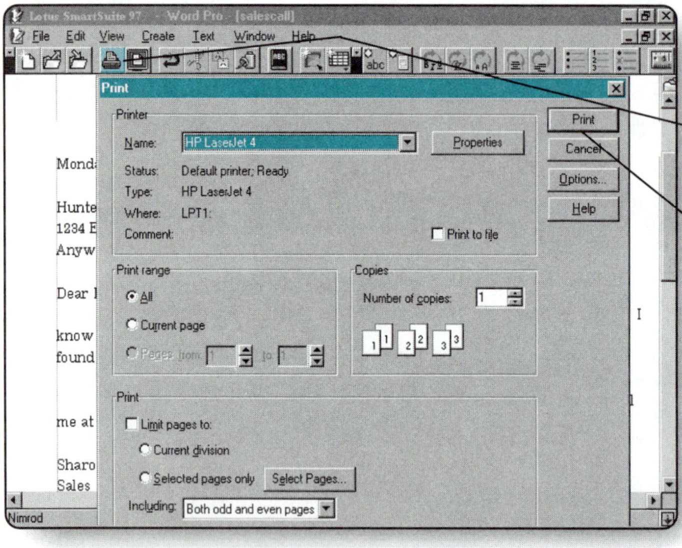

Printing with the Print Button

1. **Click** on the **Print button**. The Print dialog box will open.
2. **Click** on **Print**. One copy of the current document will be immediately sent to the printer.

Printing with the Print Dialog Box

At times, you may want to do more than simply print one copy of a document. You may want to print several copies of your document, or you may want to print only the second page. To do these types of things, you need to use the Print dialog box.

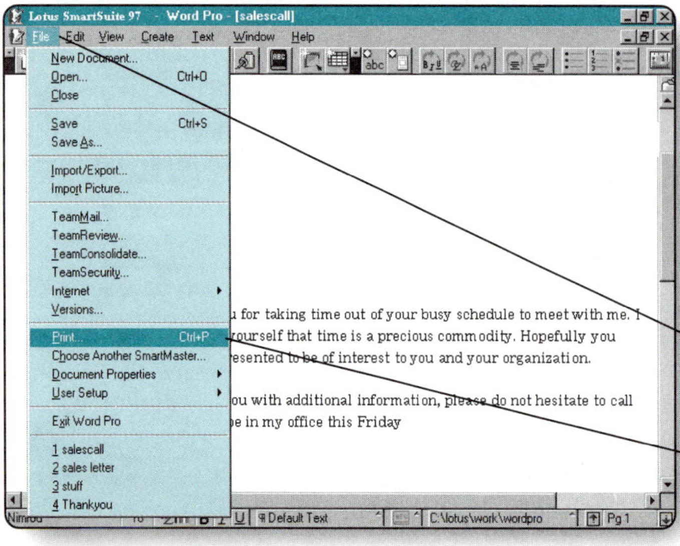

1. **Click** on **File**. The File menu will appear.
2. **Click** on **Print**. The Print dialog box will open.

3. Choose from the following **options**:

- ✦ If you are connected to more than one printer, you can choose the Name: of the printer to use for this print job. Click on the down arrow (▼) and make a selection.

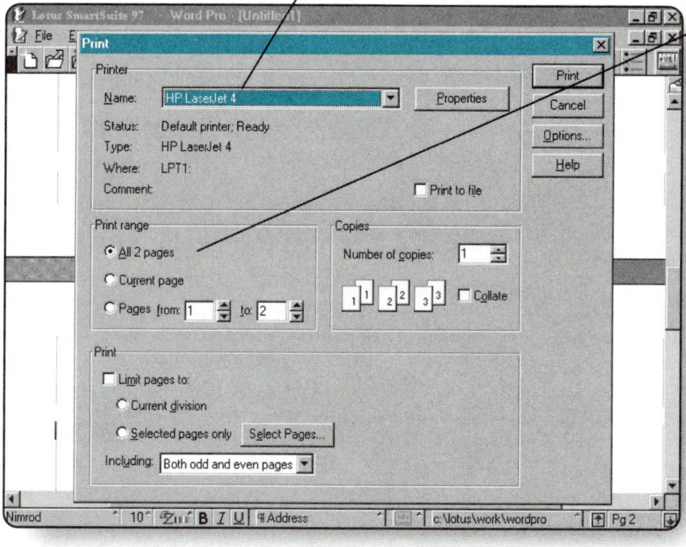

- ✦ Choose which pages of your document to print in the Print range box. You can print All, which is the preselected option. To print only the page currently displayed, click on Current page. Or if you only want to print a range of pages, click on Pages. When you click on Pages, you can select which pages to print. To select the pages to print, click on the up and down arrows (⬍) to select the beginning and ending of the range of pages to print.

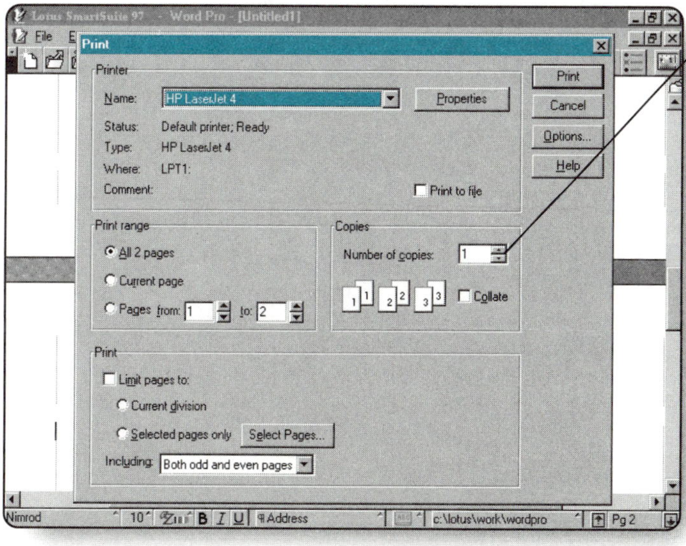

- ✦ Choose the Number of copies: to be printed by clicking on the up and down arrows (⬍) in the Copies box.

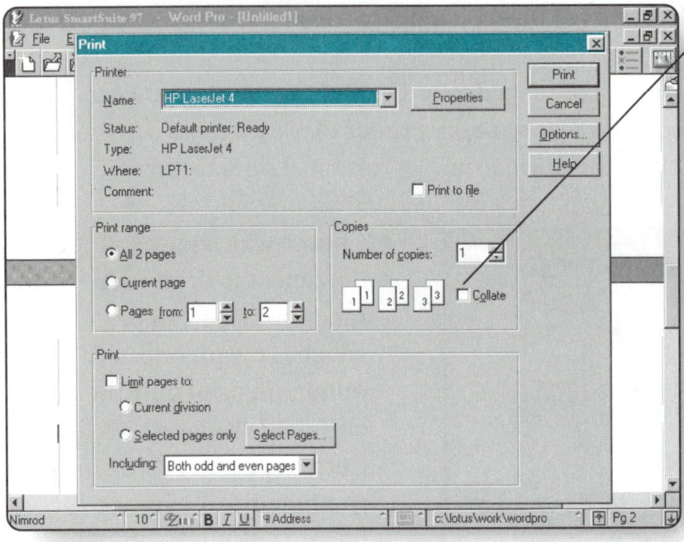

✦ Another option in the Copies box is Collate. This option is only available if there are multiple pages in your document. If you are printing more than one copy of your document, you need to decide whether you want to collate. If you ✔ Collate, pages 1, 2, 3, and so on will be printed first. Then pages 1, 2, 3, and so on will print again. This continues until all the requested copies are printed. If Collate is not checked, all the requested copies of page 1 will print, followed by all the copies of page 2, and so on.

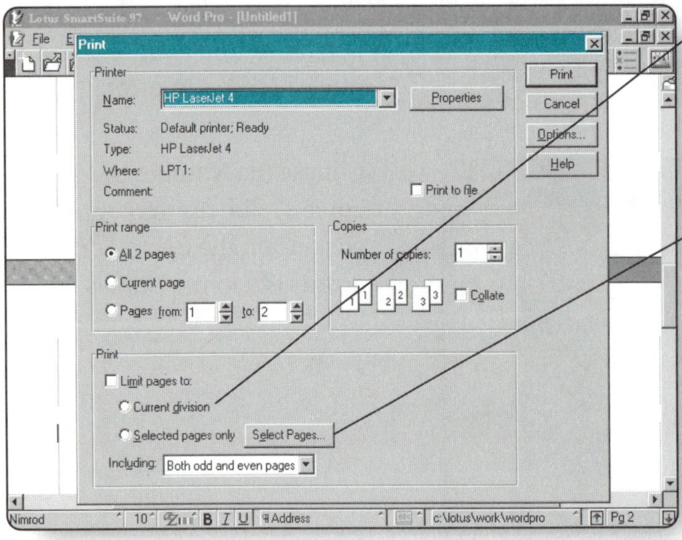

✦ If you have divided your document into divisions, you can print only the current division. Click on Current division in the Print box.

✦ You can print some of the pages in your document even if they are not in consecutive order. Click on Select Pages in the Print box. The Select Pages dialog box will open. Enter the pages you want to print in the List the pages box. Click on OK.

✦ To print just odd pages or just even pages use the Including: box. Click on the down arrow (▼) and make a selection.

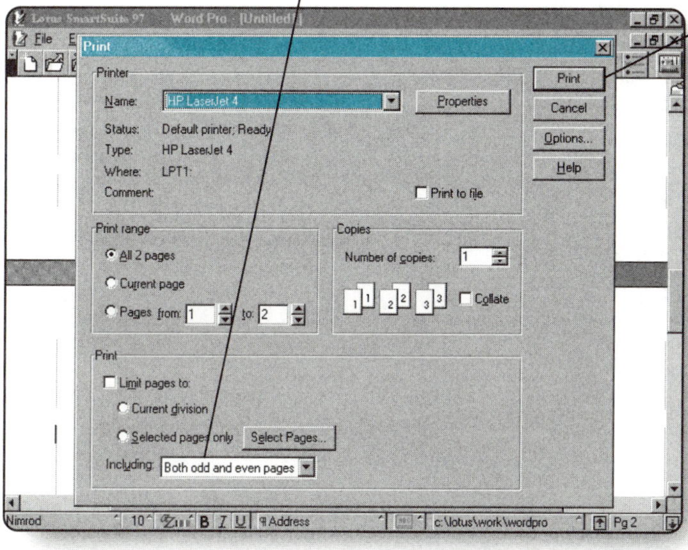

4. **Click** on **Print**, after you have made your selections. The pages will be sent to the printer.

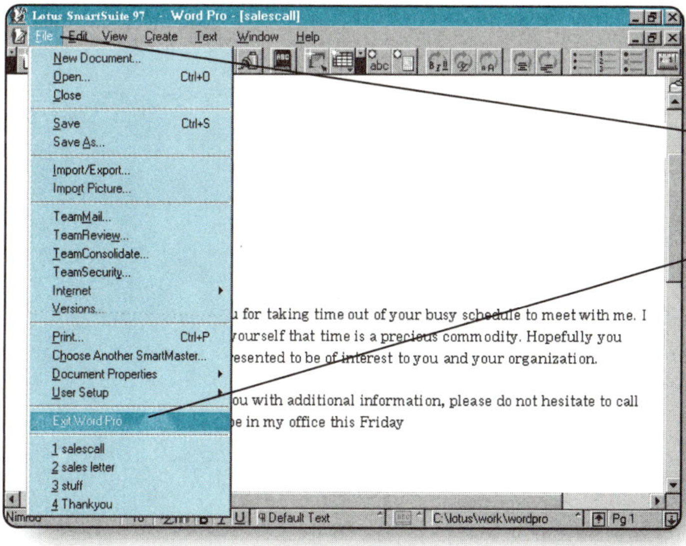

Closing a Document

1. **Click** on **File**. The File menu will appear.

2. **Click** on **Exit Word Pro**. If any documents are open that haven't been saved, Word Pro will ask you whether you want to save changes to those files.

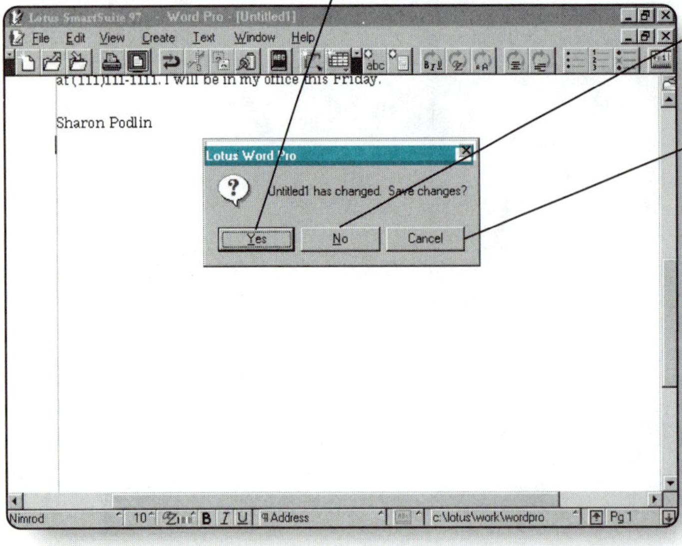

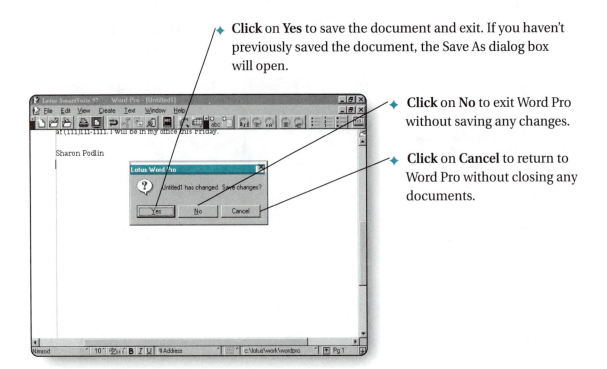

- **Click** on **Yes** to save the document and exit. If you haven't previously saved the document, the Save As dialog box will open.
- **Click** on **No** to exit Word Pro without saving any changes.
- **Click** on **Cancel** to return to Word Pro without closing any documents.

4 Formatting Word Pro Documents

Appearance is everything in this day and age. Word Pro offers several ways to improve the appearance of your document through the use of formatting. Formatting allows you to change the look of your document by changing the look of the text in that document. In this chapter, you'll learn how to:

- Work with text properties
- Insert the date and time into your document
- Insert symbols into your document
- Apply styles to your text
- Include headers and footers in your documents

WORKING WITH TEXT ATTRIBUTES

You can change the appearance of text in a variety of ways. You can make it bold, you can underline it, or you can change the font you are using. These are just a few of the text attributes you can work with.

Making Text Bold

1. **Select** the **text** you want to make bold.

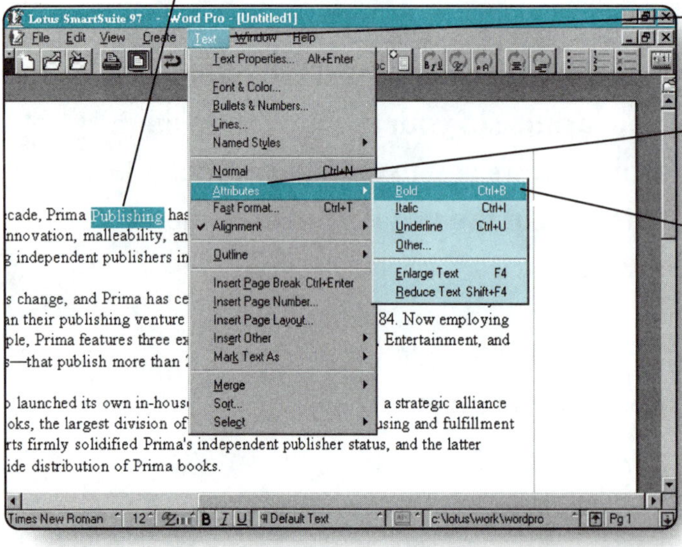

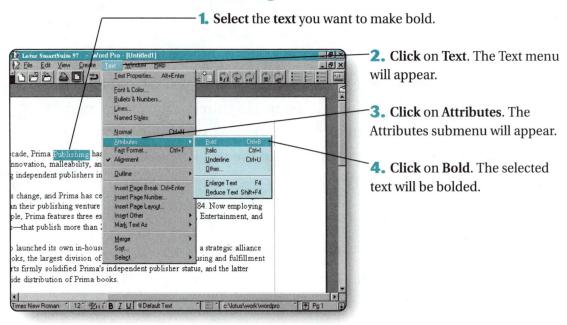

2. **Click** on **Text**. The Text menu will appear.

3. **Click** on **Attributes**. The Attributes submenu will appear.

4. **Click** on **Bold**. The selected text will be bolded.

> **TIP**
>
> A quick way to bold text using your keyboard is to select the text and press the Ctrl and B keys at the same time.

Underlining Text

1. **Select** the **text** you want to underline.

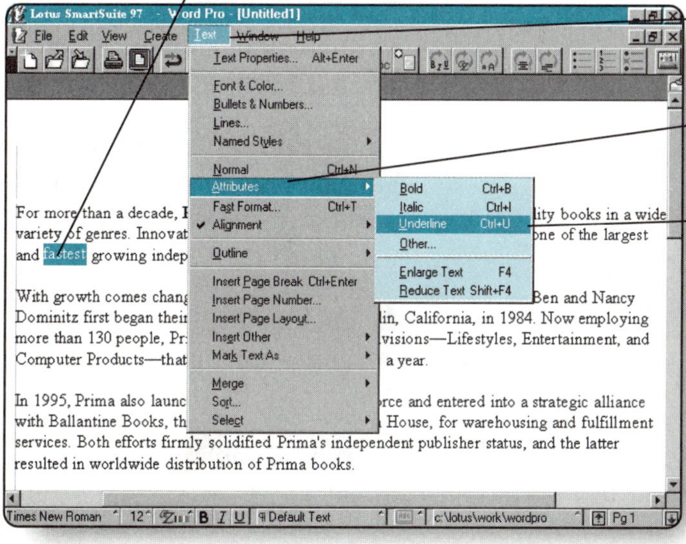

2. **Click** on **Text**. The Text menu will appear.

3. **Click** on **Attributes**. The Attributes submenu will appear.

4. **Click** on **Underline**. The selected text will be underlined.

TIP

A quick way to underline text using your keyboard is to select the text and press the Ctrl and U keys at the same time.

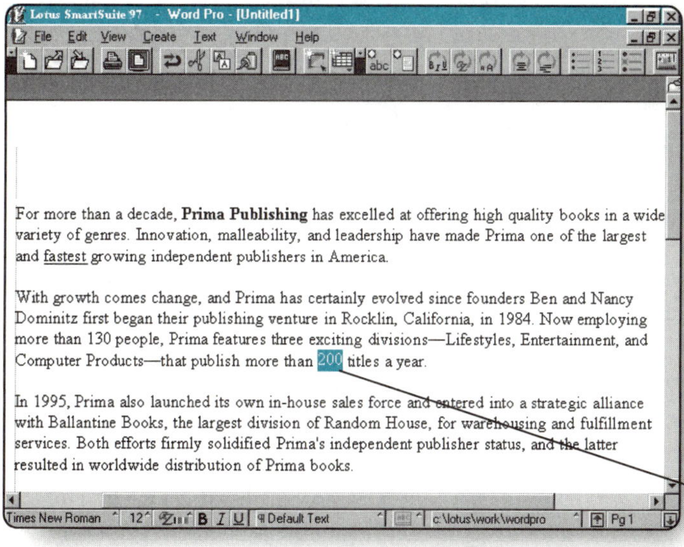

Changing Text Attributes Using the Cycle Through Attributes Options Button

You can change text attributes to text by using the Cycle Through Attributes Options button to cycle through the text attributes of bold, italic, and underline.

1. **Select** some **text**.

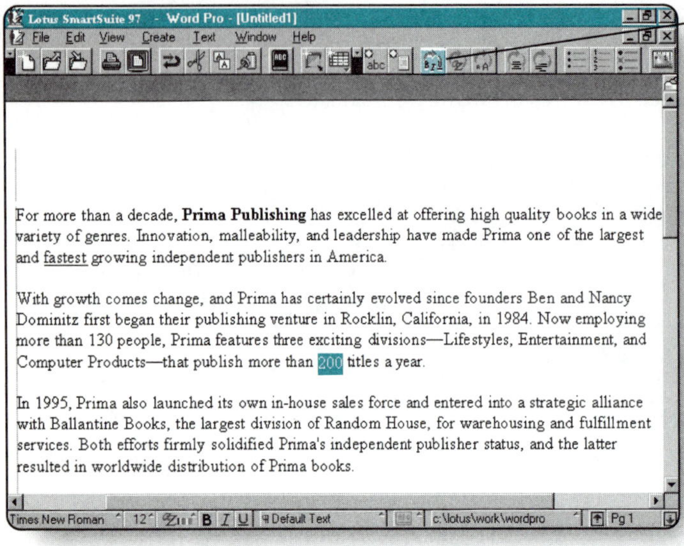

2. Click on the **Cycle through attributes options button**. The text will be bolded.

3. Click on the **Cycle through attributes options button** again. The text will be italicized.

4. Click on the **Cycle through attributes options button** again. The text will be bolded and italicized.

5. Click on the **Cycle through attributes options button** again. The text will be underlined.

6. Click on the **Cycle through attributes options button** again. The text will be made normal.

Selecting a Font Typeface

Changing the font typeface of text is another way to make it stand out from the rest of your document.

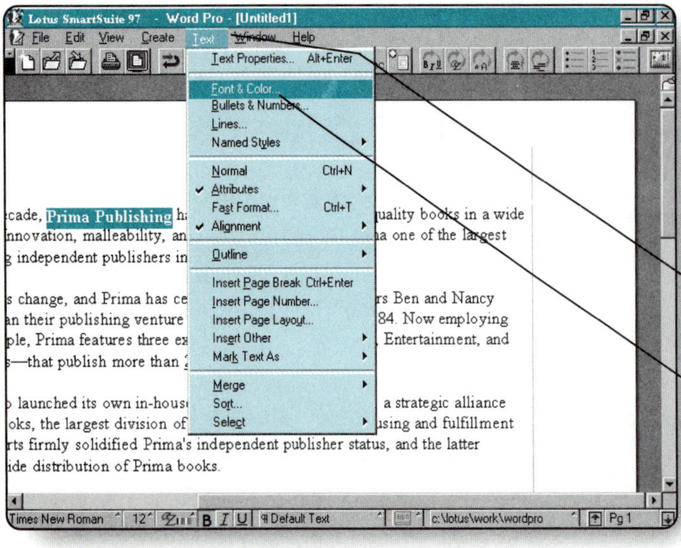

Changing the Font Typeface Using the Text Menu

1. Select the **text** whose font typeface you want to change.

2. Click on **Text**. The Text menu will appear.

3. Click on **Font & Color**. The Properties for Text dialog box will open.

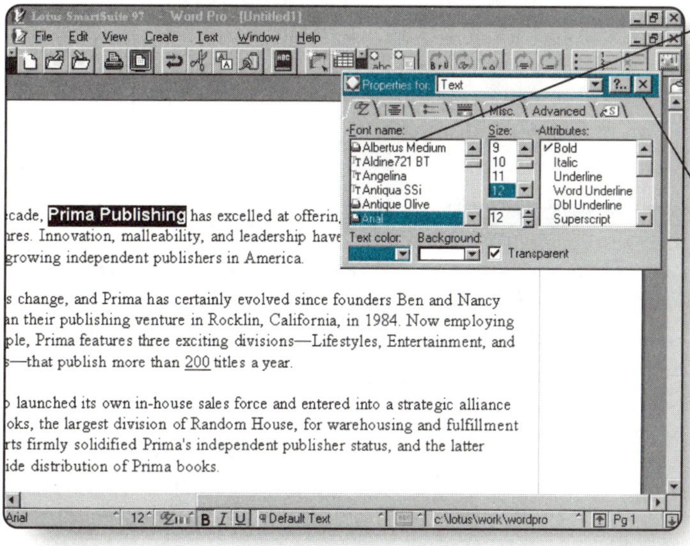

4. Click on a **font typeface name** from the Font name: list box. The font typeface change will be immediately applied to the selected text.

5. Click on the **Close button** of the Properties for Text dialog box. The dialog box will close.

Changing the Font Typeface Using the Status Bar

If you are familiar with the look of the font typefaces available on your system, you may want to use the status bar to select a new font typeface.

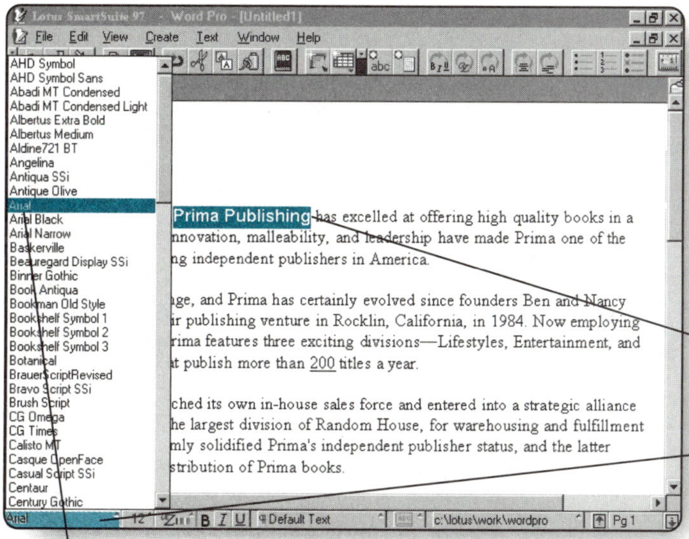

1. Select the **text** whose font typeface you want to change.

2. Click on the **Font button** in the status bar. A list of available fonts will appear.

3. Click on a new **font name**. The font change will be applied to the text.

Selecting a Font Size

You may want to make certain text larger or smaller than the rest of the text in your document.

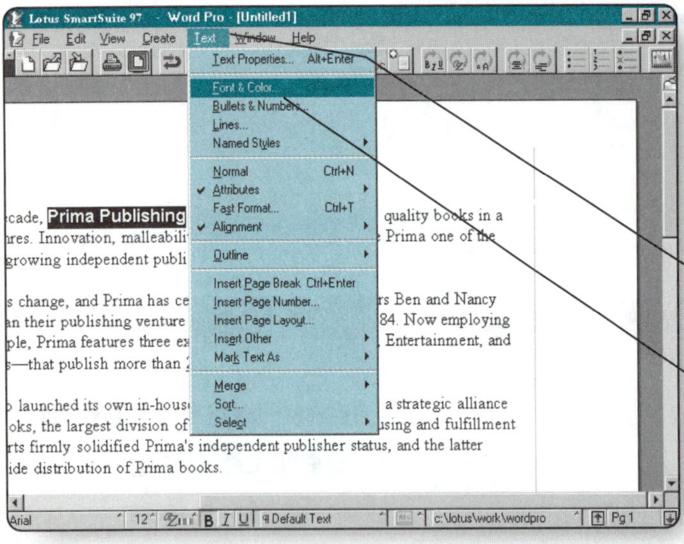

Changing the Font Size Using the Text Menu

1. Select the **text** whose font size you want to change.

2. Click on **Text**. The Text menu will appear.

3. Click on **Font & Color**. The Properties for Text dialog box will open.

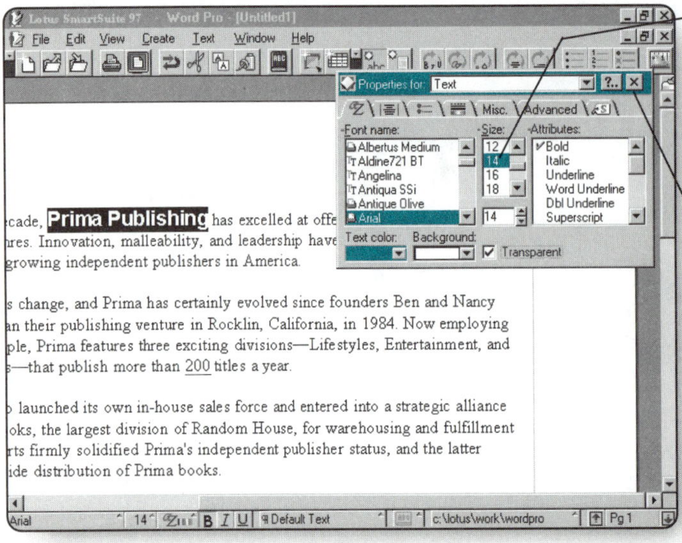

4. Click on a **font size** from the Size: list box. The larger the number, the larger the font size will be. The font size change will be immediately applied to the selected text.

5. Click on the **Close button** of the Properties for Text dialog box. The dialog box will close.

Changing the Font Size Using the Status Bar

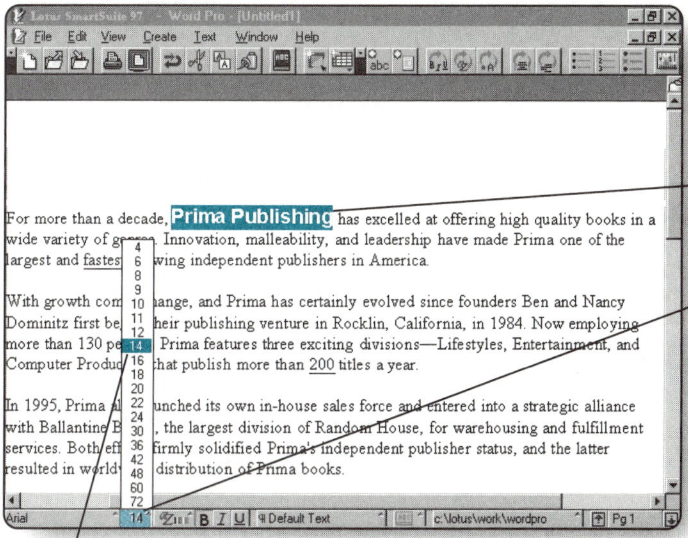

1. **Select** the **text** whose font size you want to change.

2. **Click** on the **Size button** in the status bar. A list of font sizes will appear.

3. **Click** on a **new size**. The font size change will be applied to the text.

Increasing the Font Size Using the Cycle Through Font Size Options Button

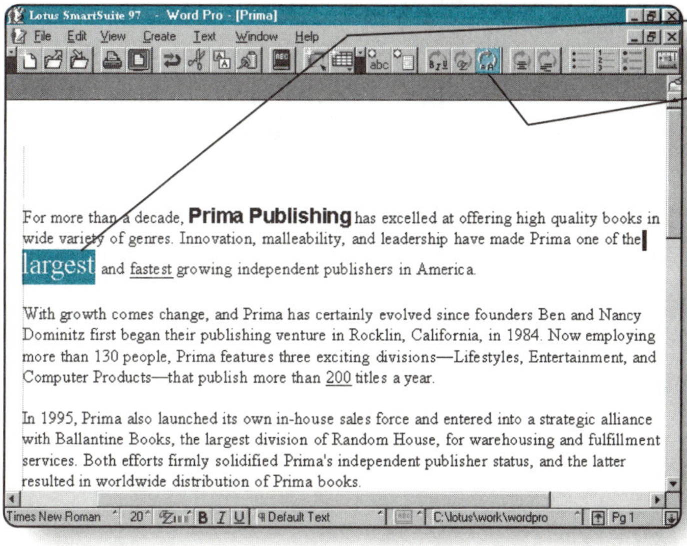

1. **Select** some **text**.

2. **Click** on repeatedly the **Cycle through font size options button** until the text becomes the desired font size.

Selecting Paragraph Alignment and Indention Options

You may want to align certain paragraphs in your documents so that they are, for example, centered on a page. For example, headings and titles are frequently centered. You also may need to indent paragraphs so that they stand out from other text.

Setting Paragraph Alignment

Four types of alignment are available: left, center, right, and full justified.

1. **Position** the **insertion point** within the **paragraph** to align.

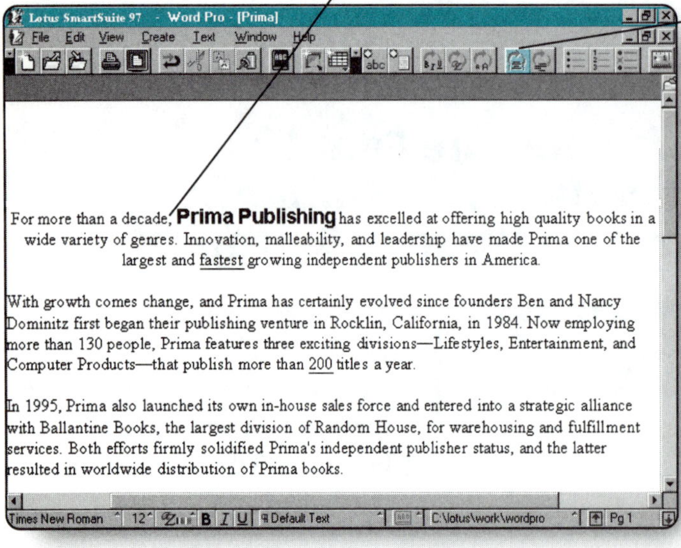

2. **Click** on the **Cycle through alignment options button**. The paragraph change its alignment.

3. **Click** on the **Cycle through alignment options button** again. The paragraph will change its alignment again.

4. **Continue clicking** on the **Cycle through alignment options button** until you have the desired alignment. The paragraph will set to that alignment setting.

TIP

To align a paragraph using your keyboard, position the insertion point in the paragraph you want to align. Press one of the following key combinations:

- To align left, press Ctrl and L at the same time.
- To align center, press Ctrl and E at the same time.
- To align right, press Ctrl and R at the same time.
- To align full justify, press Ctrl and J at the same time.

Indenting a Paragraph

Indents are set for every 1/4-inch.

1. Position the **insertion point** within the **paragraph** to indent.

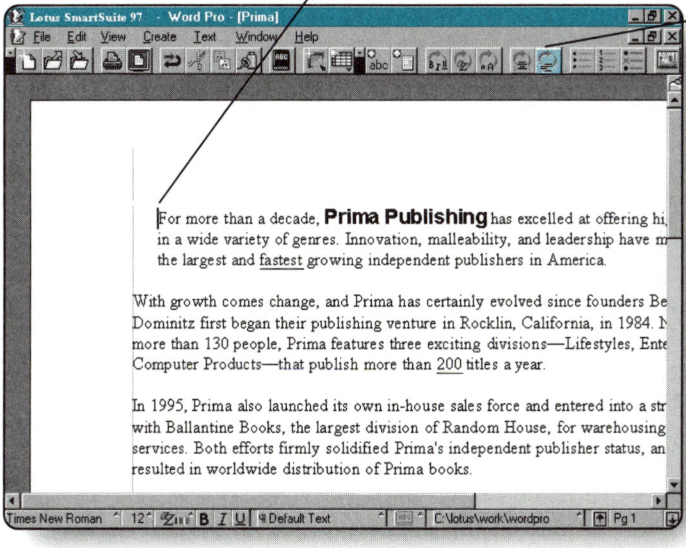

2. Click repeatedly on the **Cycle through indent options button.** The paragraph will be indented.

Working with Bullets

Word Pro supports a variety of bullet styles and makes it easy to create a bulleted paragraph.

Creating a Bulleted Paragraph

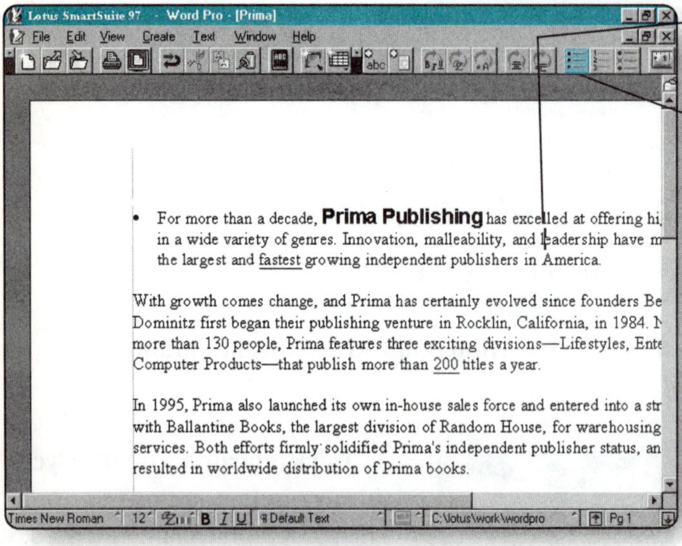

1. **Position** the **insertion point** within the **paragraph** to bullet.
2. **Click** on the **Insert default bullet button**. The paragraph will be immediately bulleted and indented.

Selecting a Bullet Style

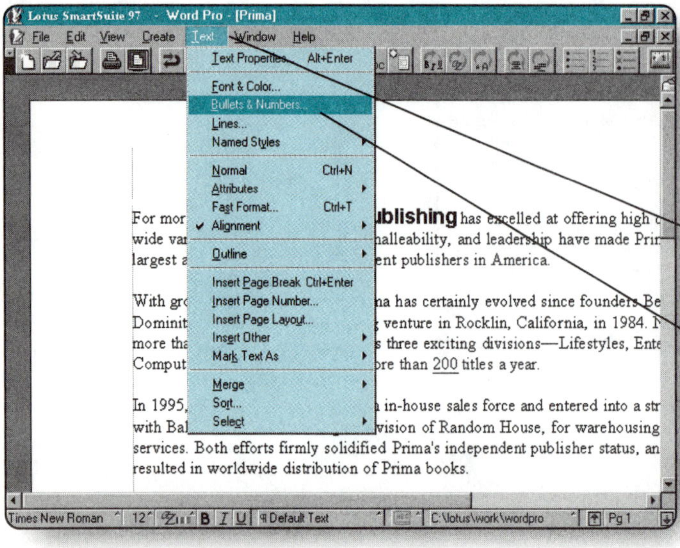

1. **Position** the **insertion point** within the **paragraph** to align.
2. **Click** on **Text**. The Text menu will appear.
3. **Click** on **Bullets & Numbers**. The Properties for Text dialog box will open.

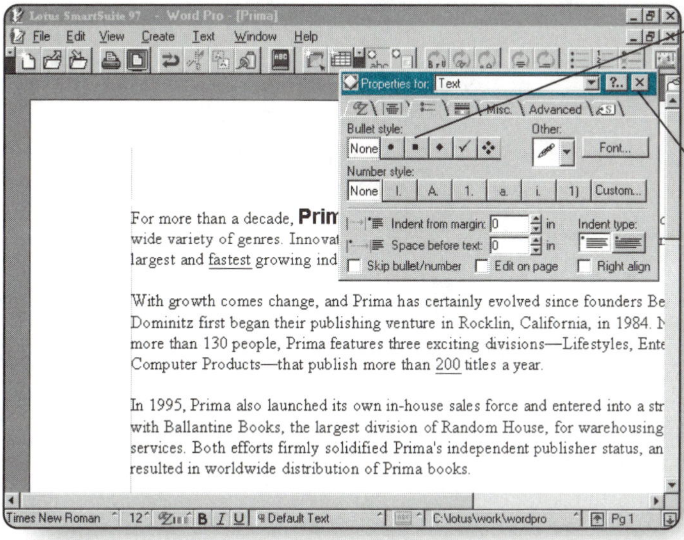

4. Click on a **bullet style button**. The bullet style will be immediately applied to the paragraph.

5. Click on the **Close button**. The Properties for Text dialog box will close.

TIP

To select from additional bullet styles, click on the down arrow (▼) by the Other drop-down list box.

Setting and Deleting Tabs

Setting and deleting tabs can be done using the ruler.

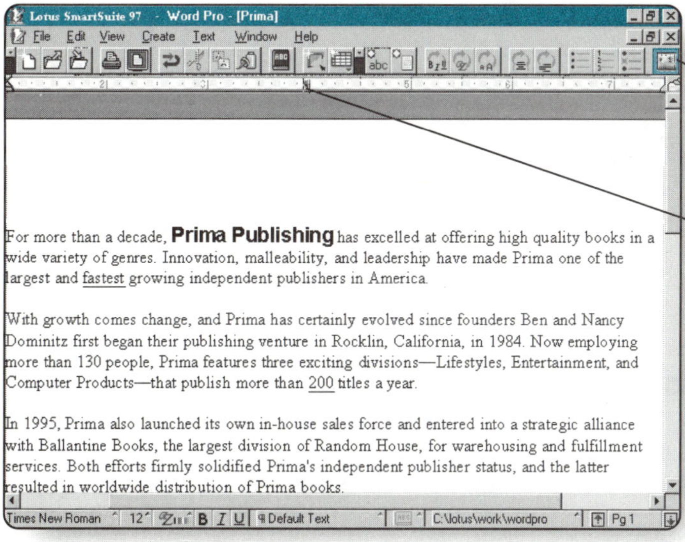

Setting Tabs

1. Click on the **Show/hide ruler button**, if the ruler is not already displayed. The ruler will display.

2. Click on the **ruler** where you want to create a new tab. The tab will be set at that point.

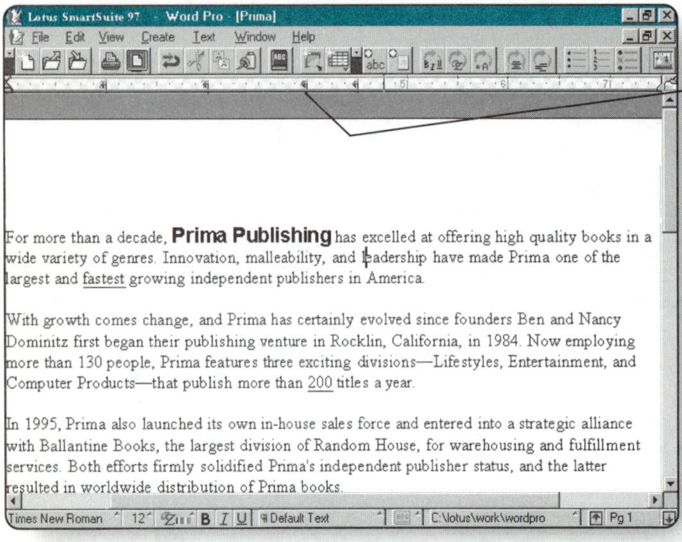

Deleting a Tab

1. **Drag** the unwanted **tab** off the ruler. The tab will be removed.

INSERTING THE DATE OR TIME

Word Pro has a great feature that will automatically insert the date or time for you.

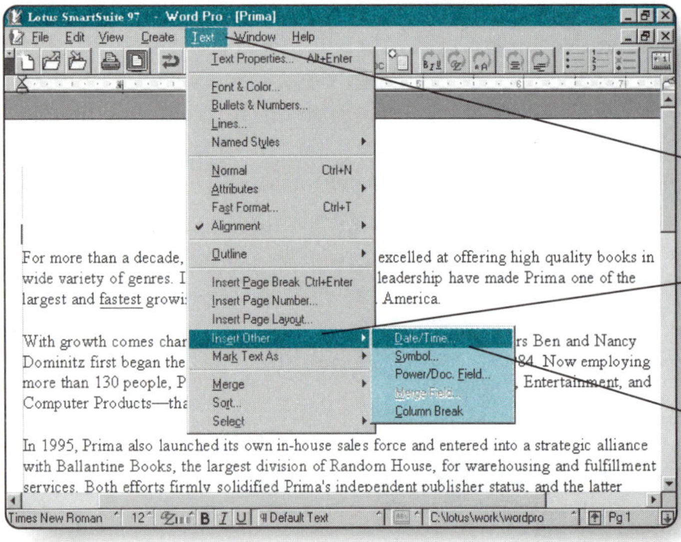

1. **Position** the insertion point where you want to place the date.

2. **Click** on **Text**. The Text menu will appear.

3. **Click** on **Insert Other**. The Insert Other submenu will appear.

4. **Click** on **Date/Time**. The Insert Date/Time dialog box will open.

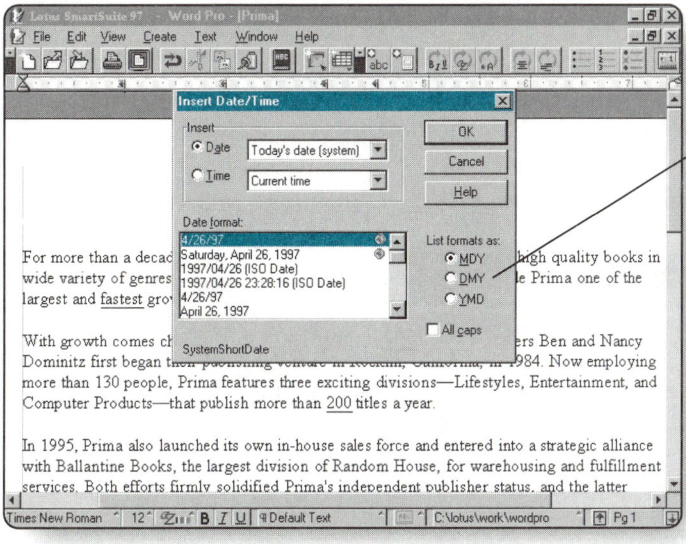

5. Select from the following **options**:

- ✦ Several types of date formats are available. You can select to list the date formats that use month, day, and year by clicking on MDY. If you want to list the formats that use day, month, and year, click on DMY. And if you want to list the formats that use year, month, and day, click on YMD.

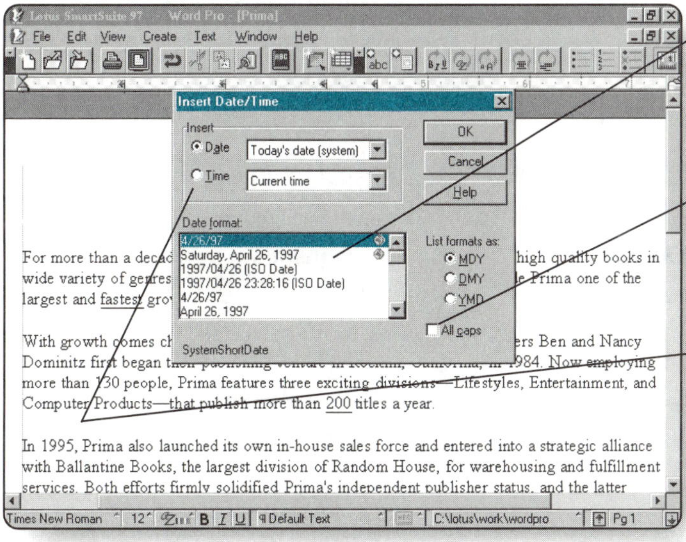

- ✦ Click on a date format from the Date format: list box to select the format you want to use.
- ✦ Place a ✔ in the All caps check box if you want the inserted date to be in a capital letters.
- ✦ Click on Time if you want to insert the time rather than the date.

6. Click on **OK**. The date or time will be inserted into your document.

INSERTING SYMBOLS

On occasion, you need to insert special symbols such as trademarks and copyright marks.

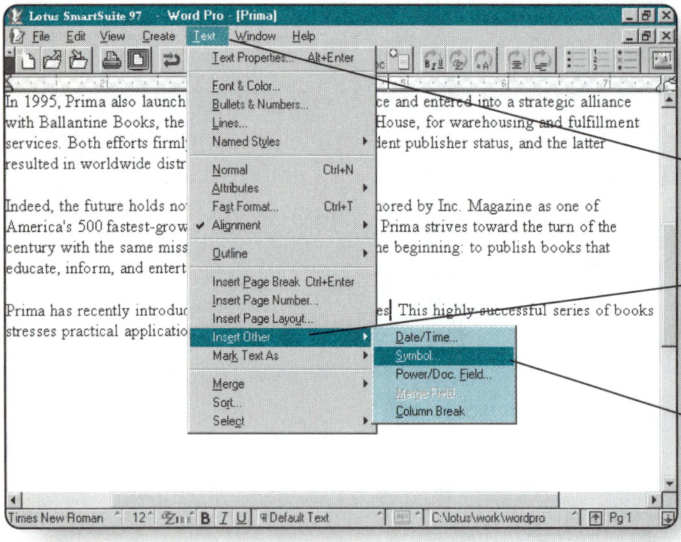

1. **Position** the **insertion point** where you want to place the symbol.

2. **Click** on **Text**. The Text menu will appear.

3. **Click** on **Insert Other**. The Insert Other submenu will appear.

4. **Click** on **Symbol**. The Insert Symbol dialog box will open.

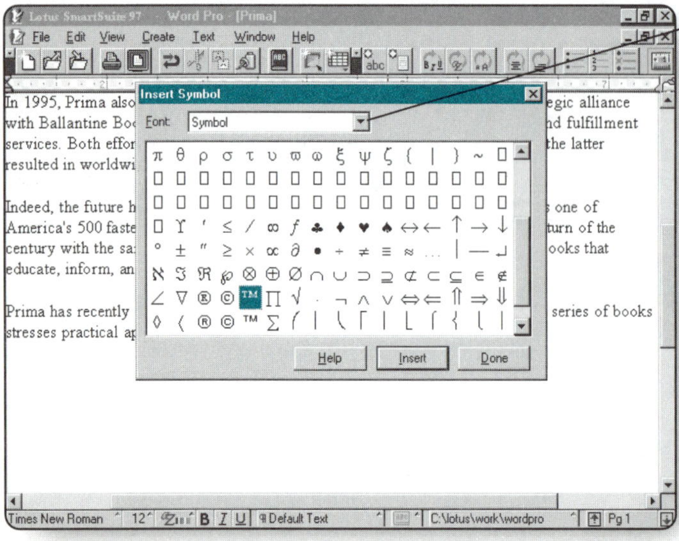

5. **Select** a **font**. Click on the down arrow (▼). A list of the fonts installed on your system will appear.

TIP

Symbol and Wingdings fonts provide many popular symbols.

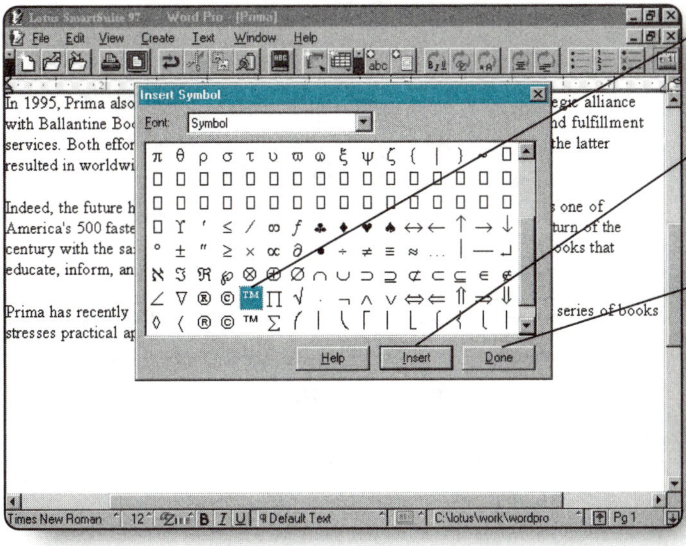

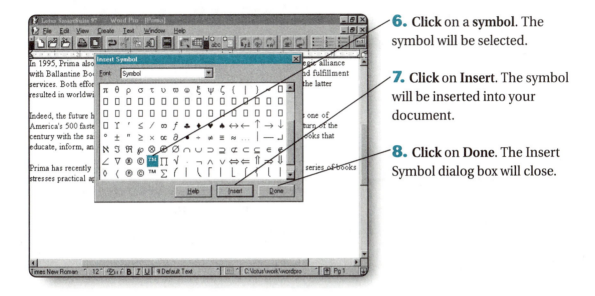

6. Click on a **symbol**. The symbol will be selected.

7. Click on **Insert**. The symbol will be inserted into your document.

8. Click on **Done**. The Insert Symbol dialog box will close.

APPLYING STYLES

You can apply text attributes to text by using the techniques presented in this chapter, or you can use styles. Styles are shortcuts to applying multiple text attributes. For example, you may want some text to use Arial Black font typeface, to have the font size of 15, and to be bold. You can code set each of these attributes individually, or you can apply the Heading 1 style. Styles make formatting text easier and provide a way to make certain elements of your document such as headings consistent in appearance. The SmartMaster template that you choose when you create a document contains predefined styles.

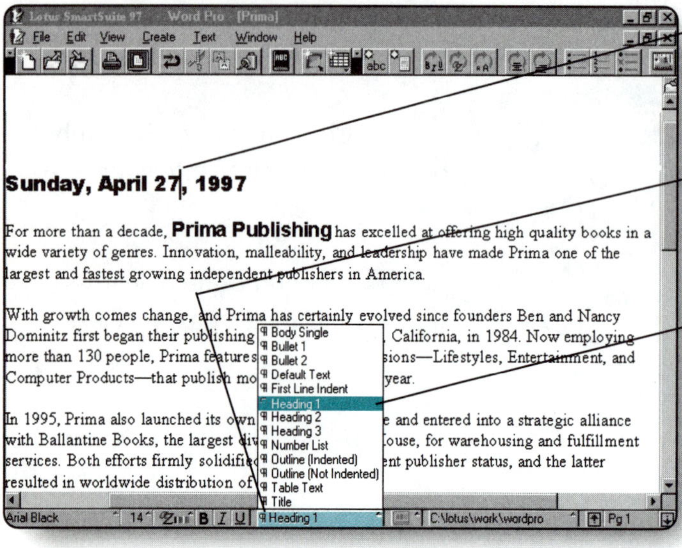

1. **Position** the **insertion point** within the **paragraph** to which you want to apply the style.

2. **Click** on the **Style Status button**. A list of available styles will appear.

3. **Click** on a **style**. The style will be immediately applied to the paragraph.

5 Working with Page Layout

One size doesn't always fit all in the world of word processing documents. You may need to adjust the size of the text area of a document. Headers and footers are often used to repeat key information on each page of a document such as a company's name or the page number. These types of page layout features give your document a professional look. In this chapter, you'll learn how to:

- Set margins
- Add borders
- Work with headers and footers

SETTING MARGINS

The size of the text area is controlled by the size of the page margins. You can set left, right, top, and bottom margins. By controlling the margins, you control the amount of text area available.

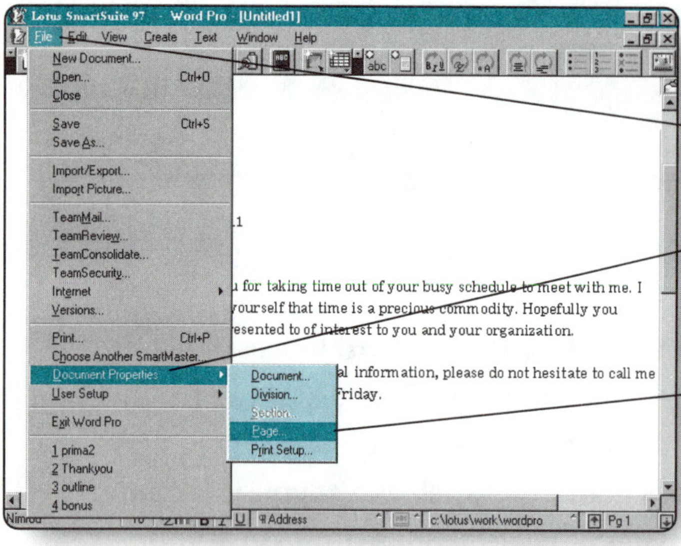

1. **Click** on **File**. The File menu will appear.

2. **Click** on **Document Properties**. The Document Properties submenu will appear.

3. **Click** on **Page**. The Properties for Page layout dialog box will open.

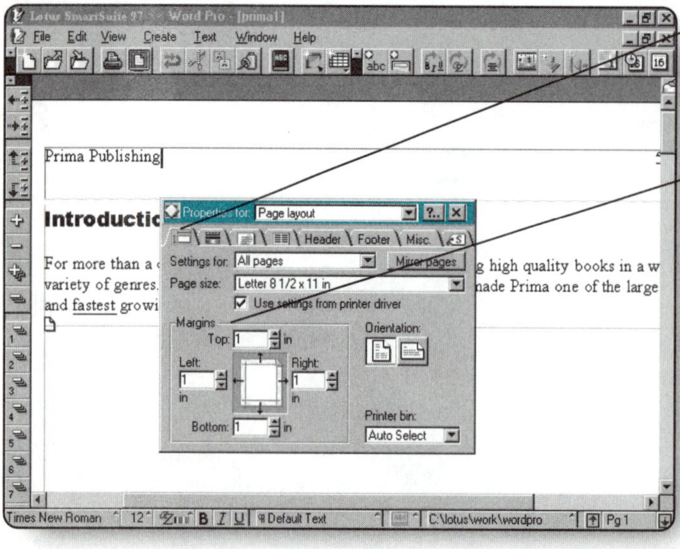

4. **Click** on the **Size and Margin tab**. The Size and Margin tab will appear.

5. **Type a value** for margins in the Top:, Left:, Right:, and Bottom: boxes. The value in these boxes is measured in inches.

6. **Click** on the **Close button**. The Properties for Page layout dialog box will close.

CHANGING THE PAGE SIZE

Word Pro lets you select from several page size options. The page size options used by Word Pro are based on the page size settings of your printer.

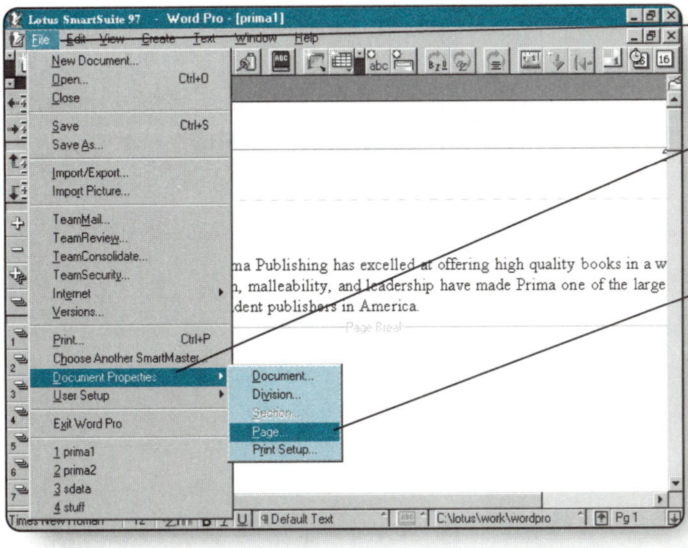

1. **Click** on **File**. The File menu will appear.
2. **Click** on **Document Properties**. The Document Properties submenu will appear.
3. **Click** on **Page**. The Properties for Page layout dialog box will open.

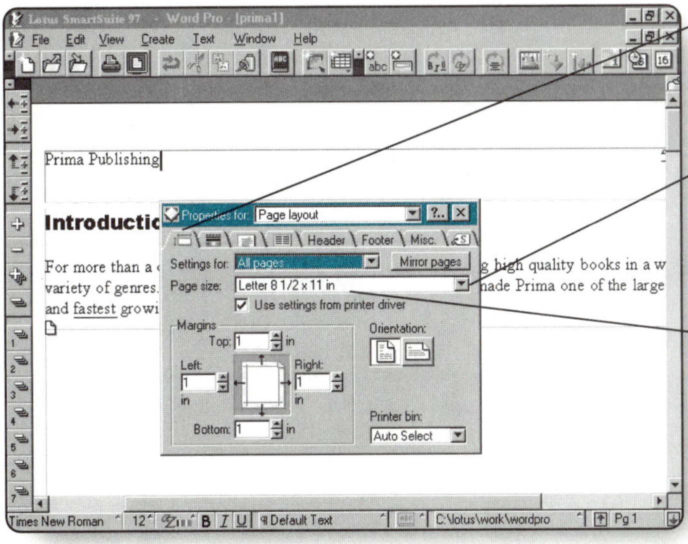

4. **Click** on the **Size and Margin tab**. The Size and Margin tab will appear.
5. **Click** on the **down arrow** (▼) in the Page size: box. The list of available page size options will appear.
6. **Click** on a **page size**. The page size will be selected.
7. **Click** on the **Close button**. The Properties for Page layout dialog box will close.

ADDING BORDERS

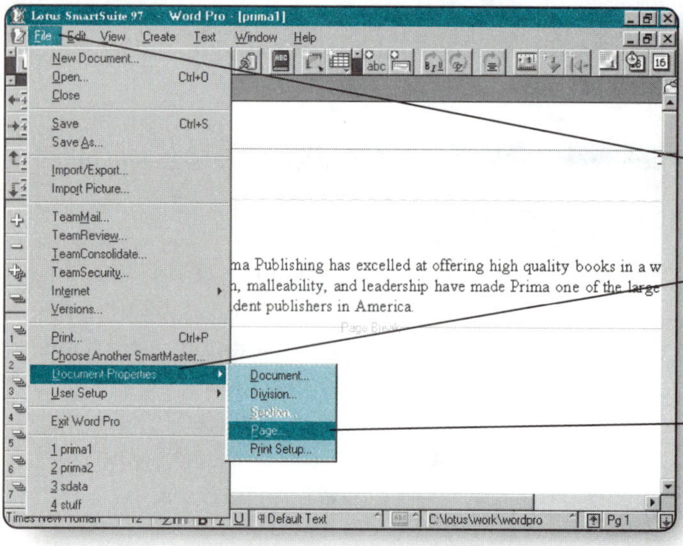

Word Pro offers a variety of borders that you can use around your page.

1. Click on **File**. The File menu will appear.

2. Click on **Document Properties**. The Document Properties submenu will appear.

3. Click on **Page**. The Properties for Page layout dialog box will open.

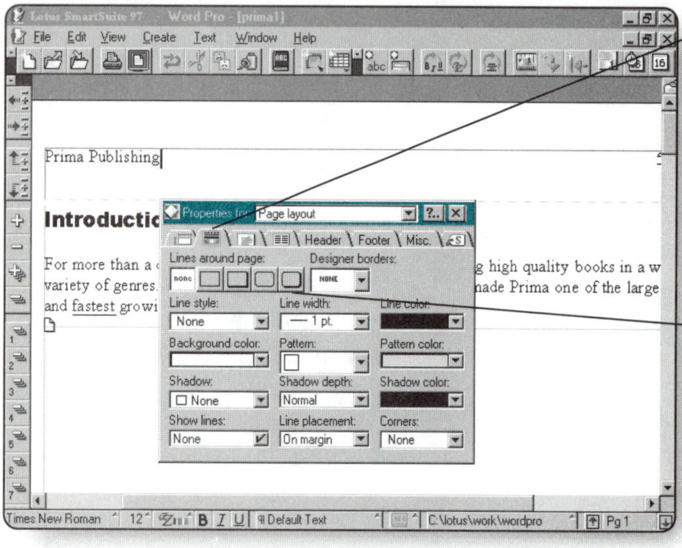

4. Click on the **Color**, **Pattern,** and **Line Style** tab. The Color, Pattern, and Line Style tab will appear.

5. Choose from the following **options**:

- ✦ If you want a simple border around your page, click on one of the buttons under Lines around page:.

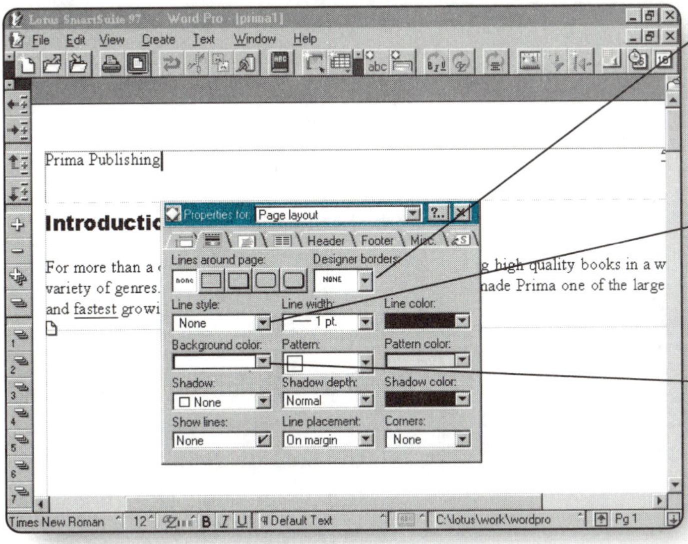

- ✦ If you want a more detailed border, click on the down arrow (▼) under Designer borders: and make a selection.
- ✦ To change the Line style: used by the border, click on the down arrow (▼) and make a selection.
- ✦ If you want to pick another Background color:, click on the down arrow (▼) and make a selection.

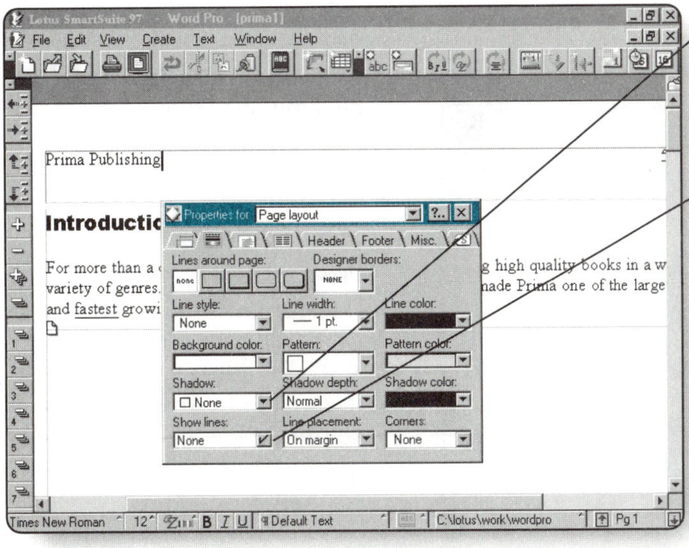

- ✦ To add a Shadow: to the border, click on the down arrow (▼) and make a selection.
- ✦ Select where to put the line by clicking the ✔ beside the Show lines: box.

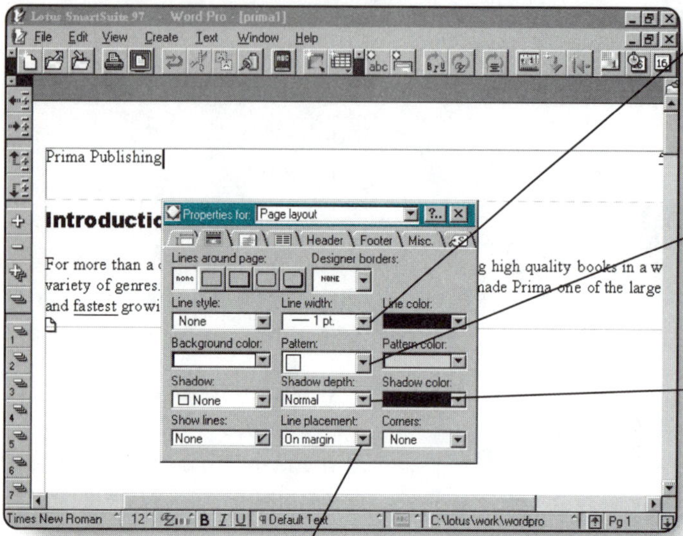

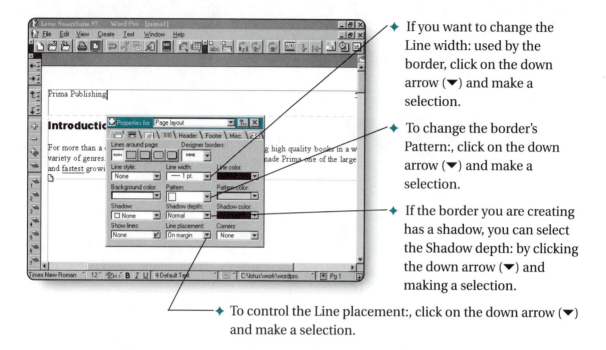

- ✦ If you want to change the Line width: used by the border, click on the down arrow (▼) and make a selection.
- ✦ To change the border's Pattern:, click on the down arrow (▼) and make a selection.
- ✦ If the border you are creating has a shadow, you can select the Shadow depth: by clicking the down arrow (▼) and making a selection.
- ✦ To control the Line placement:, click on the down arrow (▼) and make a selection.

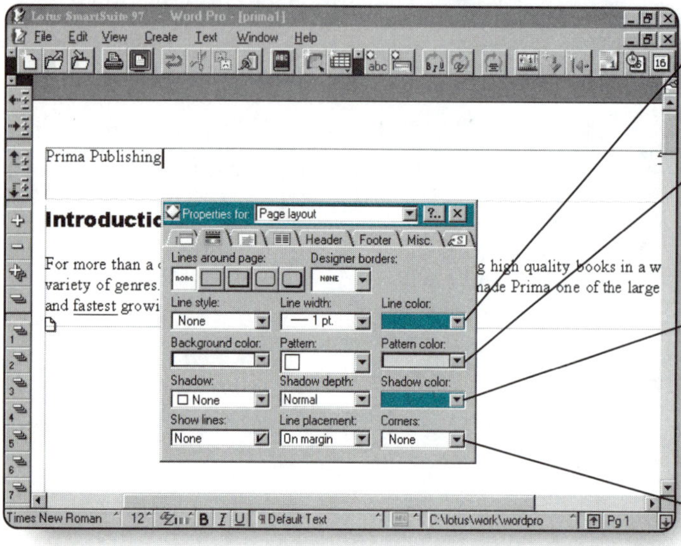

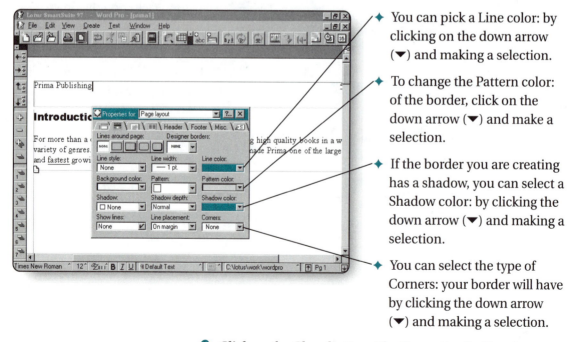

- ✦ You can pick a Line color: by clicking on the down arrow (▼) and making a selection.
- ✦ To change the Pattern color: of the border, click on the down arrow (▼) and make a selection.
- ✦ If the border you are creating has a shadow, you can select a Shadow color: by clicking the down arrow (▼) and making a selection.
- ✦ You can select the type of Corners: your border will have by clicking the down arrow (▼) and making a selection.

6. Click on the **Close button**. The Properties for Page layout dialog box will close.

SETTING A DOCUMENT'S ORIENTATION

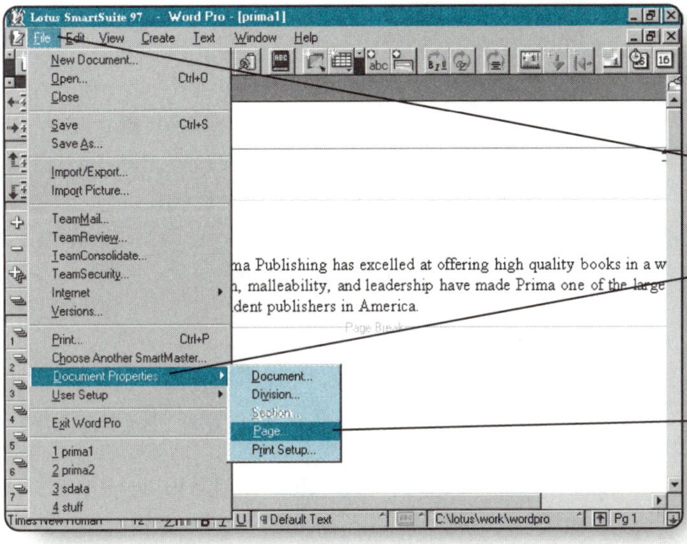

Word Pro lets you print a document using either a portrait or landscape orientation.

1. **Click** on **File**. The File menu will appear.

2. **Click** on **Document Properties**. The Document Properties submenu will appear.

3. **Click** on **Page**. The Properties for Page layout dialog box will open.

4. **Click** on the **Size and Margin tab**. The Size and Margin tab will appear.

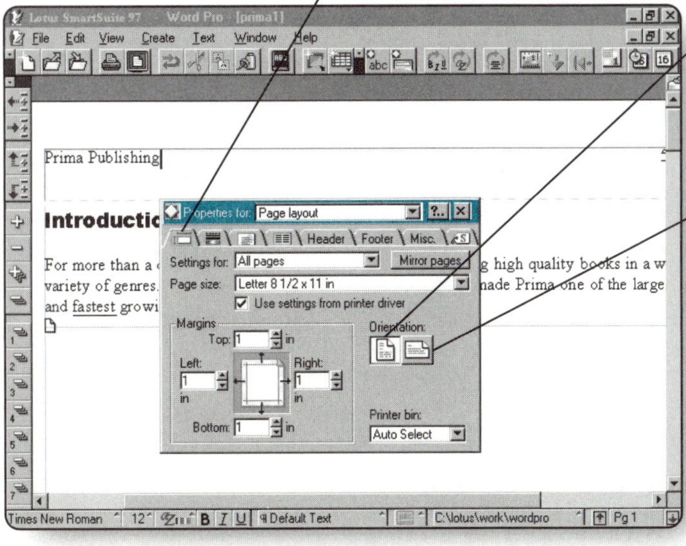

5a. **Click** on the **Portrait button**. The document's orientation will be portrait.

OR

5b. **Click** on the **Landscape button**. The document's orientation will be landscape.

6. **Click** on the **Close button.** The Properties for Page layout dialog box will close.

ADDING HEADERS AND FOOTERS

Two areas in a document are reserved for repeating text. When this text is at the top of a page it is called a header. When this text is at the bottom of a page it is called a footer. Examples of text you may want to place in a header of footer are the date the document was created, your company's name, or the current page number.

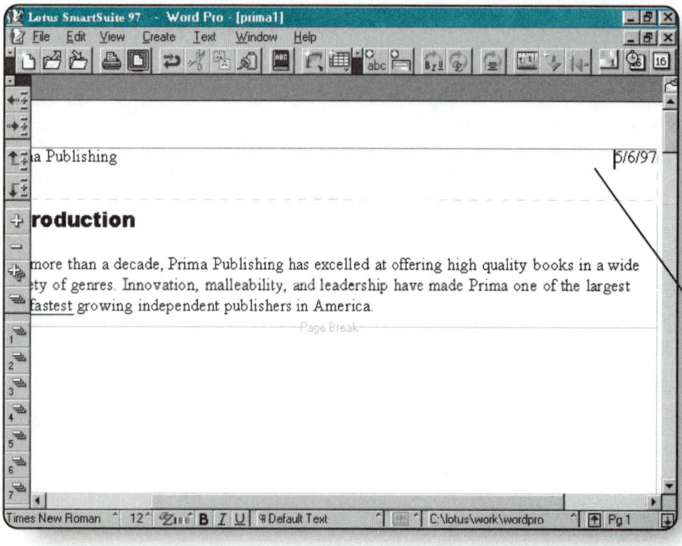

Creating a Header or Footer

1a. Click on the **header area**. The header area will be selected.

OR

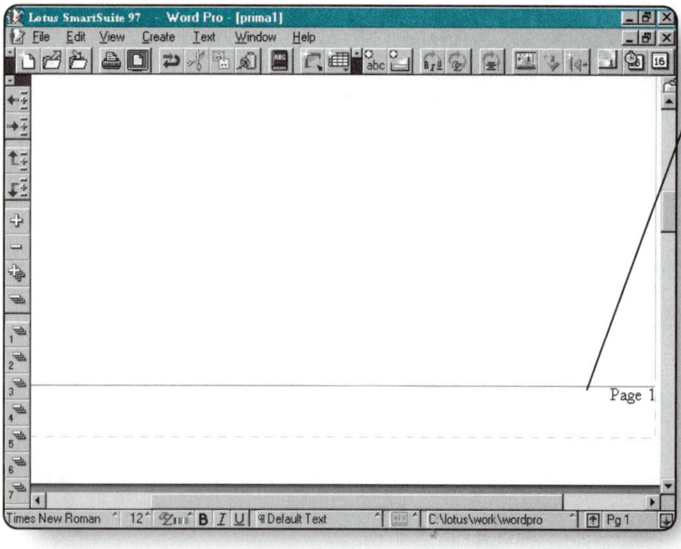

1b. Click on the **footer area**. The footer area will be selected.

2. Type some **text**. The text will be added to the header or footer.

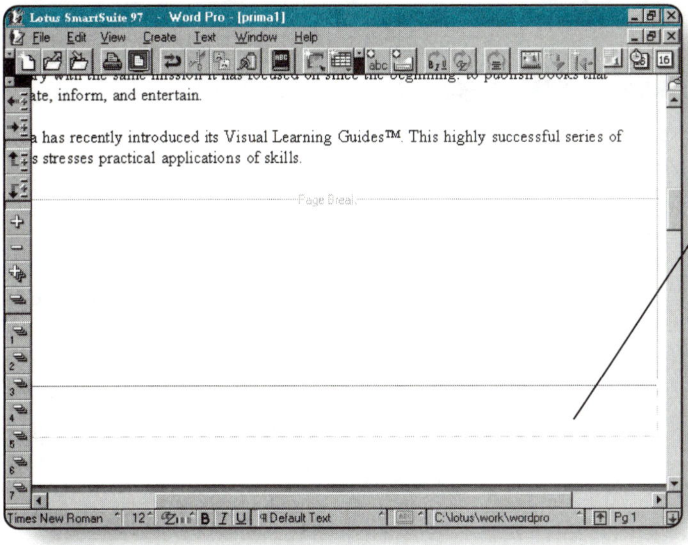

Inserting a Page Number in a Footer

1. Click on the **footer area**. The footer area will be selected.

2. Press the **Tab key** or **spacebar** to position the insertion point where you want the page number. The insertion point will move to that location.

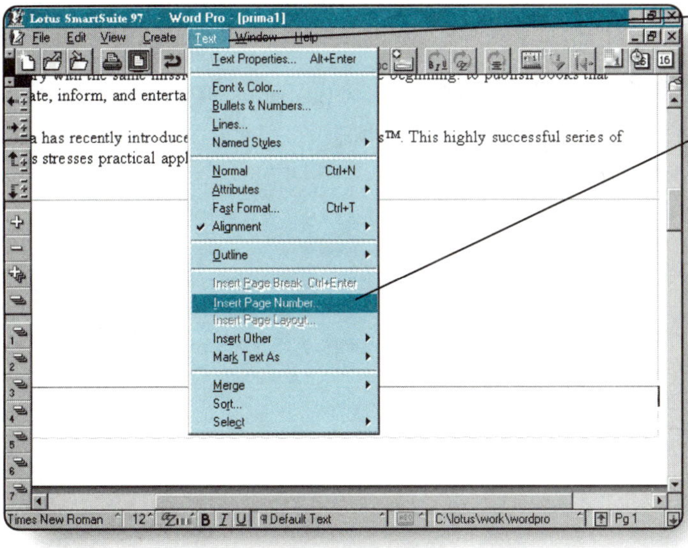

3. Click on **Text**. The Text menu will appear.

4. Click on **Insert Page Number.** The Insert Page Number dialog box will open.

5. Choose from the following **options**:

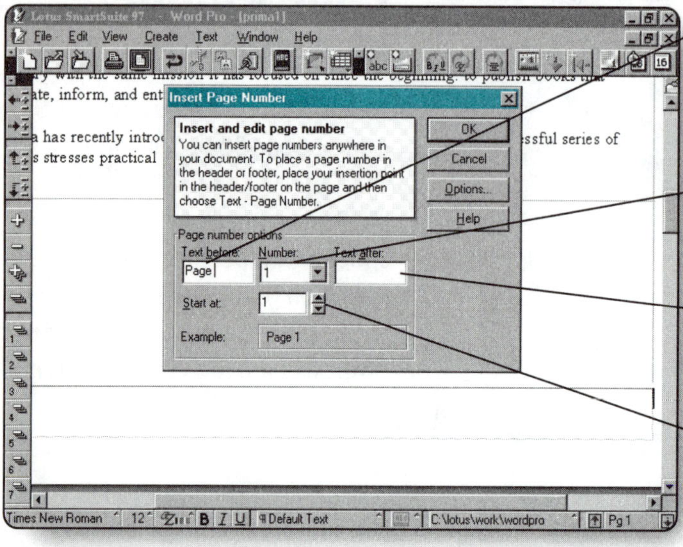

- ✦ If you want text such as Page to appear before the page number, enter text in the Text before: box.
- ✦ To pick the Number style, click the down arrow (▼) and make a selection.
- ✦ If you want text to appear after the page number, enter text in the Text after: box.
- ✦ If you want page numbering to Start at: a number other than one, click on the up and down arrows (⬍) to choose a different number.

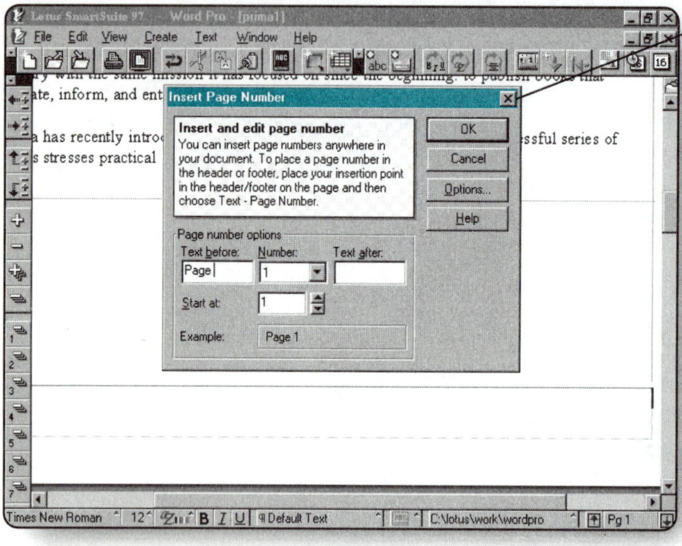

6. Click on the **Close button.** The Insert Page number dialog box will close.

6 Creating Reports

Reports are second only to letters in popularity and use. Whether you are a student, consultant, or other professional, you will have many uses for reports. Students are often called upon to do reports as part of their class work; professionals often need to do reports for a variety of reasons ranging from cost and project justifications to recommendations and strategic directions. In this chapter, you'll learn how to:

- ✦ Create and work with tables
- ✦ Use footnotes within your document
- ✦ Use Word Pro to create a table of contents for your report

WORKING WITH TABLES

Prior to tables, a typist had to spend a lot of time pressing the Tab key to line up text in columns. Tables have greatly simplified this process. Tables have columns and rows, making it easy to enter columnar text.

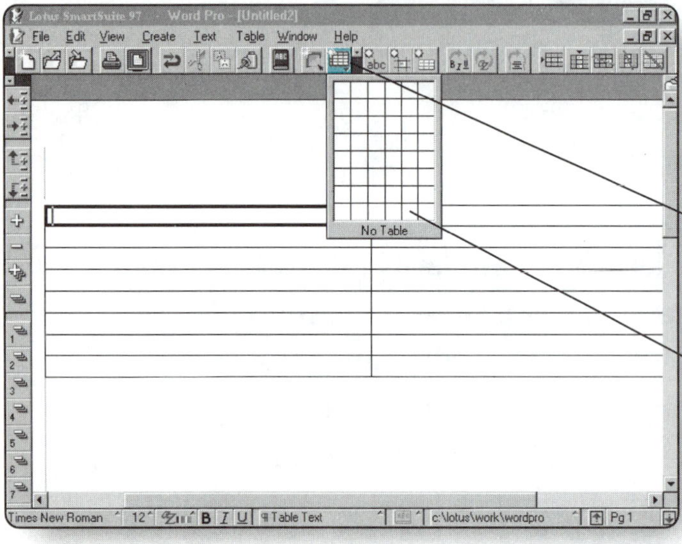

Creating a Table

Word Pro has made creating a table extremely easy through its Create table grid button.

1. Click on the **Create table grid SmartIcon**. The table grid will display.

2. Click on the **cell** representing the last cell of the table you want to create. The table will be created in your document.

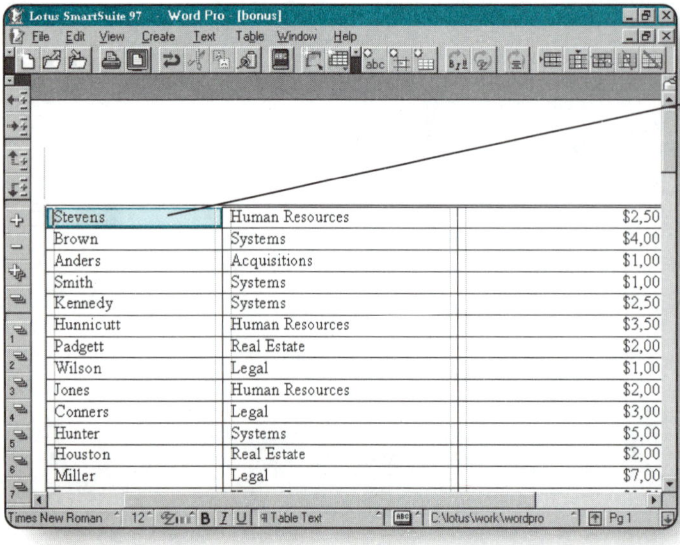

Entering Text into a Table

1. Click on the **cell** you want to enter data in. The cell will be selected.

2. Type some **text**. The text will appear in the cell.

> **TIP**
>
> To move from cell to cell going left to right, top to bottom, press the Tab key.

Modifying a Table

After you start working with a table, you may find that you need to add rows and columns. Or you may want to make a column narrower or wider based on the text in that column.

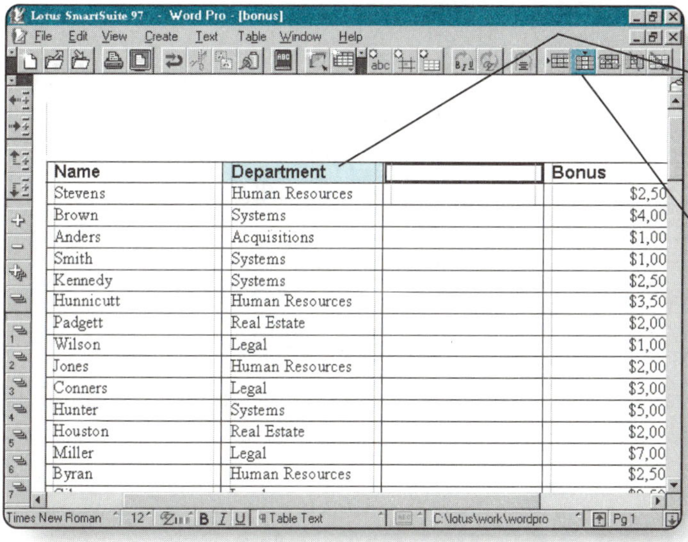

Adding Columns

1. Click on the **column** after which you want to insert a column. The column will be selected.

2. Click on the **Insert Column in Table SmartIcon**. The new column will be inserted to the right of the selected column.

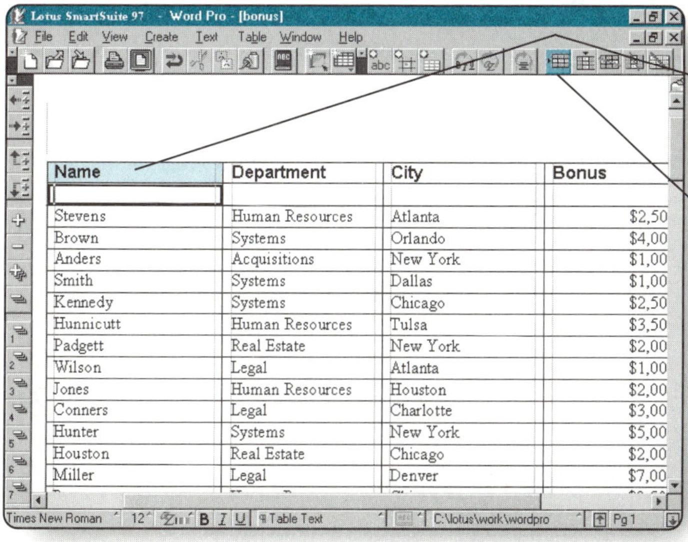

Adding Rows

1. Click on the **row** after which you want to insert a row. The row will be selected.

2. Click on the **Insert Row in Table SmartIcon**. The new row will be inserted after the selected row.

Changing the Size of a Column

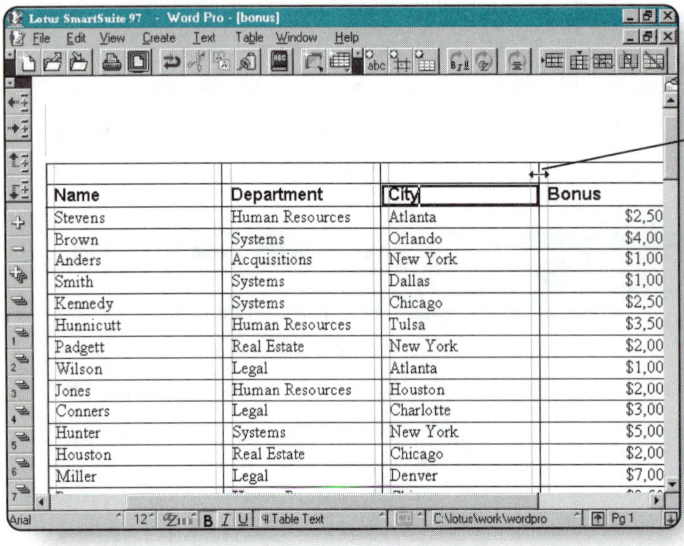

1. **Position** the **pointer** over the **right border of the column** to resize. The pointer will change to a horizontal double-headed arrow.

2. **Drag** the **border** until the column is the correct size. The column will be resized.

> **NOTE**
>
> A cell in the table must be selected before you can resize the columns in that table.

Formatting a Table

You can do several things to customize the look of your table. These include adding a border around cells and selecting a number format.

Placing a Border Around Cells

1. **Select** some **cells**.

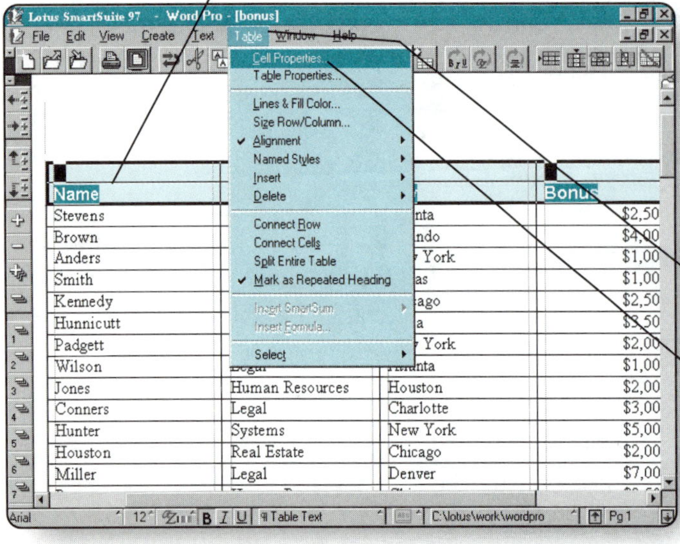

To select multiple cells, click on and hold the mouse button down on the first cell you want to work with. Drag your pointer to the last cell you want to work with. Release your mouse button. The cells will be selected.

2. **Click** on **Table**. The Table menu will appear.

3. **Click** on **Cell Properties**. The Properties for Table Cell dialog box will open.

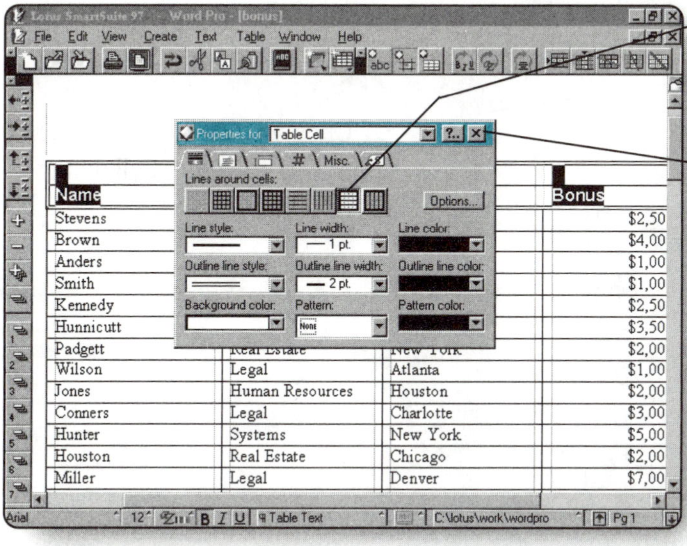

4. **Click** on a **button** under Lines around cells:. The selected border will be applied.

5. **Click** on the **Close button**. The Properties for Table Cell dialog box will close.

Selecting a Number Format for a Column

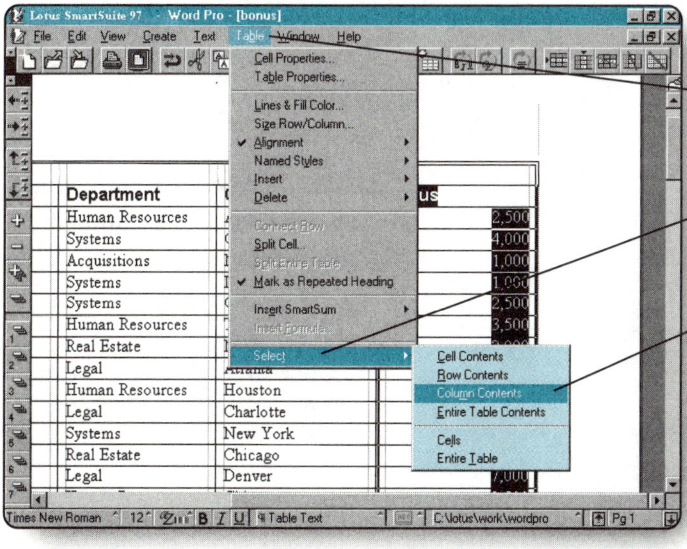

1. **Select** a **cell** in a column.

2. **Click** on **Table**. The Table menu will appear.

3. **Click** on **Select**. The Select submenu will appear.

4. **Click** on **Column Contents**. The column will be selected.

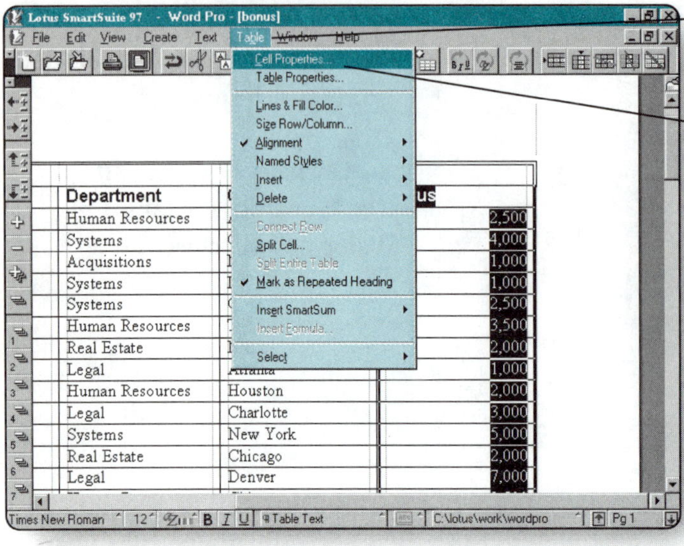

5. Click on **Table**. The Table menu will appear.

6. Click on **Cell Properties**. The Properties for Table Cell dialog box will open.

7. Click on the **Number format tab**. The Number format tab will appear.

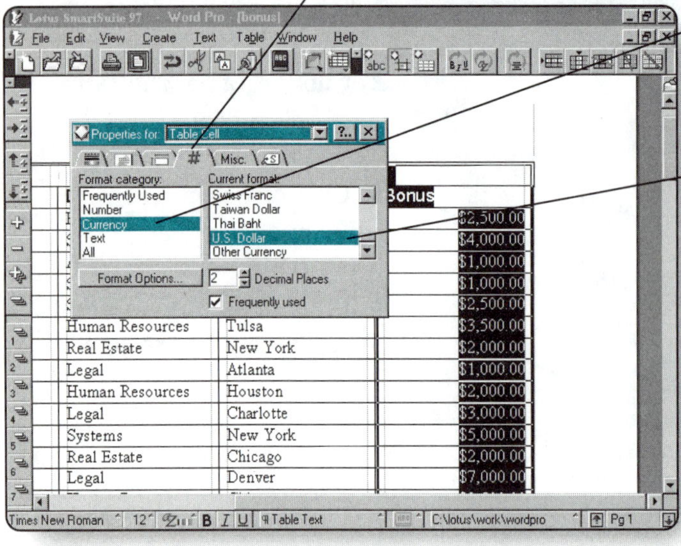

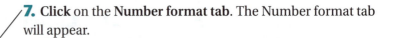

8. Click on a **Format category:**. The format category will be applied to the selected cells.

9. Click on the **Current format:** you want to use. The number format will be applied to the selected column.

10. Click on the **Close button**. The Properties for Table Cell dialog box will close.

Connecting Cells

You may want to connect cells when creating a heading for your table.

1. **Press** and **hold** the **mouse button** and **drag** across the **cells** you want to connect. The cells will be selected.

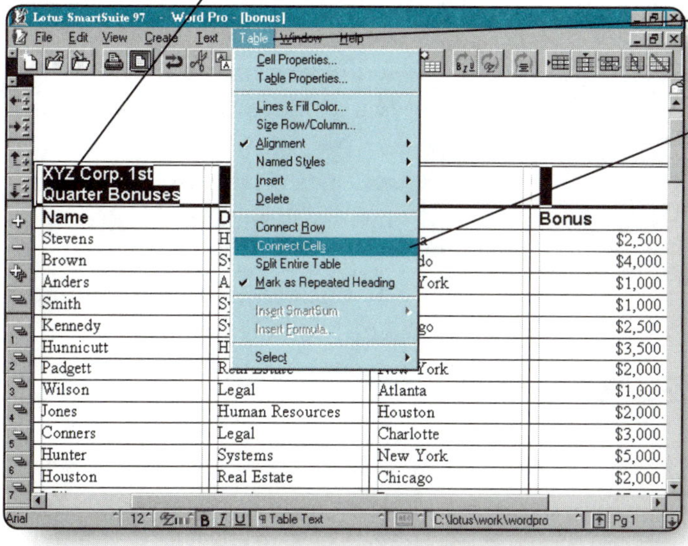

2. **Click** on **Table**. The Table menu will appear.

3. **Click** on **Connect Cells**. The cells will connect.

Creating a Repeated Heading

If you have a table that spans more than one page, you may want to mark a heading as a repeated heading. This tells Word Pro to place the marked heading at the top of each page of the table.

1. **Click** on a **cell** in the row that you want to mark as a repeated heading. The cell will be selected.

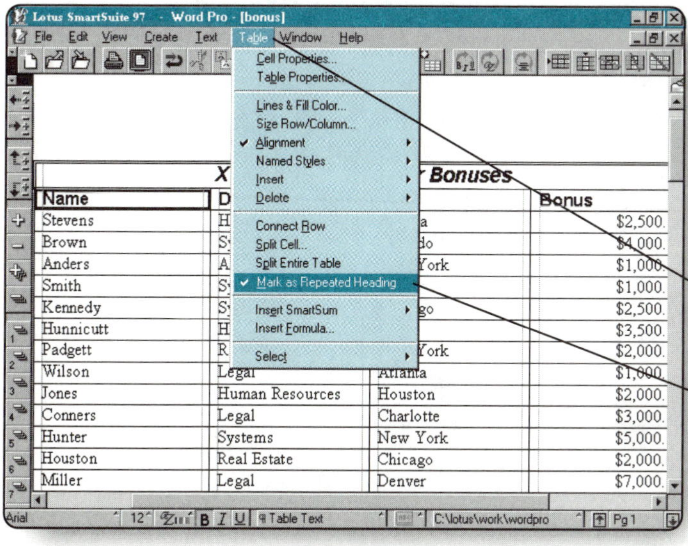

2. **Click** on **Table**. The Table menu will appear.

3. **Click** on **Mark as Repeated Heading**. The heading will automatically repeat on each page of the table.

DOCUMENTING POINTS WITH FOOTNOTES

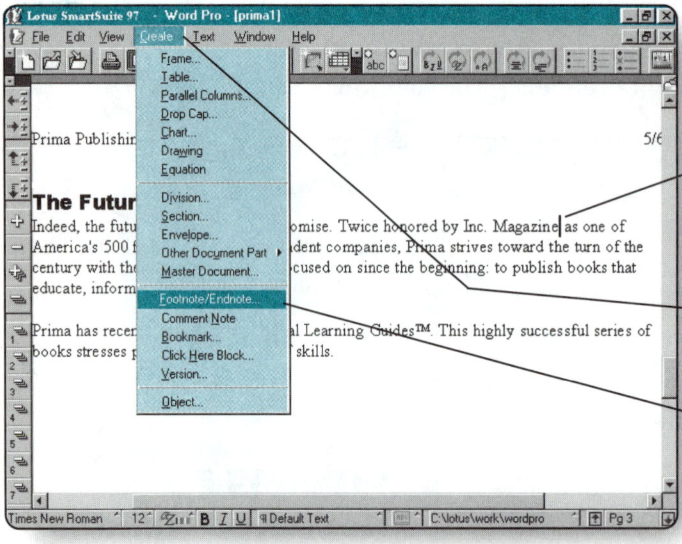

Footnotes comment on and provide reference information for the text in your document.

1. Click on the **location** for the footnote. The insertion point will be moved to that location.

2. Click on **Create**. The Create menu will appear.

3. Click on **Footnote/Endnote**. The Footnotes dialog box will open.

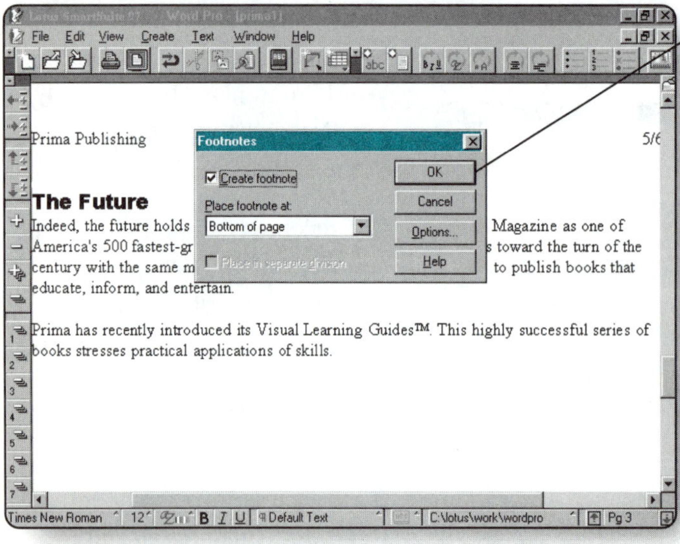

4. Click on **OK**. The footnote will be added to the document, and the Footnotes dialog box will close.

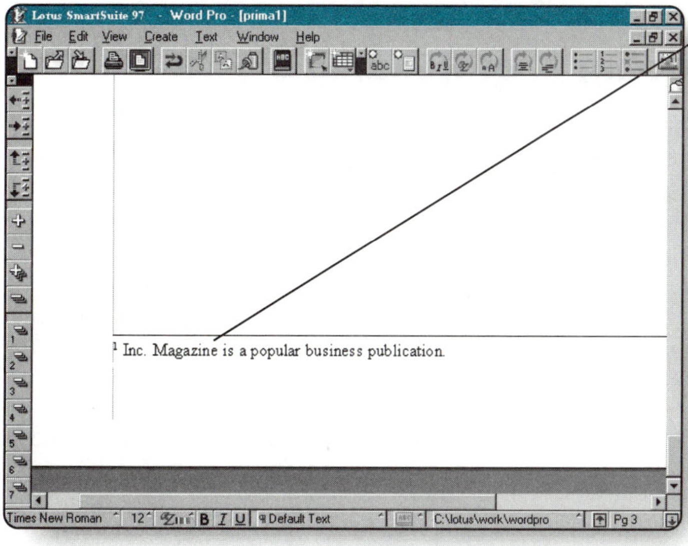

5. Type the **text** of the footnote. The text will be entered for this footnote.

6. Press the **Esc key** to return to the main text of the document.

ORGANIZING YOUR REPORT WITH A TABLE OF CONTENTS

Because reports are typically documents that contain several pages, it is useful to include a table of contents. Word Pro makes it easy to mark text for your table of contents and to generate the table of contents.

Creating a Table of Contents

Creating a table of contents requires two basic steps. The easiest way to select text for a table of contents is to use styles. Heading 1, Heading 2, and Heading 3 styles are default entries for table of contents creation. After the appropriate headings are applied, the second step is to generate the table of contents.

Applying a Heading 1, Heading 2, or Heading 3 Style

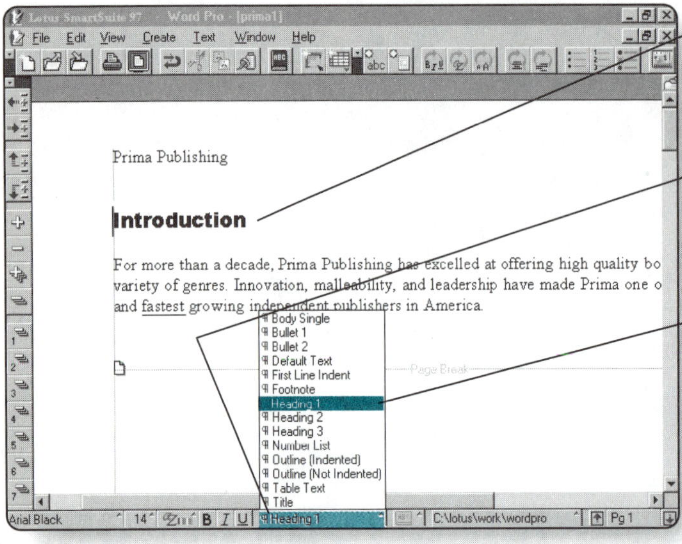

1. **Click** on the **line of text** to which you want to apply a style. The line will be selected.
2. **Click** on the **Style Status button**. The available styles will be listed.
3. **Click** on a **style**. You should use either Heading 1, Heading 2, or Heading 3. The style will be applied to the entire paragraph.

Generating the Table of Contents

1. **Click** on **Create**. The Create menu will appear.

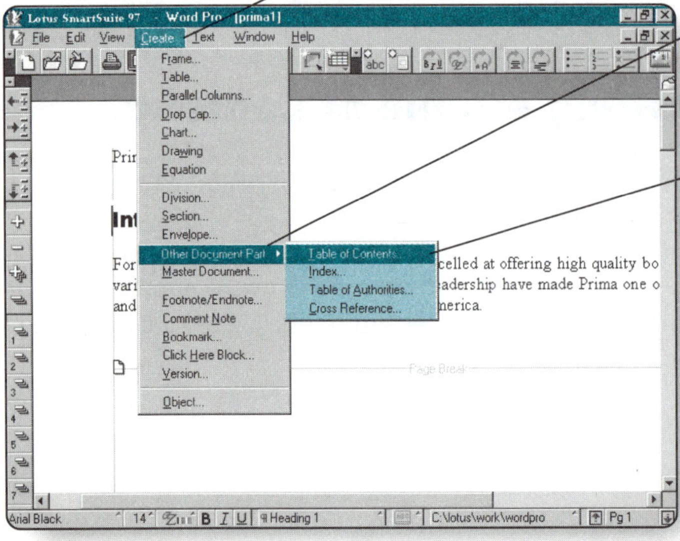

2. **Click** on **Other Document Part**. The Other Document Part submenu will appear.
3. **Click** on **Table of Contents**. The Table of Contents Assistant dialog box will open.

4. **Choose** from the following **options**:

- ✦ Choose the Table of contents look: by clicking on one from the list box.

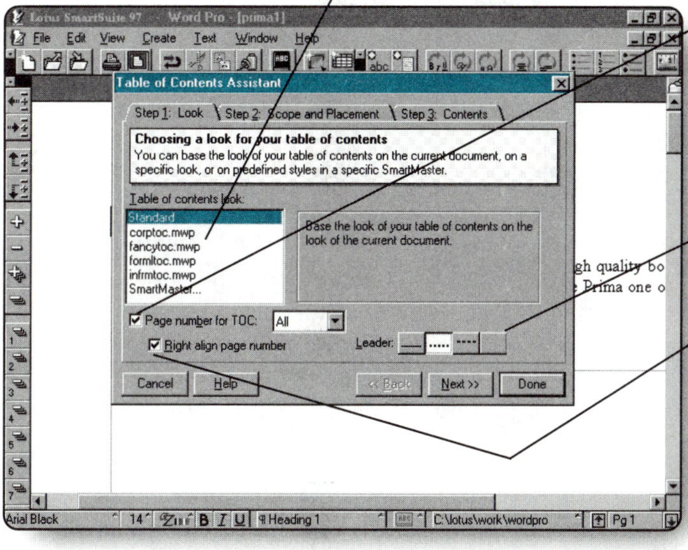

- ✦ If you do not want to include page numbers in your table of contents, click the Page number for TOC: check box to remove the ✔.
- ✦ Click on one of these buttons to select a Leader:.
- ✦ If you do not want to right align the page numbers in your table of contents, click on the Right align page number check box to remove the ✔.

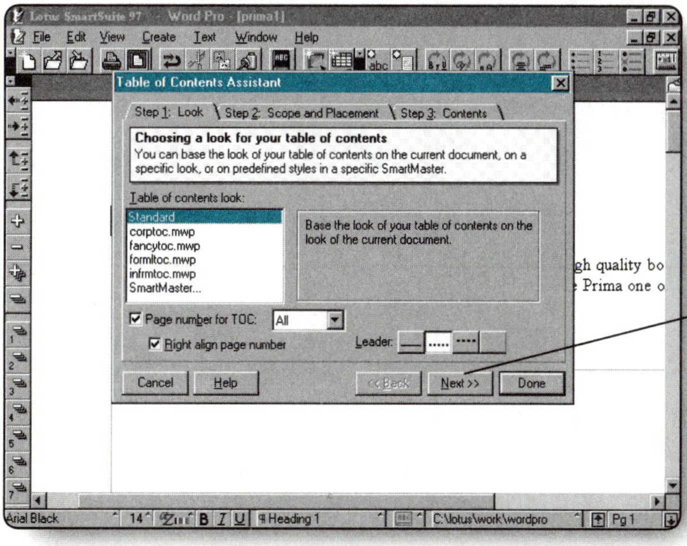

TIP

To select individual entry levels to have page numbers, different leaders, and whether to right align their page numbers, click on the down arrow (▼) in the Page number for TOC: box.

5. **Click** on **Next**. The Step 2 page will appear.

6. **Choose** from the following **options**:

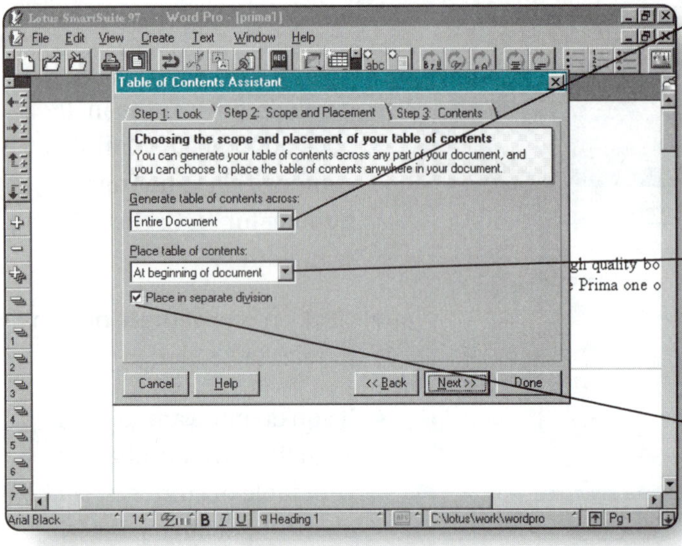

- To change the scope of the table of contents, choose what to Generate the table of contents across: by clicking on the down arrow (▼) and making a selection.
- To select where to Place table of contents:, click on the down arrow (▼) and make a selection.
- If you do not want the TOC to be in a section by itself, remove the ✔ from the Place in separate division check box.

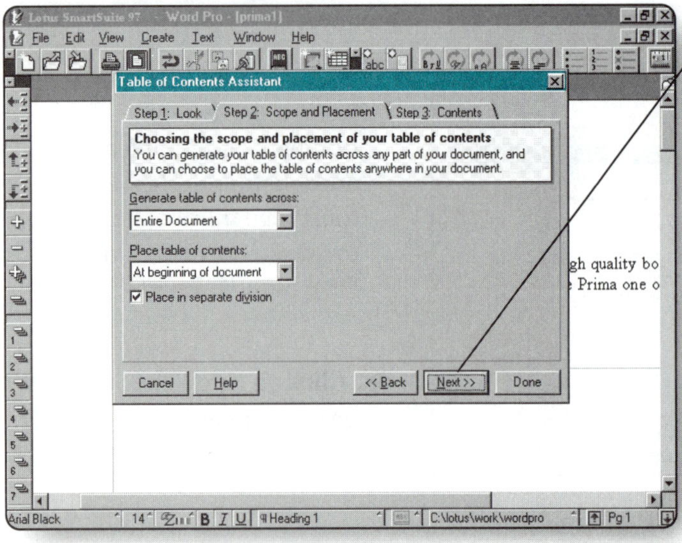

7. **Click** on **Next**. The Step 3 page will appear.

8. Choose from the following **options**:

- Choose a style to work with by clicking on it from the Text to include in table of contents: list box.

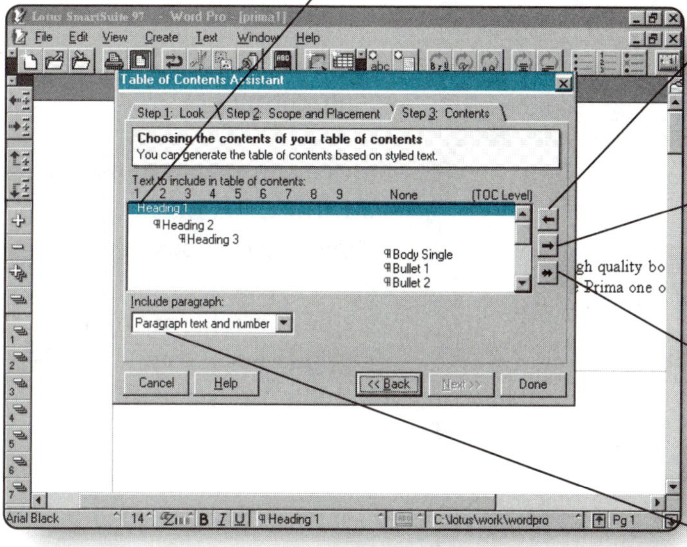

- Clicking the left arrow button moves the selected style into the table of contents hierarchy.
- Clicking the right arrow button moves the selected style down in the table of contents hierarchy.
- You can remove the selected style from the table of contents hierarchy by clicking the double arrow button.
- If you numbered the heading styles, you can decide whether to Include Paragraph: numbering by clicking the down arrow (▼) and making a selection.

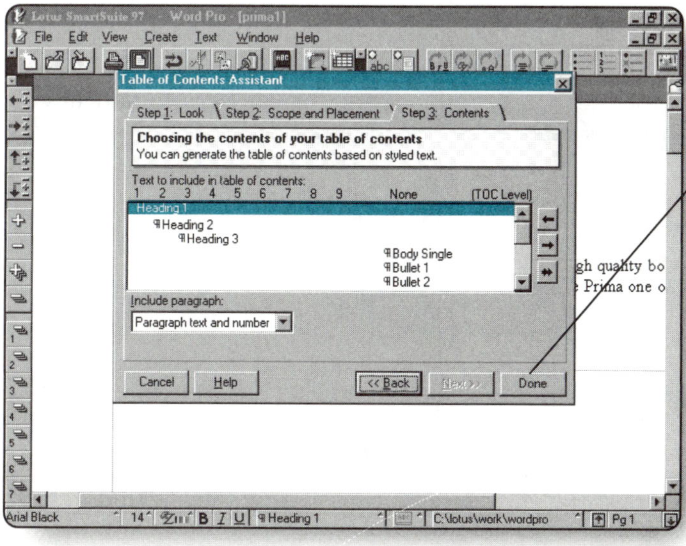

9. Click on **Done**. The table of contents will be automatically generated.

Updating Your Table of Contents

If you make changes by adding to or deleting from the items to be included in the table of contents, you will need to update the table of contents.

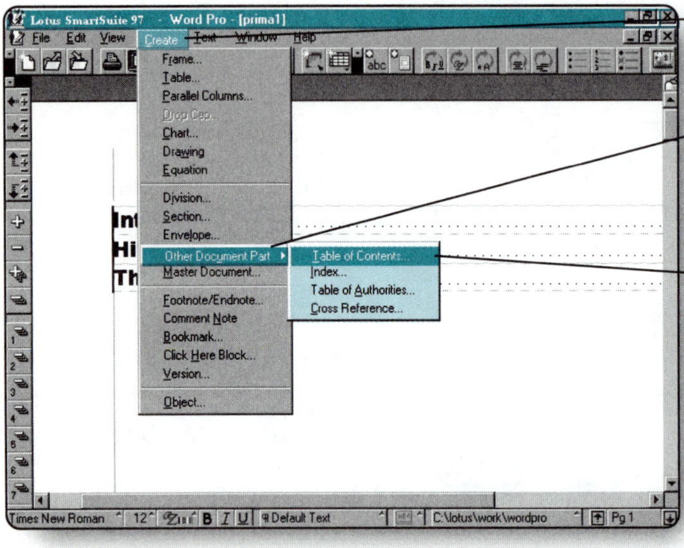

1. **Click** on **Create**. The Create menu will appear.

2. **Click** on **Other Document Part**. The Other Document Part submenu will appear.

3. **Click** on **Table of Contents**. The Update or create Table of Contents dialog box will open.

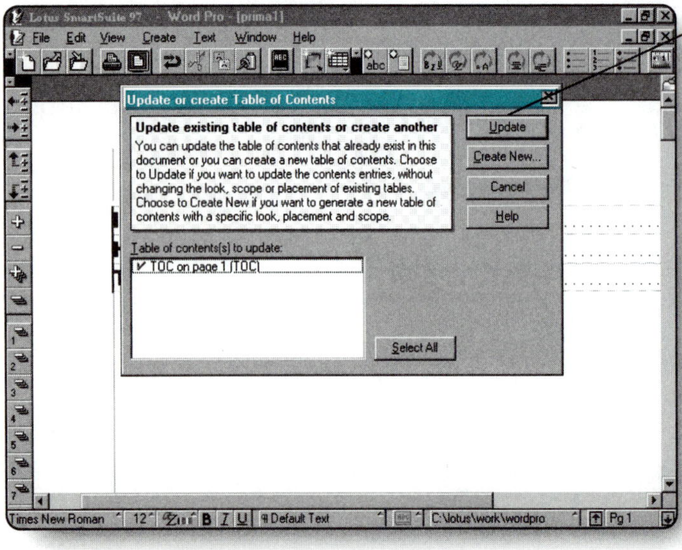

4. **Click** on **Update**. The table of contents will be automatically updated.

7 Improving Your Writing with Word Pro

Word Pro's goal is to make document creation as easy as possible. To reach this goal, several features have been included in Word Pro to improve your writing. You probably misspell a word now and then. Or you may have a grammar error in your document. Word Pro can catch these problems for you. If you can't think of the exact word you want to use, Word Pro's thesaurus can help you out. These and other features can be used to improve your writing style. In this chapter, you'll learn how to:

- Use Word Pro to check your spelling
- Use the thesaurus feature
- Let Word Pro check your grammar
- Create and manage outlines

USING WORD PRO'S SPELLING FEATURES

Word Pro has several spelling features. One feature corrects some of your misspelled word automatically for you. Another points out your misspelled words as you go, giving you the chance to correct them. Still another allows you to locate and correct all misspelled words after you are finished typing. Be aware that Word Pro considers any word it doesn't recognize a misspelled word. This means that proper names like your last name will probably be identified as misspelled.

What Is SmartCorrect?

SmartCorrect is a spelling feature of Word Pro that automatically corrects commonly misspelled words. For example, if you typed *teh*, SmartCorrect would automatically change it to *the*. You don't have to do anything. It is taken care of for you. Other examples of words that would be corrected if mistyped are *and*, *acceptable*, and *chief*.

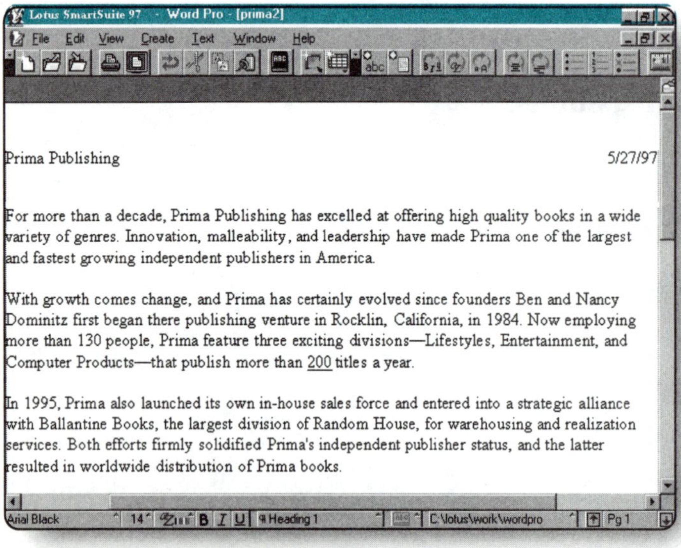

Correcting Spelling While You Type

Word Pro checks words as you type them. If it doesn't recognize the word, the Spell Check button on the status bar changes color to alert you to a possibly misspelled word.

1. **Type** some **text**. If Word Pro does not recognize a word, the Spell Check button on the status bar will change.

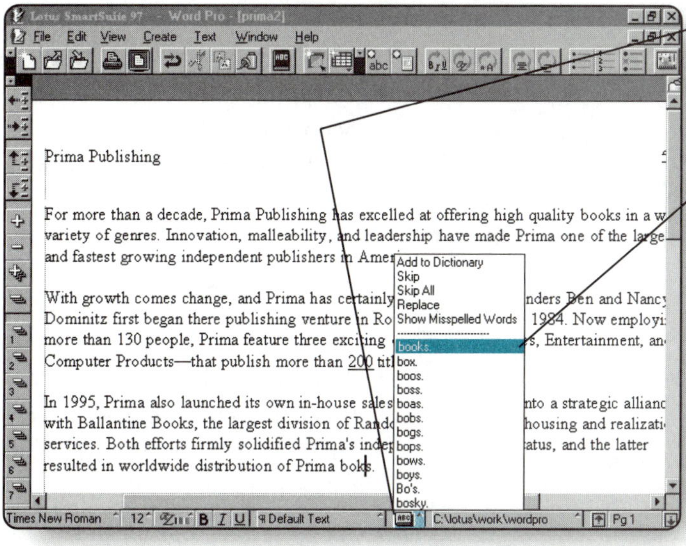

2. Click on the **Spell Check button**. A list of alternative spellings will appear.

3. Click on the **correct spelling**. The text will automatically change to reflect the selected spelling.

Using the Check Spelling Feature

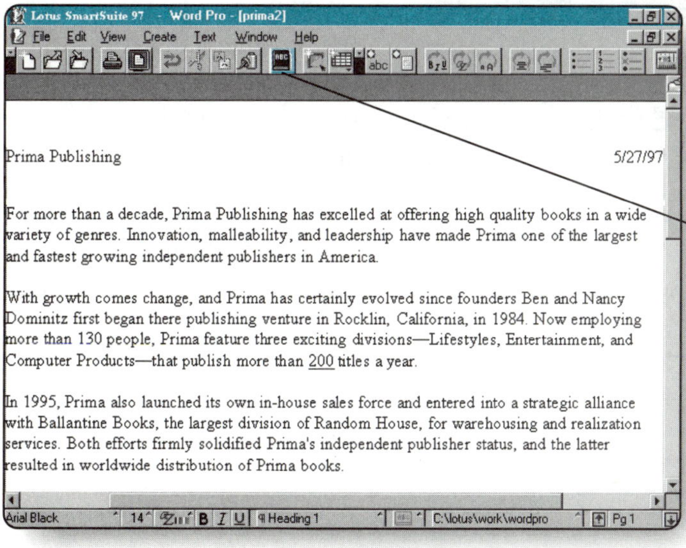

If you don't want to correct your spelling as you go, you can check your spelling when you are finished typing by using the Check Spelling feature.

1. Click on the **Check Spelling SmartIcon**. The Spell Check bar will appear. Any misspelled words will be highlighted in color. The word that Spell Check is currently working with will be highlighted in a deep color.

2. Choose from these **options**:

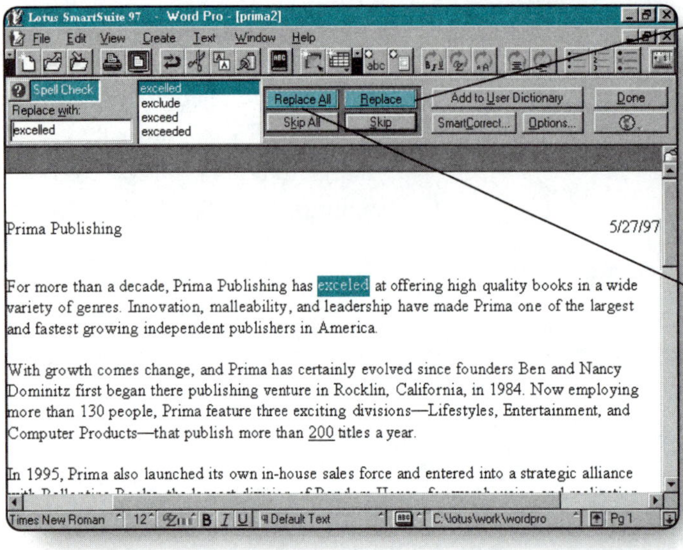

- ✦ To replace this single occurrence of this word, click on the correct spelling from the Spell Check word list and click on Replace. The word will be corrected in your document.
- ✦ To replace all occurrences of this word, click on the correct spelling of the word and then Click on Replace All.

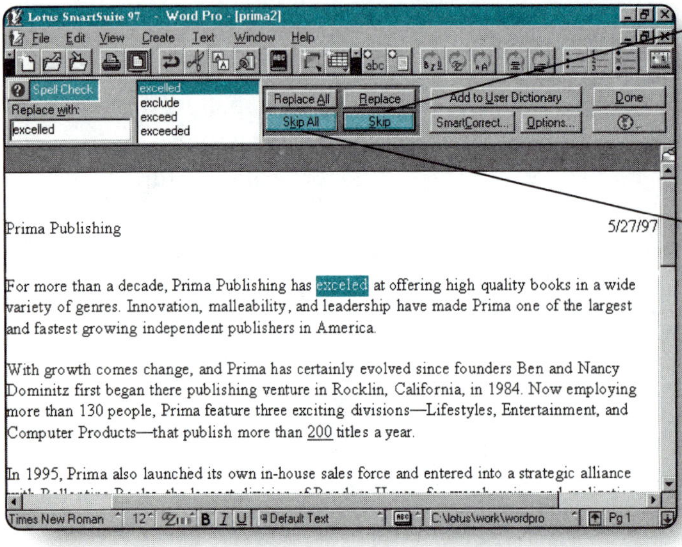

- ✦ If you do not want to change the spelling of this word and you want to skip this occurrence of this word, click on Skip.
- ✦ Click on Skip All if you do not want Spell Check to stop on any occurrences of this word.

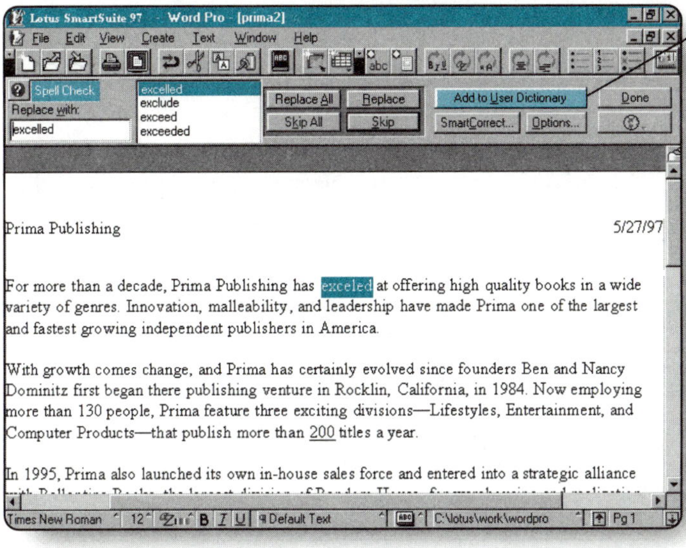

✦ If the word is correctly spelled and you want to avoid having Spell Check stop on it in the future, click on Add to User Dictionary.

3. Repeat step 2 until all the highlighted words have been checked. A message box will display letting you know that there are no more misspelled words.

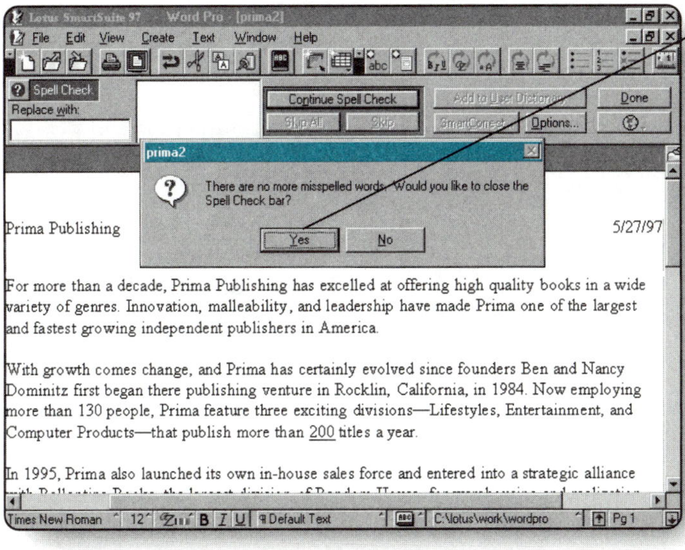

4. Click on **Yes**. The Spell Check bar will close.

FINDING JUST THE RIGHT WORD

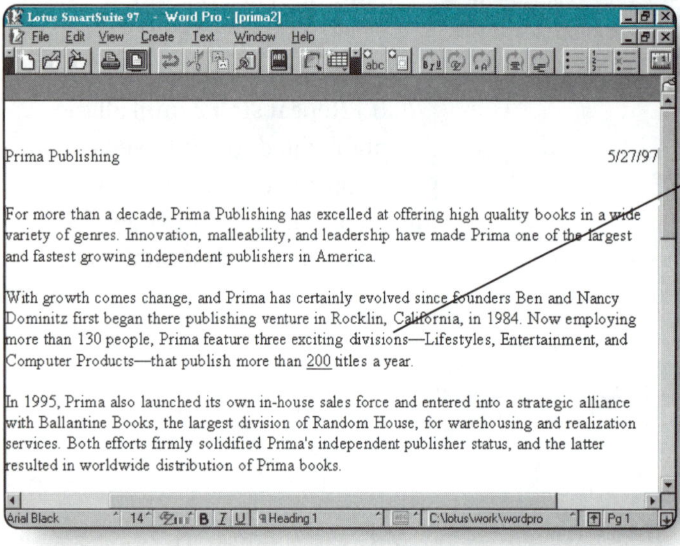

Word Pro's thesaurus gives you an easy way to find just the right words to use in your document.

1. **Position** the **insertion point** in the word you want to replace.

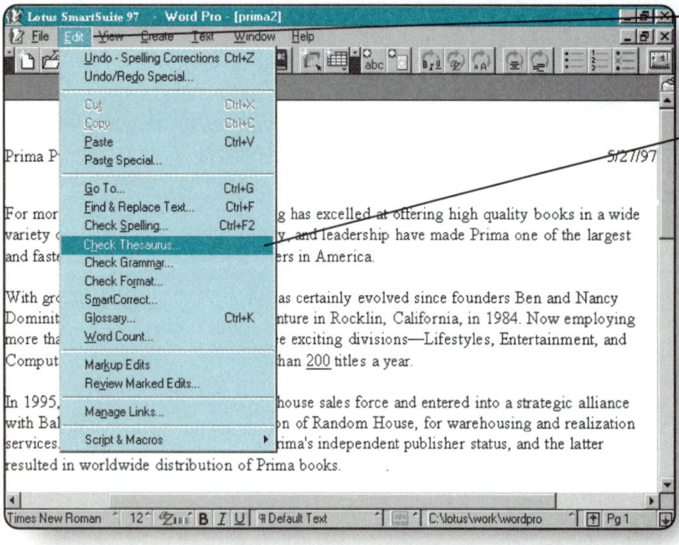

2. **Click** on **Edit**. The Edit menu will appear.

3. **Click** on **Check Thesaurus**. The Thesaurus dialog box will open.

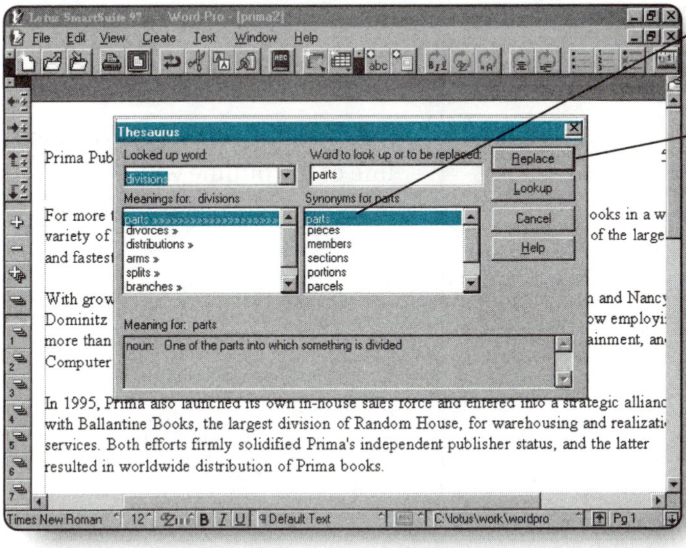

4. **Click** on a **word** from the Synonyms list box.

5. **Click** on **Replace**. The word will be immediately replaced in the document.

6. **Click** on the **Close button**. The Thesaurus dialog box will close.

WORKING WITH OUTLINES

In the olden days of the typewriter, typing an outline was a dreaded task. With Word Pro, outlines are quick to enter and easy to modify. You can create outlines using Word Pro in a couple of ways. The easiest way is with the outline styles and the outline tools.

Using Outline Styles

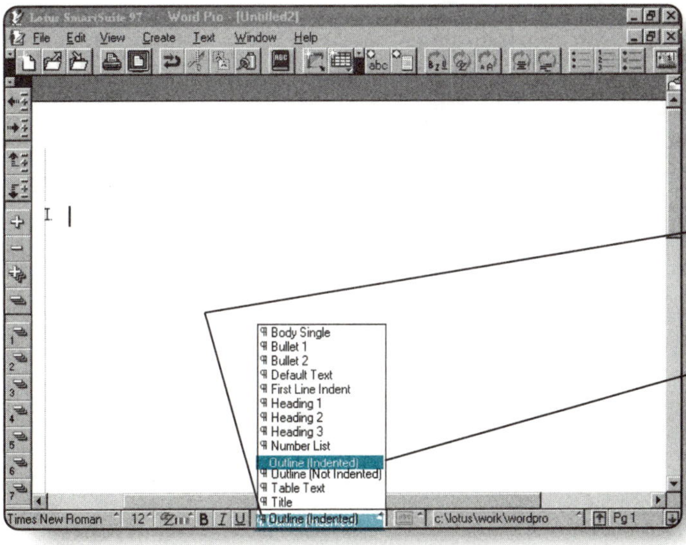

The two outline styles are Outline (Indented) and Outline (Not Indented). To start an outline, apply the Outline (Indented) style.

1. **Click** on the **Style Status button**. A list of available styles will appear.

2. **Click** on **Outline (Indented)**. The style will be applied to the current paragraph. The paragraph will begin with a Roman numeral one (I.)

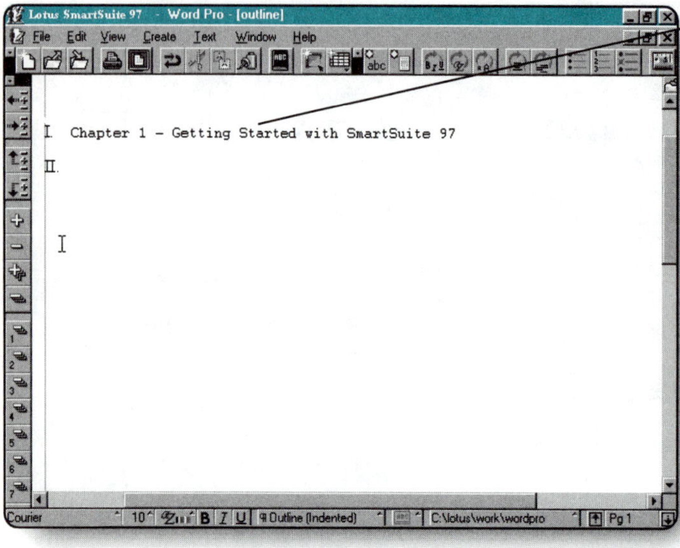

3. Type some **text** for the first line of the outline.

4. Press the **Enter key**. The next line of the outline will automatically be numbered II.

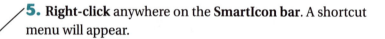

5. Right-click anywhere on the **SmartIcon bar**. A shortcut menu will appear.

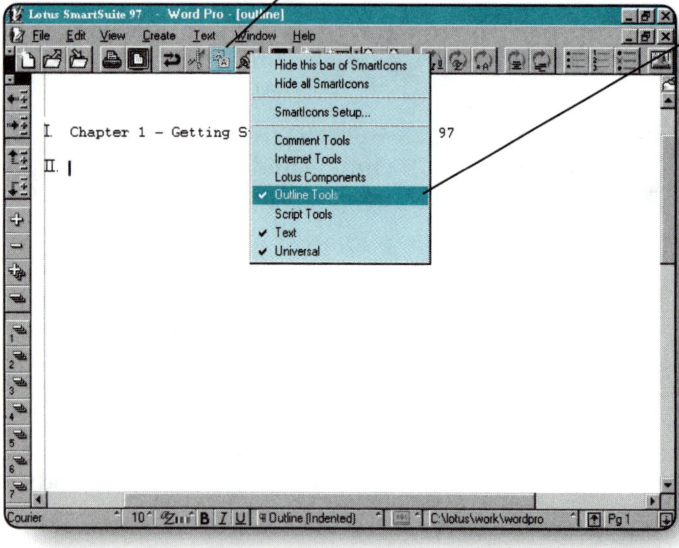

6. Click on **Outline Tools**. The Outline Tools bar will appear.

7a. Click on **Demote in Outline Level,** if you want to demote this line of the outline. The line will be demoted in the outline hierarchy.

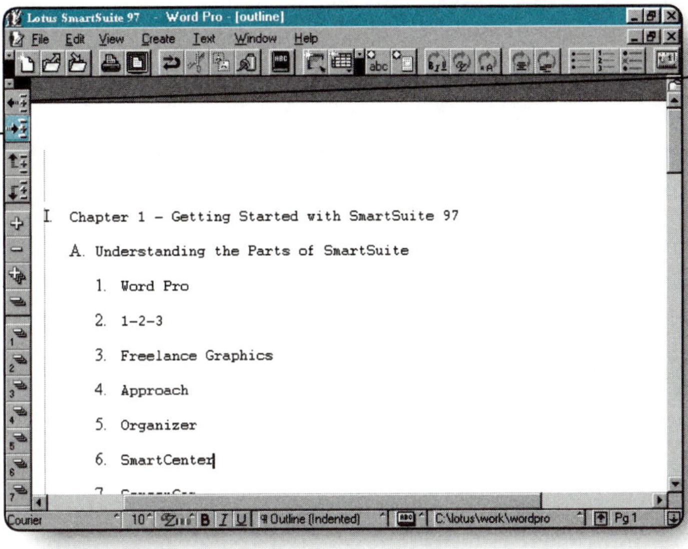

OR

7b. Click on **Promote in Outline Level,** if you want to promote this line of the outline. The line will be promoted in the outline hierarchy.

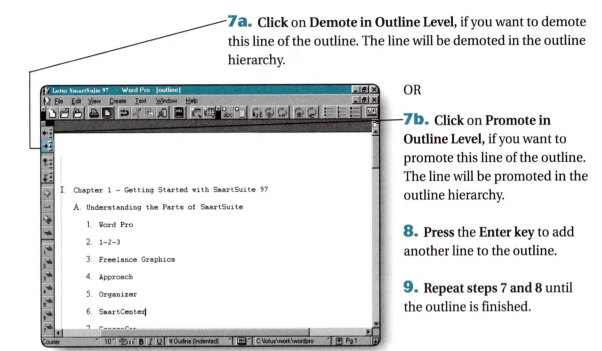

8. Press the **Enter key** to add another line to the outline.

9. Repeat steps 7 and 8 until the outline is finished.

Using the Expand and Collapse Outline Tools

If you do not want to see all the detail in an outline, you collapse it. This hides levels of detail. To see the collapse level of detail, you expand the outline.

Collapsing Part of an Outline

If the current line of the outline has nested levels under it, you can collapse that part of the outline so that you are viewing one less level of detail.

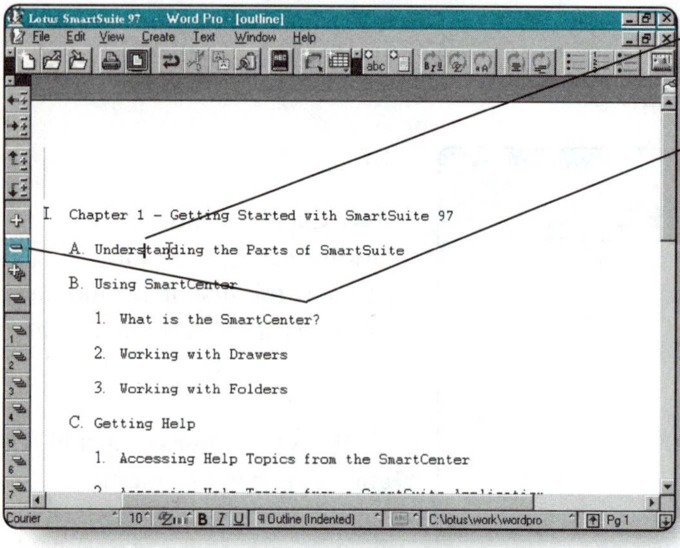

1. Click on the **line** where you want to collapse the outline.

2. Click on the **Collapse button** until all the levels of detail you don't want to see are hidden.

Expanding Part of an Outline

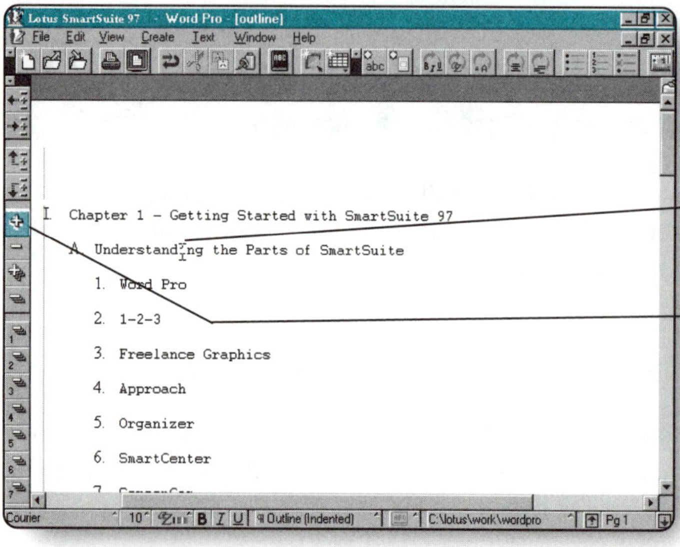

The opposite of collapsing an outline is expanding an outline. This displays hidden levels of detail in an outline.

1. Click on the **line** where you want to expand the outline.

2. Click on the **Expand button** until all the levels of detail you want to see are shown.

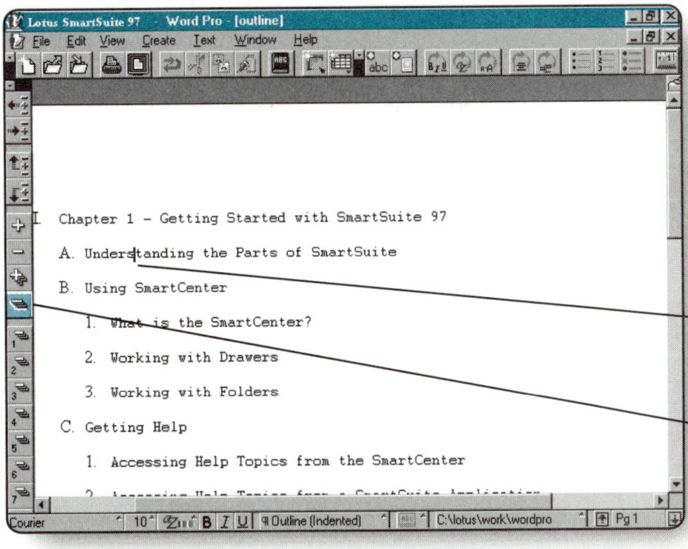

Collapsing All Levels of Detail

If part of your outline has several levels of detail and you want to collapse them all, you can do so using the Collapse All button.

1. Click on the **line** where you want to collapse the outline.

2. Click on the **Collapse All button**. All levels of detail for that part of the outline are hidden.

Expanding All Levels of Detail

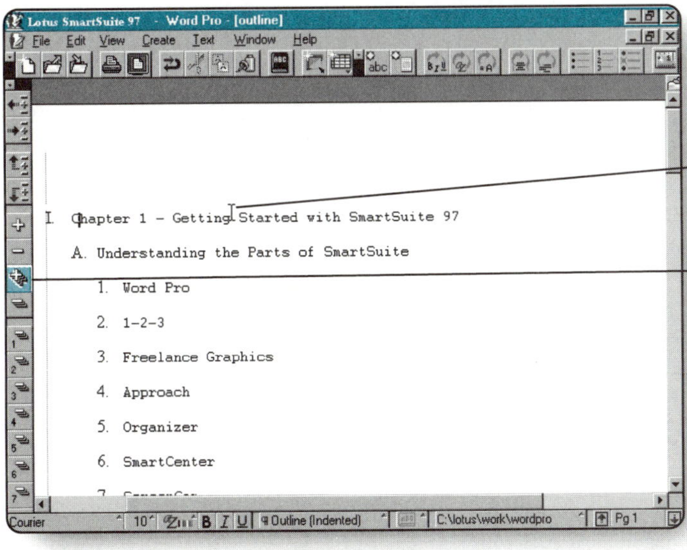

To show the all the hidden levels of detail, use the Expand All button.

1. Click on the **line** where you want to expand the outline.

2. Click on the **Expand All button**. All levels of detail for that part of the outline are shown.

8 Merging Files

If you ever have to mail the same basic letter to several people, you will find mail merge an invaluable tool. Let's say that you are sending out your resume to several companies, and you want to include a cover letter. The cover letter needs to be the same except for the address of the company receiving the letter. This is a perfect example of when to merge files. In this chapter, you'll learn how to:

- Create a data file
- Create the letter to merge
- Perform the merge

CREATING A DATA FILE

The first step to performing a merge is creating the merge data file. This file contains the data to be used to customize your letter. This file contains records. A record is a collection of information about one subject. For example, the data about one person or company would be stored in a record. Records are broken into fields. Fields contain one part of a record's information. ZIP code, phone number, last name, and company name are examples of fields.

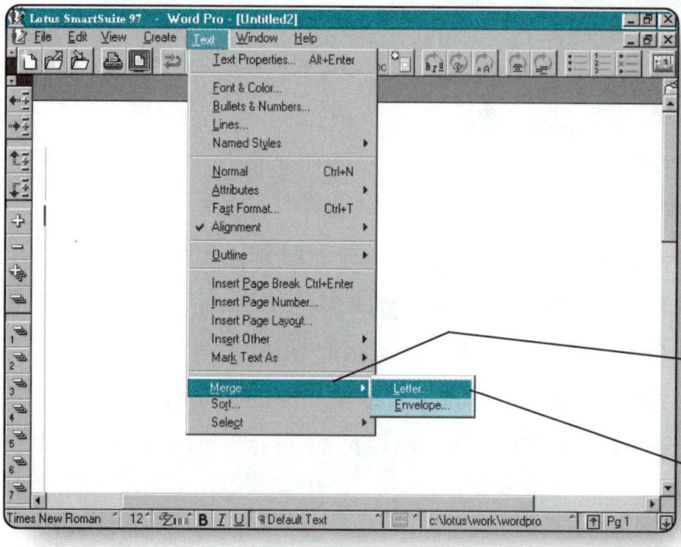

1. **Click** on **Text**. The Text menu will appear.

2. **Click** on **Merge**. The Merge submenu will appear.

3. **Click** on **Letter**. The Mail Merge Assistant will open.

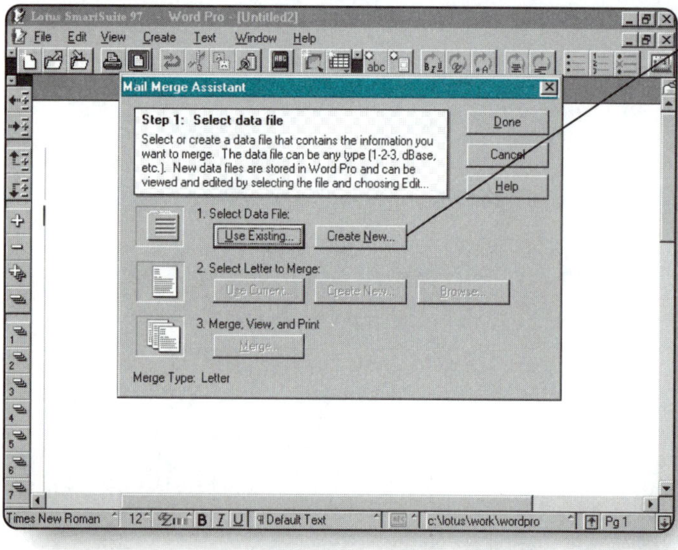

4. **Click** on **Create New**. The Create Data File dialog box will open.

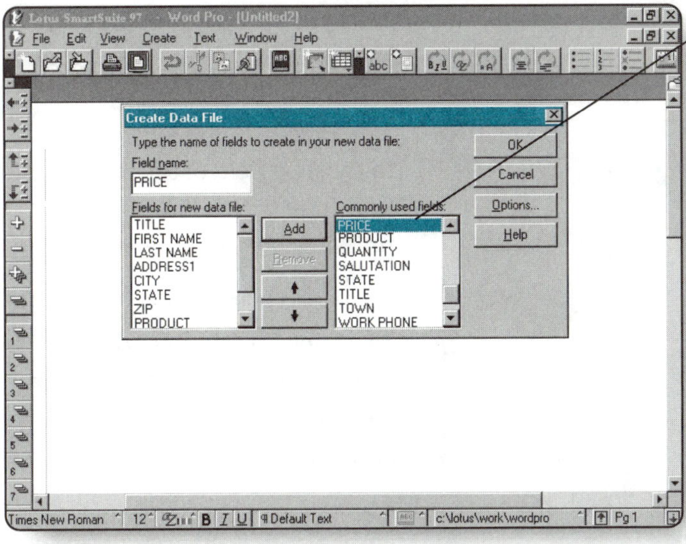

5. **Click** on a **field name** from the Commonly used fields: list box. The field will be selected.

TIP

If you cannot find a field name you want to use in the Commonly used fields: list box, type the name of the field you want in the Field name: text box. You can use letters, numbers, or spaces in your field names.

6. **Click** on **Add**. The field will be added to the Fields for new data file: list box.

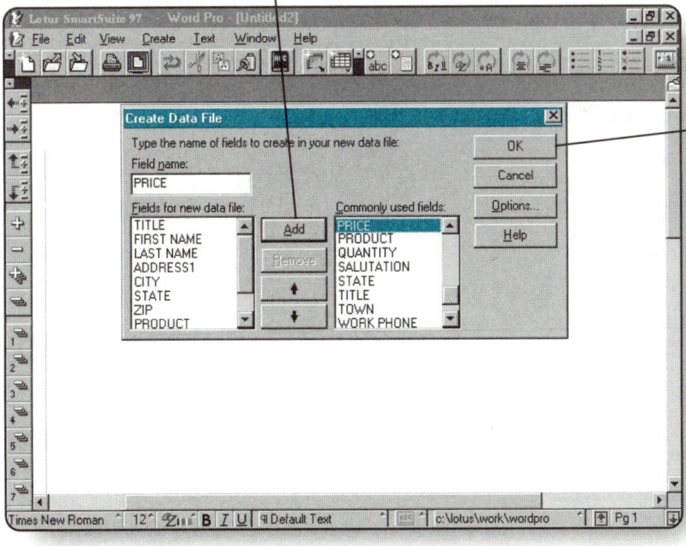

7. **Repeat steps** 3 and 4 for each field you want to add.

8. **Click** on **OK**. The Edit Data File dialog box will open.

9. **Type** some **data** for the first field of the record in the **text box.** The data will be entered for that field.

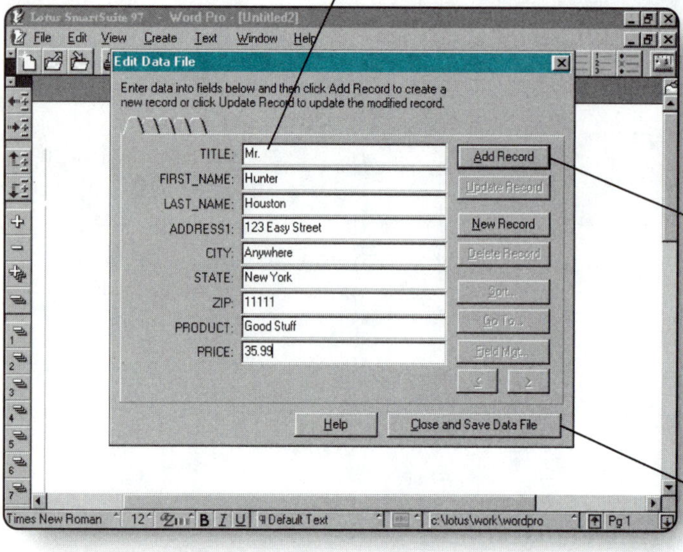

10. **Press** the **Tab key** to move to the next field of the record. Continue typing data and pressing Tab until the fields are complete.

11. **Click** on **Add Record**. The record will be added to the data file, and then a new record will appear.

12. **Repeat steps 7** through **9** until all the records are added.

13. **Click** on **Close and Save Data File**. A message box will appear letting you know that the current data file has changed.

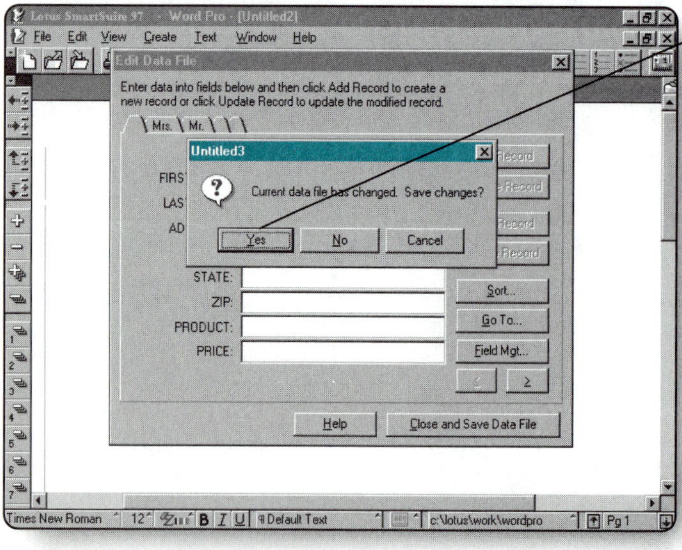

14. **Click** on **Yes**. The Save As dialog box will open.

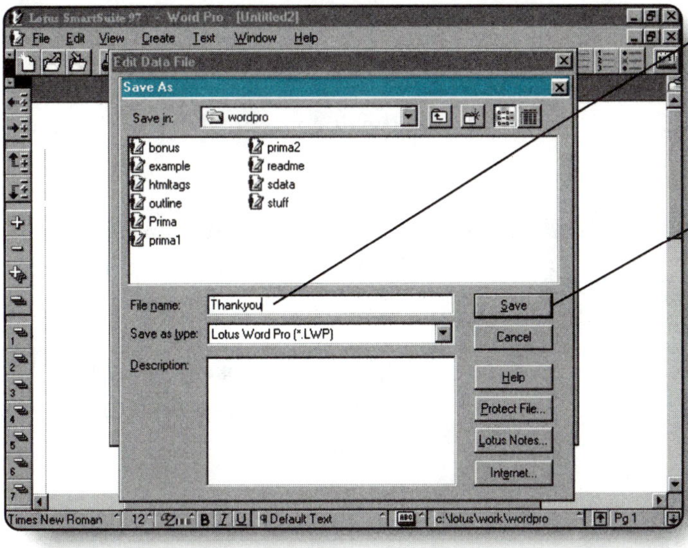

15. **Type** a **name** for the data file in the File name: text box. The text will be entered for the name.

16. **Click** on **Save**. The Mail Merge Assistant dialog box will open.

CREATING LETTER TO MERGE

After the fields are defined, you can create the letter to merge.

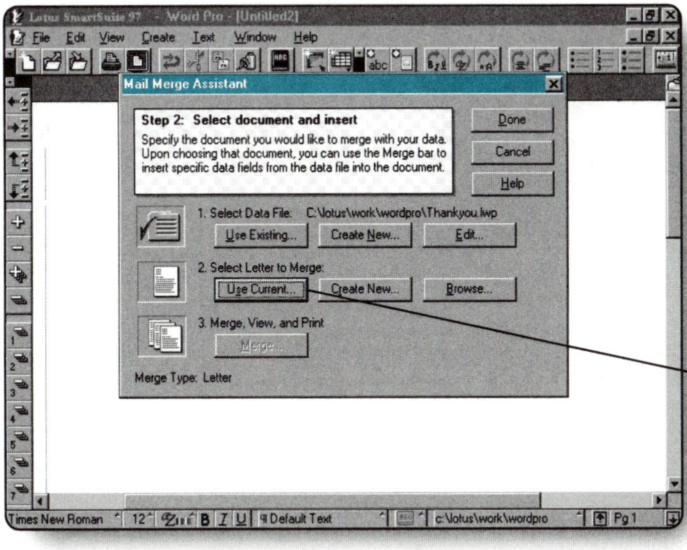

NOTE

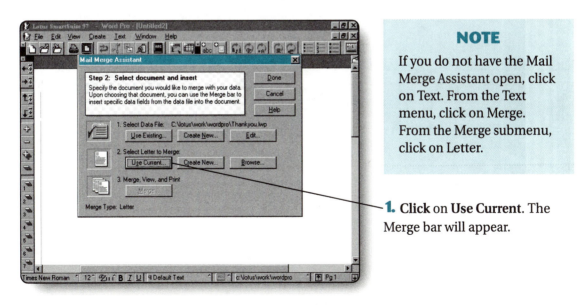

If you do not have the Mail Merge Assistant open, click on Text. From the Text menu, click on Merge. From the Merge submenu, click on Letter.

1. **Click** on **Use Current**. The Merge bar will appear.

2a. Type some **text** for the letter.

OR

2b. Click on the **location** in the document where you want to place a field.

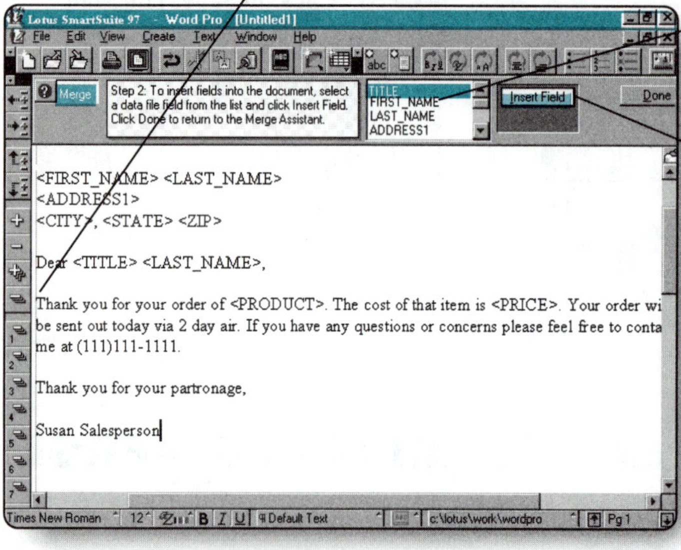

3. Click on a **field name** from the Merge bar's list box. The field name will be selected.

4. Click on **Insert Field.** A field code will be inserted into the document.

5. Repeat steps 2 through **5** until the letter is complete.

> **TIP**
>
> You can insert the same field in more than one location.

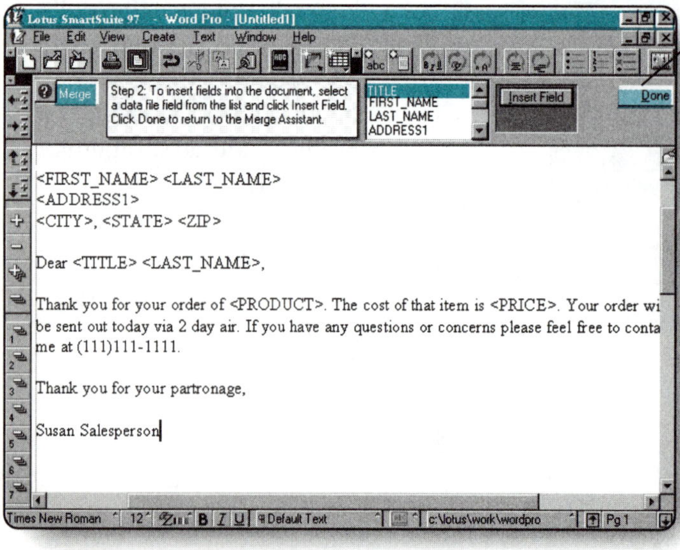

6. Click on **Done**. The Mail Merge Assistant dialog box will close.

PERFORMING THE MERGE AND PRINTING THE LETTERS

You can either view the merged documents on the screen before printing them or you can print them directly to a printer.

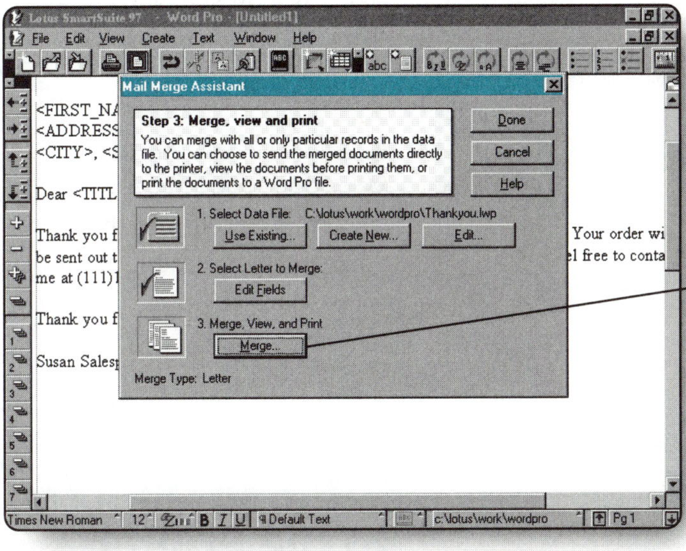

Viewing the Merged Documents On-Screen Before Printing Them

1. **Click** on **Merge**. The Merge, View and Print dialog box will open.

> **NOTE**
>
> If you do not have the Mail Merge Assistant open, then click on Text. From the Text menu, click on Merge. From the Merge submenu, click on Letter.

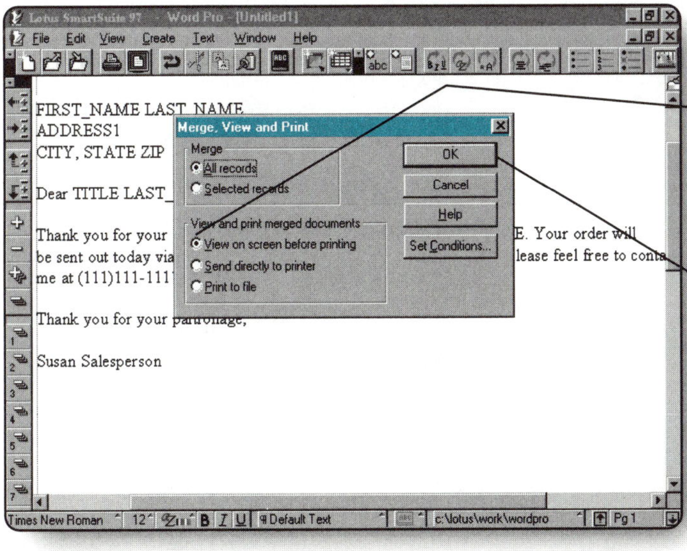

2. **Click** on **View on screen before printing**. The View and print merge documents option will be set.

3. **Click** on **OK**. The Merge bar and the first merged document will appear.

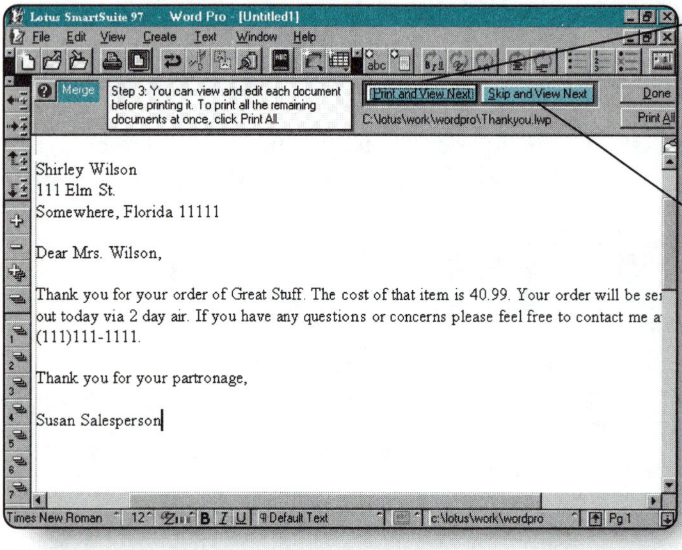

4a. Click on **Print and View Next**. The current document will print, and the next merged document will appear.

OR

4b. Click on **Skip and View Next**. The next merged document will appear.

5. Repeat step 4 until the Merge bar is no longer displayed. This means that all the merged documents have been displayed.

NOTE

If you decide you do not want to view and print all the merged documents, click Done to close the Merge bar.

Printing Directly to the Printer

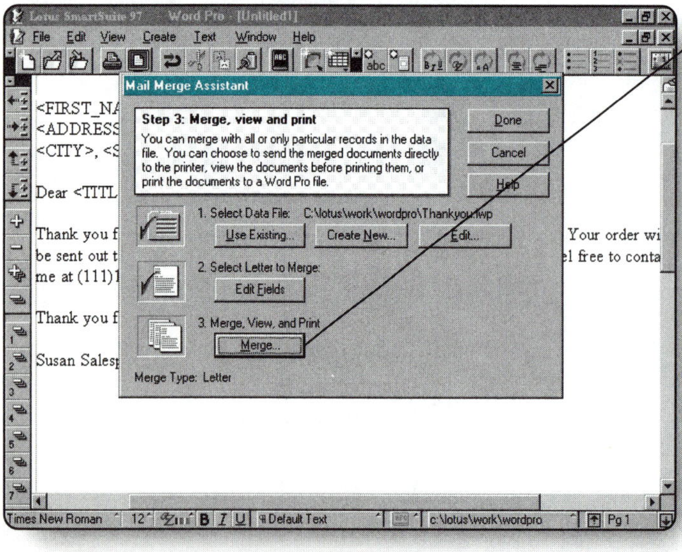

1. Click on **Merge**. The Merge, View and Print dialog box will open.

NOTE

If you do not have the Mail Merge Assistant open, then click on Text. From the Text menu, click on Merge. From the Merge submenu, click on Letter.

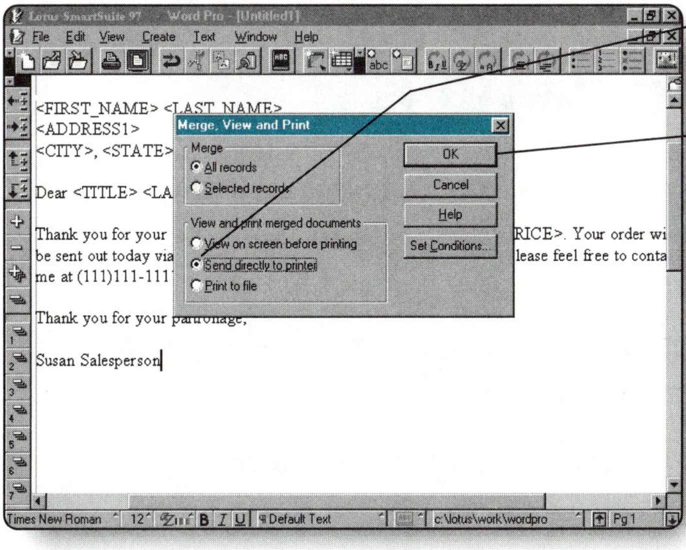

2. **Click** on **Send directly to printer**.

3. **Click** on **OK**. The merged documents will print on your printer.

PART II REVIEW QUESTIONS

1. **How would you create a letter that already had some of the text and formatting done for you?** ***See "Working with SmartMasters" in Chapter 2***
2. **How would you get to the end of a document?** ***See "Navigating in a Word Pro Document" in Chapter 2***
3. **How would you move text from one part of a document to another?** ***See "Cutting, Copying, and Pasting Text" in Chapter 2***
4. **What happens when you click the Print button?** ***See "Printing Your Document" in Chapter 3***
5. **How can you print just one page of a document?** ***See "Printing Your Document" in Chapter 3***
6. **How would you center a paragraph?** ***See "Selecting Paragraph Alignment and Indention Options" in Chapter 4***
7. **Why would you use a style?** ***See "Applying Styles" in Chapter 4***
8. **How would you include a copyright symbol in your document?** ***See "Inserting Symbols" in Chapter 4***
9. **What would you use if you needed the same text to repeat at the top of every page of your document?** ***See "Adding Headers and Footers" in Chapter 5***
10. **What is the best way to enter text that needs to have multiple columns?** ***See "Working with Tables" in Chapter 6***

PART III

Using 1-2-3

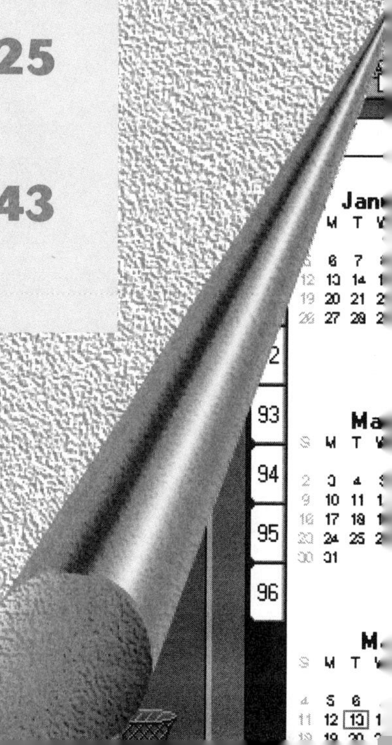

9 Creating a Simple Workbook

If you have ever used a columnar pad to work with numbers, you know what a time-consuming and tedious job it can be. Working with the columnar pad, a pencil, and a calculator, you may have had to do a budget, a timesheet, an expense report, or other dreaded task. These tasks are remarkably easier, and a lot less dreaded, using 1-2-3. In this chapter, you'll learn how to:

- Start Lotus 1-2-3 using SuiteStart
- Create a simple worksheet
- Edit data in a worksheet

STARTING LOTUS 1-2-3 USING SUITESTART

When you start your computer, two Lotus tools automatically load for you, SmartCenter and SuiteStart. In Chapter 1, you saw how to start an application using SmartCenter. Here you will start an application, in this case 1-2-3, using SuiteStart.

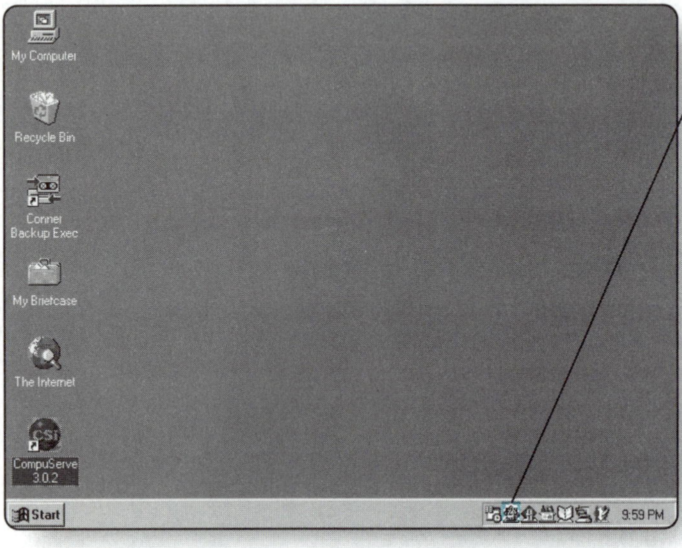

1. **Click** on the **Lotus icon** from the SuiteStart icon palette.

CREATING A WORKBOOK

When you start 1-2-3, it gives you the option to create a new workbook. You can also create a new workbook by using the File menu.

Creating a Workbook from the Welcome to 1-2-3 Dialog Box

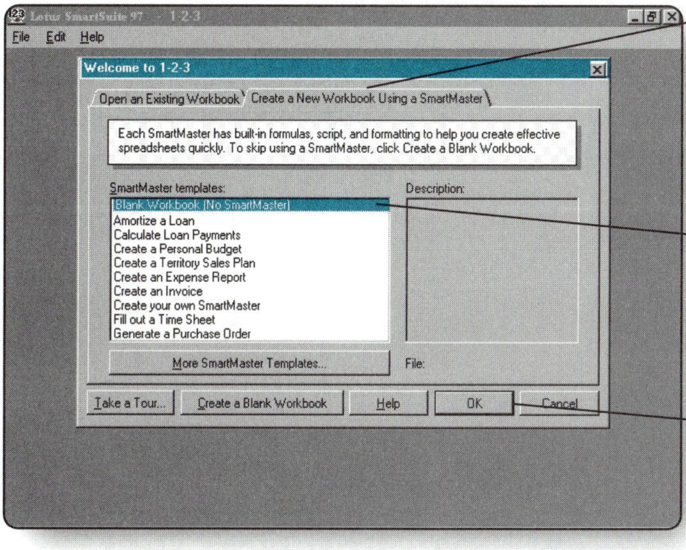

1. **Click** on the **Create a New Workbook Using a SmartMaster tab.** The Create a New Workbook Using a SmartMaster tab will appear.
2. **Click** on a **SmartMaster** from the SmartMaster templates: list box. The SmartMaster will be selected.
3. **Click** on **OK**. A new workbook will appear.

Creating a Workbook from the File Menu

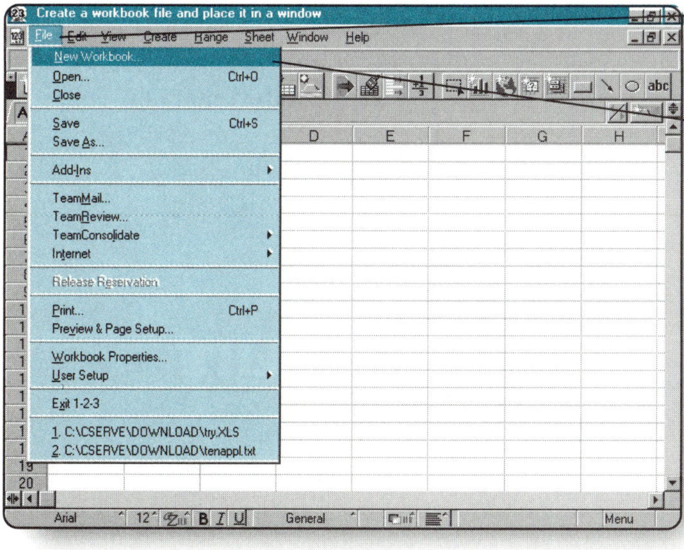

1. **Click** on **File**. The File menu will appear.
2. **Click** on **New Workbook.** The New Workbook dialog box will open.

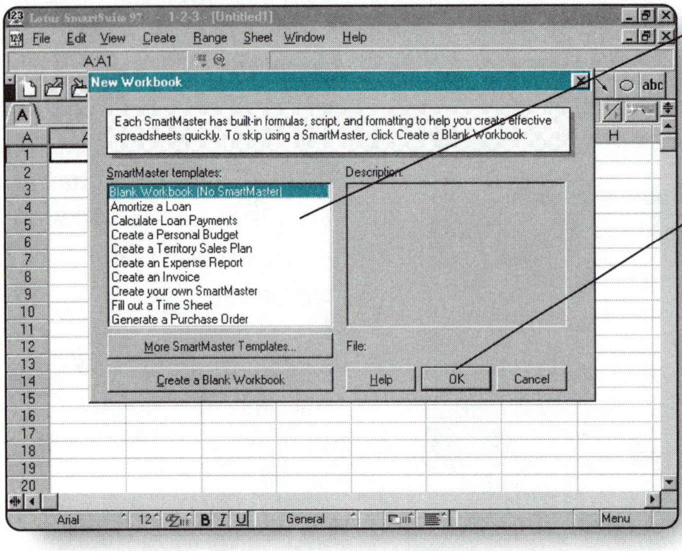

3. **Click** on a **SmartMaster** from the SmartMaster templates: list box. The SmartMaster will be selected.

4. **Click** on **OK**. A new workbook will appear.

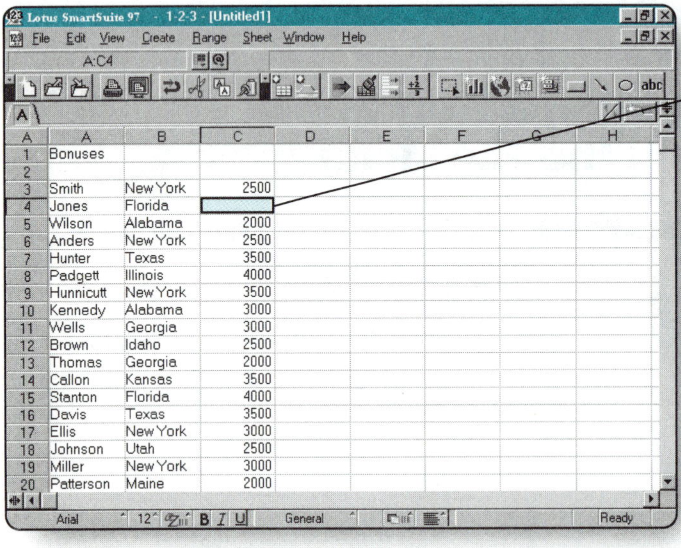

Entering Text

1. **Click** on a **cell**. The cell will be selected.

2. **Type** some **text**. The text will appear in the selected cell.

3. **Press** the **Enter key**. The text will be entered in the selected cell.

EDITING DATA

You can edit your data in a variety of ways. You may need to change the contents of a cell. Or you may want to move the data to another part of the worksheet.

Making Changes

You can make changes to the contents of a cell in two ways. One is by typing over the contents of a cell. The other is by modifying the contents of a cell.

Typing Over the Contents of a Cell

1. Click on a **cell**. The cell will be selected.

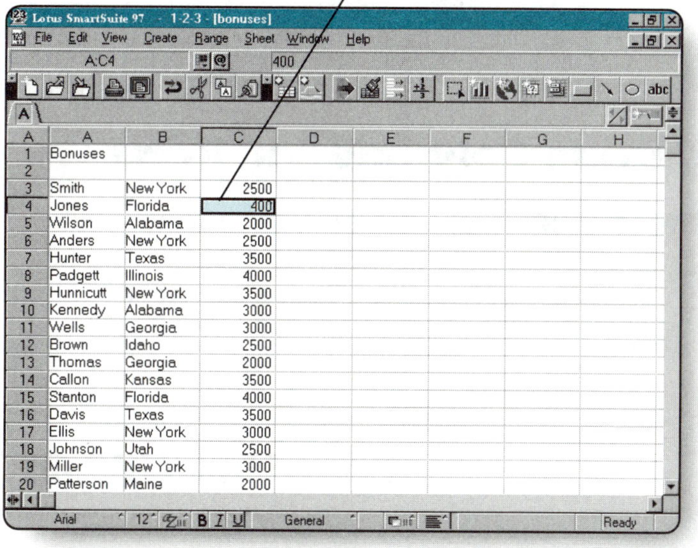

2. Type some new **text**. The text will appear in the cell.

3. Press the **Enter key**. The text will be entered in the selected cell.

Editing the Contents of a Cell

1. Click on a **cell**. The cell will be selected.

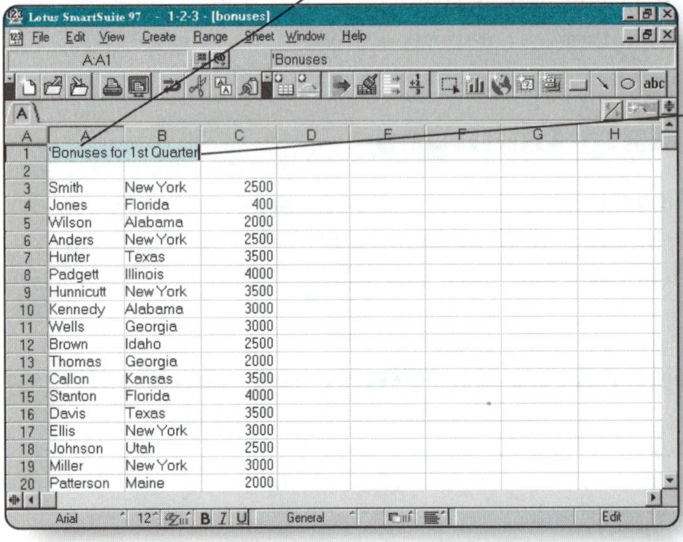

2. Press the **F2 key**. The cell will be placed in edit mode.

3. Position the **insertion point** within the cell by using the Right and Left Arrow keys. The insertion point will be relocated within the current cell.

4. Type the **changes**. The changes will appear in the current cell.

5. Press the **Enter key**. The changes will be entered into the current cell.

Inserting Columns and Rows

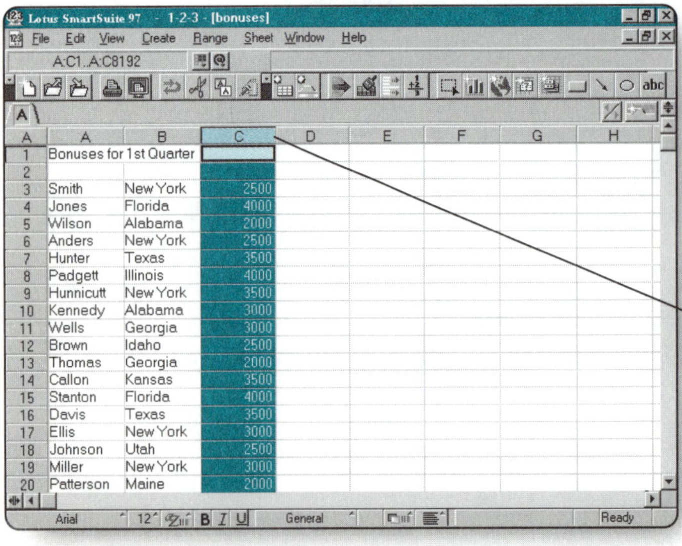

Often after you have entered data into your workbook, you find that you need to add a column or row. This is done using the Range menu.

Inserting a Column

1. Click on the **column heading** of the column you want to insert to the left of. The column will be selected.

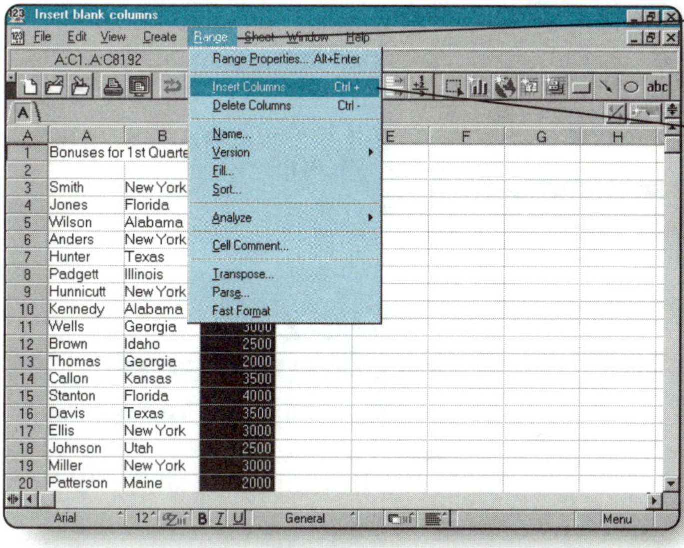

2. **Click** on **Range**. The Range menu will appear.

3. **Click** on **Insert Columns.** A new column will be inserted into the worksheet.

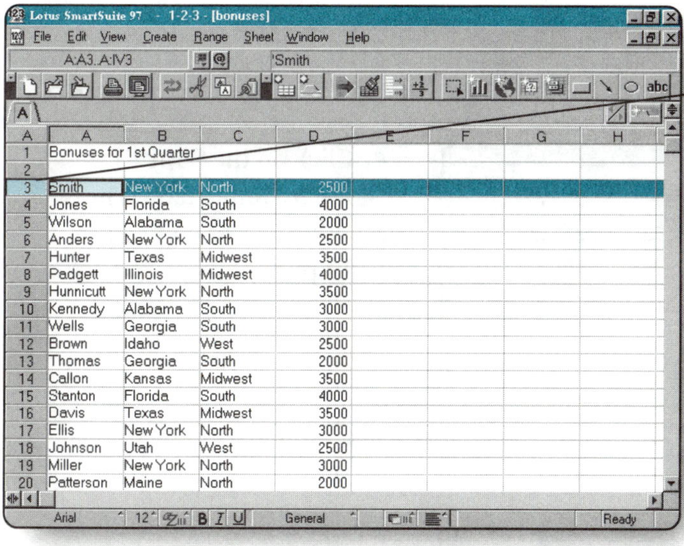

Inserting a Row

1. **Click** on the **row heading** above which you want to insert a new row. The row will be selected.

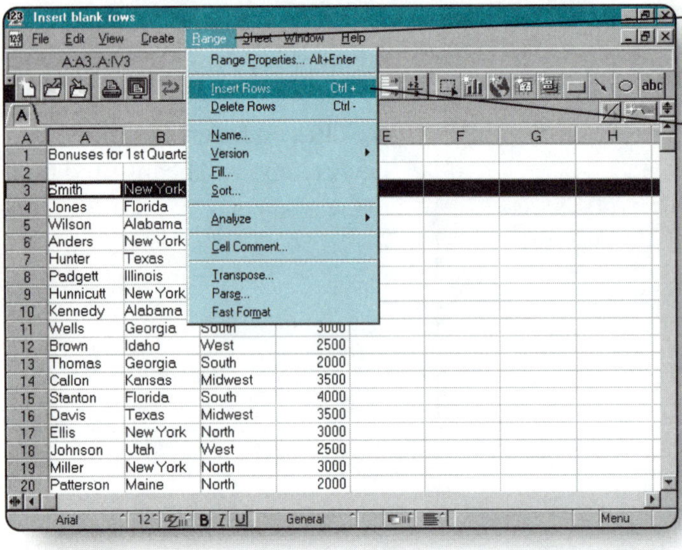

2. **Click** on **Range**. The Range menu will appear.

3. **Click** on **Insert Rows**. A new row will be inserted into the worksheet.

Copying, Cutting, and Pasting Data

Copying, cutting, and pasting data in 1-2-3 is done using the same basic steps you used in Word Pro.

Copying and Pasting Cells

1. **Select** the **cells** you want to copy.

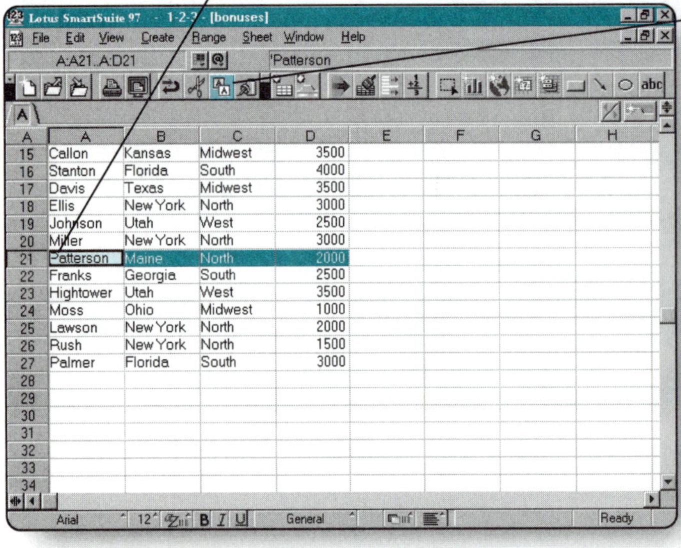

2. **Click** on the **Copy to Clipboard SmartIcon**. The selection will be copied to the Clipboard.

3. **Click** on the **starting cell** for the location for the copied cells. The cell will be selected.

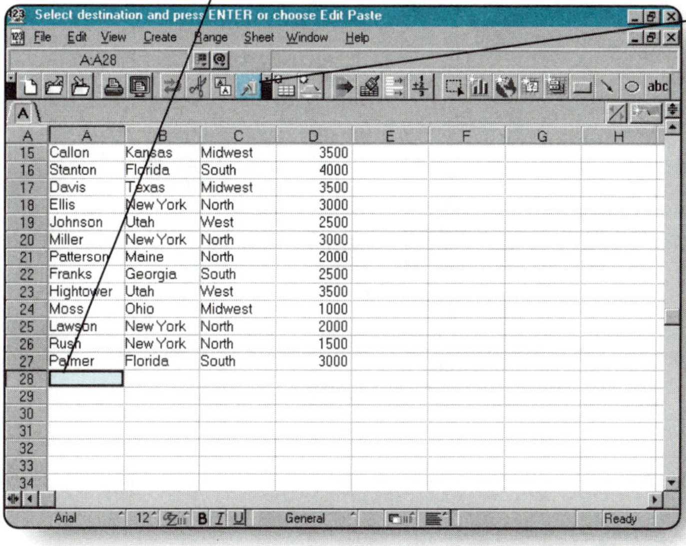

4. **Click** on the **Paste Clipboard Contents SmartIcon**. The cells will be copied to the selected location.

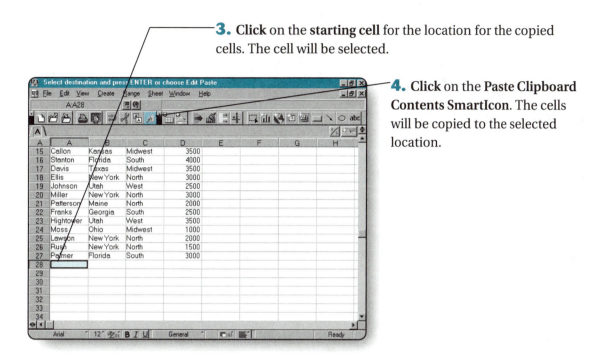

Cutting and Pasting Cells

Cutting and pasting cells is one way to move cells to a new location.

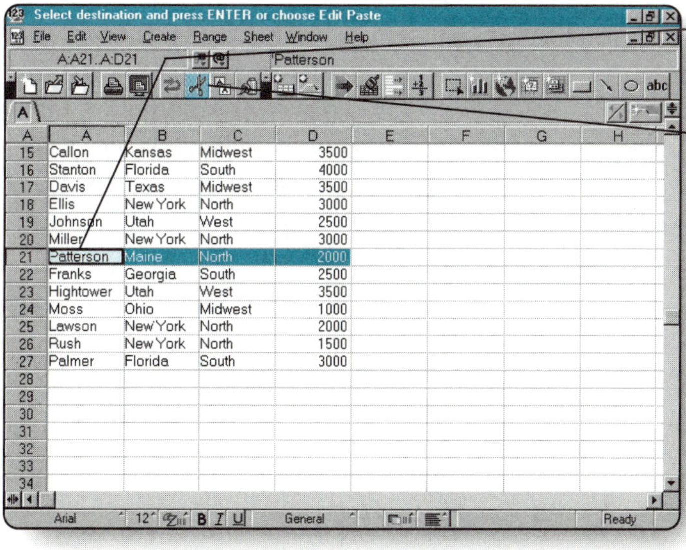

1. **Select** the **cells** you want to move.

2. **Click** on the **Cut to Clipboard SmartIcon**. The selection will be removed from the worksheet and copied to the Clipboard.

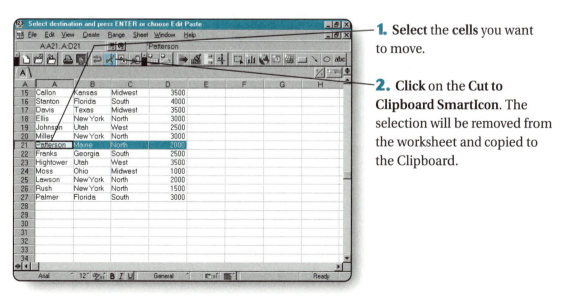

3. **Click** on the **starting cell** for the new location for the cells. The cell will be selected.

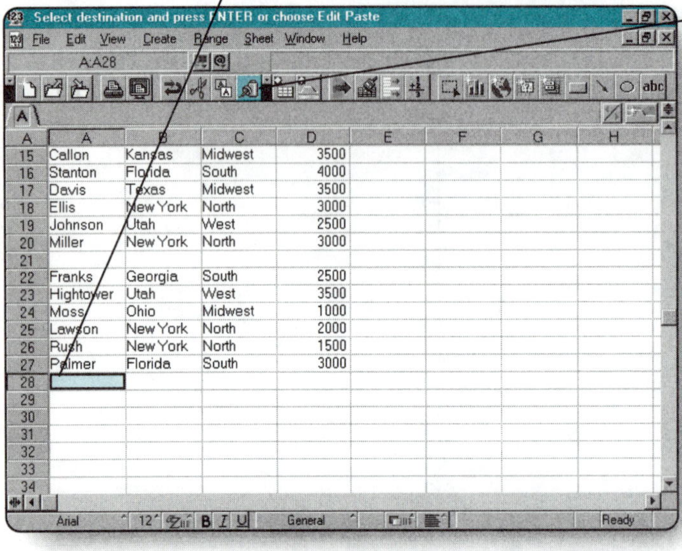

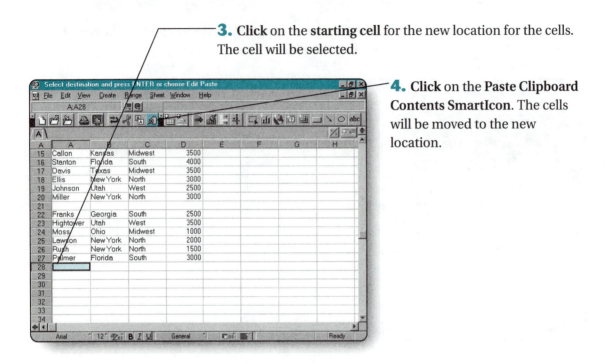

4. **Click** on the **Paste Clipboard Contents SmartIcon**. The cells will be moved to the new location.

Moving Data

Another way to move data is to drag it to another location.

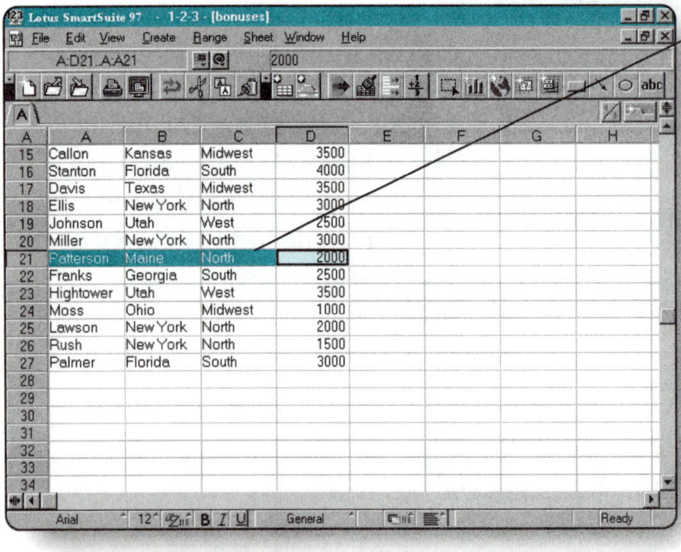

1. **Select** some **cells** to move.

2. **Position** the **pointer** over the **top border** of the selected cells. The pointer will change to look like a hand.

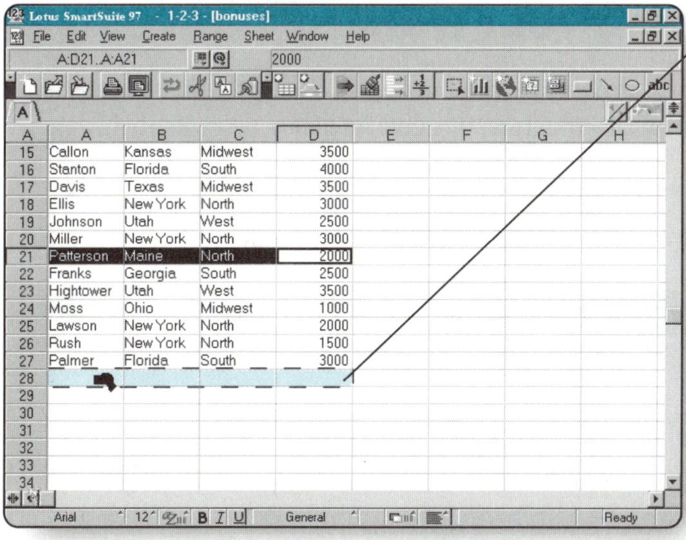

3. Drag the **cells** to their new location. The cells will be relocated.

PRINTING AND SAVING YOUR WORK

Printing using 1-2-3 is similar to printing in Word Pro. Remember that 1-2-3 is a WYSIWYG (What You See Is What You Get) environment, meaning that your worksheet will print out just as it looks on the screen. As with any application, it is important to save your work frequently while working with 1-2-3.

Printing Using 1-2-3

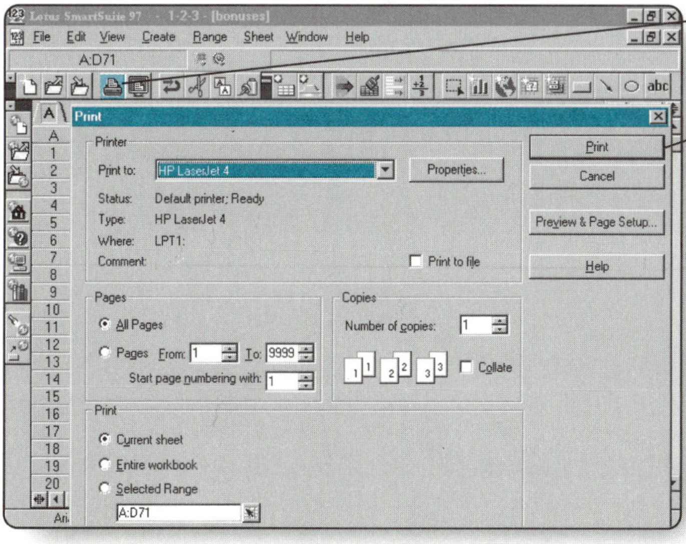

1. Click on the **Print SmartIcon**. The Print dialog box will open.

2. Click on **Print**. The workbook will be sent to the printer.

Saving Your Work

1. Click on the **Save the Current File SmartIcon**. If the file has not been saved before, the Save As dialog box will open.

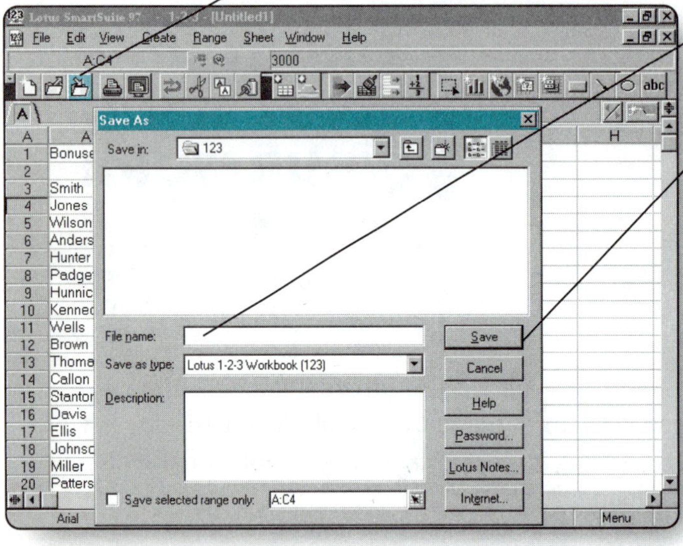

2. Type a **name** for the file in the File name: text box.

3. Click on **Save**. The workbook will be saved.

10 Working with @Functions and Formulas

1-2-3's strength lies in its capability to handle a variety of formulas. You can create your own formulas or use the formulas built into 1-2-3. Another major strength of 1-2-3 is its three-dimensional nature. You are not limited to working on just one worksheet. You can work on as many as you need. In this chapter, you'll learn how to:

- Enter formulas
- Use 1-2-3's built-in formulas
- Copy formulas

USING BUILT-IN @FUNCTIONS

1-2-3 has built-in functions known as @functions. They are called @functions because to use one of these functions you must start by typing the @ sign. 1-2-3 supports literally hundreds of @functions. An example of an @function is @Sum. This function adds all the values for multiple cells, called a range, and returns the total.

Selecting a Commonly Used @Function

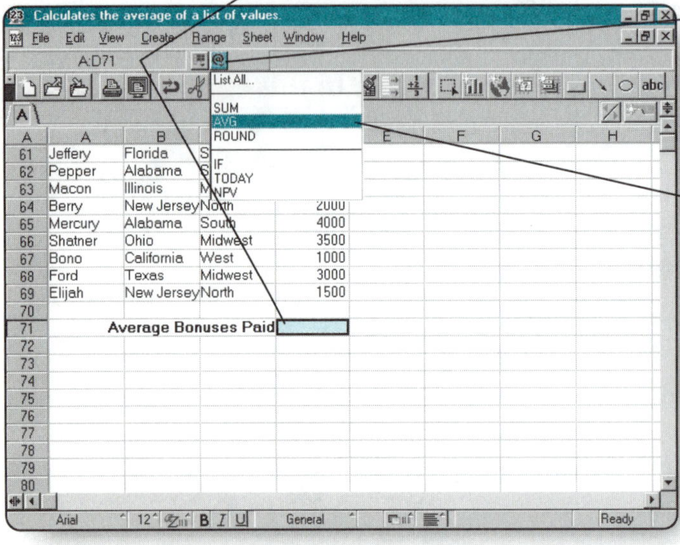

1. **Click** on the **cell** where the formula will go. The cell will be selected.

2. **Click** on the **@function selector**. A menu of the most frequently used @functions will appear.

3. **Click** on a **function**. The function will be inserted in the selected cell.

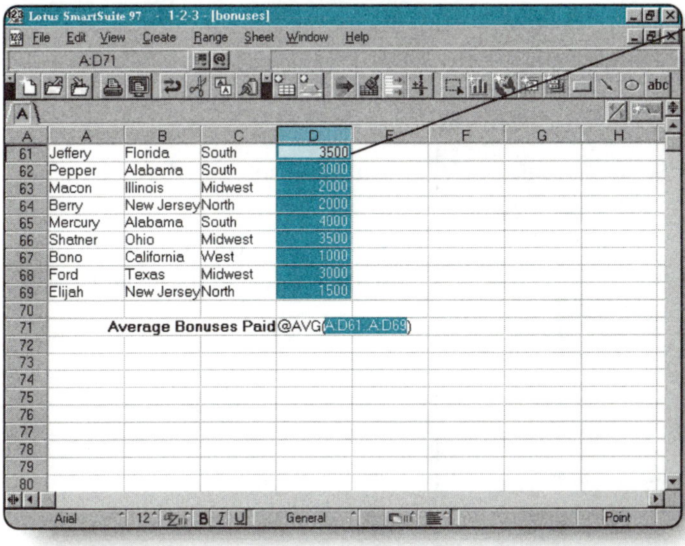

4. **Select** the **cells** to be used by the @function. If there are multiple cells, denoted by the word *list* in the @function, select the cells by clicking on the first cell and dragging to the last cell. If a single cell needs to be referenced in the @function, denoted by a letter such as *x* or *y*, then replace the letter with a cell address.

5. **Press** the **Enter key** when you are finished selecting the cells for the @function. The result of the function will be displayed.

Selecting Other @Functions

1. **Click** on the **cell** where the formula will go. The cell will be selected.

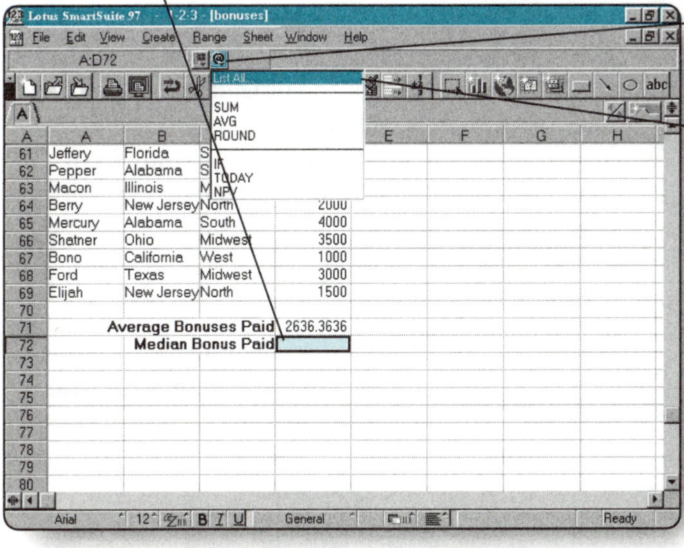

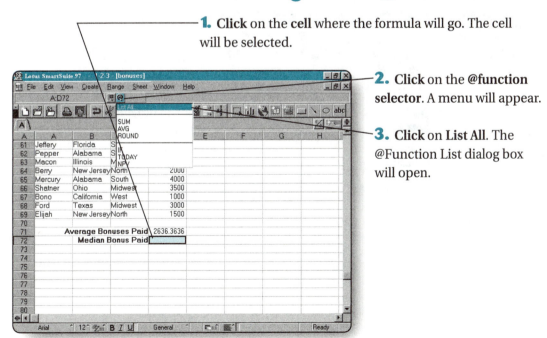

2. **Click** on the **@function selector**. A menu will appear.

3. **Click** on **List All**. The @Function List dialog box will open.

4. Click on the **down scroll bar arrow** (▼) until the @function you want appears.

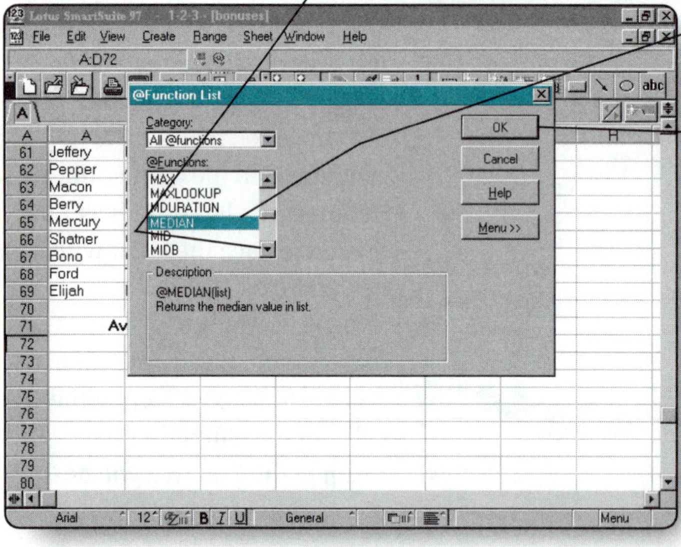

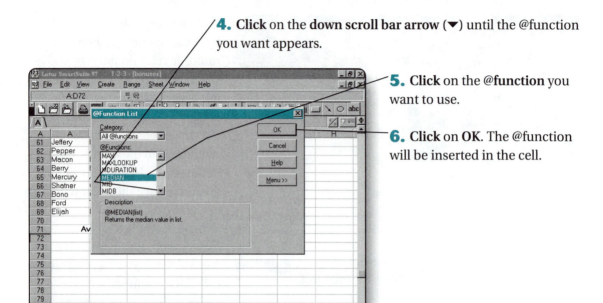

5. Click on the **@function** you want to use.

6. Click on **OK**. The @function will be inserted in the cell.

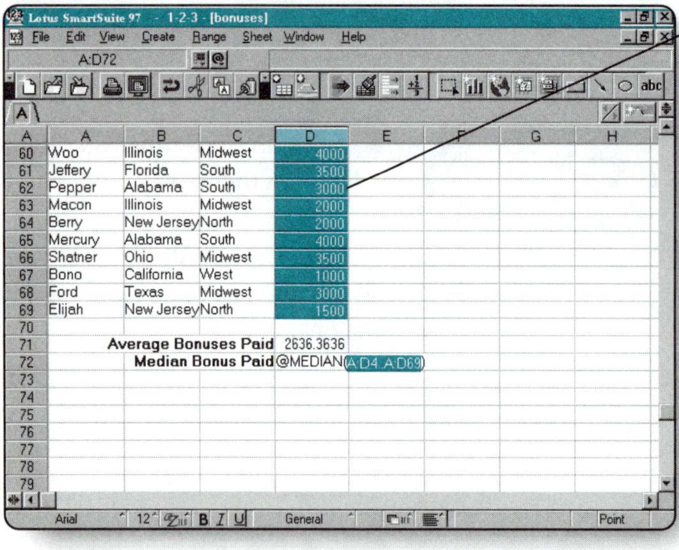

7. Select the **cells** to be used by the @function. If there are multiple cells, denoted by the word *list* in the @function, select the cells by clicking on the first cell and dragging to the last cell. If a single cell needs to be referenced in the @function, denoted by a letter such as *x* or *y*, then replace the letter with a cell address.

8. Press the **Enter key** when you are finished selecting the cells for the @function. The result of the function will be displayed.

ENTERING FORMULAS

If you need to use a formula that is not one of the built-in @functions, you can create your own from scratch. To let 1-2-3 know that you are entering a formula, you must type a plus sign (+) as the first character in the cell. You then enter the first cell you need to use to perform your calculation. You build a formula by combining cell references and operators. To do addition, use +; to do subtraction, use -; to do multiplication, use *; and to do division, use /. Using cell references and operators, you can make a formula as simple or as complex as you need.

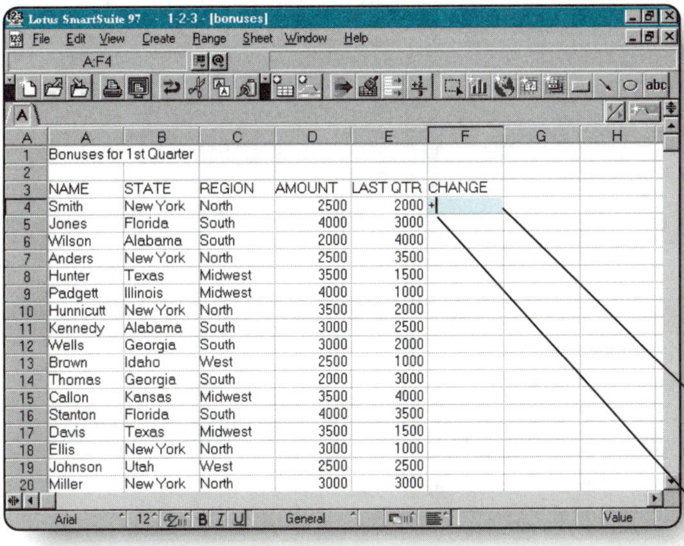

Creating Your Own Formulas

1. **Select** the **cell** where you want the formula.
2. **Type** + (plus sign). This will let 1-2-3 know you are entering a formula.

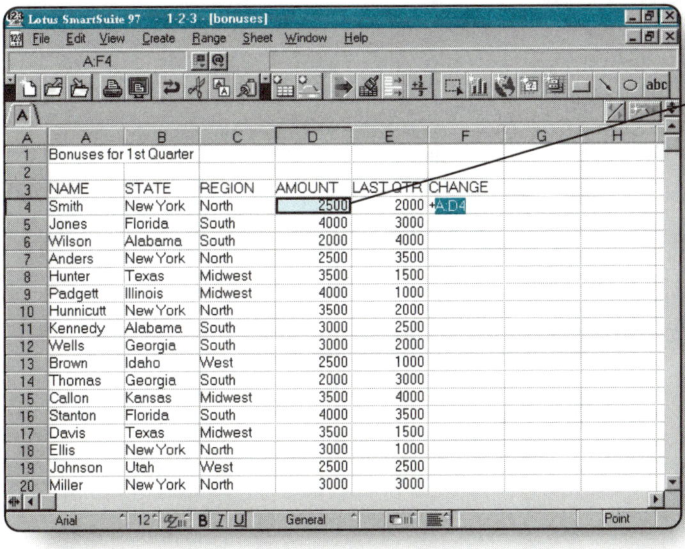

3. **Click** on the **cell** containing the first number you want to use. 1-2-3 will enter the cell address in the formula.

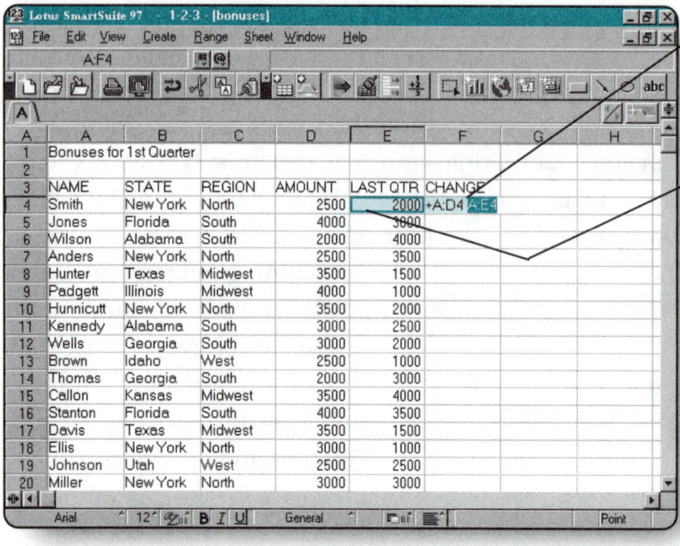

4. Type an **operator**. The operator will appear in the formula.

5. Click on the **cell** with the next value you want to use in your calculation. The cell's address will appear in the formula.

6. Continue entering operators and clicking on cells until the formula is complete.

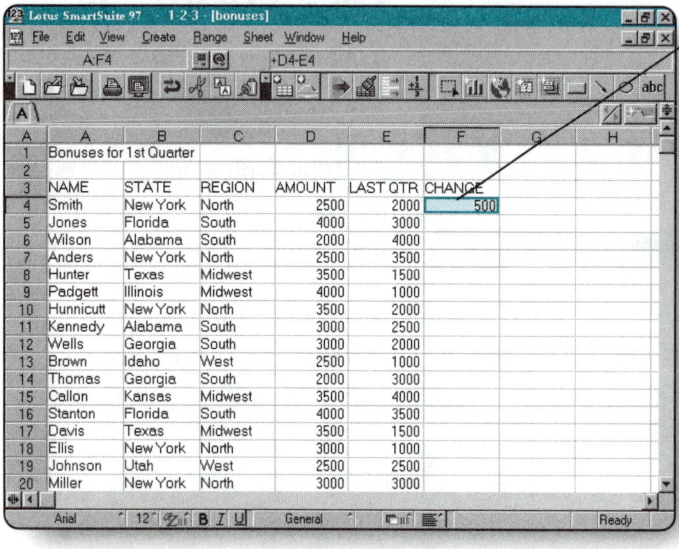

7. Press the **Enter key**. The result will appear in the selected cell.

Using Named Ranges

Cell addresses are one way to reference a particular cell in a formula. If you have a formula such as +A1-B1, you might not understand the intent of the calculation. On the other hand, if you have +SecondQtr-FirstQtr, you would know that you are trying to find the difference between two quarters. The second formula illustrates the use of *named ranges.* A named range is a name given to a range of cells, where a range can be one or more cell. Named ranges can be used in formulas and as a way to locate specific areas in a workbook.

Naming a Range

1. **Select** a **range** to name. Using this technique you can name a single cell or multiple cells. 1-2-3 considers one or more cells to be a range.

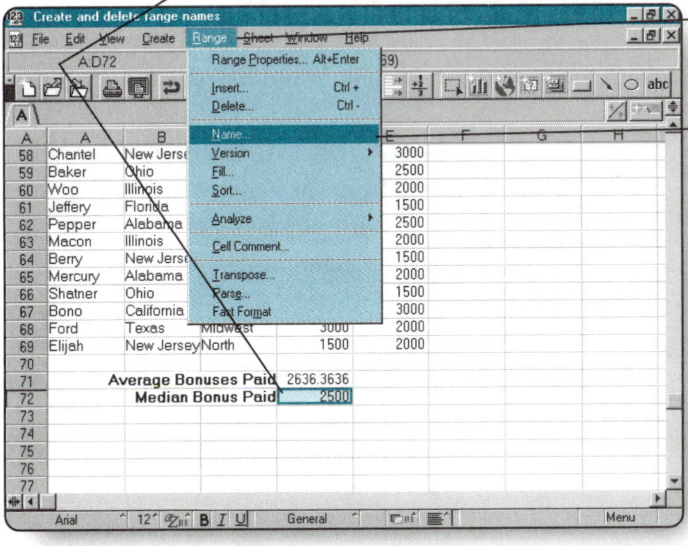

2. **Click** on **Range**. The Range menu will appear.

3. **Click** on **Name**. The Name dialog box will open.

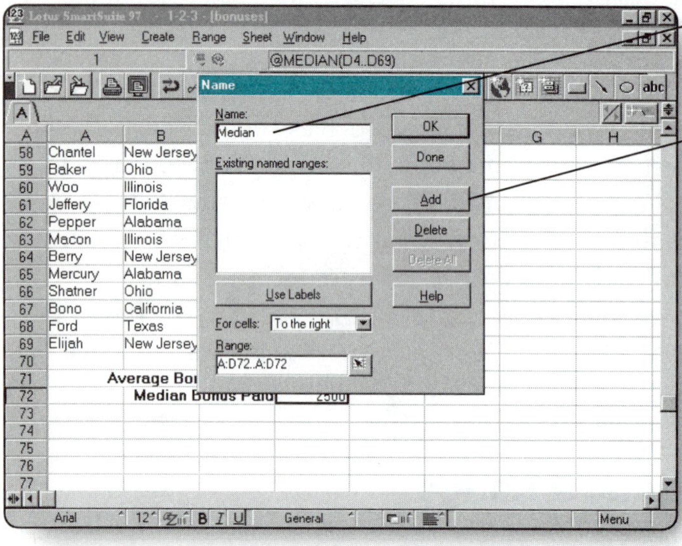

4. **Type** a **name** for the range in the Name: text box.

5. **Click** on **Add**. The name will be added to the workbook.

6. **Click** on **OK**. The Name dialog box will close.

Using the Navigator to Access a Named Range

1. **Click** on the **Navigator**. The Navigator list will appear.

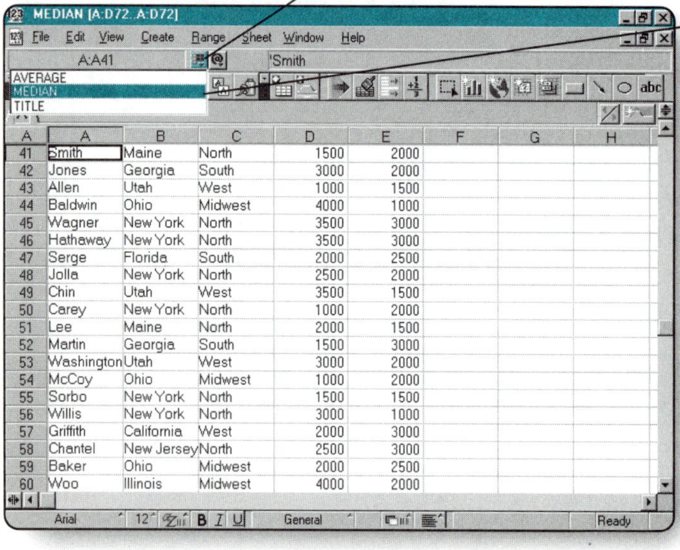

2. **Click** on the **named range** from the Navigator list. The current range will become the selected range.

COPYING FORMULAS

Formulas are copied from cell to cell just like you would copy any other data. There is one difference you need to be aware of. Cell references by default are *relative*. When a cell reference is relative, it means that it is relative to the current location in the workbook. If, for example, you have a formula of +A1-B1 in cell C1 and you copied it to cell C2, 1-2-3 automatically changes the formula to +A2-B2 to make it relative to its new location.

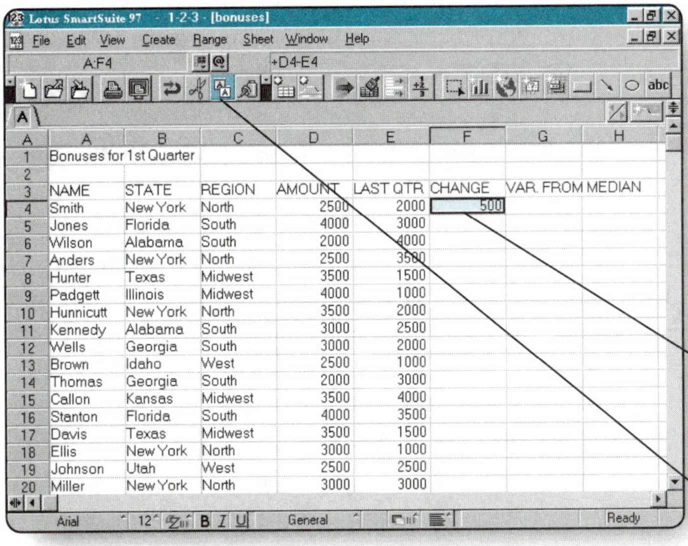

Copying a Formula with Relative Cell References

1. **Click** on the **cell** with the formula you want to copy. The cell will be selected.
2. **Click** on the **Copy to Clipboard SmartIcon**. The selection will be copied to the Clipboard.

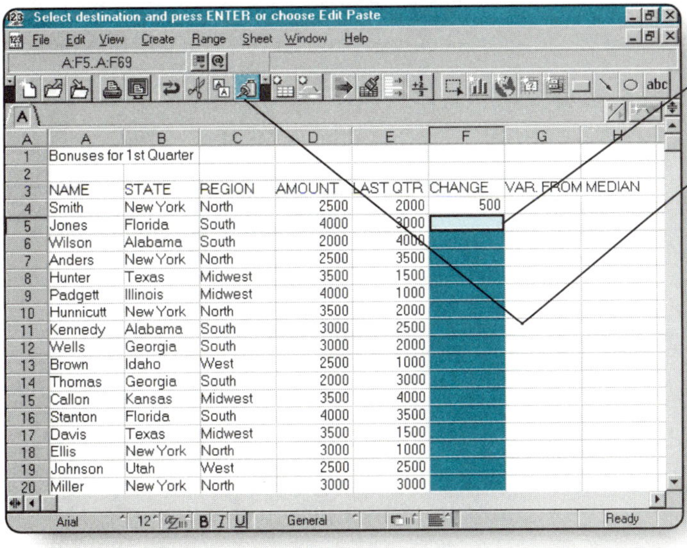

3. **Select** the **range** you want to copy the formula to.
4. **Click** on the **Paste Clipboard Contents SmartIcon**. The formula will be copied to the selected range.

Select a cell from the range where the formula was copied to, and you will notice that 1-2-3 adjusted the formula so that its cell references are relative to the new location.

Copying a Formula with Absolute Cell References

Sometimes you will not want 1-2-3 to adjust cell references in your formulas so that they are relative to their new location. You may have a formula that needs to always refer to a specific cell. To do this, you need to use an *absolute* reference. An absolute reference does not change when moved or copied to a new location. If you have a formula that divides A1 by B1 and you want to always divide by the value in B1, no matter where the formula is moved or copied to, then you must make B1 an absolute reference. To make a reference absolute, you use the $ sign. A $ in front of the column portion of a cell address, $A1 for example, makes the column portion of the address absolute. A $ in front of the row portion of the cell address, A$1 for example, makes the row absolute. If you want cell itself to absolute, place a $ before the column and row reference, A1 for example.

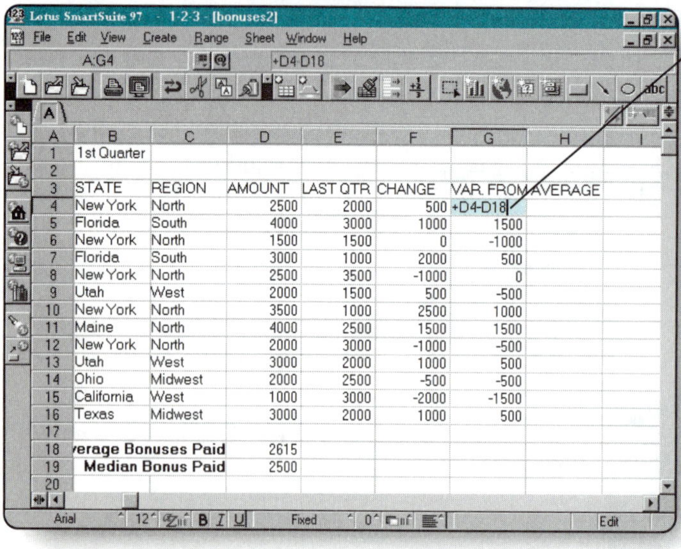

1. **Click** on a **cell** whose formula needs a cell absolute reference. The cell will be selected.

2. **Press F2** to edit the cell's contents. The cell will be placed in edit mode.

3. **Press** the **right and left arrow keys** to move to the location where you need to enter a $ (dollar sign).

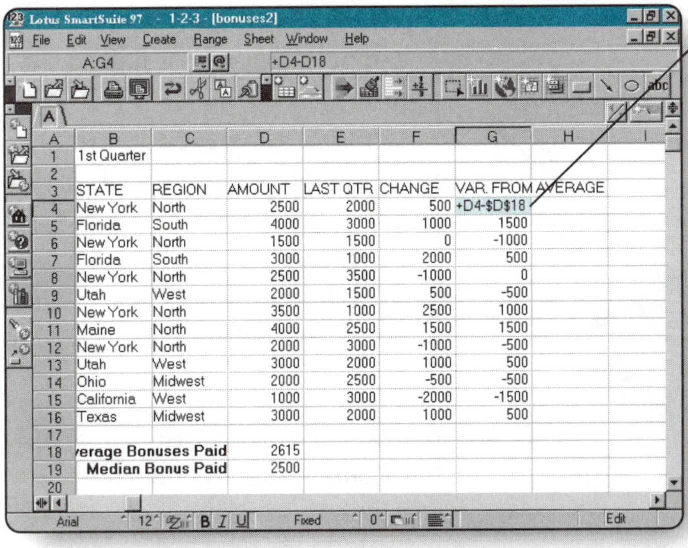

4. Type $ (dollar sign).

5. Repeat steps 3 and **4**, if necessary.

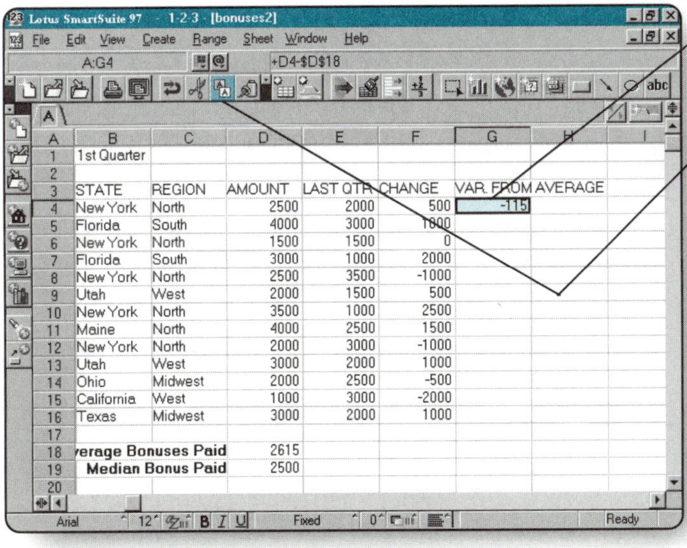

6. Press the **Enter key**. The cell formula will reflect the change.

7. Click on the **Copy to Clipboard SmartIcon**.

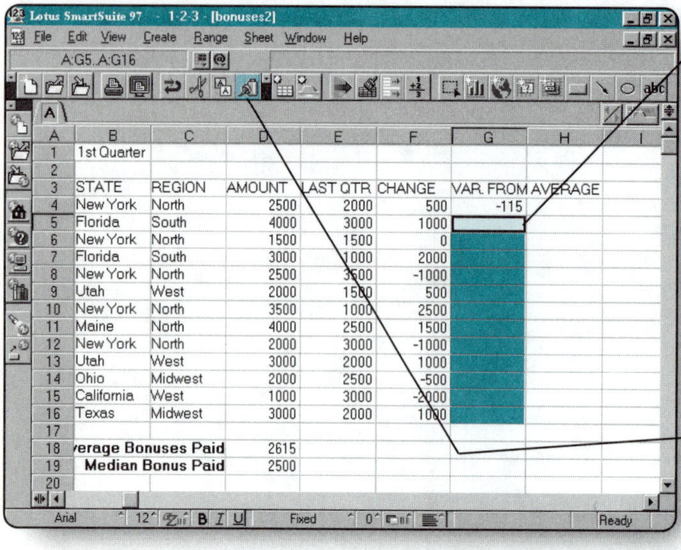

8. **Select** the **range** where you want to copy the formula to.

NOTE

If you copied the formula to cells before you made changes to an absolute reference, you need to recopy the formula.

9. **Click** on the Paste **Clipboard Contents SmartIcon**. The formula will be copied to the selected range.

11 Formatting Worksheets

Gone are the days when a simple printed worksheet will do. As with most things, the appearance of the data is as important as the data itself. If someone doesn't read your worksheet, what is the point of creating one? This chapter focuses on worksheet formatting. In this chapter, you'll learn how to:

- Format cells
- Resize columns and rows
- Work with multiple worksheets
- Check your spelling
- Use templates

FORMATTING CELLS

You are probably familiar with formatting as it applies to a word processing document. 1-2-3 supports formatting as well. Cells can have different colors, fonts, number formats, borders, and alignments.

In the 1-2-3 environment, each cell has a format associated with it. If you wanted to, you could give every cell on your worksheet a different format, though it would make for a very busy and probably ugly worksheet!

Changing the Appearance of Cells

To change the appearance of cells, you select the cells and then work with the range's properties. This can be done through the 1-2-3 status bar buttons or through the Range Properties dialog box.

Selecting a Font Type and Font Size

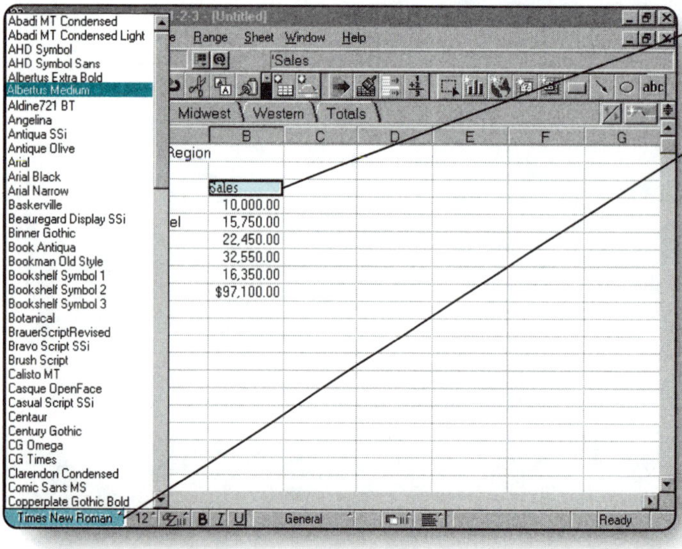

1. Select a **range**. The range will be selected.

2. Click on the **Font name status bar button**. A list of font names available on your system will appear.

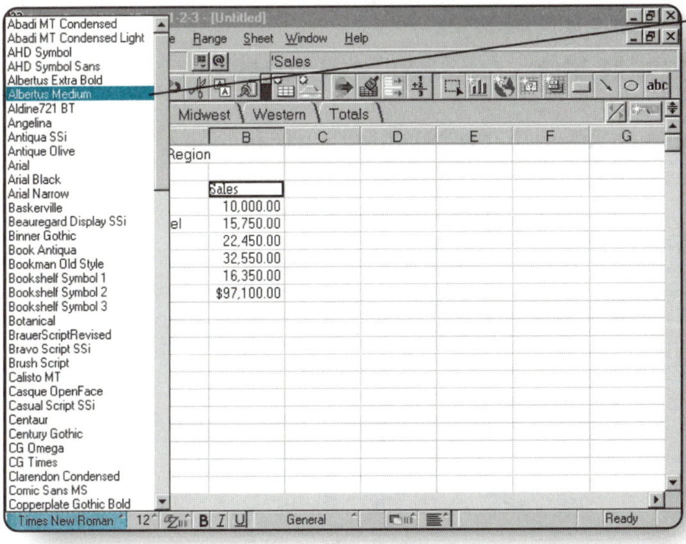

3. Click on the **font** you want. The range's font will become the same as the selected font.

4. Click on the **Point size status bar button**. A list of font sizes will appear.

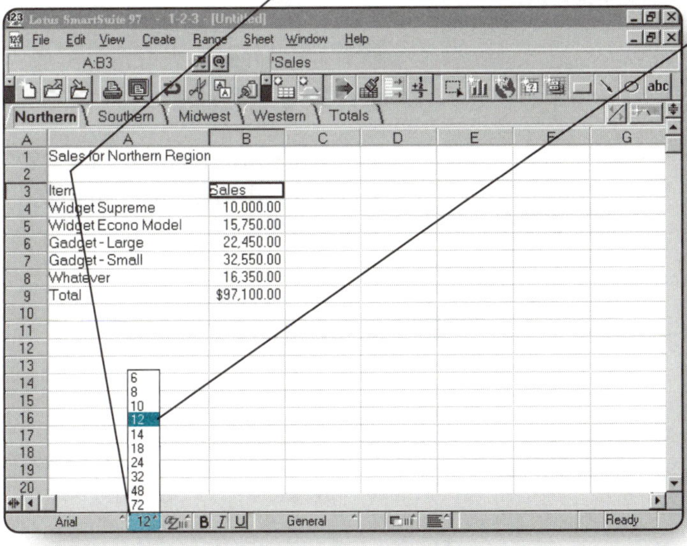

5. Click on the **point size** you want. The range's font size will become the same as the one you selected.

Making a Range Bold, Italic, or Underlined

1. Select a **range** that you want to make bold, italic, or underlined.

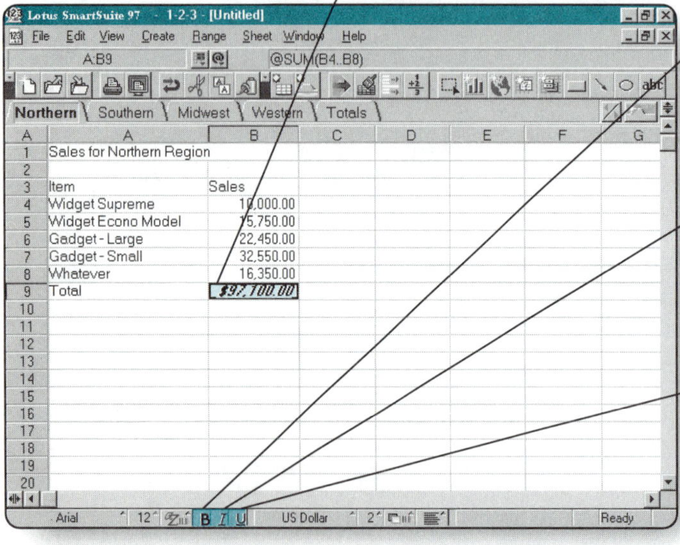

2a. Click on the **Bold button**. The selected range will become bolded.

OR

2b. Click on the **Italic button**. The selected range will become italicized.

OR

2c. Click on the **Underline button**. The selected range will become underlined.

Working with Colors

You may want to change the background color of a range to make it stand out more.

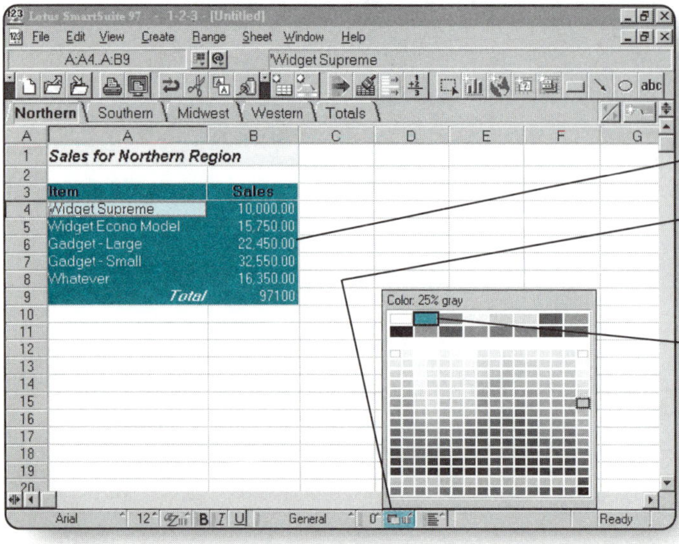

1. Select a **range**.

2. Click on the **Background color button**. A palette of colors will appear.

3. Click on the **color** you want. The selected range's background will become that color.

Using Borders

Borders can be used to make a range of cells stand out or to divide parts of your worksheet.

1. **Select** a **range.**

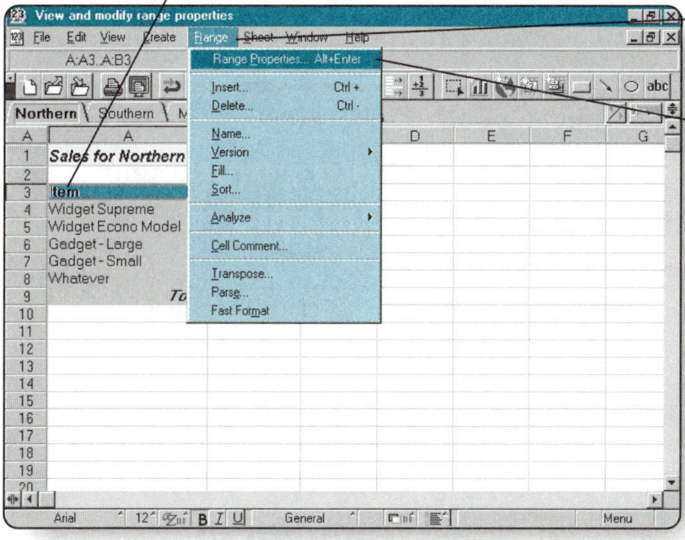

2. **Click** on **Range**. The Range menu will appear.

3. **Click** on **Range Properties**. The Properties for Range dialog box will open.

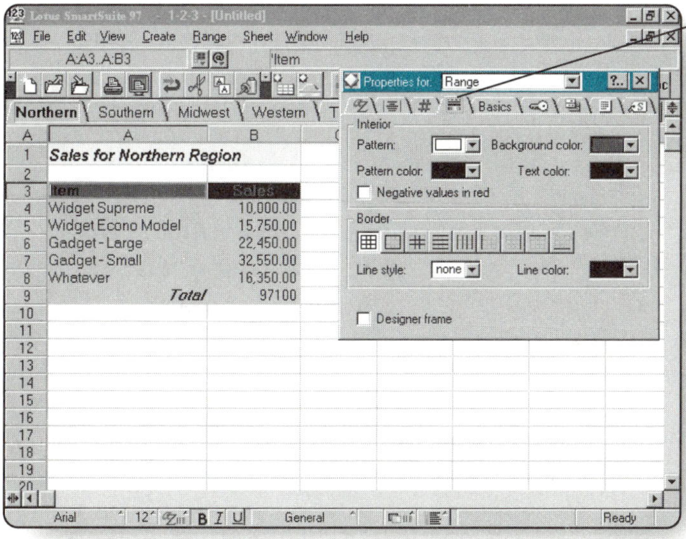

4. **Click** on the **Color, pattern, and line style tab**. The Color, pattern, and line style tab will appear.

5. Choose from the following **options**:

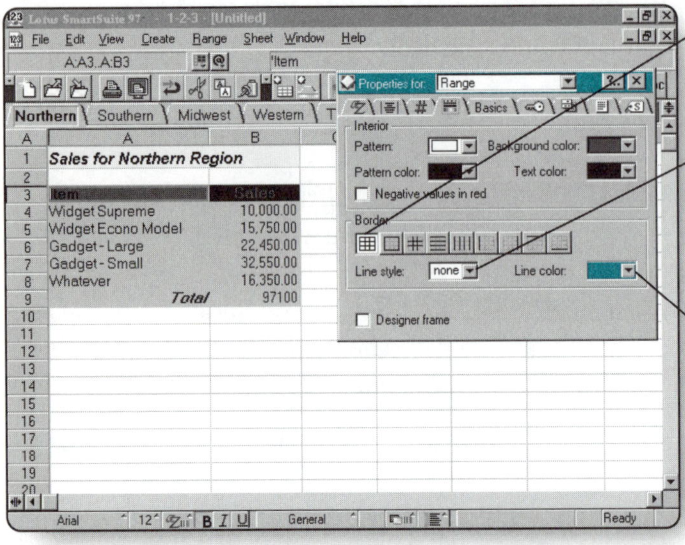

- Click on a Border button to apply a border to the selected range.
- To select a different Line style:, click on the down arrow (▼) to display a list of styles. Click on the line style you want.
- Click on the down arrow (▼) to select a different Line color:.

6. Click on the **Close button**. The dialog box will close.

Setting Cell Alignment

As a default, 1-2-3 aligns text to the left. Numbers are right aligned. You can change this using the Alignment button.

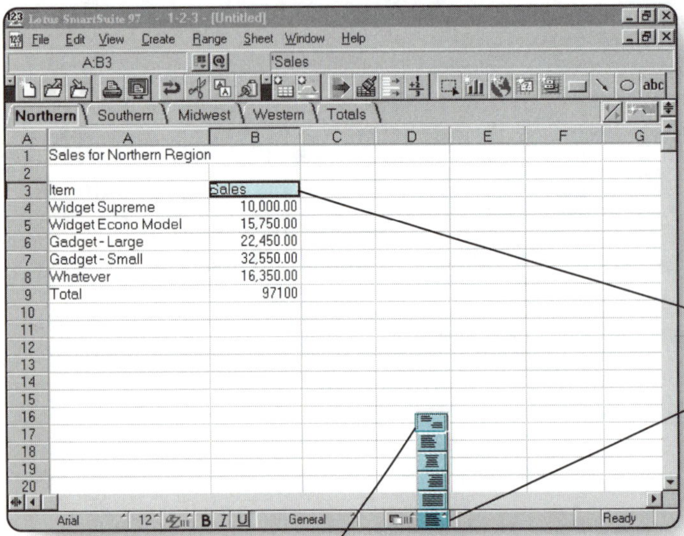

1. Select a **range**.

2. Click on the **Alignment button**. A menu of alignment buttons will appear.

3. Click on the **alignment** you want. The range's alignment will change to that of the selected alignment.

Formatting Numeric Data

When you enter numbers or formulas, the values displayed in a cell use a format called general. The general format displays values the same way that they are entered. If you want numbers to display with, for example, dollar signs, commas, and a certain number of decimals, use a number format.

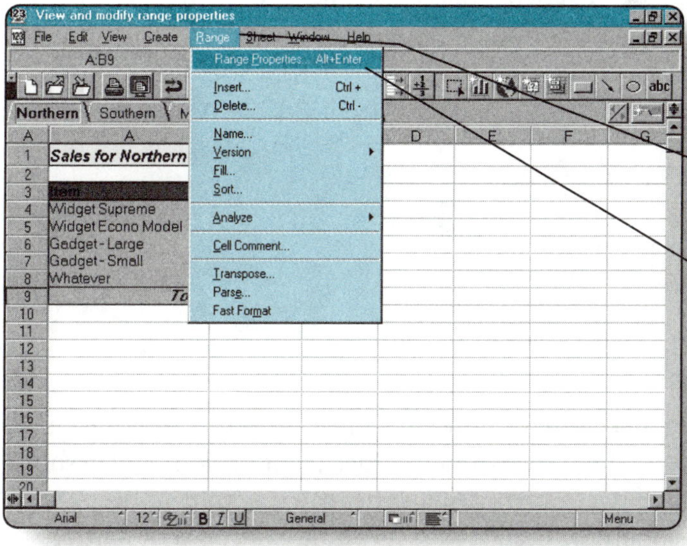

1. **Select** a **range**.
2. **Click** on **Range**. The Range menu will appear.
3. **Click** on **Range Properties**. The Properties for Range dialog box will open.

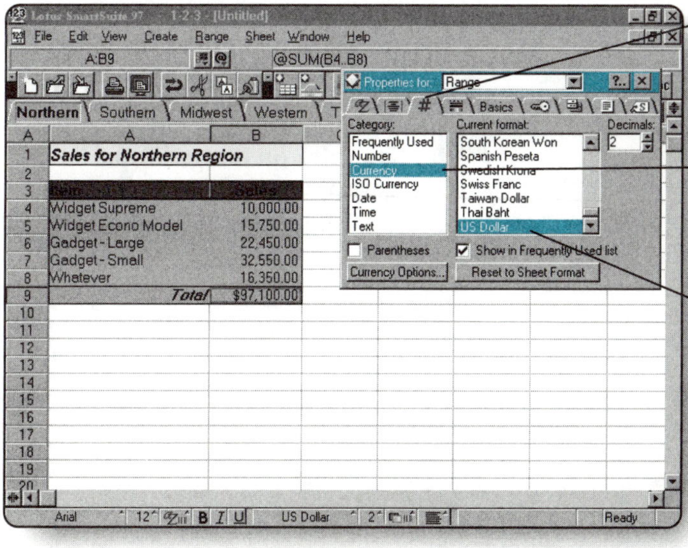

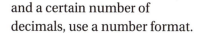

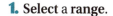

4. **Click** on the **Number format tab**. The Number format tab will appear.
5. **Click** on a **category** from the Category: list. The formats for that category will appear.
6. **Click** on the **format** you want from the Current format: list. The format will be applied to the selected cells.

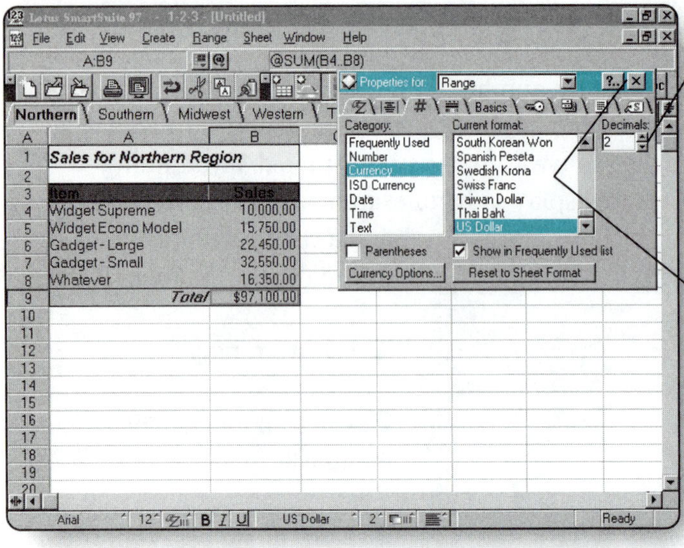

7. **Click** on the **up and down arrows** (♦) if you want to change the number of Decimals: displayed. This option is only available if you selected a format that uses a fixed number of decimal places.

8. **Click** on the **Close button**. The dialog box will close.

Applying Named Styles

1-2-3 supplies you with several named styles that you can apply to a range. These styles apply borders, fonts, colors, and in some cases, number formats. Using styles can give your worksheets a professional appearance with very little work on your part.

1. **Select** a **range**.

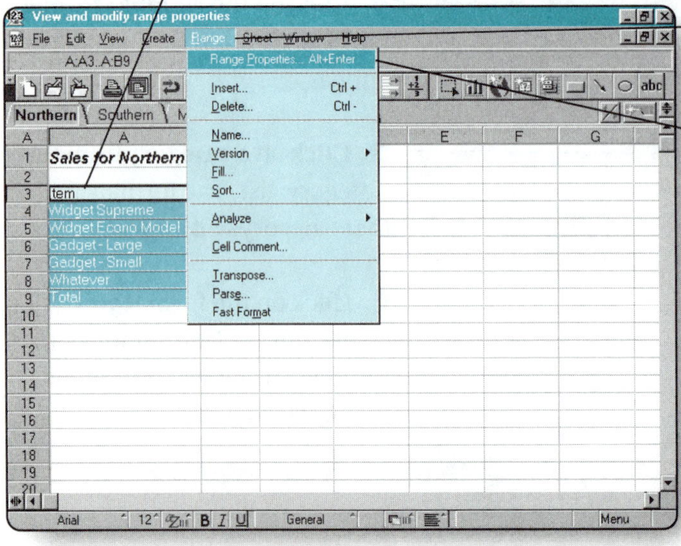

2. **Click** on **Range**. The Range menu will appear.

3. **Click** on **Range Properties**. The Properties for Range dialog box will open.

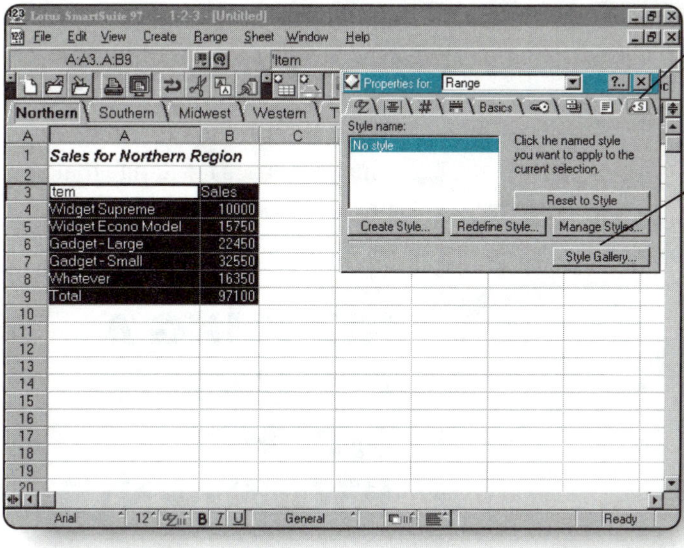

4. Click on the **Named style tab**. The Named style tab will appear.

5. Click on **Style Gallery**. The Style Gallery dialog box will open.

6. Move the **scroll bar button**. This will scroll through the list of available style templates.

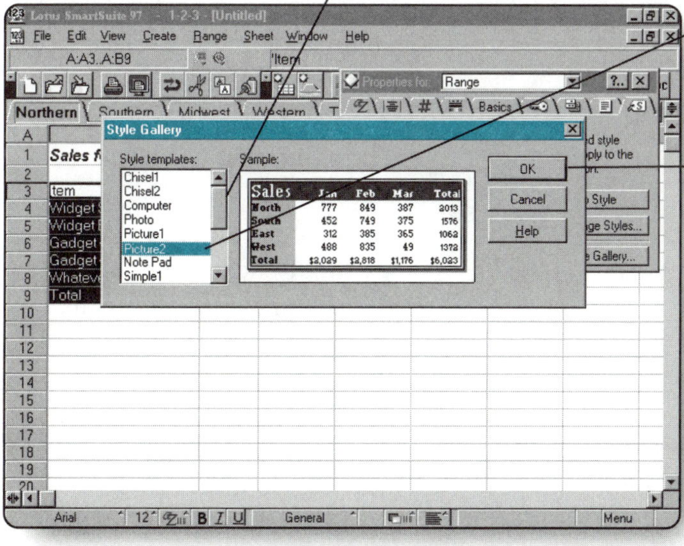

7. Click on the **style** you want to use. The selected style template will appear in the Sample: box.

8. Click on **OK**. The style will be applied to the selected range.

9. Click outside the selected range. The range will be deselected so that you can see the style applied to the range.

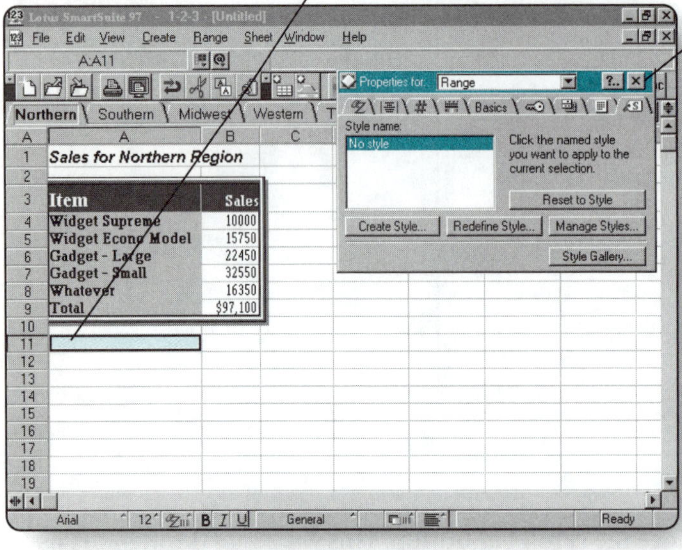

10. Click on the **Close button**. The Properties for Range dialog box will close.

RESIZING A COLUMN TO FIT THE WIDEST ENTRY

1-2-3 allows you to resize a column to fit the widest entry in that column. This allows you to make your columns as small as possible without hiding any of the contents of the cells in that column.

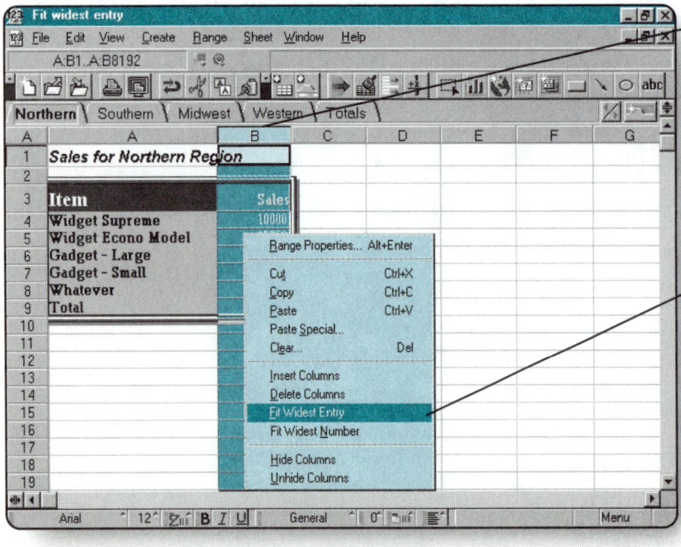

1. Click on a **column's heading**. The entire column will be selected.

2. Right-click on the **column**. A shortcut menu will appear.

3. Click on **Fit Widest Entry**. The column will be automatically resized.

WORKING WITH MULTIPLE SHEETS

A task you may need to do frequently is consolidate the information from several sheets. For example, you may need to find the grand total of all the sales from all of your regions. The easiest way to do this is by adding sheets to your workbook. In this case, each region could have its own sheet, and another sheet would be used for the totals. This type of use can apply to many applications. You may, for example, want to have a workbook that has a separate sheet for each product your company sells or a workbook with a sheet for each of your employees so that you can track their hours.

Adding a Sheet to a Workbook

You can add up to 256 sheets to a single workbook.

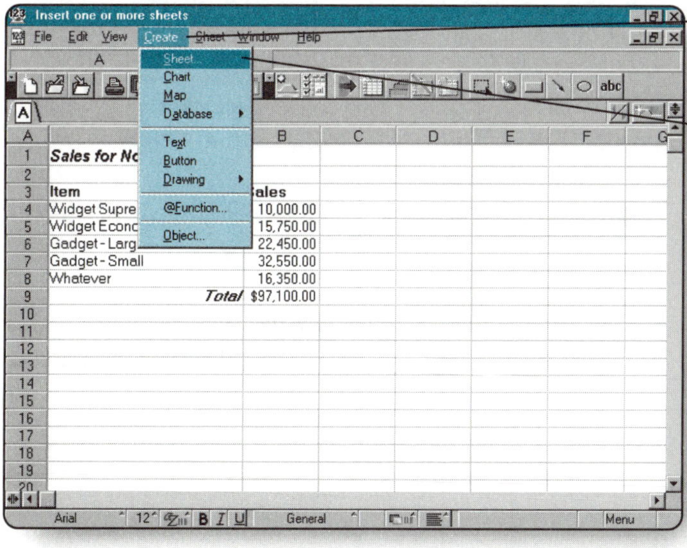

1. **Click** on **Create**. The Create menu will appear.

2. **Click** on **Sheet**. The Create Sheet dialog box will open.

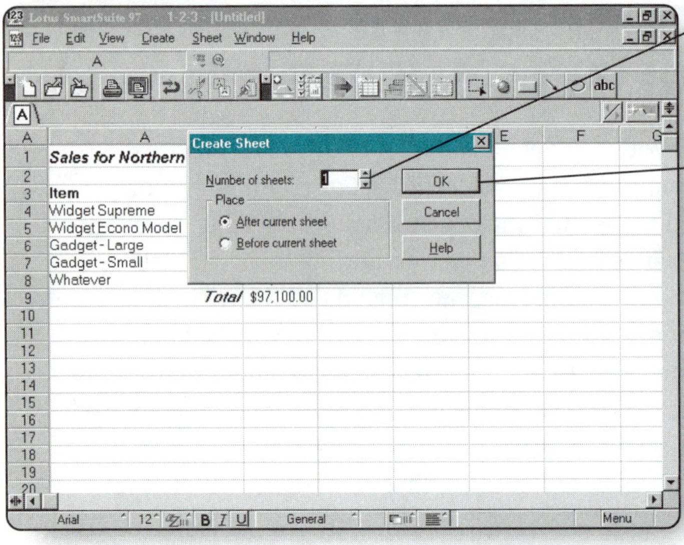

3. **Click** on the **up and down arrows** (⬍) to select the Number of sheets: you want to create.

4. **Click** on **OK**. The sheets will be created in the current workbook.

Renaming a Sheet

When a sheet is first created, it has a less than exciting name like A or B. Renaming a sheet makes it easier to use.

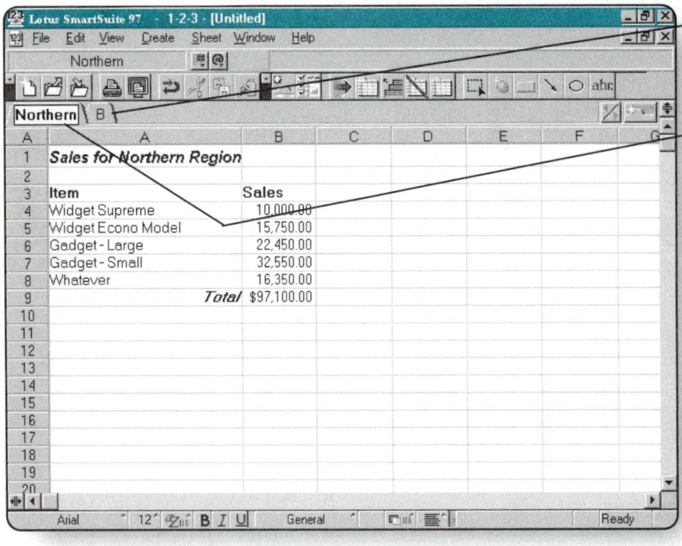

1. **Double-click** on the sheet's **tab**.

2. **Type** the new **name** of the sheet.

3. **Press** the **Enter key**. The new sheet name will be displayed.

Creating a Formula Using Multiple Sheets

To create a formula using multiple sheets, you perform the same basic steps as when you are working on a single sheet. The only difference is that instead of selecting a range on the current sheet, you select a range on another sheet. This creates a *three-dimensional formula.*

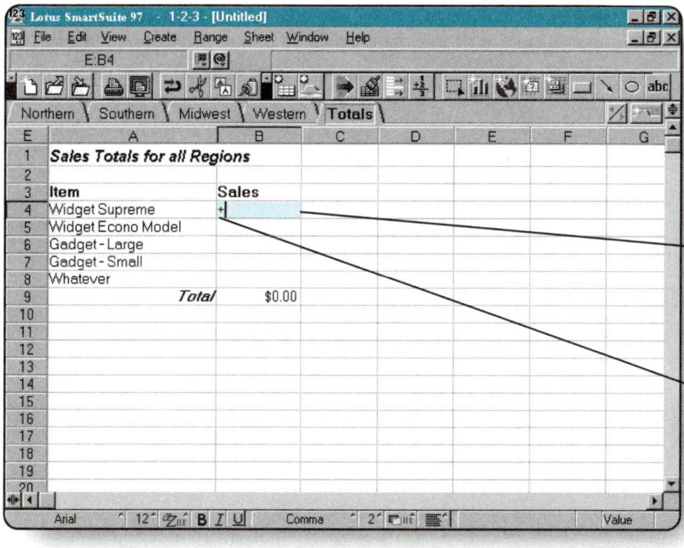

1. Click on the **cell** where you want to create the formula. The cell will be selected.

2. Type + (plus sign). This will let 1-2-3 know that you are creating a formula.

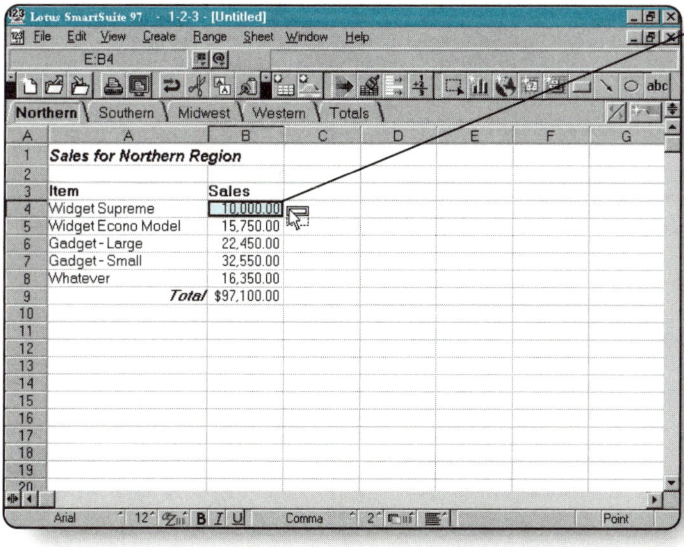

3. Select the first **cell or range** you need in your formula.

If this is on a different sheet, click on the sheet tab where the range or formula is located first.

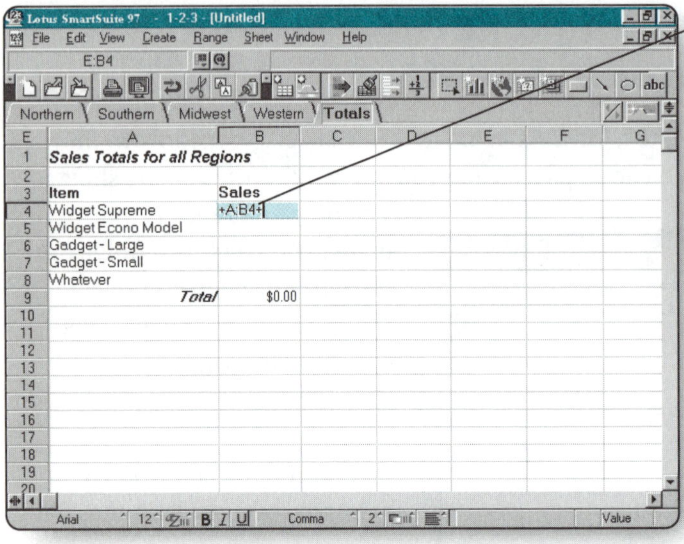

4. **Type** an **operator**.

5. **Repeat steps** 3 and 4 until the formula is complete.

6. **Press** the **Enter key**. The formula will be entered.

CHECKING SPELLING

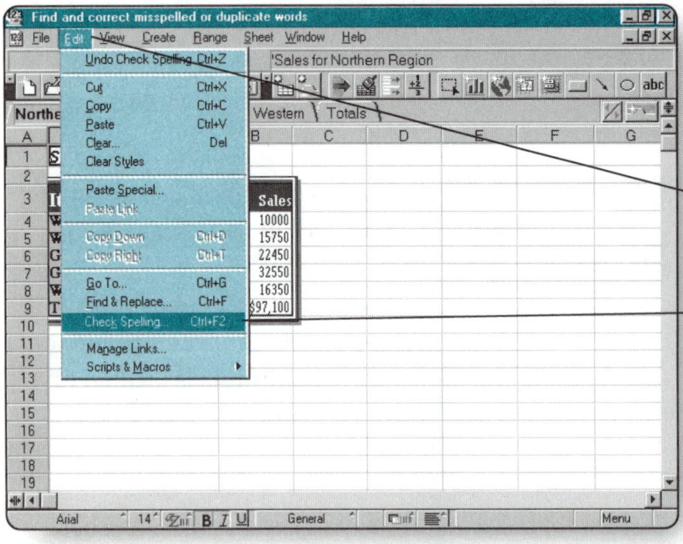

Because worksheets include text in them, it is a good idea to check the spelling for the contents of your workbook.

1. **Click** on **Edit**. The Edit menu will appear.

2. **Click** on **Check Spelling**. The Check Spelling dialog box will open.

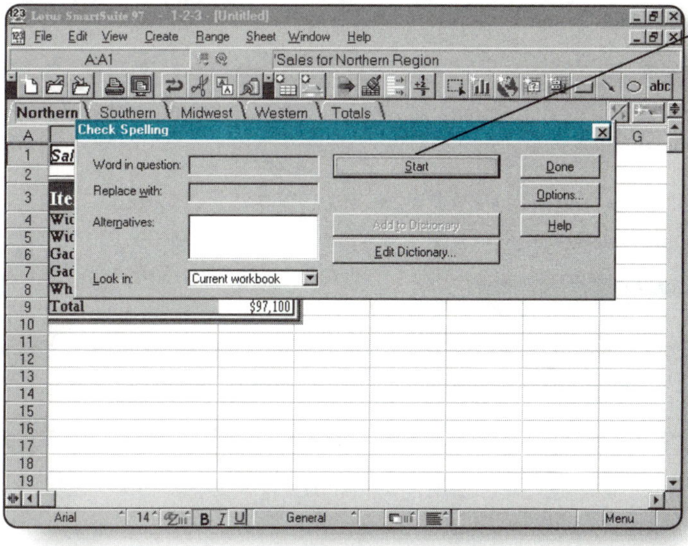

3. **Click** on **Start**. 1-2-3 will start checking your spelling.

The word currently being checked as possibly misspelled will be displayed in the Word in question: box.

4. **Choose** from these **options**:

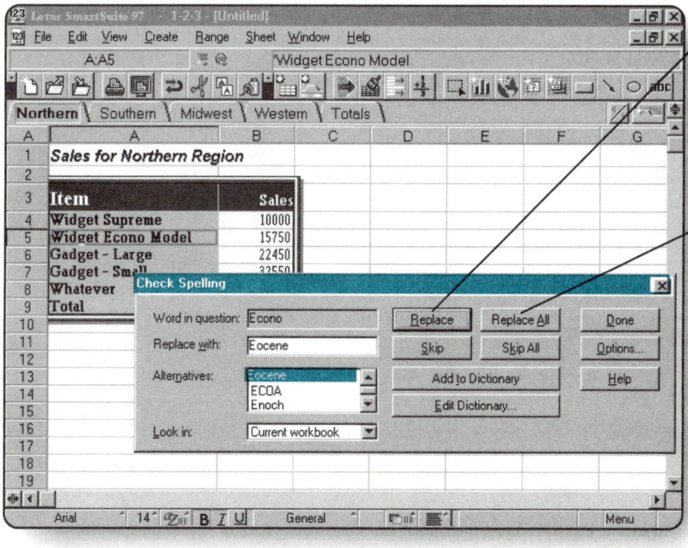

- Select the correct spelling for the word from the Alternatives: list and click Replace to replace this single occurrence.
- Select the correct spelling for the word from the Alternatives: list and click Replace All to replace all occurrences in this workbook.

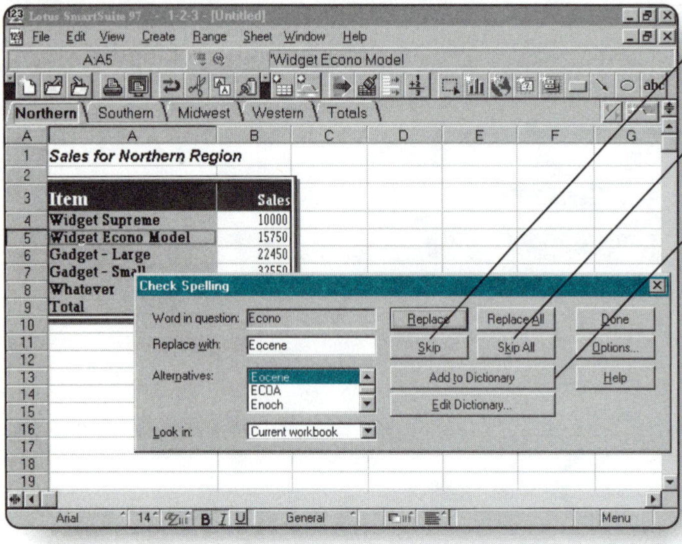

- ✦ To skip this occurrence, click on Skip.
- ✦ To skip all occurrences, click on Skip All.
- ✦ If the word is spelled correctly, you may want to add it to the dictionary. If a word is added to the dictionary, it will not be stopped on in the future when you check spelling. To do this, click on Add to Dictionary.

After you choose one of these options, the next word in question will be identified.

5. **Repeat step 4** until the message box displays saying the search is complete.

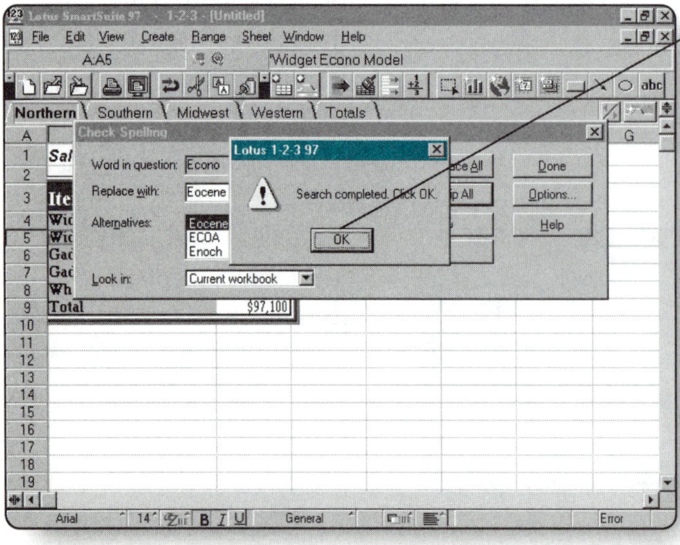

6. **Click** on **OK**. The Check Spelling dialog box will appear.

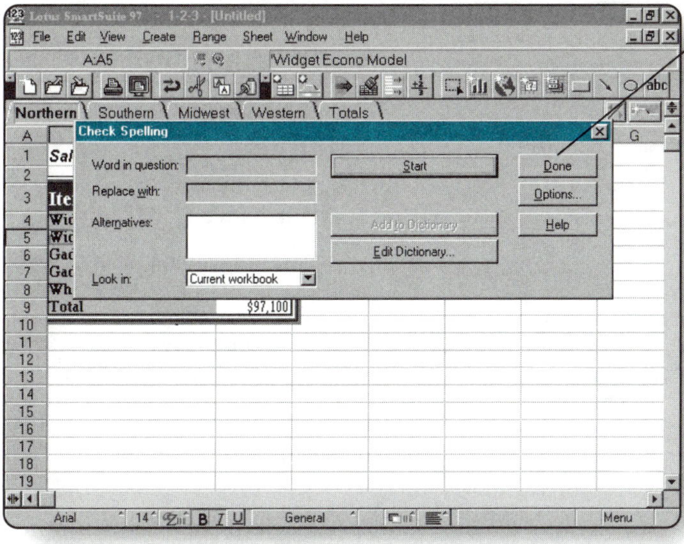

7. Click on **Done**. The Check Spelling dialog box will close.

USING SMARTMASTERS TO SAVE TIME

A quick and painless way to create workbooks complete with formulas and formatting is to use 1-2-3's SmartMasters. SmartMasters are template workbooks set up for commonly used reports and forms such as budgets. Each SmartMaster has sample data for you to use as a model and instructions that show you how the SmartMaster should be used. Just type your own data; everything else is taken care of for you.

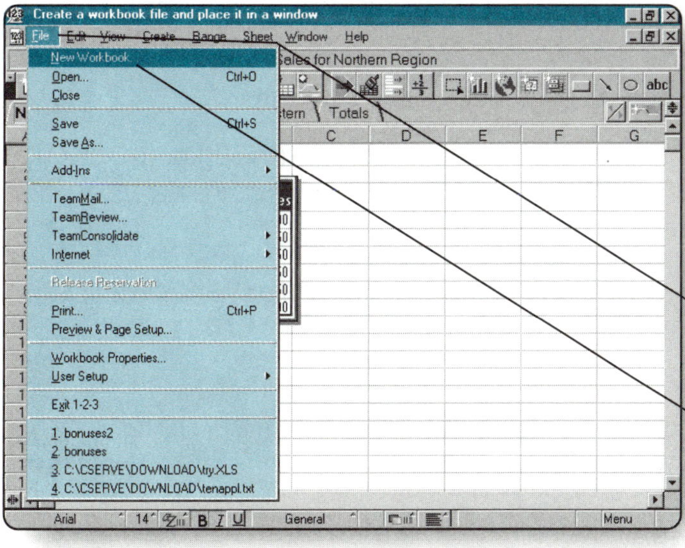

1. Click on **File**. The File menu will appear.

2. Click on **New Workbook**. The New Workbook dialog box will open.

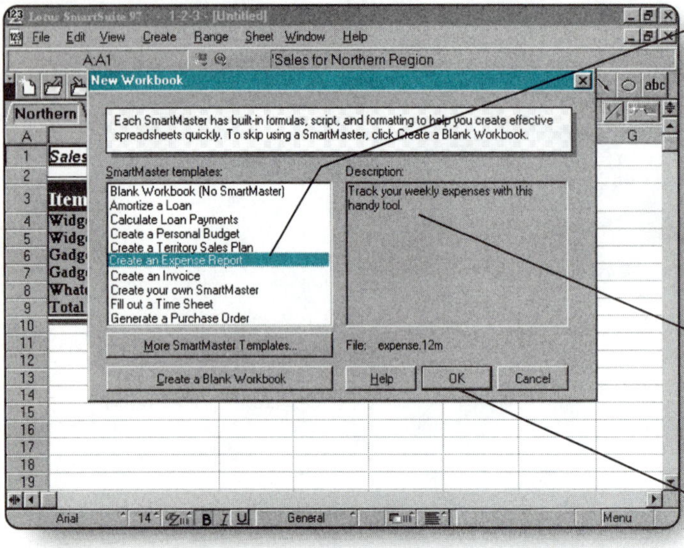

3. **Click** on a **SmartMaster** from the SmartMaster templates: list box.

NOTE

Do not select Blank Workbook (No SmartMaster).

When you click on a SmartMaster, a description of that SmartMaster will appear in the Description: box.

4. **Click** on **OK**. A new workbook will be created using the selected SmartMaster.

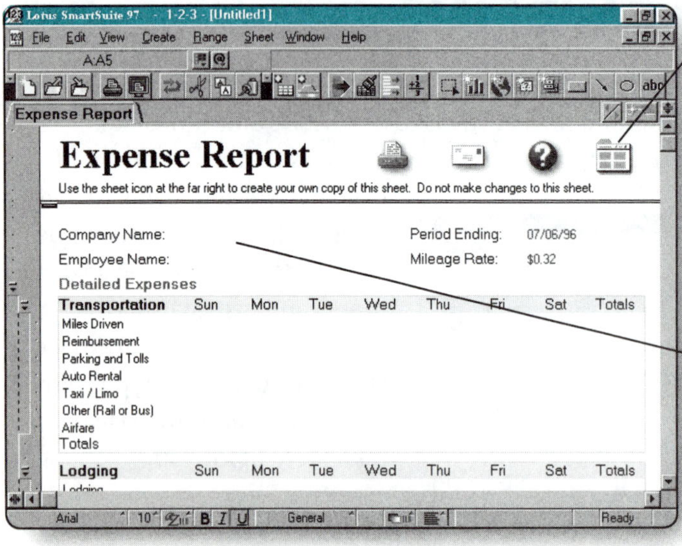

5. **Click** on the **sheet icon**. A copy of the sheet will be created so that the original will not be modified.

Most SmartMasters have this icon. The most notable exception is the personal budget SmartMaster.

6. **Type** the appropriate **data** into the yellow areas of the sheet.

Sample data will appear in a blue font.

You can work with the workbook as you would any workbook—changing formatting, entering data, and performing calculations.

12 Creating Charts

A chart is a powerful tool for the presentation of information. One chart can make more of an impact than endless pages of numbers. This is demonstrated by the fact that in our two most popular news media, television and newspapers, charts are used extensively. In this chapter, you'll learn how to:

- Create a chart
- Enhance the appearance of a basic chart

CREATING A CHART

Creating a chart is just a two-step process using 1-2-3. All you need to know is what you want to chart and where you want to put the chart.

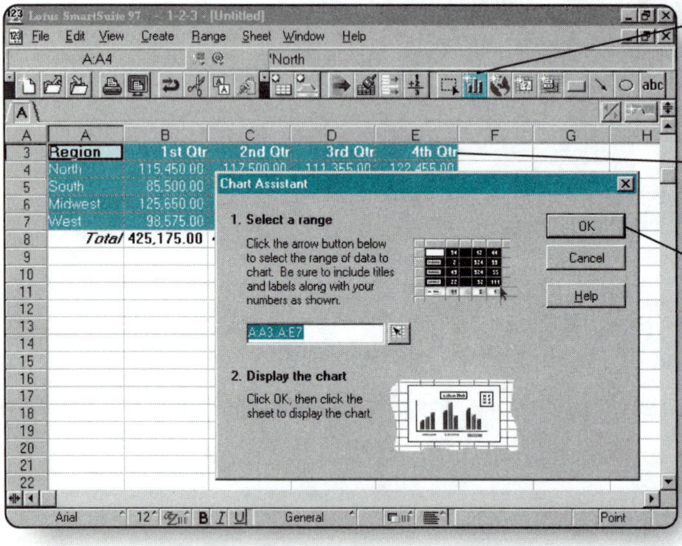

1. **Click** on the **Create a Chart SmartIcon**. The Chart Assistant dialog box will open.
2. **Select** the **range** you what to chart.
3. **Click** on **OK**. The Chart Assistant dialog box will close, and the pointer will change to look like a small bar chart.

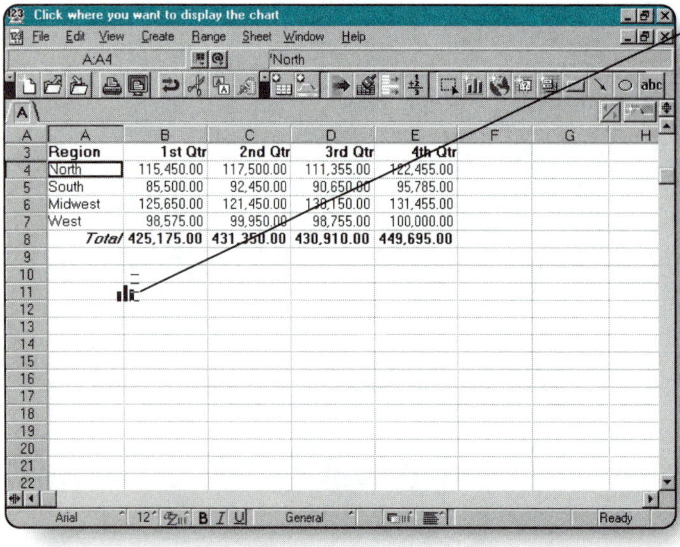

4. **Click** on the **worksheet** where you want the chart to go. The chart will be created.

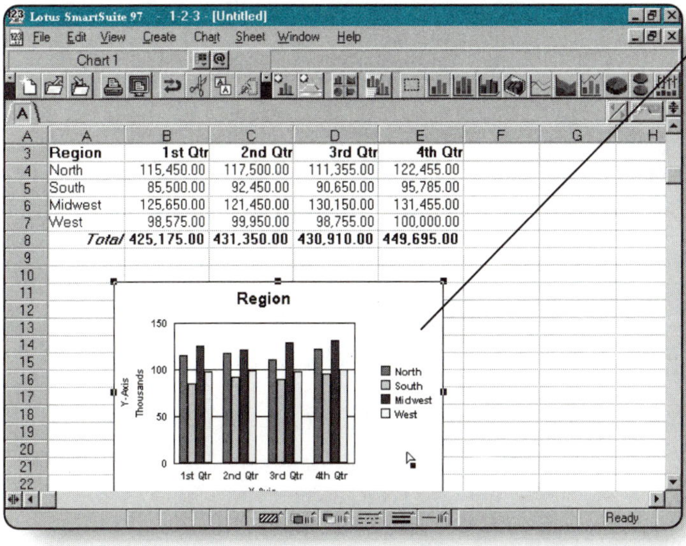

The chart is created with its upper left corner positioned where you clicked the worksheet. The type of chart created is a bar chart.

Selecting the Chart Type

If you do not want a simple bar chart, you can change the chart type. Chart types that you can select from include stacked bar, area, pie, and line as well as others.

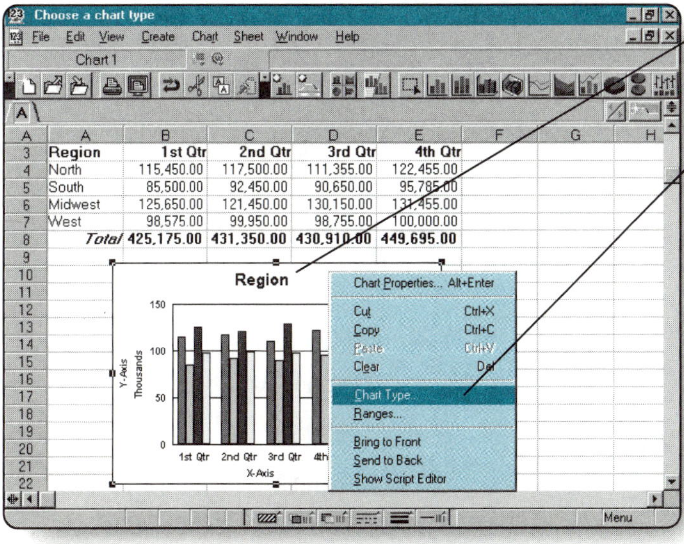

1. **Right-click** on the **chart**. A shortcut menu will appear.

2. **Click** on **Chart Type**. The Properties for Chart dialog box will open.

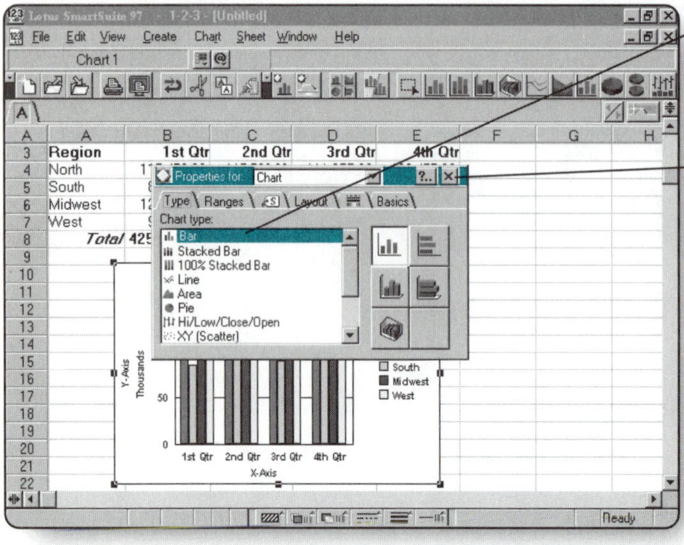

3. **Click** on the **Chart type:** you want. The chart will reflect that selection.

4. **Click** on the **Close button**. The Properties for Chart dialog box will close.

Enhancing a Chart

With very little effort, you now have a chart. As matter of fact, creating a chart is so simple it probably made you want to enhance the chart to improve its appearance. You can create a 3-D chart. You may want to use styles to change the color and appearance of a chart. You can also select the color and pattern for each individual series or slice, depending on whether the chart is a bar or pie chart.

Making a Chart 3-D

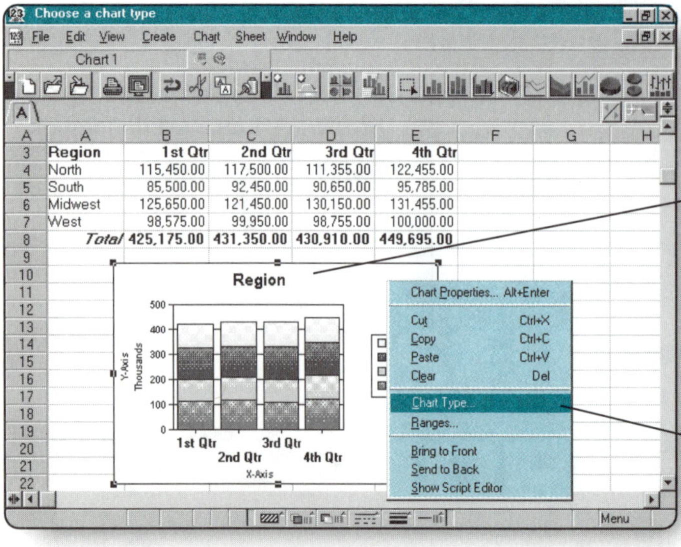

Three-dimensional charts are more dramatic in appearance and are often more visually pleasing.

1. **Right-click** on the **chart's background**. Do not click on any of the chart's elements such as its legend, bars, slices, or axis. The chart will be selected, and a shortcut menu will appear.

2. **Click** on **Chart Type**. The Properties for Chart dialog box will open.

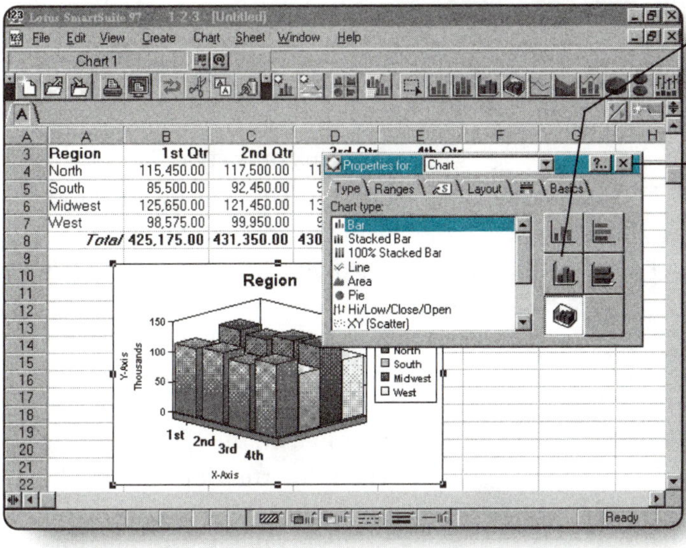

3. **Click** on a **3-D button**. The chart will change appearance to reflect your selection.

4. **Click** on the **Close button**. The Properties for Chart dialog box will close.

Using Styles

Styles are a quick way to change the appearance of your chart. By applying a style, you can change the color and pattern for the series or slices in your chart.

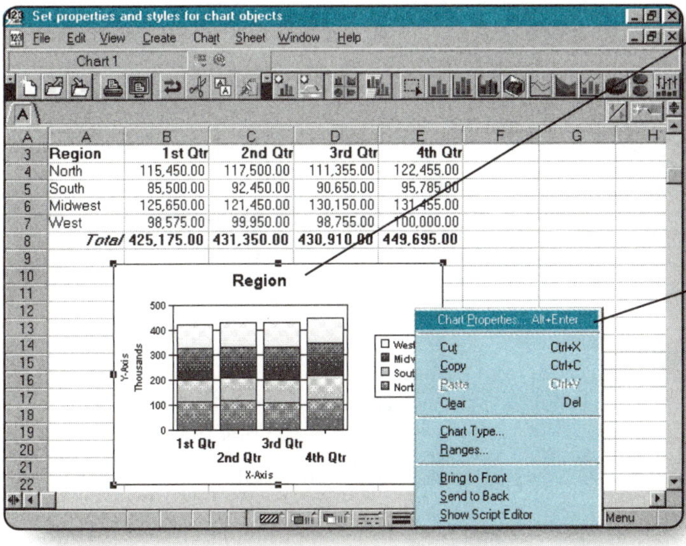

1. **Right-click** on the **chart's background**. Do not click on any of the chart's elements such as its legend, bars, slices, or axis. The chart will be selected, and a shortcut menu will appear.

2. **Click** on **Chart Properties**. The Properties for Chart dialog box will open.

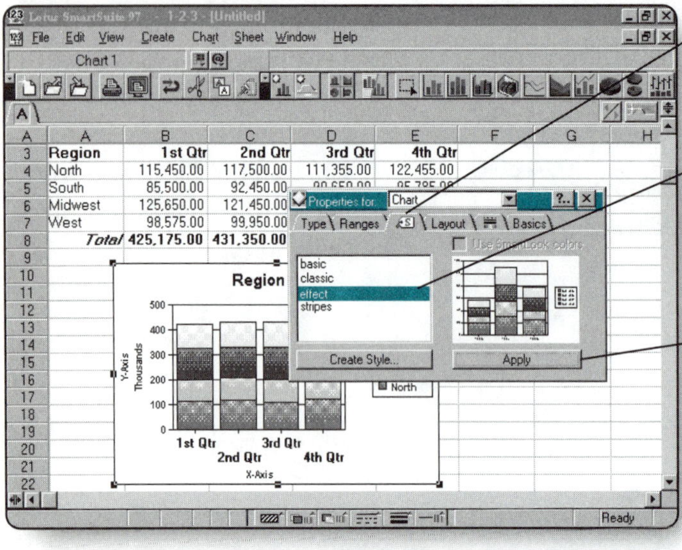

3. **Click** on the **Named style tab**. The Named style tab will appear.

4. **Click** on a **style**. The chart will be previewed in the window on the right side of the dialog box.

5. **Click** on **Apply**. The style will be applied to the selected chart.

6. **Click** on the **Close button**. The Properties for Chart dialog box will close.

Changing the Color of a Single Series or Slice

If you do not find a style that uses the color and patterns you want, you can change the color of individual series and slices.

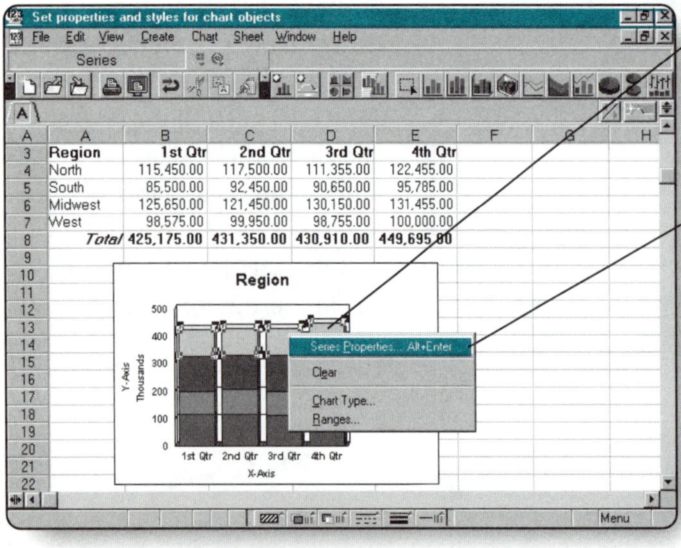

1. **Right-click** on the **series or slice** whose color you want to change. A shortcut menu will appear.

2a. **Click** on **Series Properties**. The Properties for Series dialog box will open.

OR

2b. **Click** on **Slice Properties**. The Properties for Slice dialog box will open.

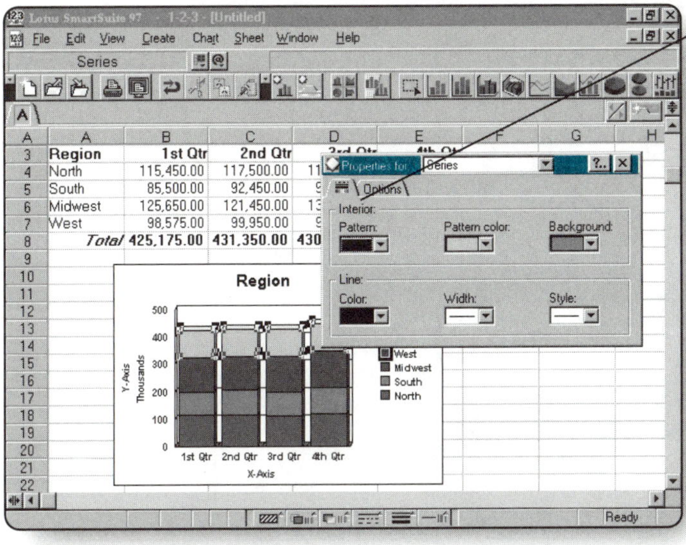

3. Click on the **Color, pattern, and line style tab**. The Color, pattern, and line style tab will appear.

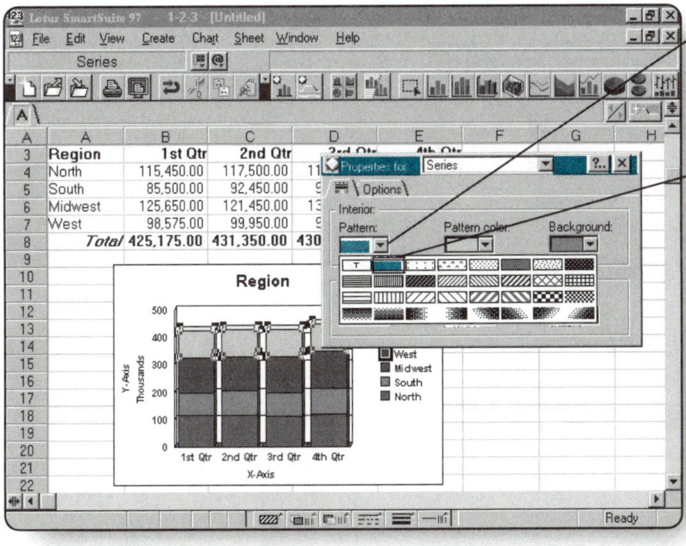

4. Click on the **down arrow** (▼) under the Pattern:. The pattern palette will appear.

5. Click on a **pattern**. The pattern palette will close, and the pattern will be applied to the selected series or slice.

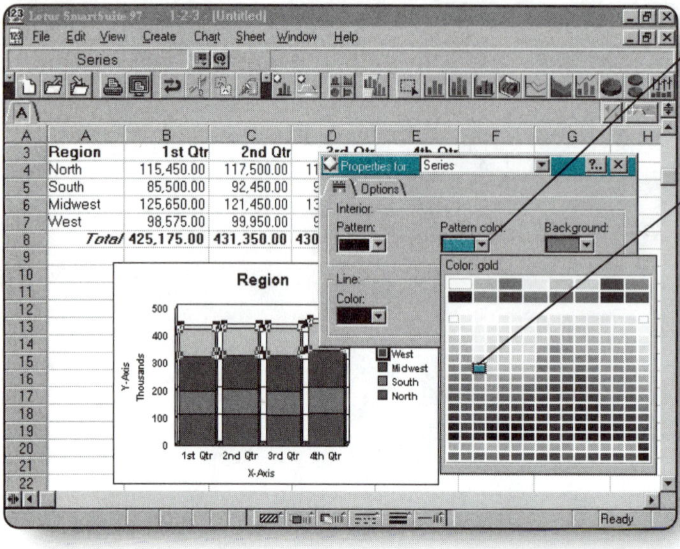

6. Click on the **down arrow** (▼) under the Pattern color:. The color palette will appear.

7. Click on a **color**. The color palette will close, and the color will be applied to the selected series or slice.

8. Choose from the following **options**:

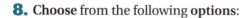

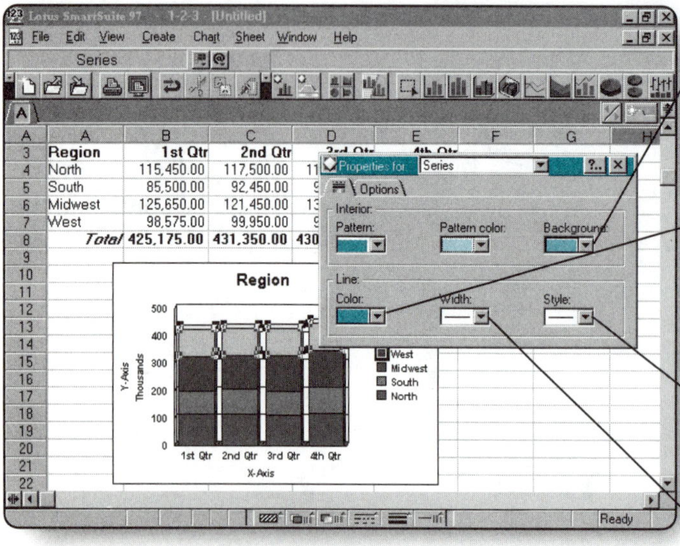

- ✦ If you selected a pattern other than solid, you can select the Background: of the pattern by clicking on the down arrow (▼).
- ✦ To change the Color: of the line that outlines the series or slice, click on the down arrow (▼) and select a color from the color palette.
- ✦ Click on the down arrow (▼) to choose a different Style: for the line.
- ✦ The Width: of the line that outlines the series or slice change be changed by clicking on the (▼) and selecting a different width from the list.

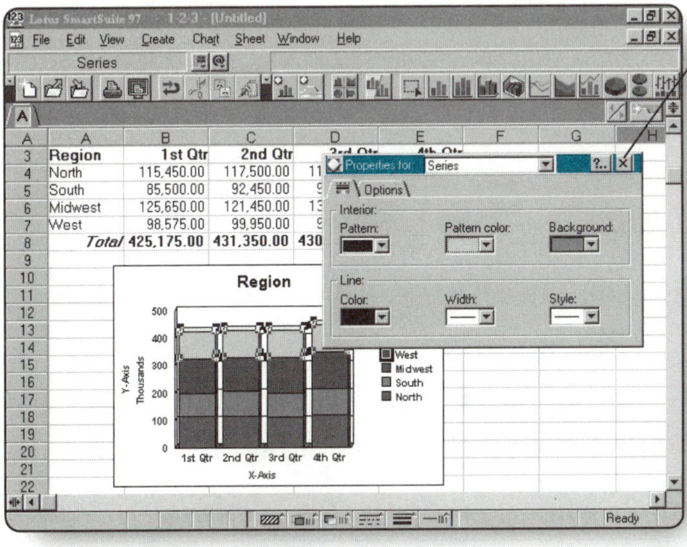

9. **Click** on the **Close button**. The Properties dialog box will close.

NOTE

You do not have to close the Properties for series or slice dialog box to change the color of another series or slice. With the Properties dialog box open, click on another series or slice.

PART III REVIEW QUESTIONS

1. **What happens if you press the F2 key while in 1-2-3?** ***See "Making Changes" in Chapter 9***
2. **How would you move the contents of a cell to a new location?** ***See "Moving Data" in Chapter 9***
3. **Do you need to create your own formula to total a column of numbers?** ***See "Using Built-In @Functions" in Chapter 10***
4. **What happens to a formula when you copy it?** ***See "Copying Formulas" in Chapter 10***
5. **What does a $ mean in a cell reference?** ***See "Copying Formulas" in Chapter 10***
6. **What would you do to make sure that there aren't misspelled words in your workbook?** ***See "Checking Spelling" in Chapter 11***
7. **Does 1-2-3 use styles?** ***See "Changing the Appearance of Cells" in Chapter 11***
8. **How would you put a border around cells?** ***See "Changing the Appearance of Cells" in Chapter 4***
9. **How many steps does it take to create a chart?** ***See "Creating a Chart" in Chapter 12***
10. **How would you make a 2-D chart a 3-D chart? See** ***"Making the Chart 3-D" in Chapter 12***

PART IV

Using Freelance

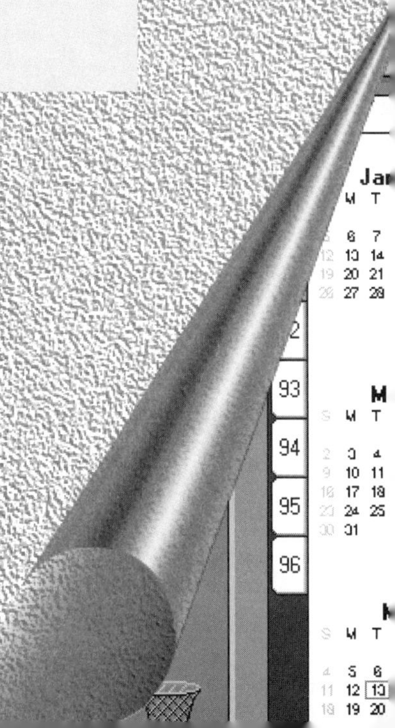

13 Creating a Simple Presentation

Freelance Graphics is a tool that aids you in creating presentation graphics. Using Freelance, you can create slides and speaker notes. Freelance provides you with SmartMasters to help you create attractive presentations. The slide you create can either be viewed on-screen or be printed out. In this chapter, you'll learn how to:

- Use SmartMasters to create a professional-looking presentation
- Work with your presentation's slides to add text and graphics

USING SMARTMASTERS

The fastest and easiest way to create a professional-looking presentation is to use one of Freelance's many SmartMasters. Freelance's SmartMasters have been designed by a professional graphic designer so that your presentations will look great with a minimum amount of effort.

Starting a Presentation

When you start Freelance, you are asked whether you want to start a new presentation. You can also start a new presentation using the File menu after you start Freelance.

Starting a Presentation When You Start Freelance

1. Start Freelance. The Welcome to Lotus Freelance Graphics dialog box will open.

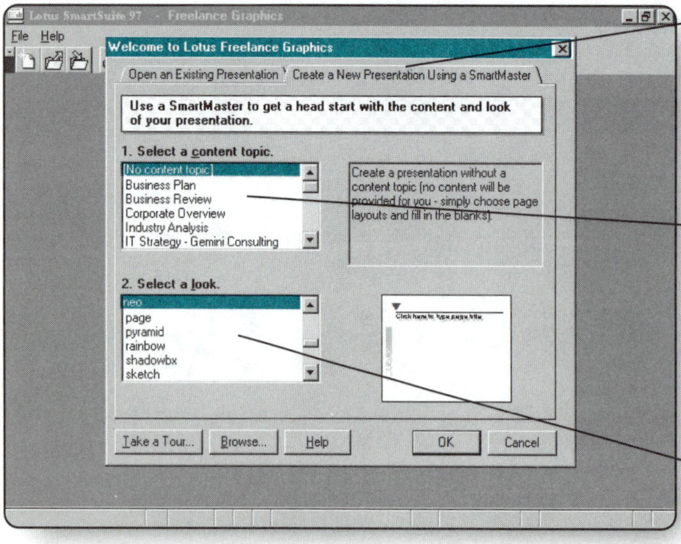

2. Click on the **Create a New Presentation Using a SmartMaster tab**. The Create a New Presentation Using a SmartMaster tab will appear.

3. Click on a **content topic** from the Select a content topic. list box. A description and preview of the proposed presentation will appear on the right side of the dialog box.

4. Click on a **look** for the presentation in the Select a look. list box. The preview of the presentation will change to match the selection.

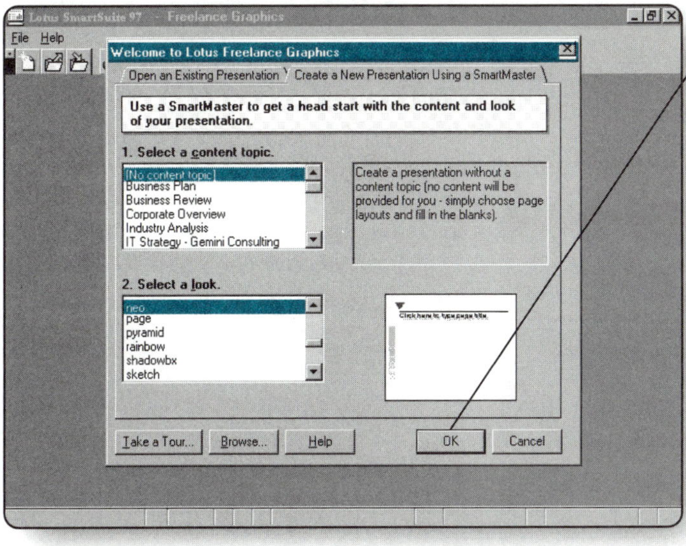

5. **Click** on **OK**. The New Page dialog box will open.

> **NOTE**
>
> Some SmartMasters may display a message box at this point informing you of the steps you need to take when using the SmartMaster. Click on OK.

6. **Select** a **content page** from the Content topic: list. The page will be added to your presentation.

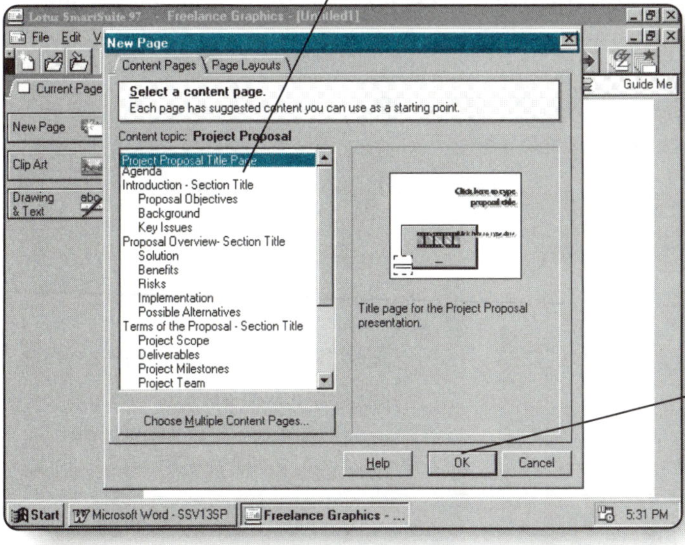

The pages in the Content topic: list are listed in the order it is recommended that you place them in your presentation. For example, the title page is at the top of the list because it is probably the first page you'll want to add to your presentation.

7. **Click** on **OK**. The page will be added to your presentation.

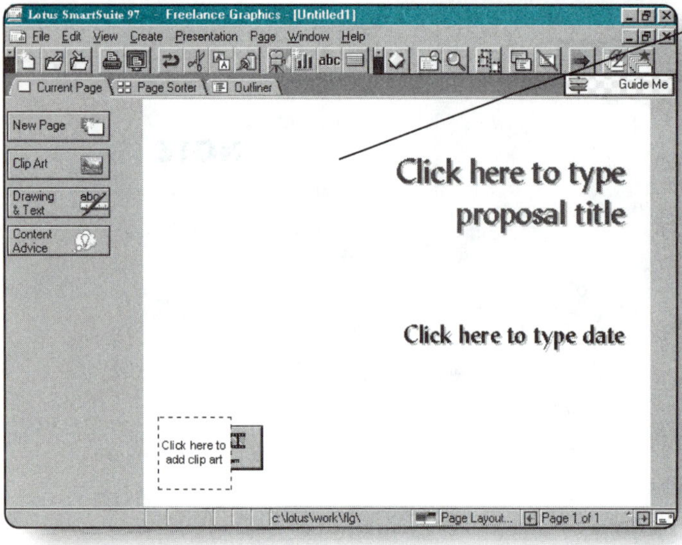

The newly added page is shown on the Current Page tab of your presentation. You are now ready to add text and graphics to the page.

Starting a Presentation After You've Started Freelance

1. **Click** on the **Create a new presentation SmartIcon**. The New Presentation dialog box will open.

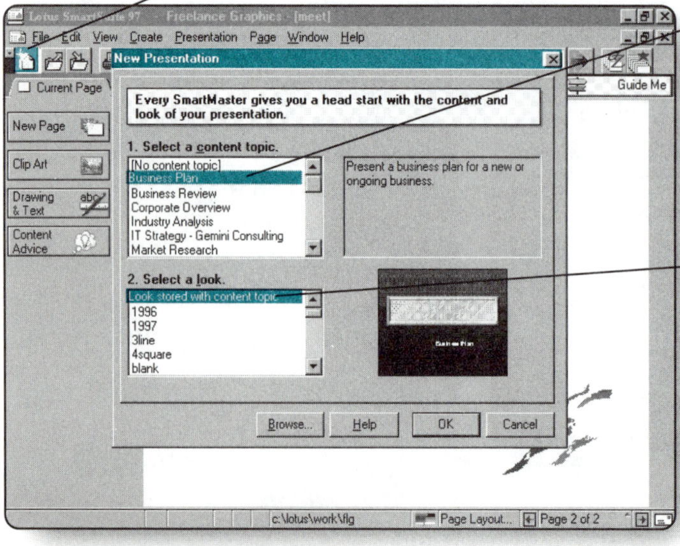

2. **Click** on a **content topic** from the Select a content topic. list box. A description and preview of the proposed presentation will appear on the right side of the dialog box.

3. **Click** on a **look** for the presentation in the Select a look. list box. The preview of the presentation will change to match the selection.

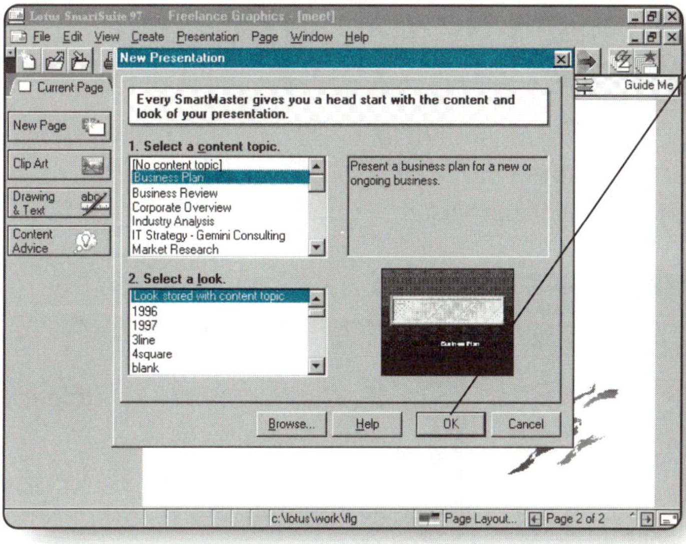

4. **Click** on **OK**. The New Page dialog box will open.

> **NOTE**
>
> Some SmartMasters may display a message box at this point informing you of the steps you need to take when using the SmartMaster. Click on OK.

5. **Select** a **content page** from the Content topic: list. The page will be added to your presentation.

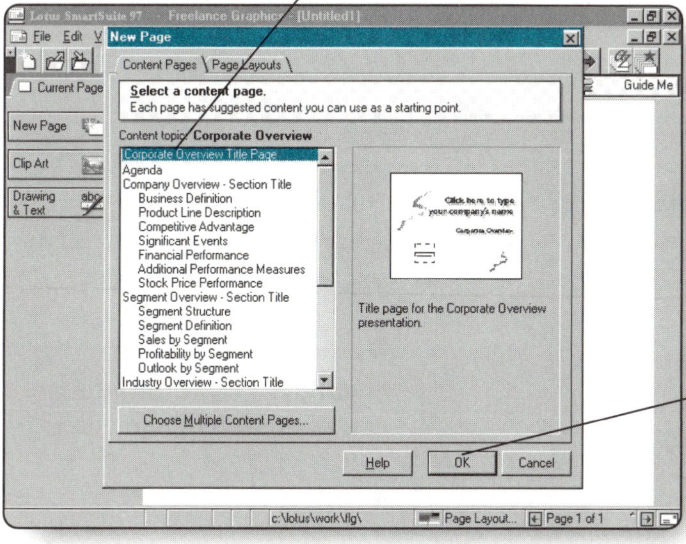

The pages in the Content topic: list are listed in the order it is recommended that you place them in your presentation. For example, the title page is at the top of the list because it is probably the first page you'll want to add to your presentation.

6. **Click** on **OK**. The page will be added to your presentation.

Applying a New SmartMaster to Your Presentation

After you create your presentation, you may find that you don't like the look of the SmartMaster you originally selected. You can apply a new SmartMaster to your presentation at any time.

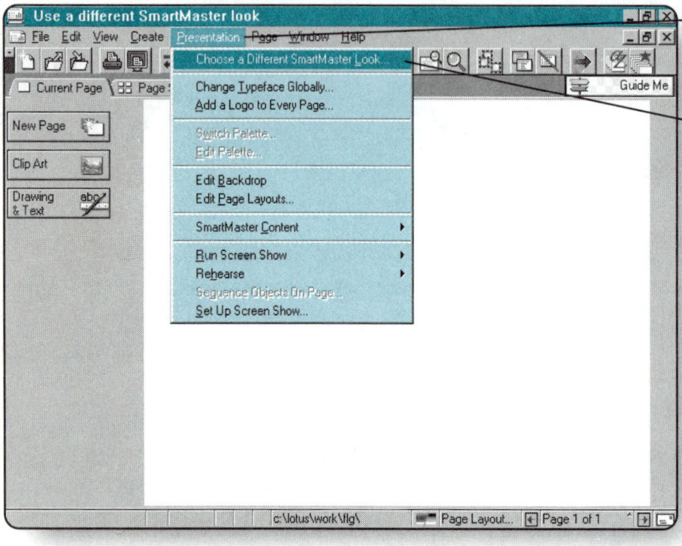

1. **Click** on **Presentation**. The Presentation menu will appear.
2. **Click** on **Choose a Different SmartMaster Look**. The Choose a Look for Your Presentation dialog box will open.

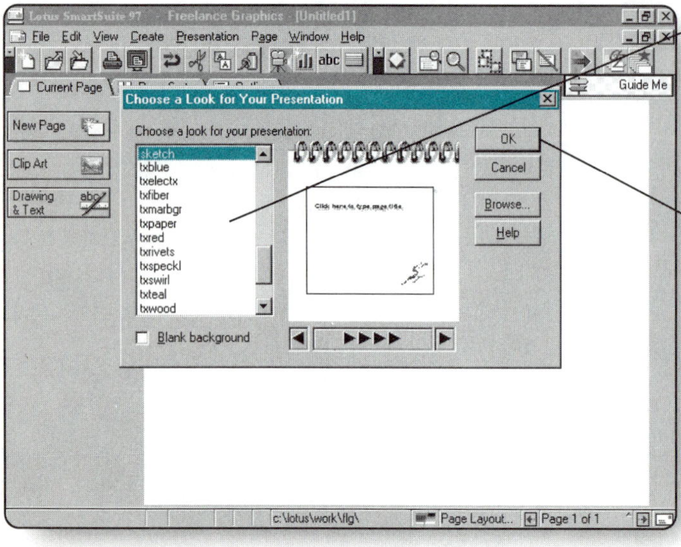

3. **Click** on a **look** for your presentation from the list. The SmartMaster's look will be previewed in the window on the right side of the dialog box.
4. **Click** on **OK**. The new SmartMaster look will be applied to your presentation.

WORKING WITH SLIDES

SmartMasters are set up so that the slides using them give you clues as to how to use them. On a slide, there will be different objects and instructions to click on those objects. Slides can have the following types of objects: text, clip art, bulleted text, chart, and table.

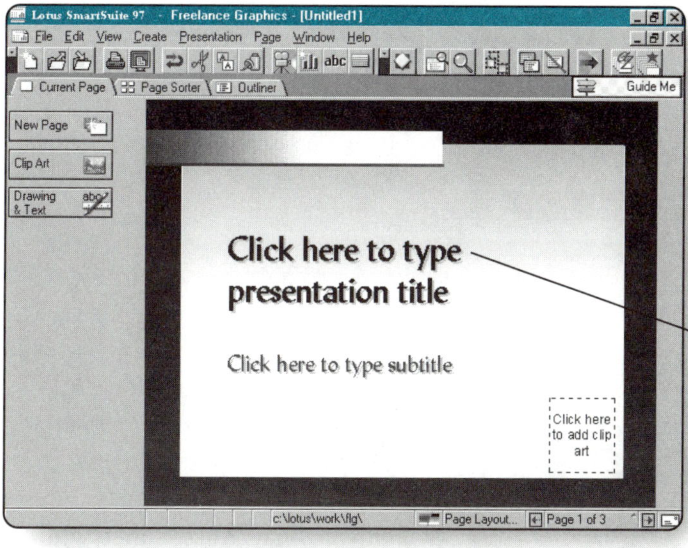

If you do not use an object, don't worry. The empty object will not appear on the final version of the slide.

Entering Text on a Slide

1. **Click** on an **object** that begins with the phrase **Click here to type**. The text area will be changed to edit mode.

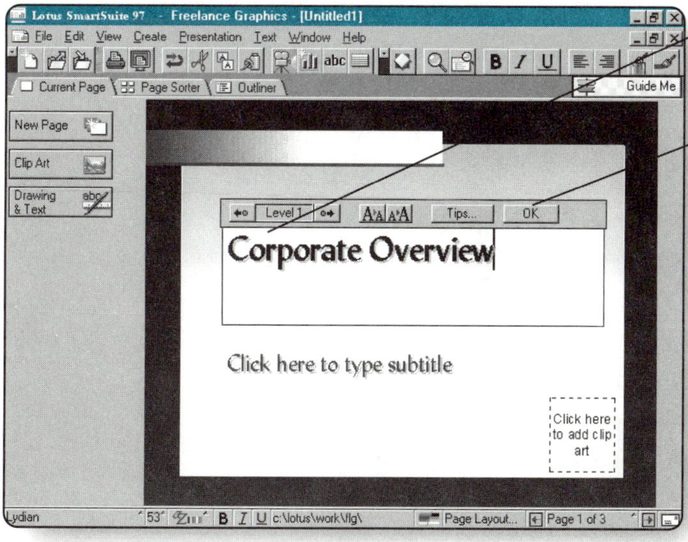

2. **Type** some **text**. The text will be entered into the slide.

3. **Click** on **OK**. The text object will no longer be in edit mode.

4. **Repeat steps 1** through **3** until all text objects are complete.

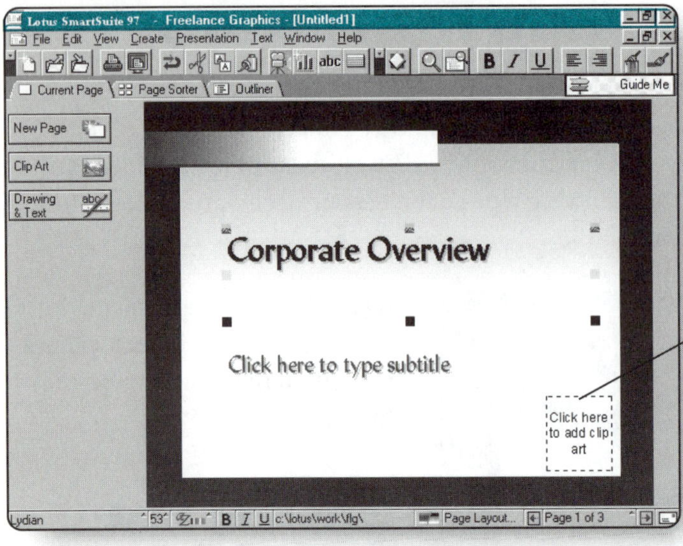

Adding Clip Art to a Slide

Some slides have objects designated for clip art. An example of this type of slide is a title slide.

1. **Click** on the **object** that says, "Click here to add clip art." The Add Clip Art or Diagram to the Page dialog box will open.

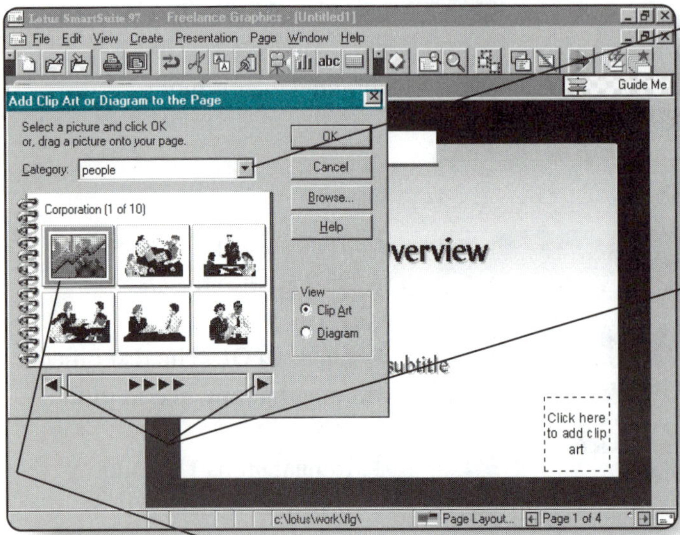

2. **Click** on the **down arrow** (▼) to select a Category: of clip art. The notebook at the bottom of the dialog box will display the clip art images associated with the selected category.

3. **Click** on the **arrow buttons** under the notebook. This will scroll through the images.

4. **Click** on the **clip art** picture you want.

5. **Click** on **OK**. The clip art will be added to the slide.

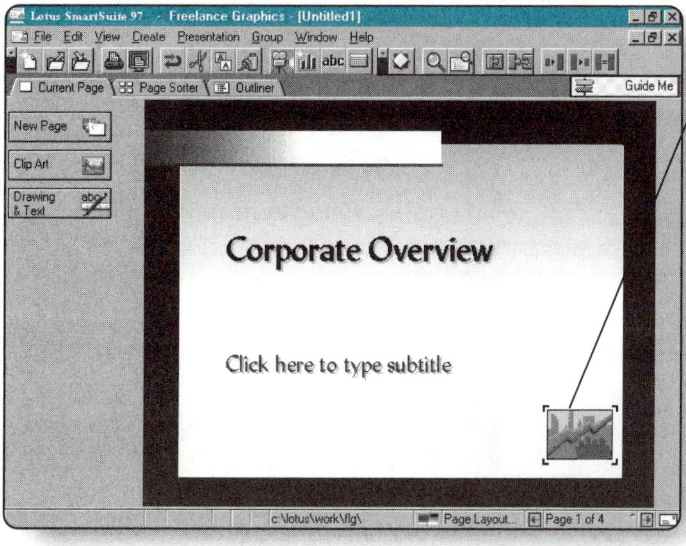

The clip art is automatically sized to fit within the clip art object.

Working with Bulleted Lists

Working with bulleted lists is similar to working with text objects. The only difference is that when you press Enter, you add another bulleted item. Before starting this process, you need to add a page with a bulleted text object. Bulleted List is an example of a page layout that has a bulleted text object.

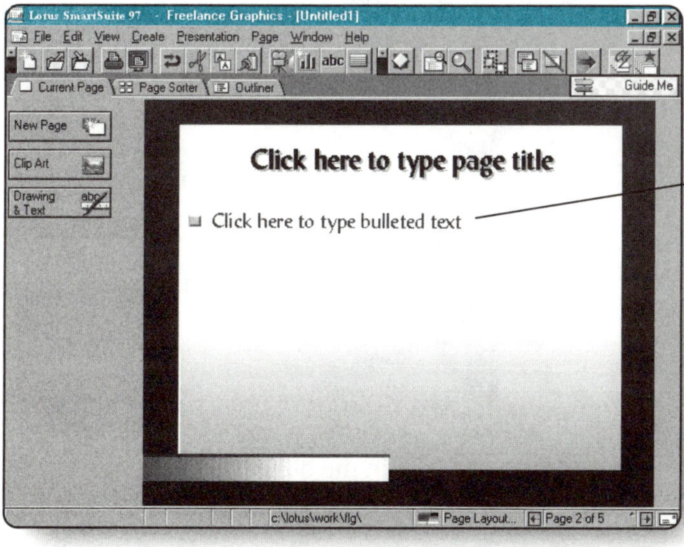

1. **Click** on an **object** that says "Click here to type bulleted text." The object will be changed to edit mode.

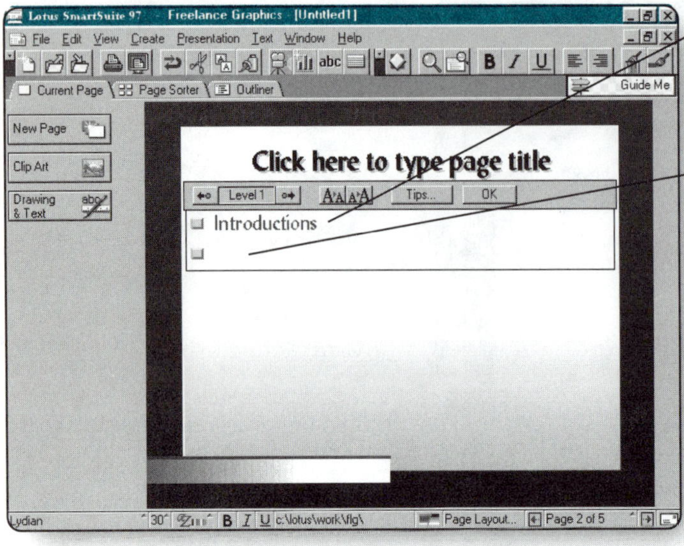

2. **Type** some **text** for the bulleted item. The text will be added to the bulleted list.

3. **Press** the **Enter key**. A new bulleted item will be added.

4a. **Type** some **text** for the bulleted item. The text will be added to the list.

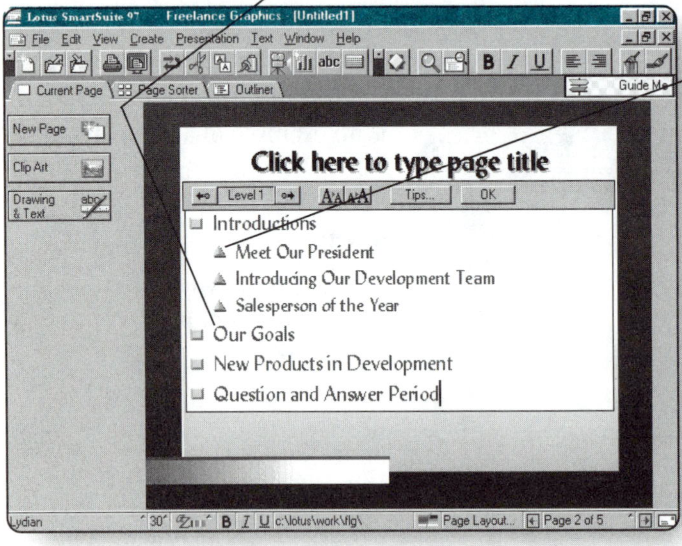

OR

4b. **Press** the **Tab key**. The next level in the bullet hierarchy will be added. **Type** some **text** for the item.

5. **Repeat steps 3** and **4** until the bulleted list is complete.

6. **Click** on **OK**. The bullet list object will not be in edit mode.

To move backwards, in other words, return to the higher level in the bullet hierarchy, press Shift and the Tab key.

Adding a Chart to a Slide

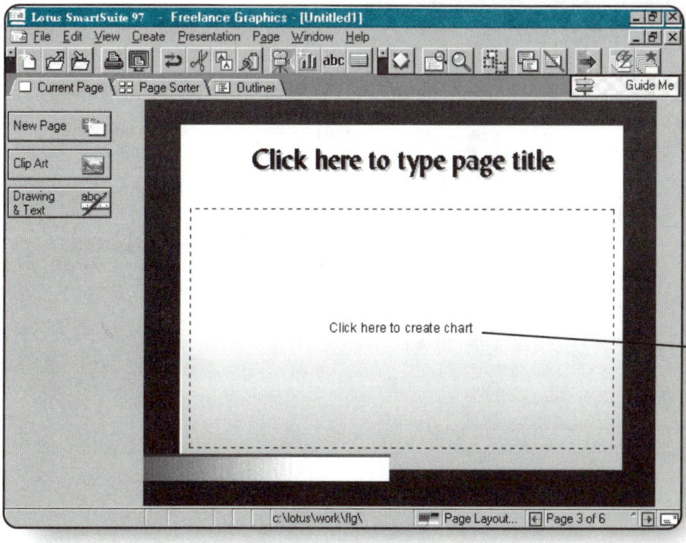

Charts are a great way to present data. Creating a chart in Freelance is similar to creating a chart in 1-2-3. Select a page layout to add that has a chart object on it. *1 Chart* is an example of a page layout with a chart object on it.

1. **Click** on the **object** that says "Click here to create chart." The Create Chart dialog box will open.

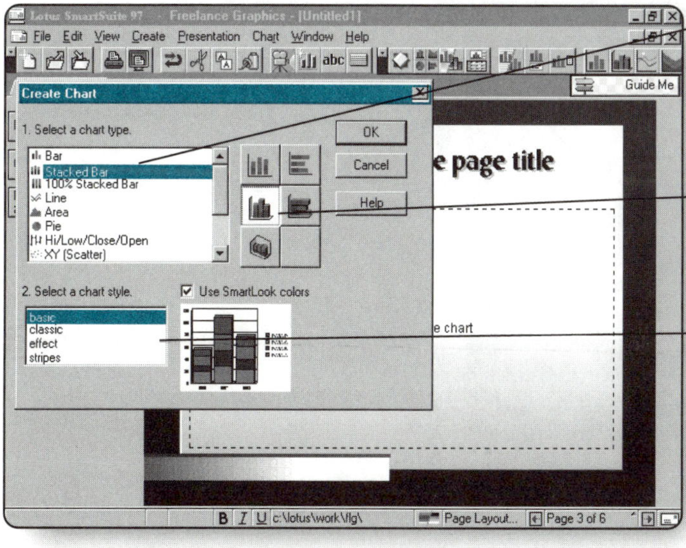

2. **Click** on a **chart type** from the list box. The chart will be previewed in the lower right corner of the dialog box.

3. **Click** on an **icon button**. The chart's orientation will be changed.

4. **Click** on **chart style** from the Select a chart style. list box. The chart's style will be changed.

5. **Click** on **OK**. The Edit Data dialog box will open.

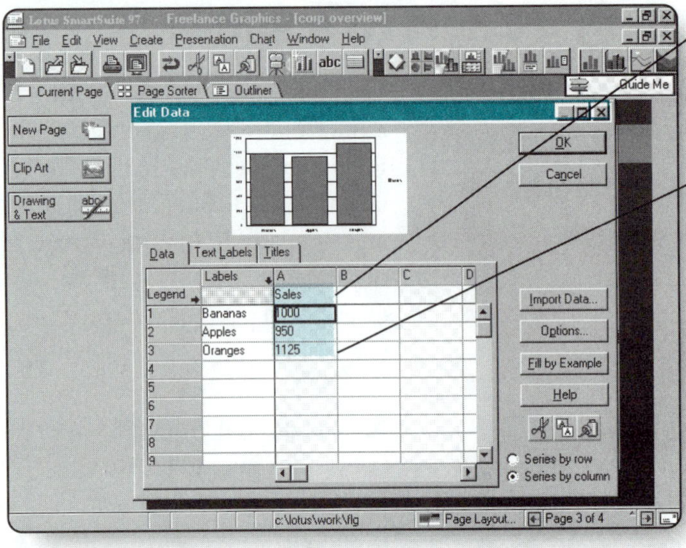

6. **Type a title** for the chart on the title row. The title will be added to the chart.

7. **Type** the **data** for the chart. As you type, the chart will be updated.

8. **Click** on **OK**. The chart is added to the slide.

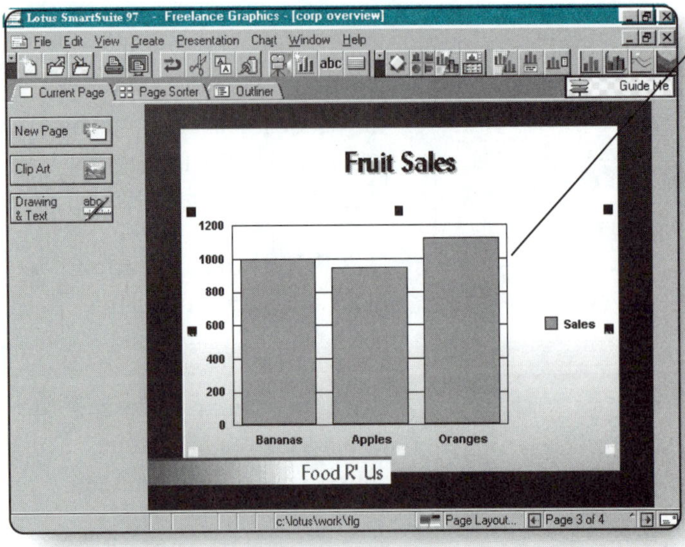

The chart automatically sizes on the slide to match the original size of the chart object.

Working with Tables

The first thing you need to know when working with tables is how many columns and rows you will need. After you create the table, you enter the data in it. You can format a table so that the headings, for example, are a different font from the rest of the table. Select a page layout to add that has a table object on it. *Table* is an example of a page layout with a table object on it.

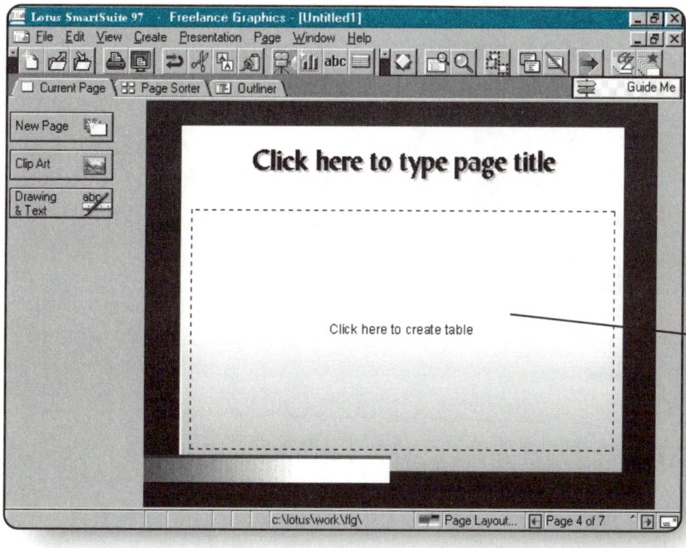

Creating a Table

1. **Click** on the **object** that says "Click here to create table." The Table Gallery dialog box will open.

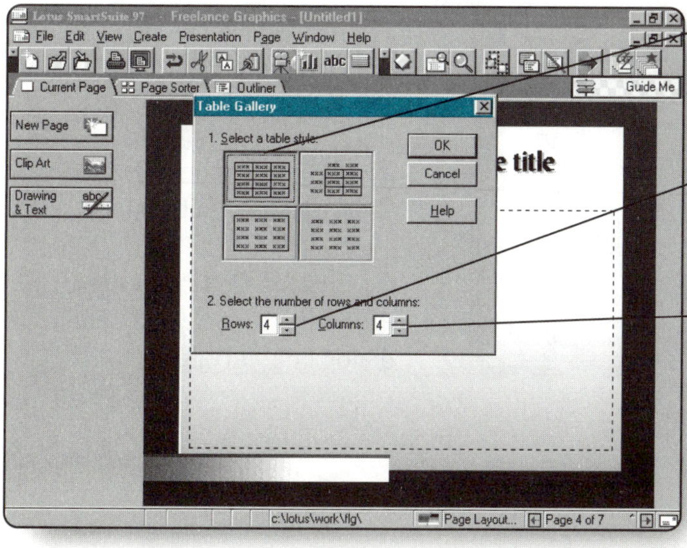

2. **Click** on a **table type button**. This will set the table type of the table you are creating.

3. **Click** on the **up and down arrows** (⬍) to set the number of Rows:.

4. **Click** on the **up and down arrows** (⬍) to set the number of Columns:.

5. **Click** on **OK**. The table will be created on the slide.

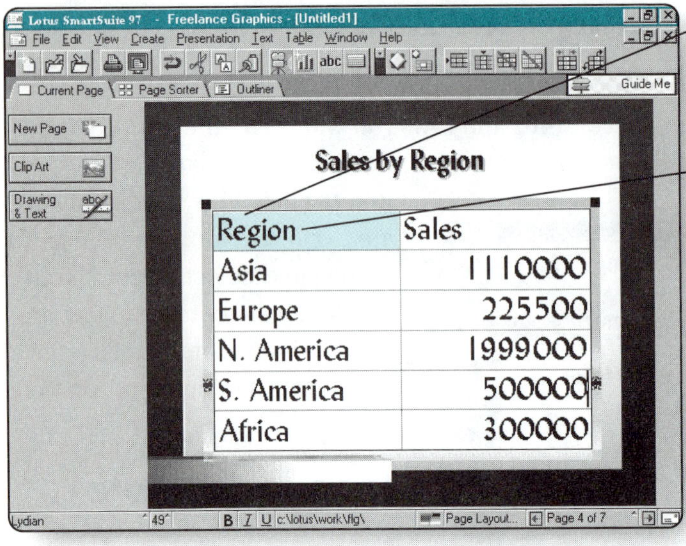

6. Click on the first **cell** in the table. The table will be changed to edit mode.

7. Type some **text**. The text will be added to the table.

8. Press the **Tab key**. The next cell in the table will be selected.

9. Repeat steps 7 and **8** until all the necessary text is added to the table.

Change the Font of Table Cells

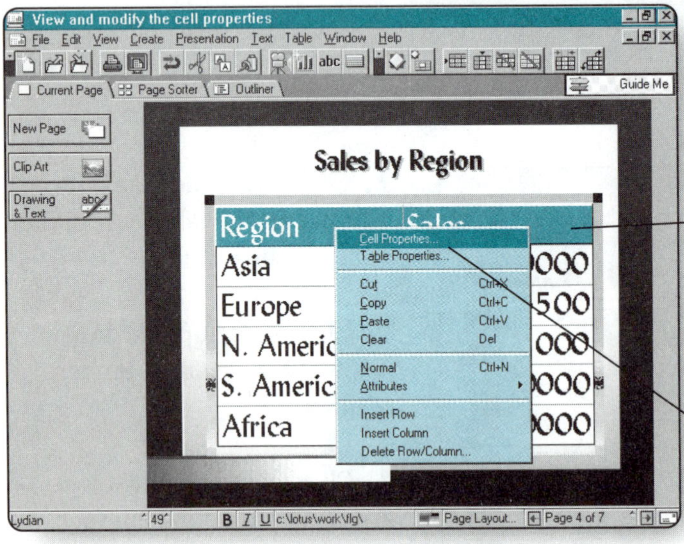

NOTE

If the table is not active, double-click on it.

1. Highlight a **cell or cells**. The cell or cells will be selected.

2. Right-click the **cells**. A shortcut menu will appear.

3. Click on **Cell Properties**. The Properties for Selected Cell(s) dialog box will open.

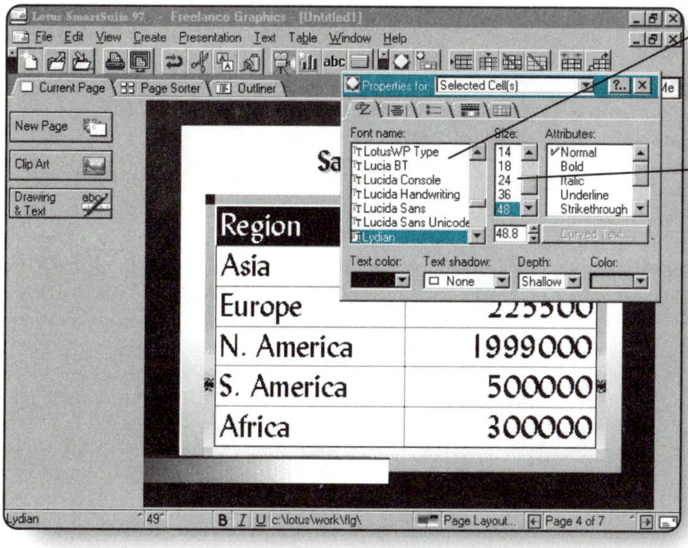

4. **Click** on a **font** from the Font name: list. The font will be applied to the selected cells.

5. **Click** on a **size** from the Size: list. The font size of the selected cells will change.

6. **Click** on the **Close button**. The dialog box will close.

ADDING SLIDES

You can add as many slides as you want to your presentation. Each slide has a page layout associated with it. The page layout determines the role of the slide in the presentation and the objects on the slide.

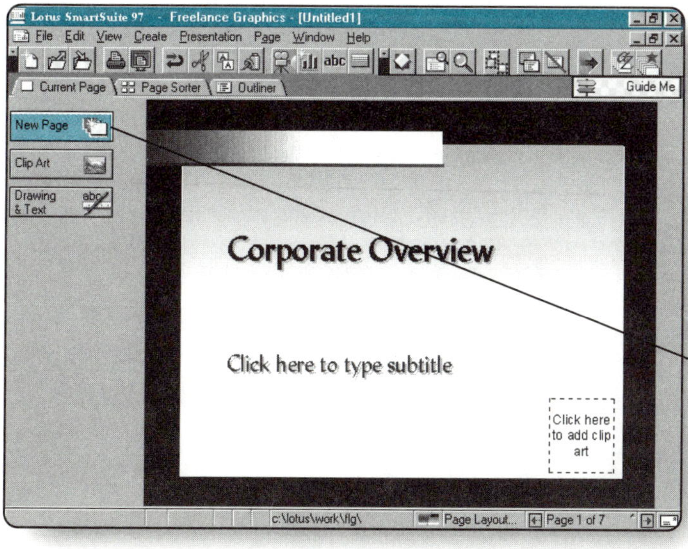

Adding a New Slide Based on a Page Layout

If you want a slide without content suggestions, you need to create one using a page layout.

1. **Click** on **New Page**. The New Page dialog box will open.

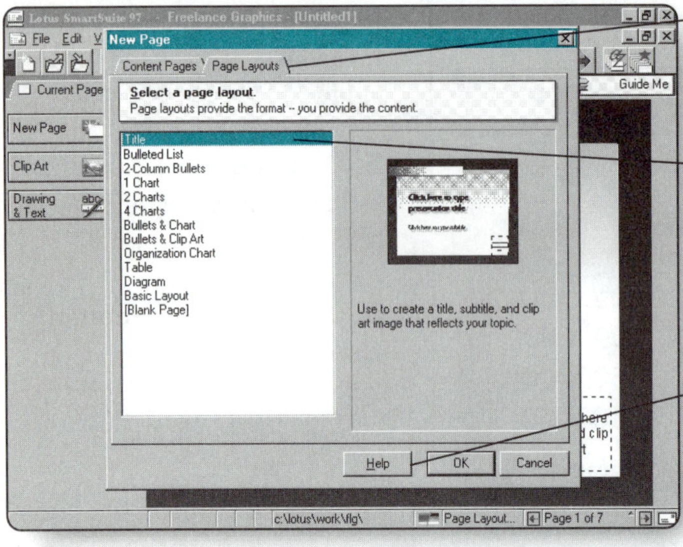

2. Click on the **Page Layouts tab**. The Page Layouts tab will appear.

3. Click on a **page layout** from the list. A slide using that page layout will appear in the preview window on the right side of the dialog box.

4. Click on **OK**. The slide will be added.

Adding a New Slide Using Content Pages

If you want a suggestion as to where and what type of things to place on a slide, use a content page to create it.

1. Click on **New Page**. The New Page dialog box will open.

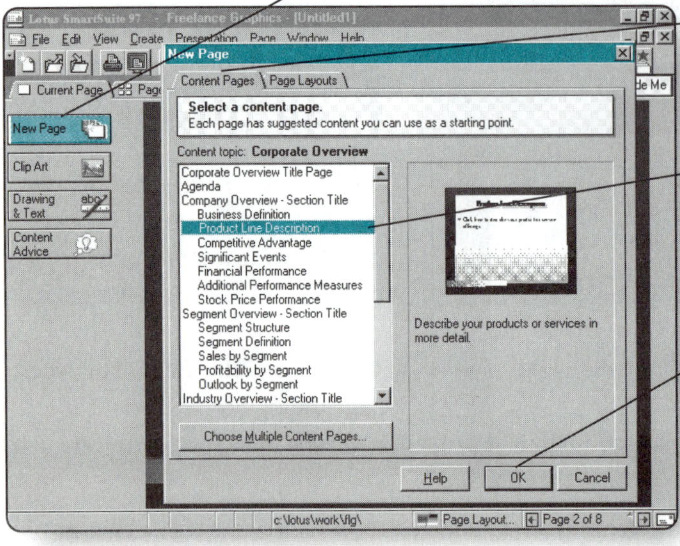

2. Click on the **Content Pages tab**. The Content Pages tab will appear.

3. Click on a **content page**. A preview of a slide using the selected content page will appear.

4. Click on **OK**. The slide will be added to your presentation.

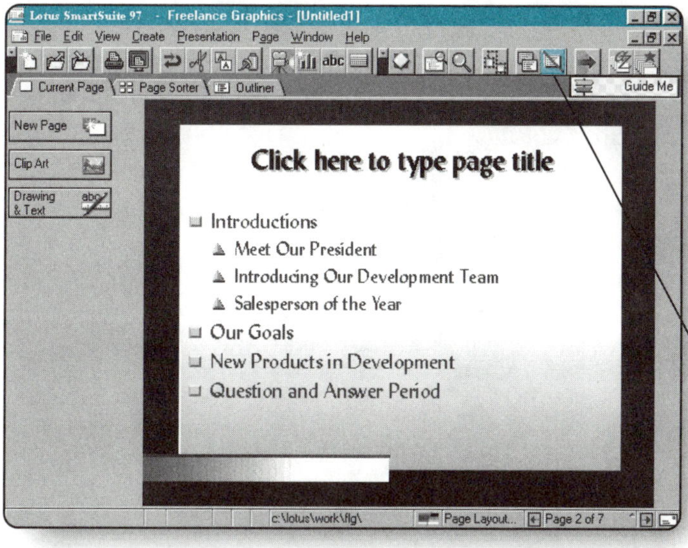

DELETING SLIDES

If you do not want a slide to be a part of your presentation, delete it.

1. Move to the **slide** to be deleted. The slide will appear.

2. Click on the **Delete Pages SmartIcon**. The Slide will be deleted from the presentation.

> **NOTE**
>
> If the Delete Pages SmartIcon is not displayed, click the edge of the slide so that no objects are selected.

MOVING AROUND IN YOUR PRESENTATION

There are several ways to move from slide to slide in your presentation by using the status bar navigation buttons or by using the Page Sorter.

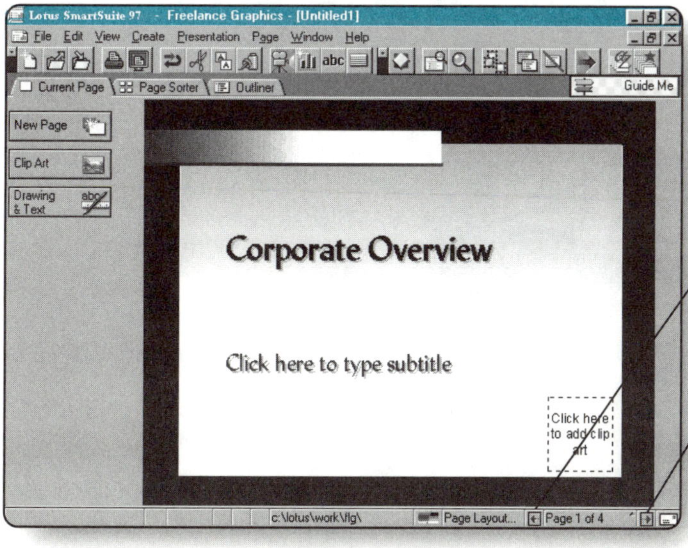

Using the Status Bar Navigation Buttons to Move to a Slide

1. Click on the **previous slide button**. The previous slide in the presentation will appear.

2. Click on the **next slide button**. The next slide in the presentation will appear.

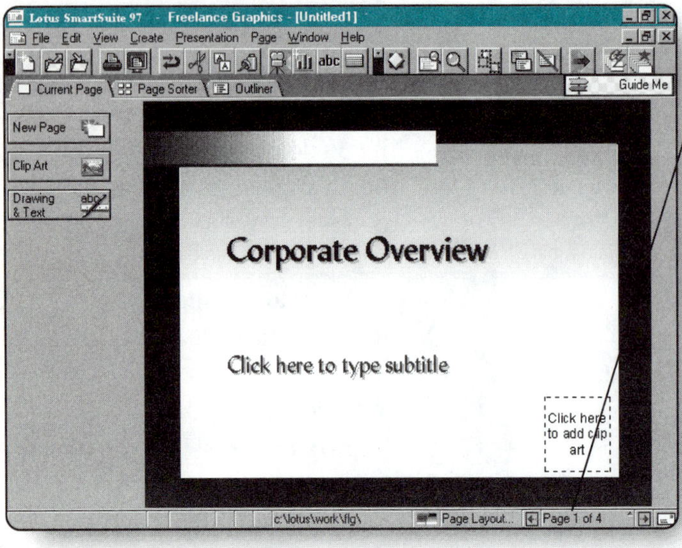

3. **Click** on the **page number button**. A menu listing the pages in the presentation will appear.

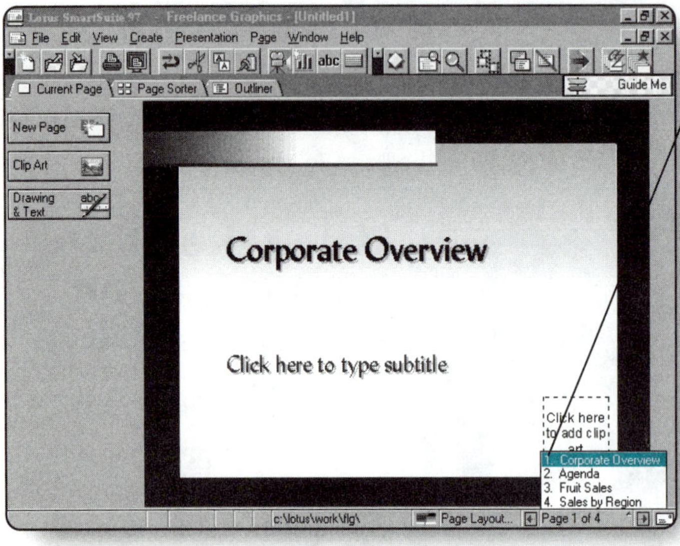

4. **Click** on a **slide**. The slide will appear.

Moving to a Slide Using Page Sorter

The Page Sorter is used for a variety of things including to move to a page in the presentation.

1. **Click** on the **Page Sorter tab**. The Page Sorter tab will appear.

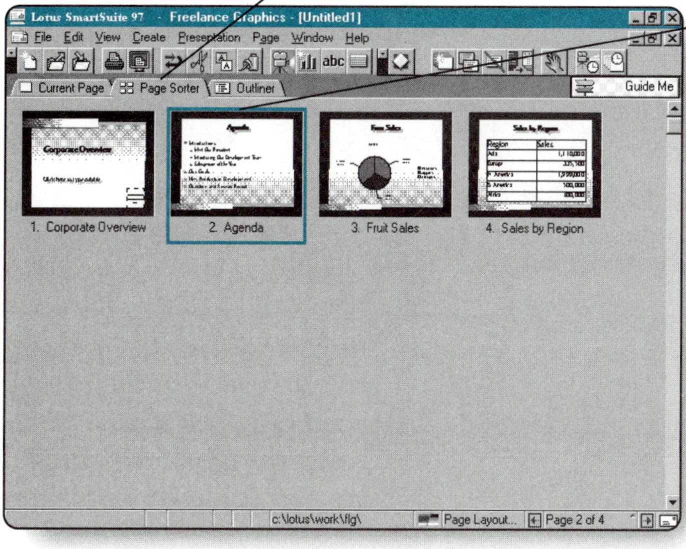

2. **Double-click** on the **slide** you want to go to. The slide will appear.

14 Making Professional Slide Shows

After you create your presentation, you'll want to show it. You may need to print a copy of your presentation or show it on a monitor or both. Freelance provides you with tools to create a professional and visually interesting slide show. In this chapter, you'll learn how to:

- Add speaker notes to your presentation
- Print your slide show
- Show your presentation

WORKING WITH SPEAKER NOTES

Speaker notes can be added to any slide in your presentation. After the notes have been added, you can print them. Printed speaker notes have the slide on the top half of the page and the note on the bottom half.

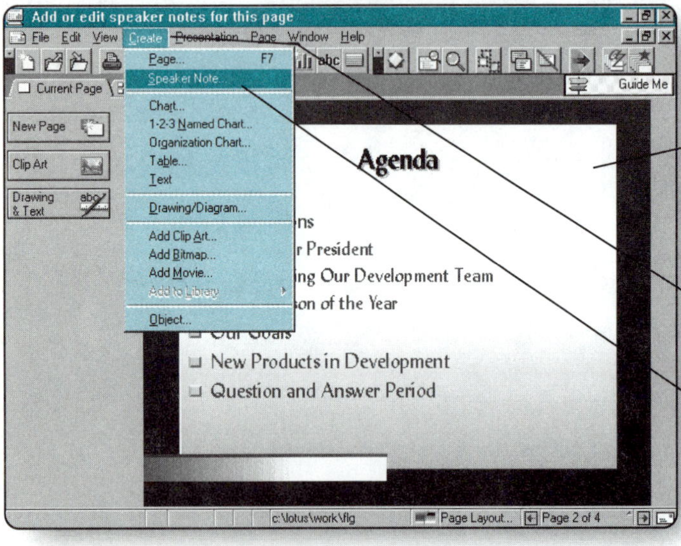

Adding a Speaker Note

1. **Select** a **slide** to which you want to add the speaker note. The slide will become the current slide.
2. **Click** on **Create**. The Create menu will appear.
3. **Click** on **Speaker Note**. The Speaker Note dialog box will open.

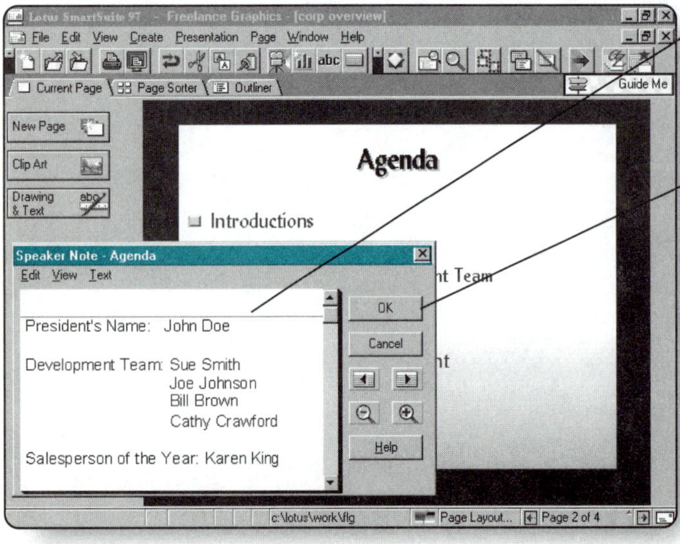

4. **Type** the **text** of the speaker note. The text will appear in the text box.
5. **Click** on **OK**. The speaker note will be added to the slide.

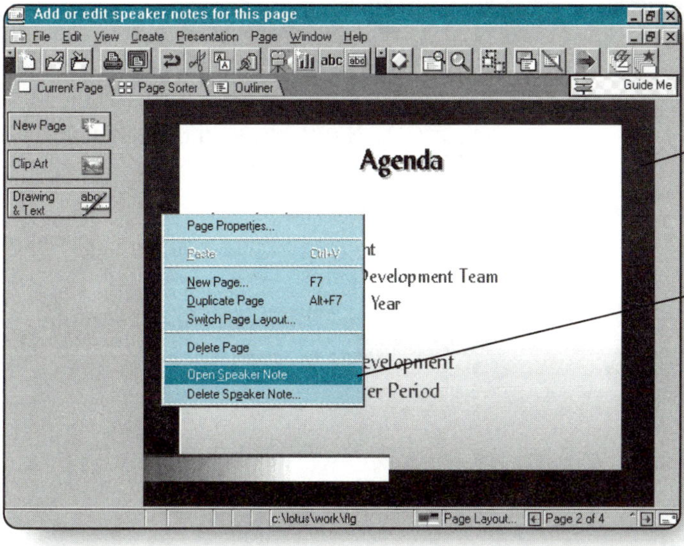

Editing a Speaker Note

1. **Right-click** on the **border area** of the slide. A shortcut menu will appear.
2. **Click** on **Open Speaker Note**. The Speaker Note dialog box will open.

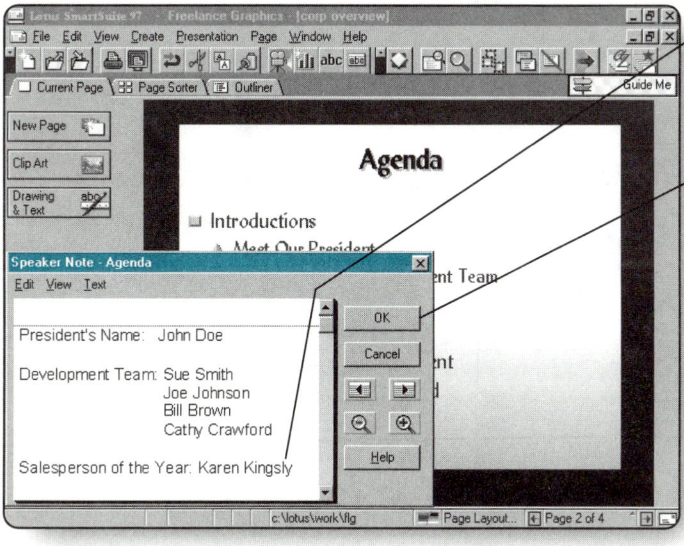

3. **Type** the **changes** to the speaker note. The change will be reflected in the text box.
4. **Click** on **OK**. The speaker note will be updated.

Deleting a Speaker Note

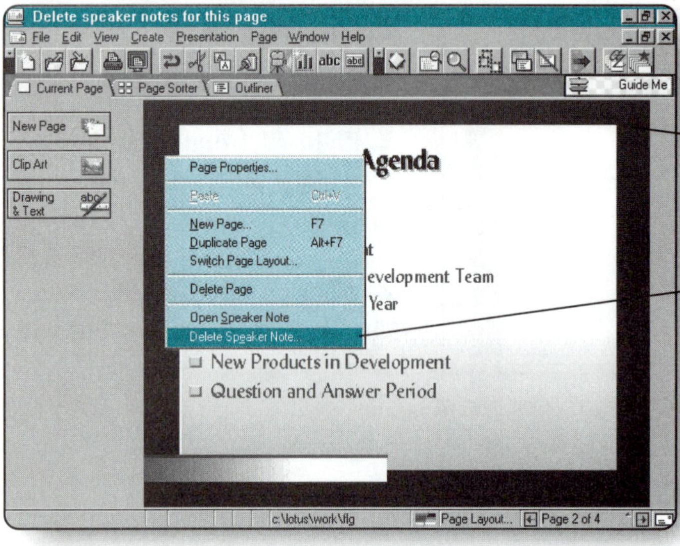

1. **Right-click** on the **border area** of the slide. A shortcut menu will appear.
2. **Click** on **Delete Speaker Note**. The Delete Speaker Note dialog box will open.
3. **Choose one** of the following:

- ✦ If you want to delete the speaker note from this page only, click on Current page.

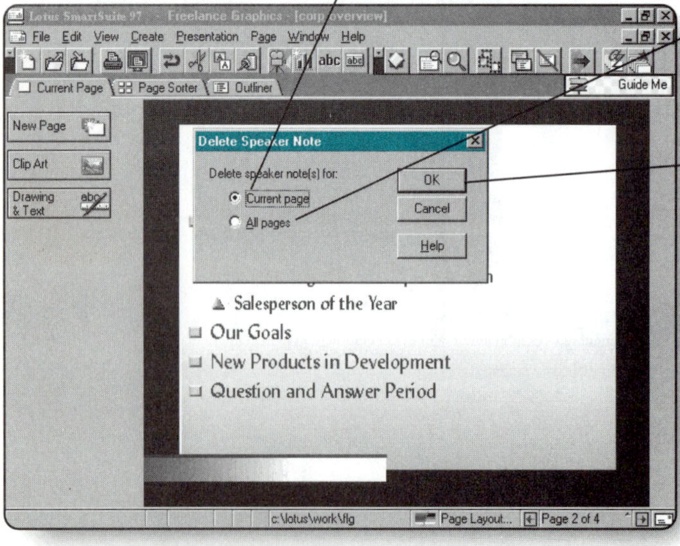

- ✦ If you want to delete all the speaker notes, click on All pages.

4. **Click** on **OK**. A warning message box will appear.

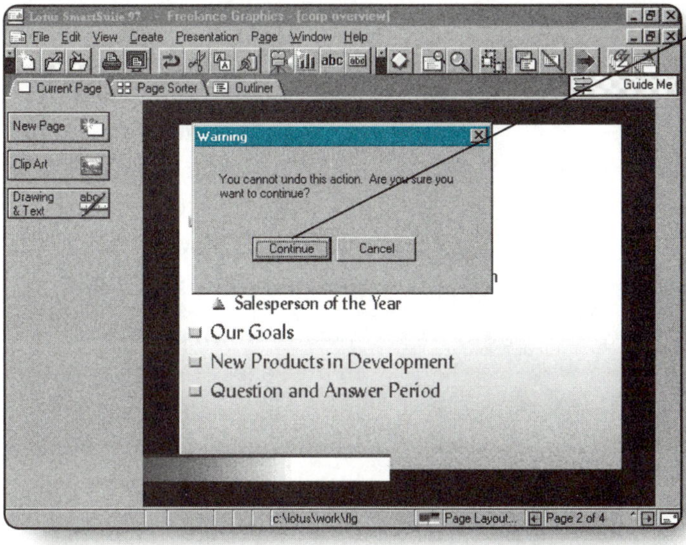

5. Click on **Continue**. The speaker note will be deleted.

PRINTING YOUR SLIDE SHOW

Freelance provides four types of formats for your printed slide show: full page, handouts, speaker notes, and audience notes.

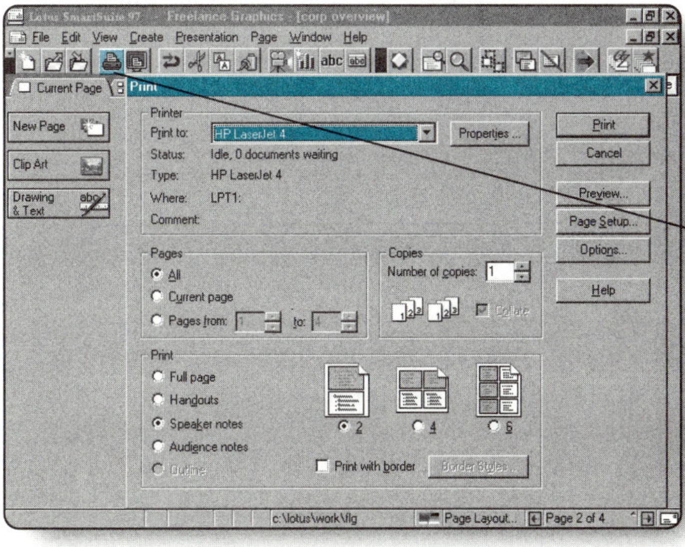

Handouts can be printed one, two, four, or six to a page. Speaker notes and audience notes can be printed one, two, or three to a page.

1. Click on the **Print SmartIcon**. The Print dialog box will open.

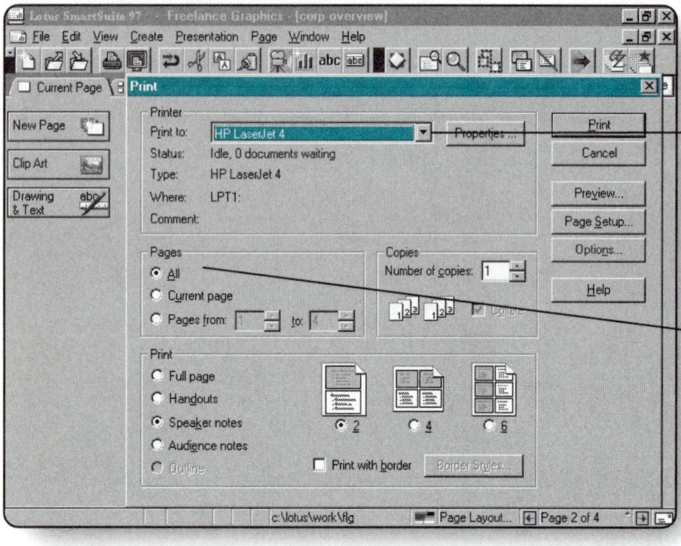

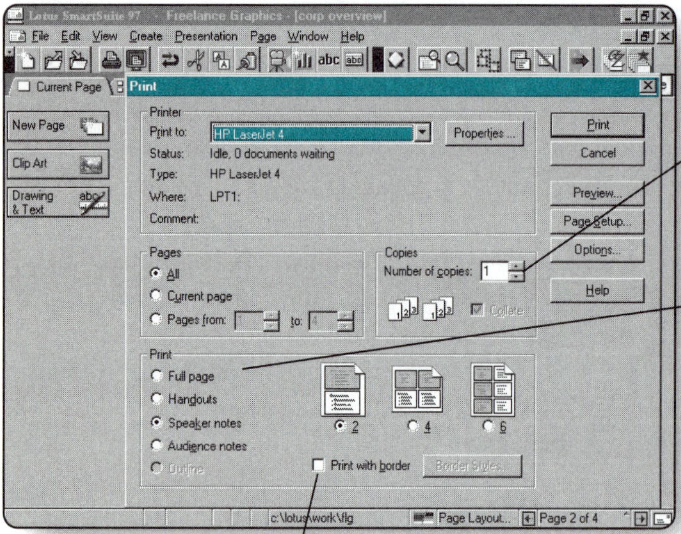

2. Choose from the following **options**:

- ✦ If you are connected to more than one printer, you can choose where to Print to: by clicking the down arrow (▼) and making a selection.
- ✦ Choose which pages to print in the Pages box. You can print All, which is the preselected option; you can print just the Current page; or you can print a specific page by clicking Pages. To print a specific range of pages, click on the up and down arrows (⬍) to select the beginning and ending pages of the range.
- ✦ Choose the Number of copies: to be printed by clicking the up and down arrows (⬍) in the Copies box.
- ✦ In the Print box, you can select what to print. If you want to print one slide per page, select Full page. If you want to print multiple slides per page, select Handouts and then click on 2, 4, or 6. If you want to print out your speaker notes, select Speaker notes and then click on 1, 2, or 3. Another option is to print audience notes. Audience notes have the slide on one part of the page and a ruled area like notebook paper for the audience to take notes. To do this, click on Audience notes and click on 1, 2, or 3.
- ✦ If you want a border, (✔) Print with border.

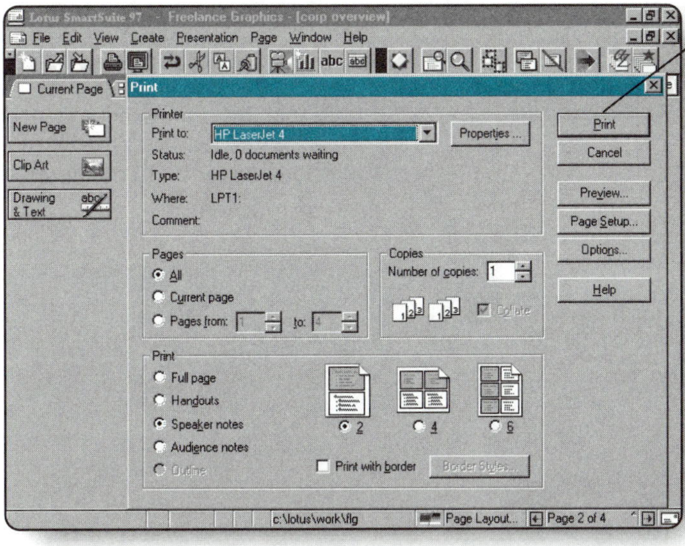

3. Click on **Print**. The pages will be sent to the printer.

SHOWING THE PRESENTATION

Instead of discussing your presentation from printed handouts or overhead slides, you may want to present your slides on a computer monitor or television hooked up to your computer. This gives you more flexibility and impact than a printed media can.

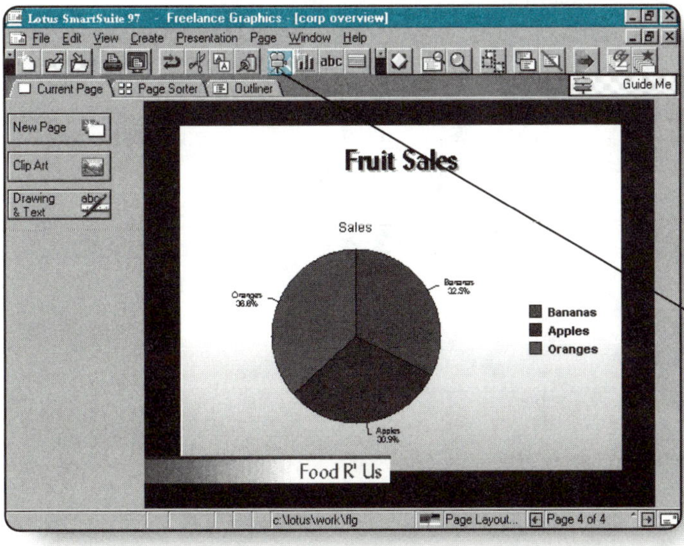

Running the Standard Slide Show

You can run your slide show at any time with just a click of a button.

1. Click on the **Run screen show from beginning SmartIcon**. The slide show will appear.

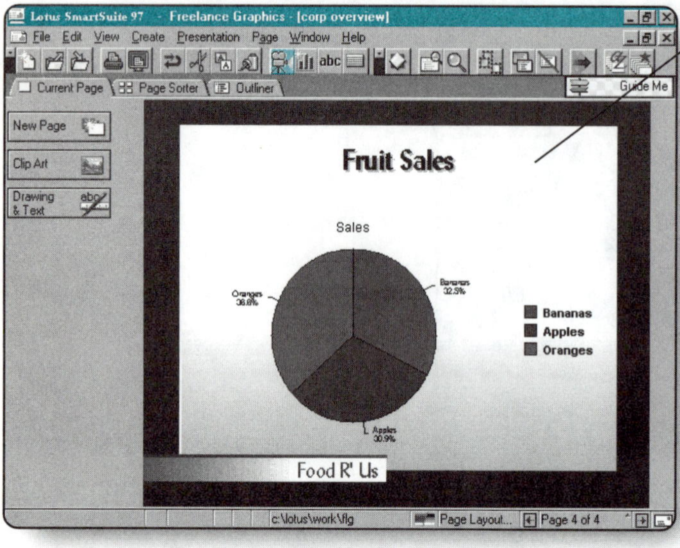

2. **Click** on the **slide**. The next slide in the presentation will appear.

3. **Repeat step 2** until the slide show is complete.

> **TIP**
>
> To exit from a slide show before the last slide, press the Esc key.

Rearranging Slides

If you do not like the current order of the slides in your presentation, change it! This can be done easily using the Page Sorter.

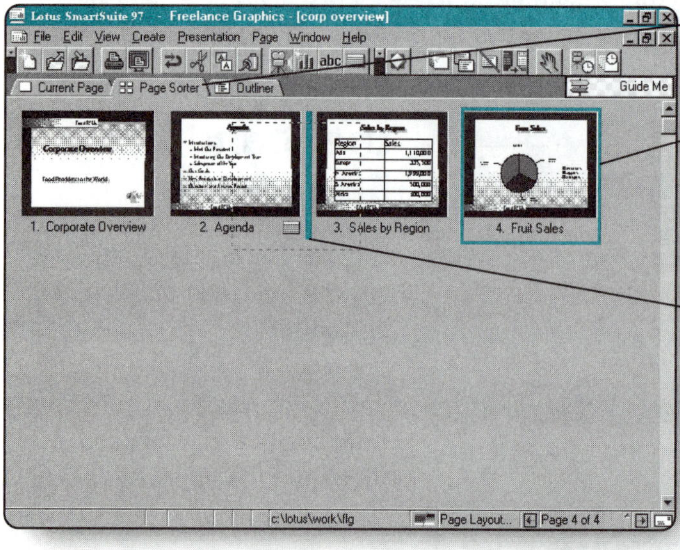

1. **Click** on the **Page Sorter tab**. The Page Sorter tab will appear.

2. **Click** and **drag** the **slide** you want to move. A bar will appear to identify the new location of the slide.

3. **Release** the **mouse button**. The slide will move to its new location.

Setting a Slide's Trigger

When a slide is triggered, it closes so that the next slide can display. A slide can have a manual trigger, which means you have to click your mouse or press a key to move to the next slide. Or you can have an automatic trigger where the slide closes after a certain number of seconds.

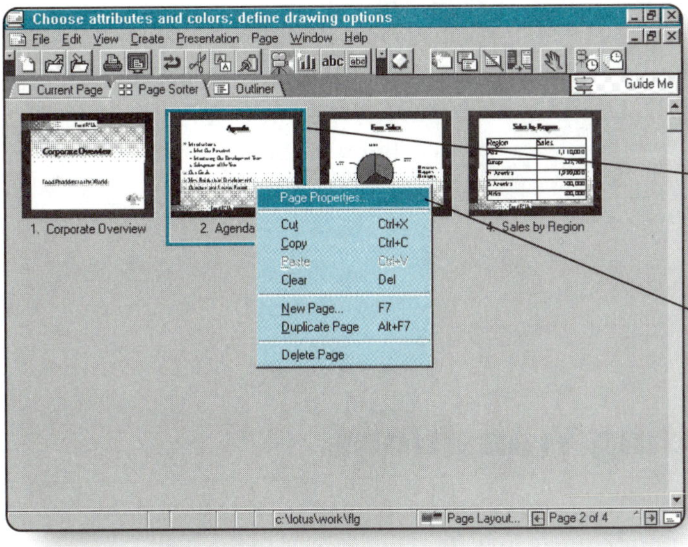

1. **Right-click** the **slide** for which you want to set a trigger. A shortcut menu will appear.

2. **Click** on **Page Properties**. The Properties for Page dialog box will open.

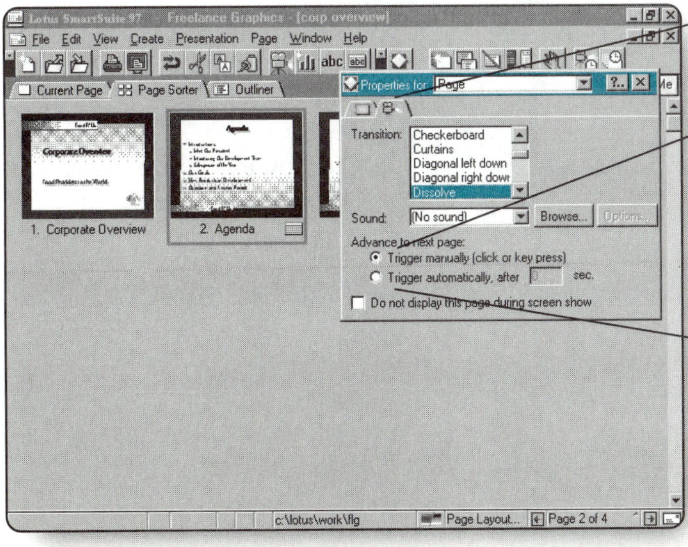

3. **Click** on the **Slide Show tab**. The Slide Show tab will appear.

4a. **Click** on **Trigger manually**. A manual trigger will be set for this slide.

OR

4b. **Click** on **Trigger automatically**. An automatic trigger will be set for this slide.

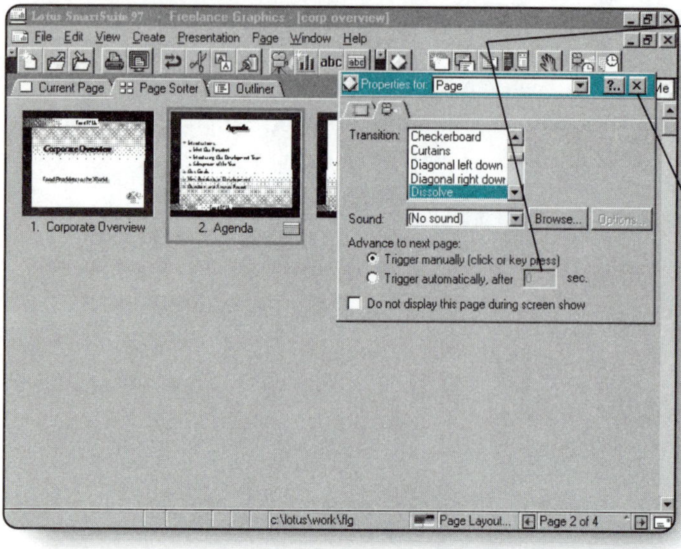

Three seconds has been preset for the amount of time for the automatic trigger. If you don't want the time to be three seconds, **type** a new **value** in the text box.

5. Click on the **Close button**. The Properties for Page dialog box will close.

Adding Transitions

Transitions can add visual excitement to your slide show. Transitions control how one slide moves to the next.

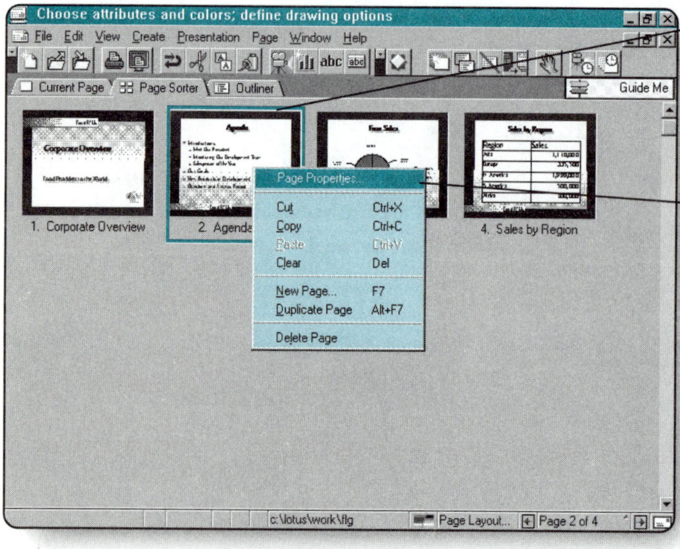

1. Right-click the **slide** for which you want to set a transition. A shortcut menu will appear.

2. Click on **Page Properties**. The Properties for Page dialog box will open.

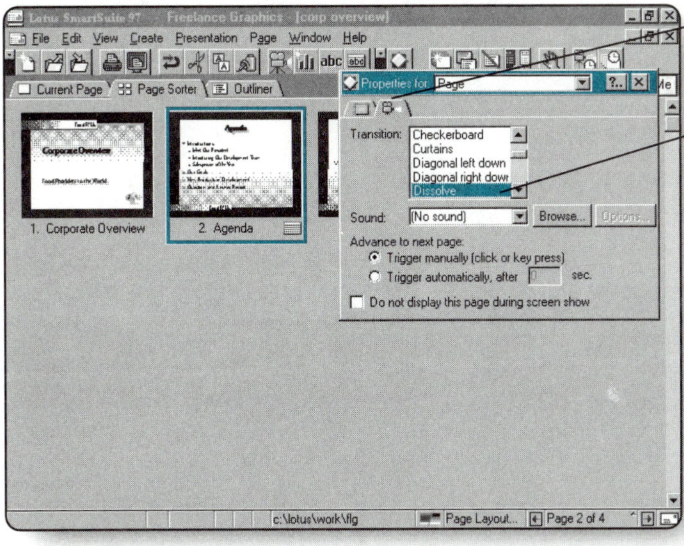

3. **Click** on the **Slide Show tab**. The Slide Show tab will appear.

4. **Click** on a **Transition**: from the list box. The transition will be applied to the selected slide.

5. **Click** on the **Close button**. The Properties for Page dialog box will close.

PART IV REVIEW QUESTIONS

1. **How do you add a page to your presentation?** ***See "Adding Slides" in Chapter 13***
2. **Does the typical presentation have different kinds of pages?** ***See "Adding Slides" in Chapter 13***
3. **What are Click here blocks used for?** ***See "Working with Slides" in Chapter 13***
4. **What happens when you first start Freelance?** ***See "Starting a Presentation" in Chapter 13***
5. **How do you move from one slide to another when you are creating your pages?** ***See "Working with Slides" in Chapter 13***
6. **What does pressing the Esc key do when you are viewing a slide show?** ***See "Showing the Presentation" in Chapter 14***
7. **How do you move from slide to slide in a slide show?** ***See "Showing the Presentation" in Chapter 14***
8. **How would you provide your audience with printed copies of the slides that also provide for a note taking area?** ***See "Printing Handouts and Speaker Notes" in Chapter 14***
9. **What do you use to rearrange the slides in a slide show?** ***See "Rearranging Slides" in Chapter 14***
10. **How do you add visual effects to your slide show?** ***See "Adding Transitions" in Chapter 14***

PART V

Using Organizer

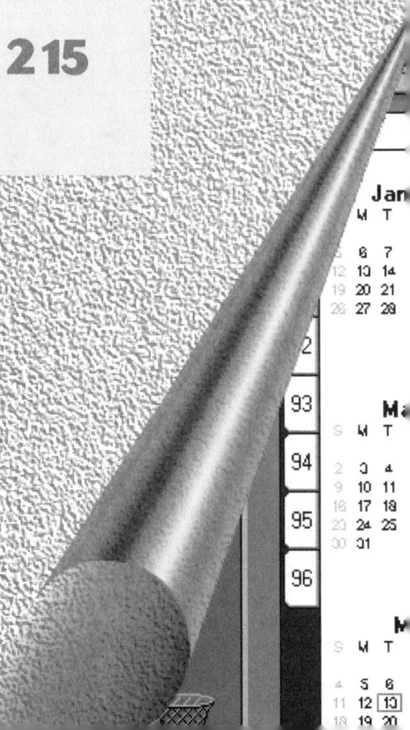

15 Working with your Calendar

Organizer is designed to replace the traditional paper-based appointment book, address book, and to do list. Not only is it the electronic equivalent of these three things, it also is a phone call manager, planner, notepad, and anniversary reminder.

The Calendar portion of Organizer is full-featured, yet remarkably easy to use. You can track appointments and meetings just as you would in its paper-based counterpart. In this chapter, you'll learn how to:

- Add an appointment
- Modify an appointment
- Print your appointments
- Change the Calendar view

ADDING AN APPOINTMENT

As far as Organizer is concerned, an appointment is anything that requires your time during a specific period. Meetings are appointments. Client calls are appointments. Interviews are appointments.

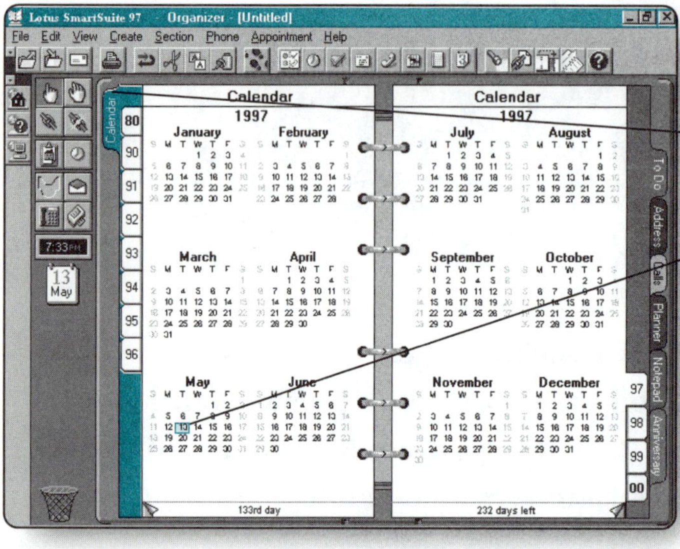

1. **Click** on the **Calendar tab**. A calendar of this year will appear.
2. **Click** on the **date** the appointment takes place. The date will be selected.

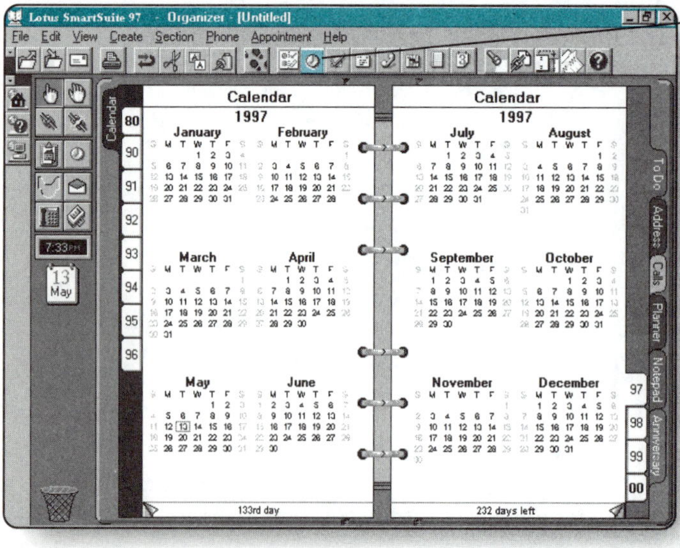

3. **Click** on the **Create an Appointment SmartIcon**. The Create Appointment dialog box will appear.

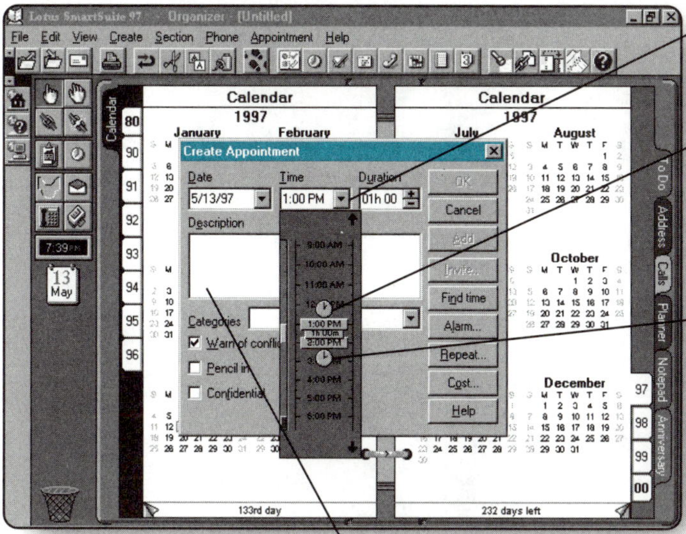

4. Click on the **down arrow** (▼). A timeline will appear.

5. Drag the **top clock** to the starting time of the appointment. This will set the beginning of the appointment.

6. Drag the **bottom clock** to the ending time of the appointment. This will set the ending of the appointment and will calculate the duration.

7. Click on the **Description** text box. The text box will be selected.

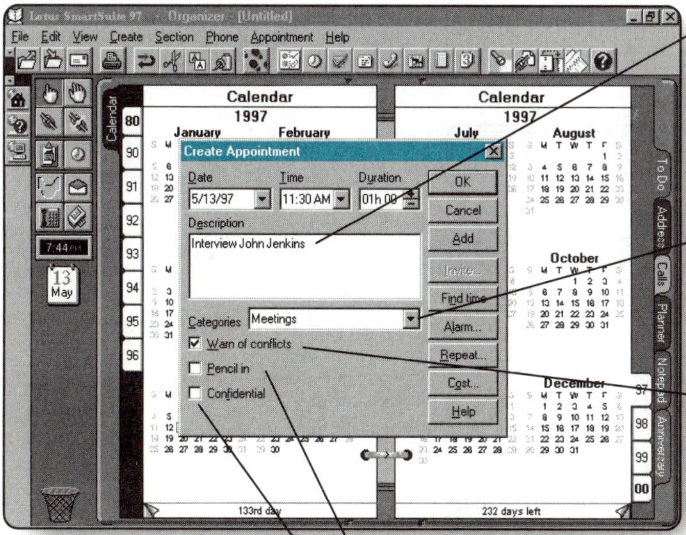

8. Type the **text** for the Description.

9. Choose from the following **options**:

- ✦ If you want to assign a Categories entry to organize your entries, click on the down arrow (▼).
- ✦ Warn of conflicts is preselected for you. If you do not want Organizer to warn you of conflicts, click the check box to remove the ✔.
- ✦ To mark this appointment as tentative, ✔ Pencil in.
- ✦ To make this a confidential appointment, ✔ Confidential.

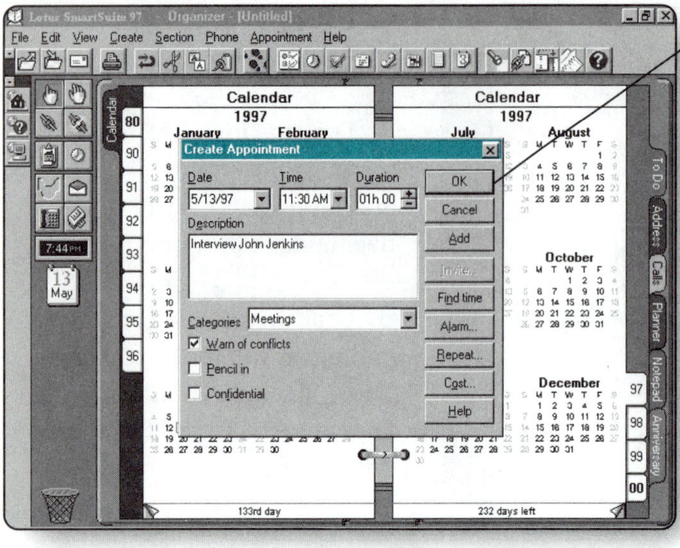

10. Click on **OK**. The appointment will be added.

CHANGING THE VIEW

When you click on the Calendar tab, a calendar of the current year appears. The Calendar can be viewed by the day, by the work week, by a calendar week, or by the month.

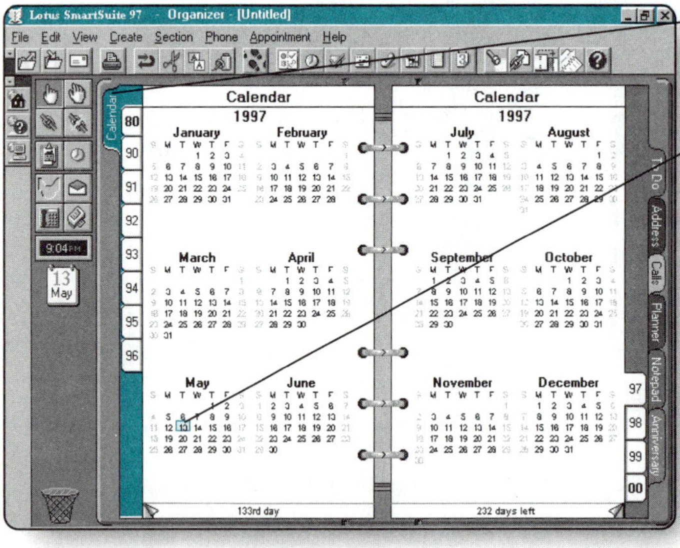

1. **Click** on the **Calendar tab**. The Calendar page will appear.

2. **Double-click** on the **date** you want to view. The date's appointment will appear.

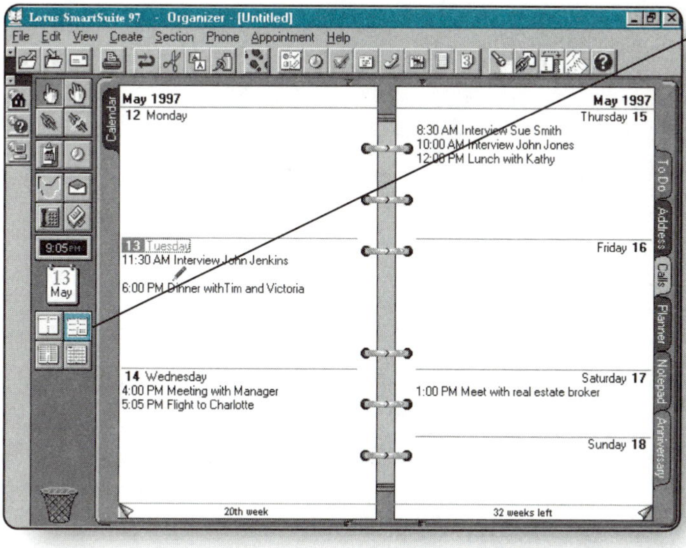

3. Click on a **View icon**. The view will change to reflect the selected icon.

MODIFYING AN APPOINTMENT

Appointments change. This is one of the truths of life. Often a meeting or interview is rescheduled. Or you may need to change the description of an appointment.

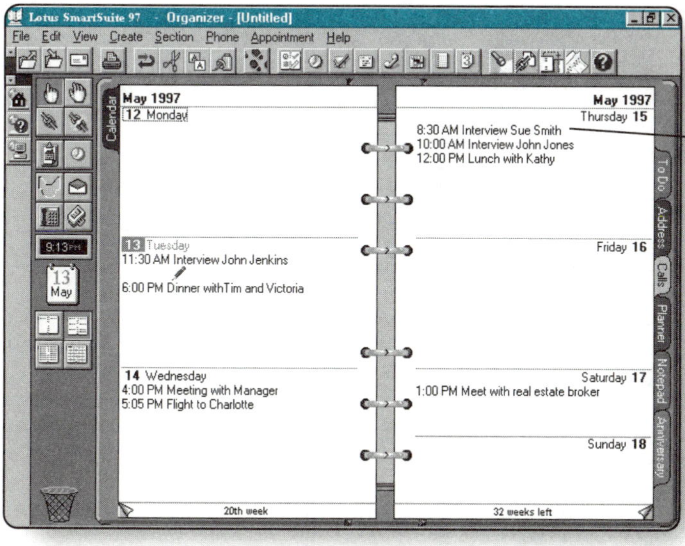

Editing an Appointment

1. Double-click the **appointment** you want to edit. The Edit Appointment dialog box will open.

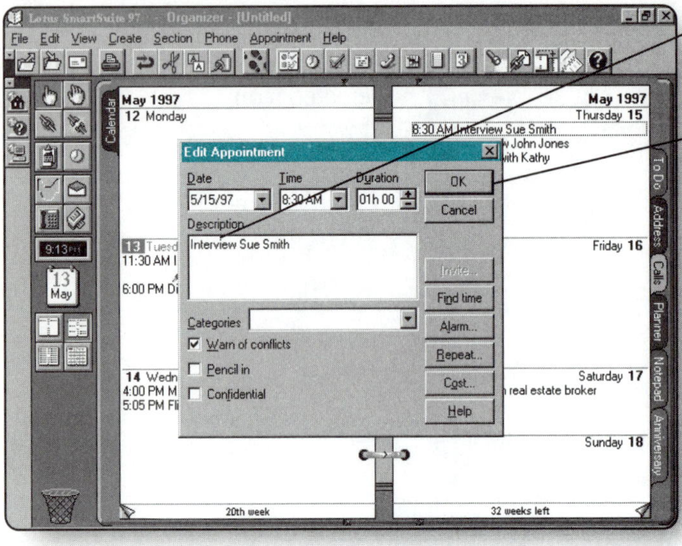

2. **Make** the necessary **changes** to the appointment.

3. **Click** on **OK**. The appointment will be updated.

Moving an Appointment

Instead of editing an appointment to reschedule it, you can drag it to a new time slot.

1. **Position** the **pointer** over the time portion of the appointment. The pointer will change to a pointing finger.

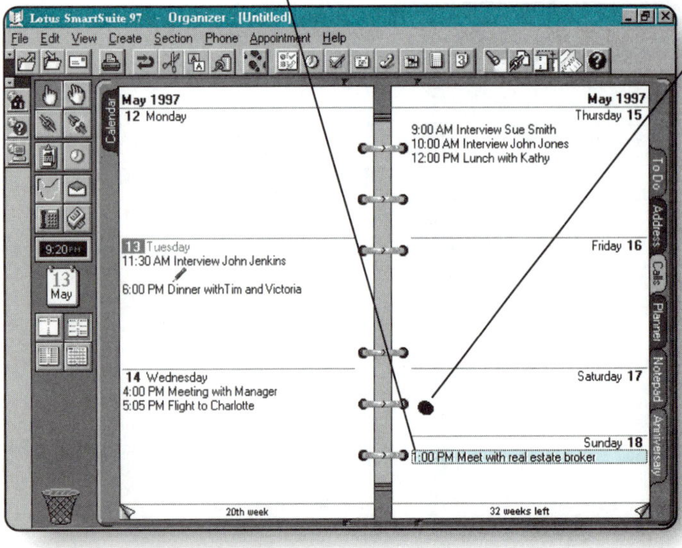

2. **Click** and **drag** the **appointment** to its new time period. The pointer will change to a clock.

Adding an Alarm to an Appointment

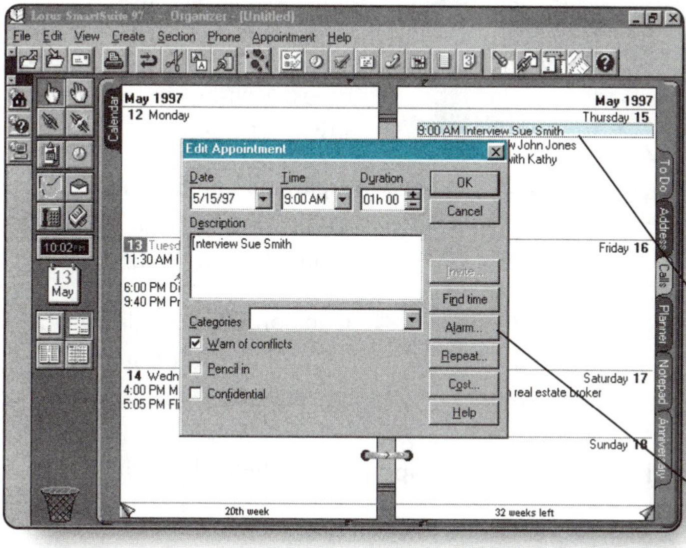

If you want Organizer to remind you of an appointment, you can set an alarm. At the assigned time before the appointment, an alarm will sound, and a dialog box will appear.

Setting the Alarm

1. Double-click the **appointment** you want to edit. The Edit Appointment dialog box will open.

2. Click on **Alarm.** The Alarm dialog box will appear.

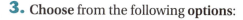

3. Choose from the following **options**:

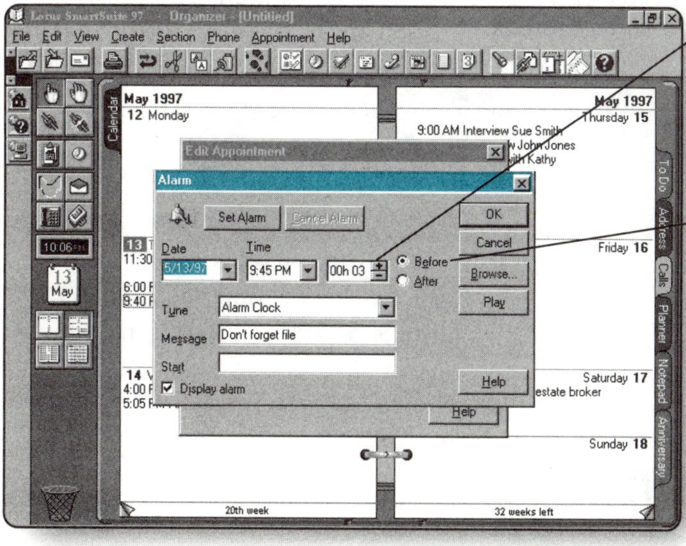

- Click on the plus and minus buttons to set the amount of time before or after the appointment you want the alarm to go off.
- To select whether the alarm occurs Before or After the start of the appointment, click on the appropriate option button.

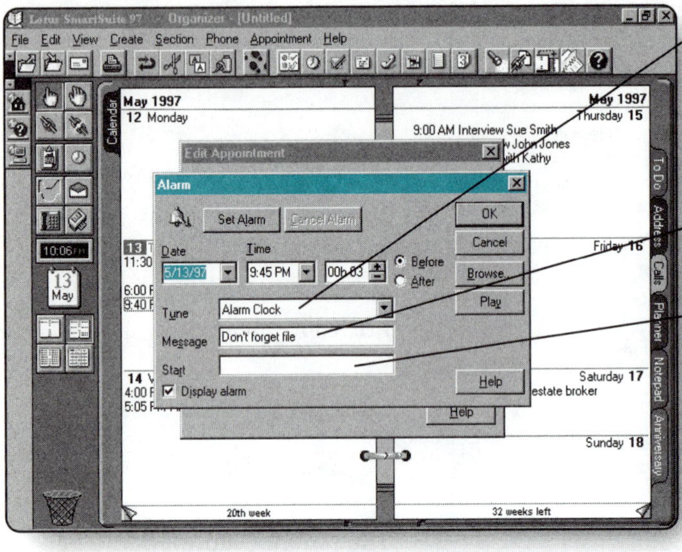

- ✦ The preselected Tune that plays is Alarm Clock. To select a different tune, click on the down arrow (▼) and select from the list.
- ✦ Type a Message in the text box.
- ✦ Organizer can Start an application for you. Type the application in the text box.

4. **Click** on **OK**. The alarm will be set, and the Edit Appointment dialog box will reappear.

5. **Click** on **OK**. The Edit Appointment dialog box will close.

Responding to an Alarm

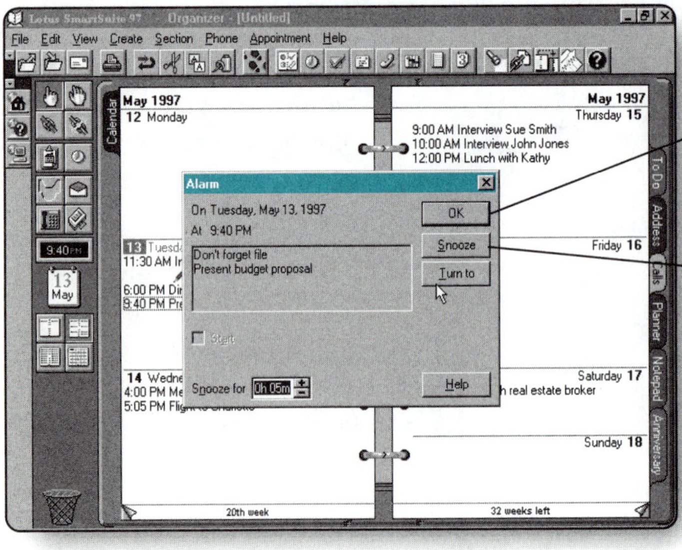

When the alarm you set goes off, a dialog box appears.

1a. **Click** on **OK**. The alarm will be dismissed.

OR

1b. **Click** on **Snooze**. The alarm will repeat again after the amount of time specified in the Snooze for box has elapsed.

Creating a Repeating Appointment

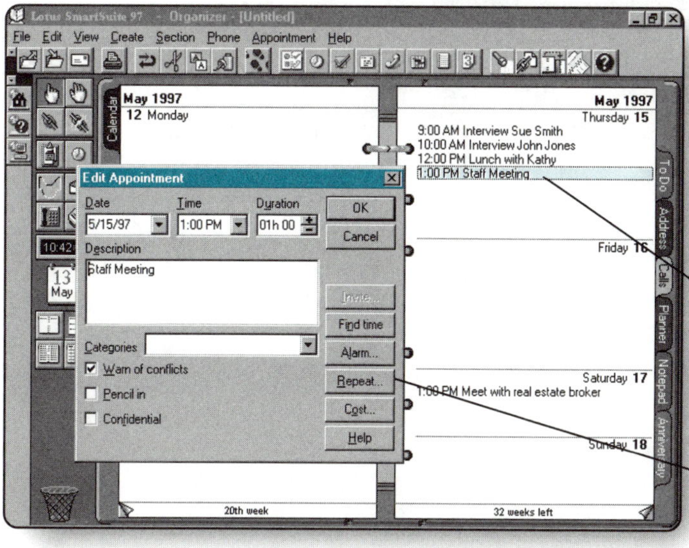

A repeating appointment is one that you tell Organizer to schedule at the same time every day, week, month, and so on. This saves you the effort of having to enter the appointment repeatedly.

1. **Double-click** the **appointment** you want to edit. The Edit Appointment dialog box will open.

2. **Click** on **Repeat**. The Repeat dialog box will open.

3. **Choose** from the following **options**:

- Click on the down arrow (▼) beside the first list box in the Repeats group. Select the time period for the repeat from the list.

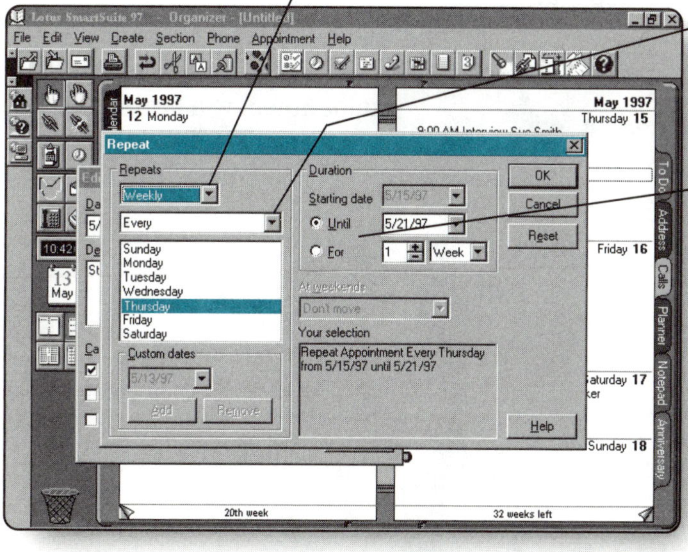

- Click on the down arrow (▼) beside the second list box in the Repeats group. Select a frequency from the list.
- To set the Duration of the repeating appointment, click either Until or For. If you selected Until, click on the down arrow (▼) beside the list box and select the ending date for the repeat. If you selected For, click on the plus and minus buttons to set the numeric frequency and click on the down arrow (⬍) to select the period.

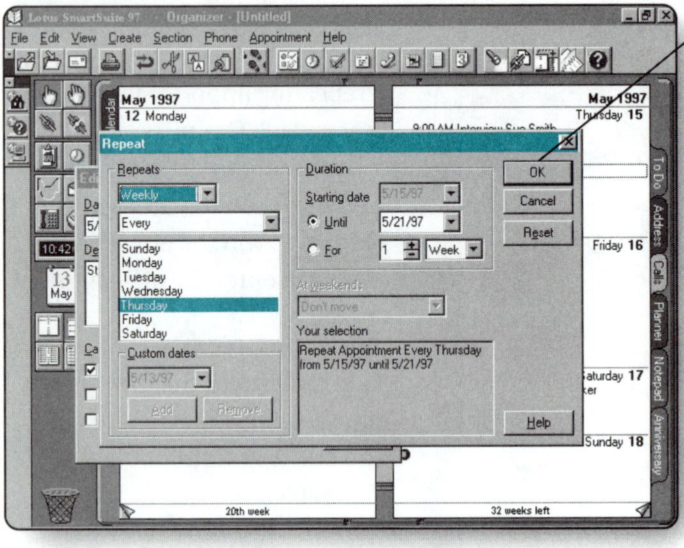

4. **Click** on **OK**. The appointment will be updated, and the Edit Appointment dialog box will reappear.

5. **Click** on **OK**. The Edit Appointment dialog box will close.

Deleting an Appointment

If an appointment is canceled, delete it.

1. **Right-click** the **appointment** to be deleted. A shortcut menu will appear.

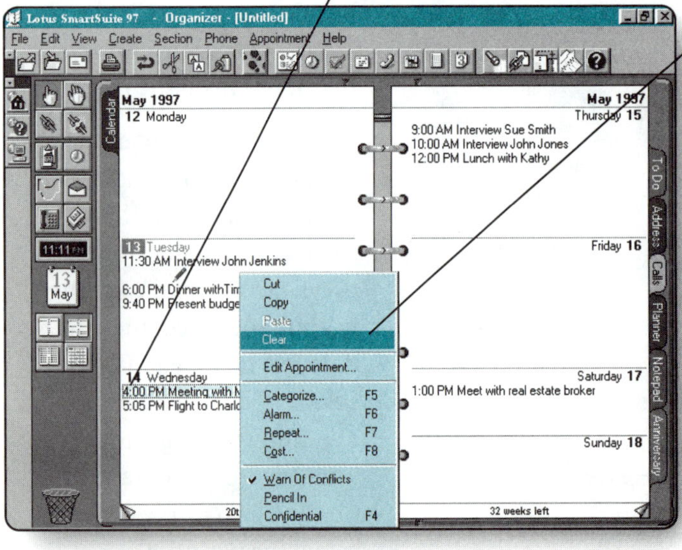

2. **Click** on **Clear**. The appointment will be deleted.

PRINTING CALENDAR INFORMATION

Organizer gives you a choice of 14 different layouts for use when printing your calendar.

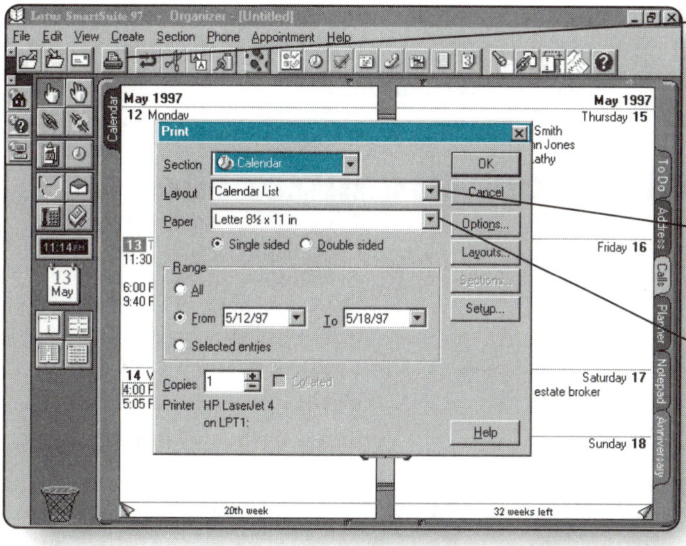

1. Click on the **Print SmartIcon**. The Print dialog box will open.

2. Choose from the following **options**:

- ✦ To choose a different Layout, click on the down arrow (▼) and make your selection.
- ✦ If you want to print to a paper size other than the stand letter size, click the down arrow(▼) of the list box next to Paper and click on the paper size you want.

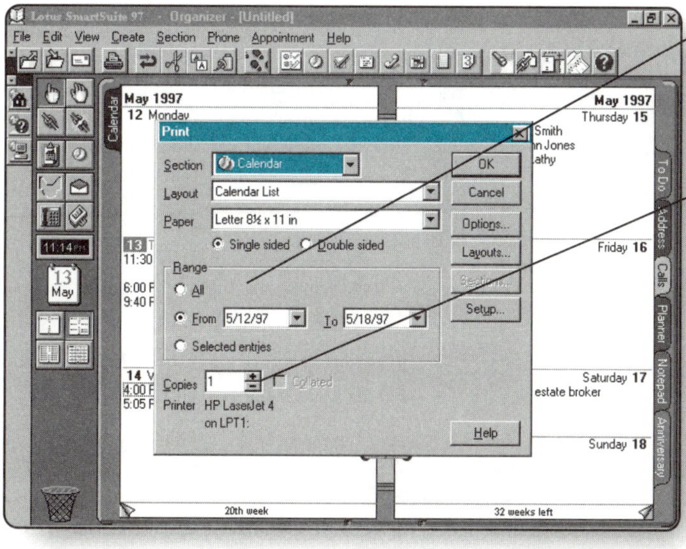

- ✦ The preselected range is the current week. You can also print All your appointments or just the Selected entries.
- ✦ To print more than one copy, click on the plus and minus buttons.

3. Click on **OK**. The appointments will be sent to the printer to print.

WORKING WITH YOUR ORGANIZER FILE

The file extension used by Organizer is .OR3. If you want, you can maintain multiple Organizer files on your system. This is a nice feature when more than one person is using your system. If you are the only or primary user of Organizer, you may want to set up Organizer to automatically open your Organizer file for you when you start Organizer.

Saving Your Organizer File

1. **Click** on the **Save the Current File SmartIcon**. The Save As dialog box will open.

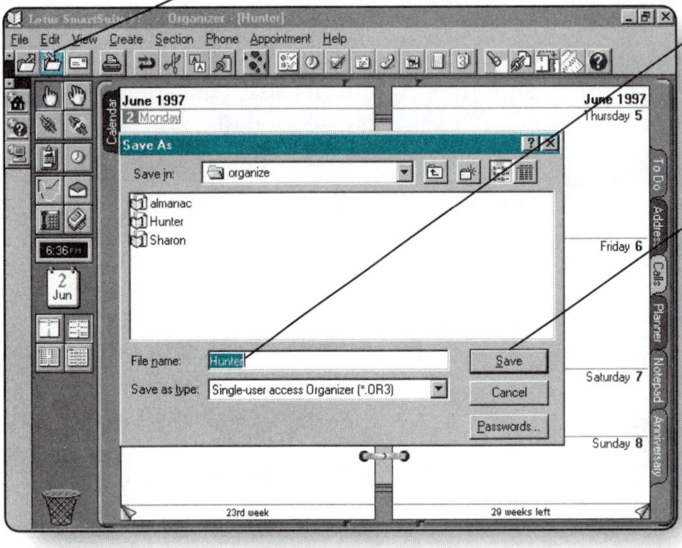

2. **Type** a **name** for the file in the File Name: text box. The entered name will appear in the text box.

3. **Click** on **Save**. The file will be saved.

Letting Organizer Automatically Save Your File

If you have made changes to your file and you exit Organizer, you will be prompted to save your file. You can set up Organizer to save your file automatically, either after every change or at a certain time interval.

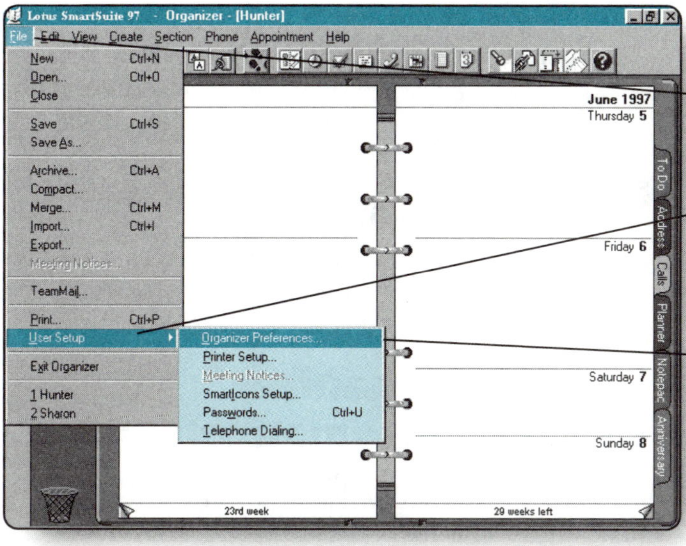

1. **Click** on **File**. The File menu will appear.

2. **Click** on **User Setup**. The User Setup submenu will appear.

3. **Click** on **Organizer Preferences**. The Organizer Preferences dialog box will open.

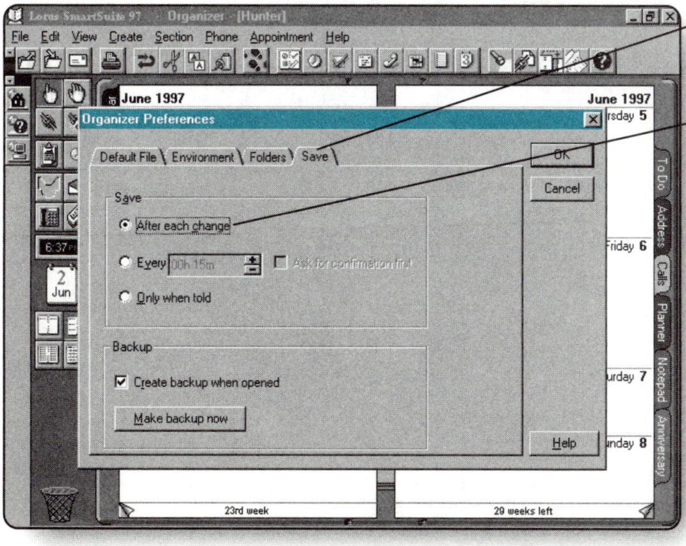

4. **Click** on the **Save tab**. The Save tab will appear.

5a. **Click** on the **After each change option button**. The option will be selected.

If you select this option, Organizer saves your Organizer file after each change you make. This helps ensure that little or none of your data will be lost in the event of equipment failure or power loss.

OR

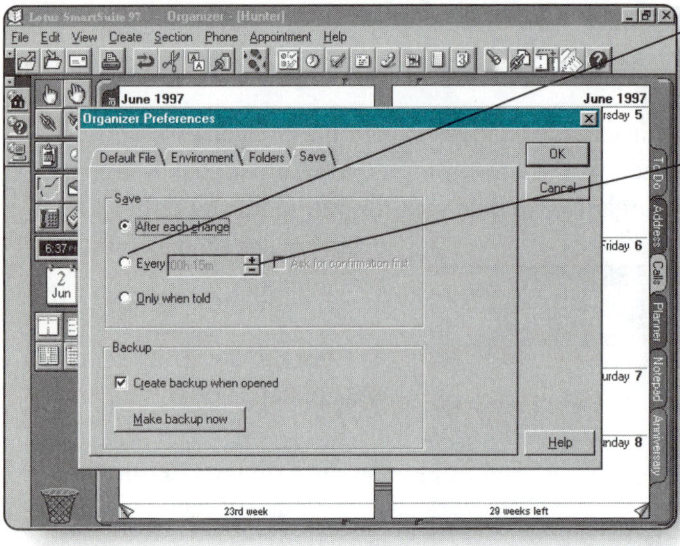

5b. **Click** on the **Every option button**. The option will be selected.

If you don't want to save after every change, select this option. Organizer will save your work every 15 minutes. If you want to save more or less often than every 15 minutes, use the + and – button to select a new time interval.

6. **Click** on **OK**. The preference will be saved.

Setting Your Organizer File to Open Automatically

Using the Organizer Preferences dialog box, you want your Organizer file to open each time you start Organizer.

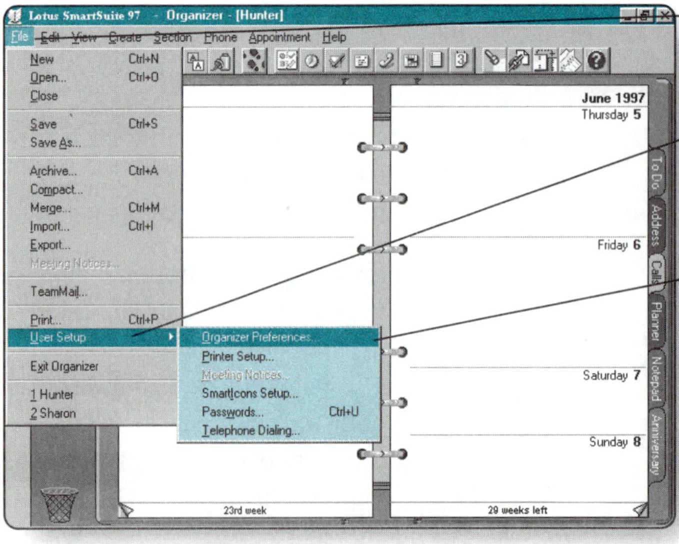

1. **Click** on **File**. The File menu will appear.

2. **Click** on **User Setup**. The User Setup submenu will appear.

3. **Click** on **Organizer Preferences**. The Organizer Preferences dialog box will open.

4. **Click** on the **Default File tab**. The Default File tab will appear.

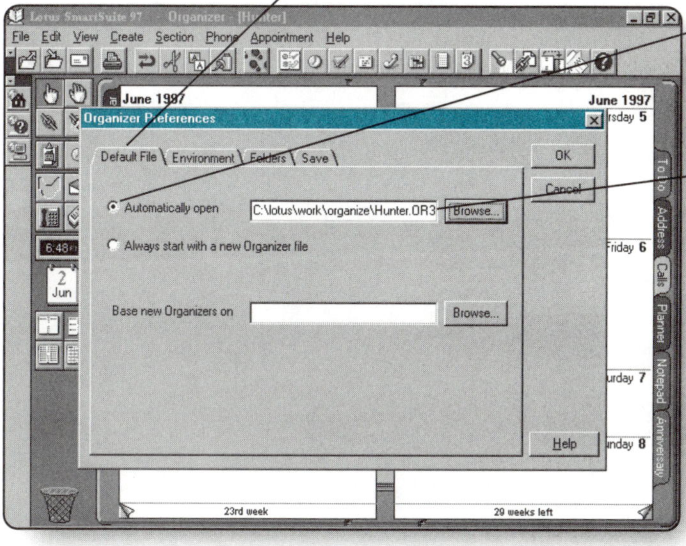

5. **Click** on the **Automatically open option button**. The option will be selected.

6. **Type** the **full path and name** of your Organizer file in the **text box** to the right of the option button. The path and name of the file will be entered.

7. **Click** on **OK**. The preference will be saved.

16 Using the To Do List

The To Do section helps you keep track of what you want to do and when you must do it. It also allows you to assign priorities and track when a to do task is completed. In this chapter, you'll learn how to:

- ✦ Enter to do tasks
- ✦ Sort your to do tasks
- ✦ Display your to do tasks on your Calendar
- ✦ Print your to do tasks

ENTERING TO DO TASKS

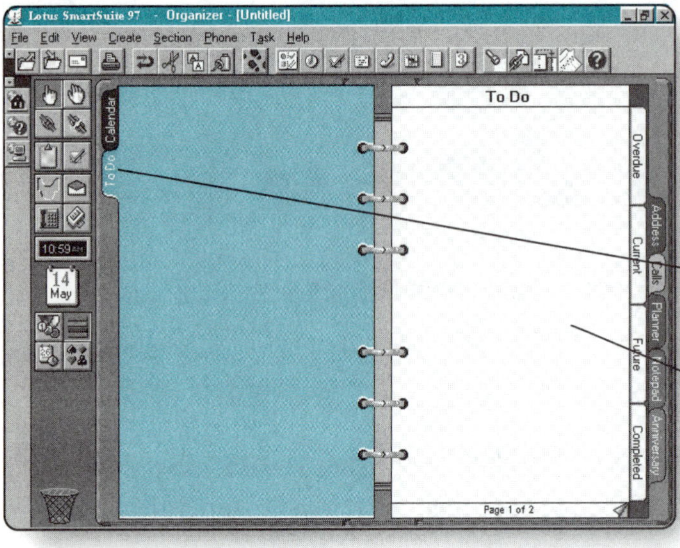

When you create an item in your to do list, you are creating a task. Each task can have a start and ending date associated with it as well as a priority and a category assigned to it.

1. Click on the **To Do tab**. The To Do tab will appear.

2. Double-click on the **To Do page**. The Create Task dialog box will open.

3. Type the **description** of the task in the Description text box.

4. Choose from the following **options**:

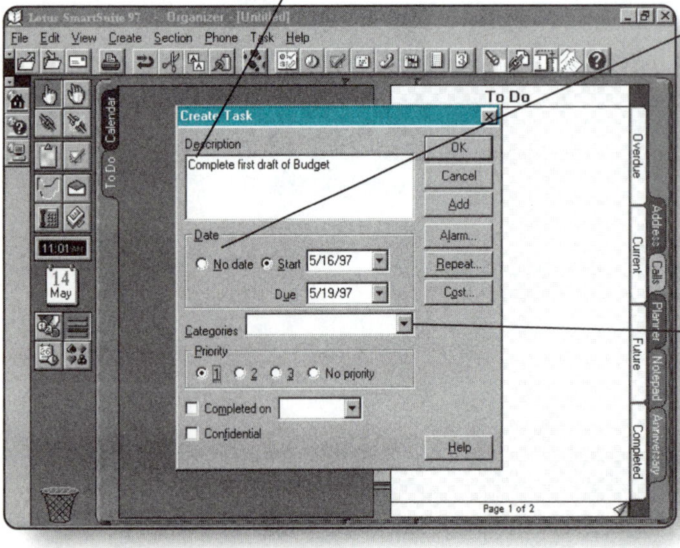

- ✦ You can choose to assign a date to the task. Click on No date if you do not want to assign a date. Click on Start if you do want to use dates with this task. You can select a starting and due date by clicking the down arrows (▼).
- ✦ If you want to be able to group your tasks by categories, click on the down arrow (▼) and select one.

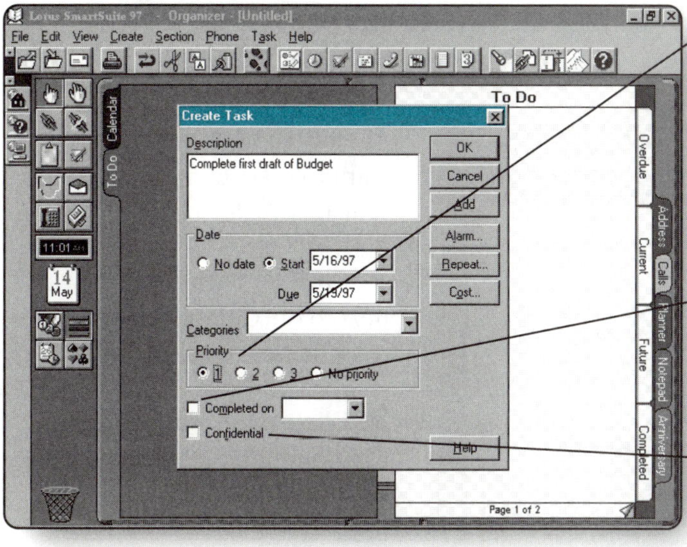

- Tasks do not have a priority assigned to them by default. The highest priority is 1; the lowest is 3. From the Priority group, click on the priority setting you want to use with this task.
- If you want mark a task as completed, ✔ Completed on and select a date by clicking the down arrow (▼).
- If this is a confidential task, ✔ Confidential.

5. **Click** on **OK**. The task will be added to the To Do list.

CHANGING THE STATUS TO COMPLETED

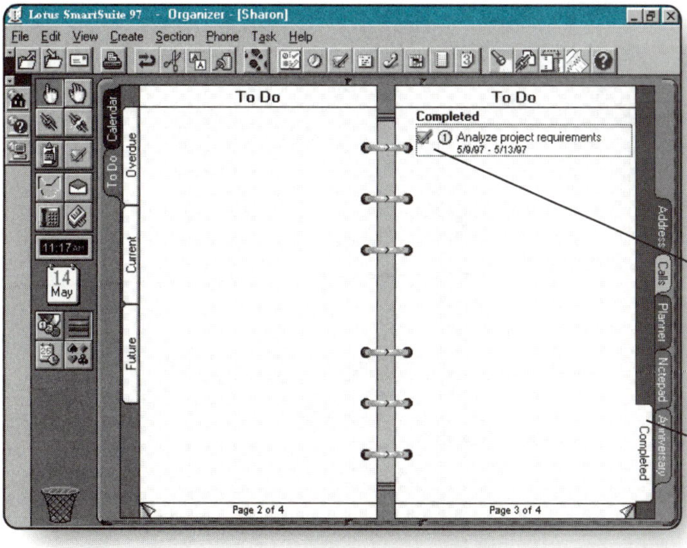

After you are finished with a task, you'll want to mark it as completed.

Marking a Task as Completed Today

1. **Click** in the **box** next to the task. A ✔ will be placed in it, and the task will be marked as completed as of today.

Completed tasks can be viewed on the Completed tab of the To Do list.

Marking a Task as Completed for a Day Other Than Today

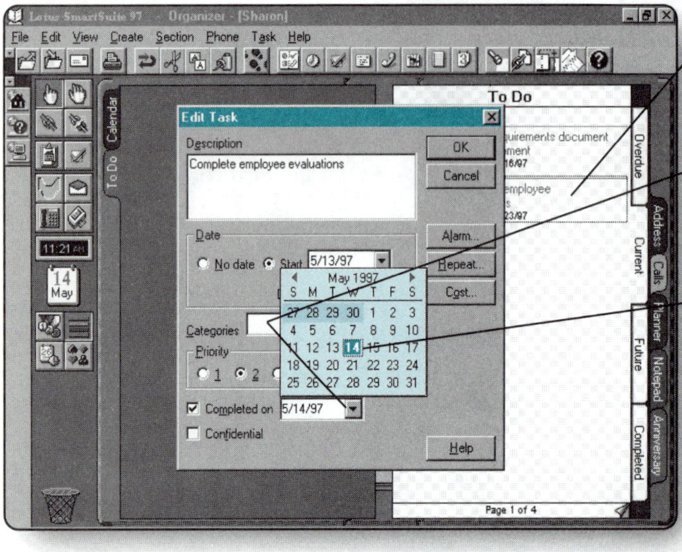

1. Double-click on the **task** you want to mark completed. The Edit Task dialog box will open.

2. Click on the **down arrow** (▼) next to the Completed on box. A calendar will appear.

3. Click on the **date** the task was completed. The date will be entered in the Completed on box.

4. Click on **OK**. The task will be updated.

SORTING TO DO TASKS AND WORKING WITH CATEGORIES

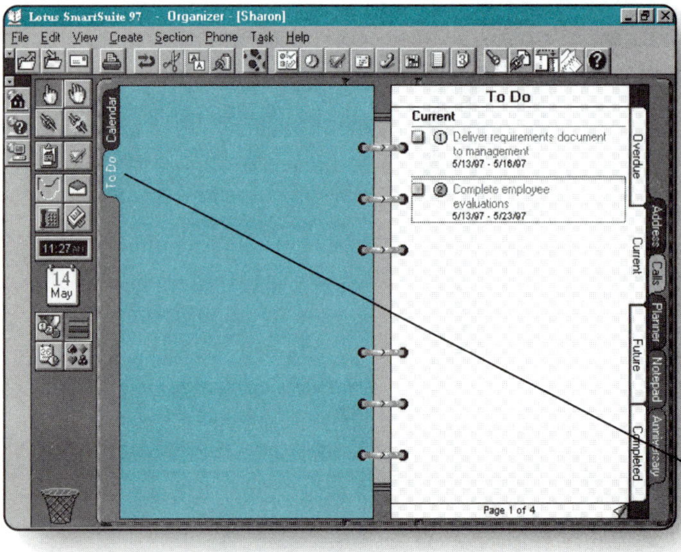

Organizer lets you sort your tasks by either priority, status, start date, or category. You do not have to use just the categories provided with Organizer. You can create your own if you want.

Sorting To Do Tasks Using the View Icons

1. Click on the **To Do tab**. The To Do tab will appear.

2. Choose one of the following **options**:

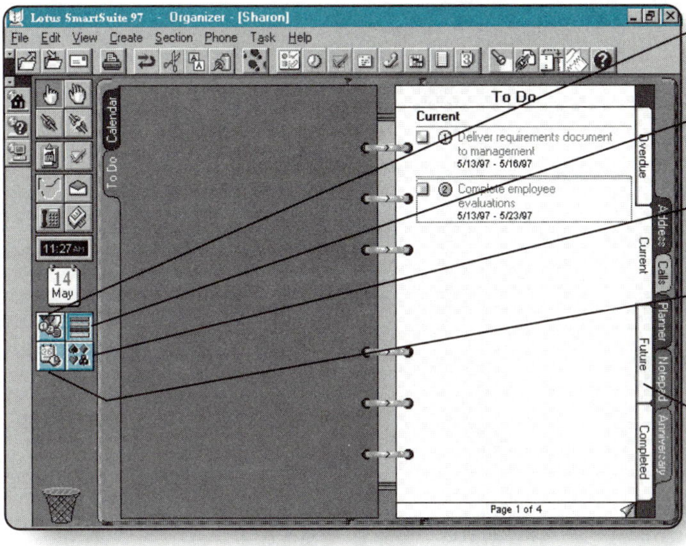

- ✦ To sort tasks by priority, click on the View by Priority icon.
- ✦ To sort tasks by status, click on the View by Status icon.
- ✦ To sort tasks by category, click on the View by Category icon.
- ✦ To sort tasks by start date, click on the View by Start Date icon.

Depending on the view you are using, different tabs will display on the vertical side of the page.

Adding a New Category

You can use categories to organize the different objects in Organizer such as tasks. If you are working on a project, for example, you may want to create a category for that project and assign the category to any appointments or tasks that you associated with that project.

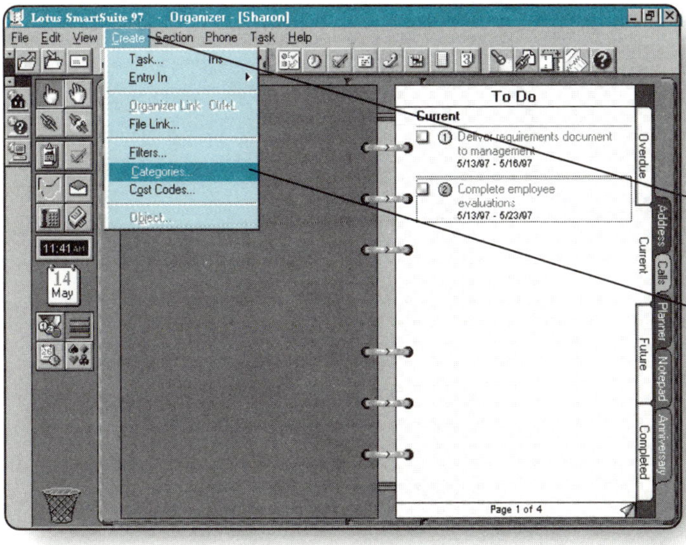

1. Click on **Create**. The Create menu will appear.

2. Click on **Categories**. The Categories dialog box will open.

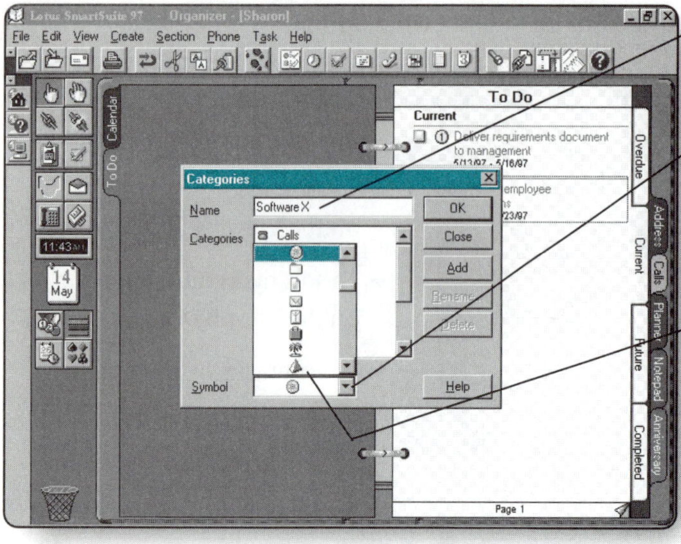

3. **Type** the **text** for the Name of the category in the text box.

4. **Click** on the **down arrow** (▼) to select a symbol for the new category. A list of symbols will appear.

5. **Click** on the **symbol** you want.

6. **Click** on **OK**. The new category will be added.

DISPLAYING TO DO TASKS IN YOUR CALENDAR

Because of the nature of tasks, you may want to display them in other parts of Organizer. For example, you may want to show your tasks in your Calendar.

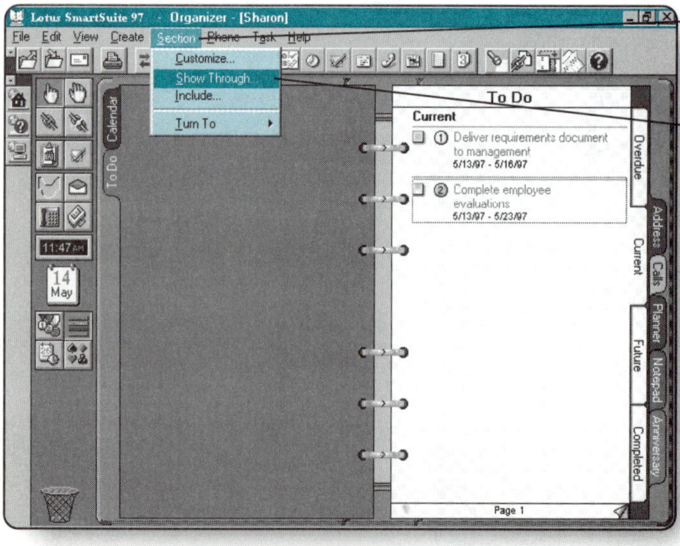

1. **Click** on **Section**. The Section menu will appear.

2. **Click** on **Show Through**. The Show Through dialog box will open.

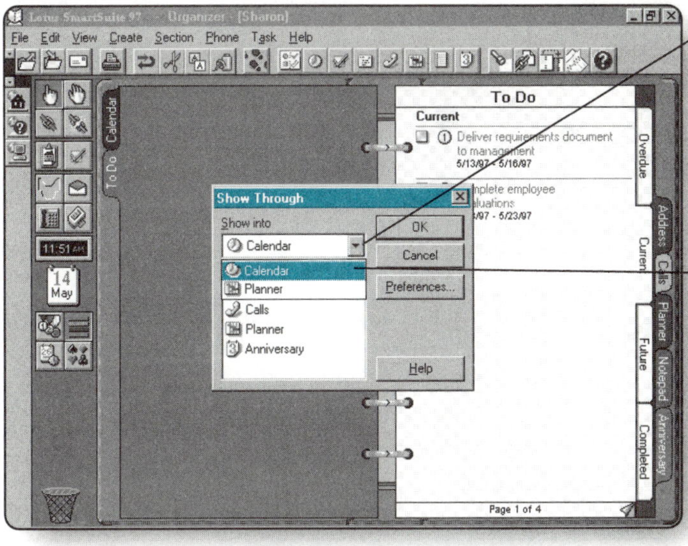

3. **Click** on the **down arrow** (▼) of the Show into box. The list of available sections will appear. There are two areas that you can show into, Calendar and Planner.

4. **Click** on a **section**. The section will be selected.

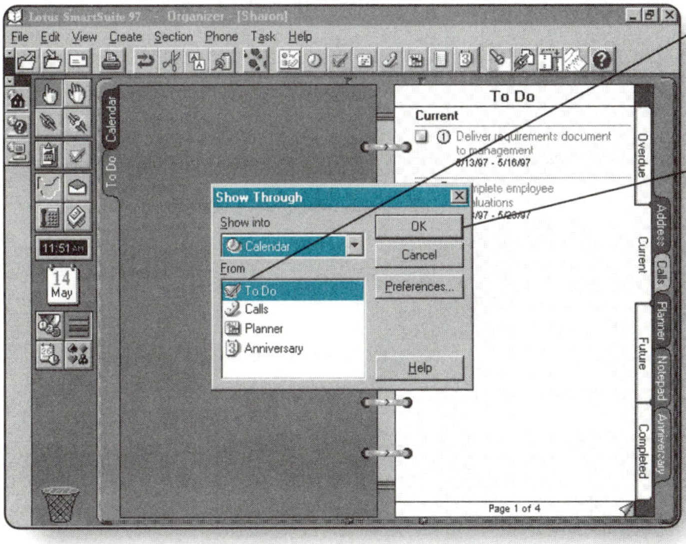

5. **Click** on a **section** in the From list box. The section will be selected.

6. **Click** on **OK**. The show through setting will be applied.

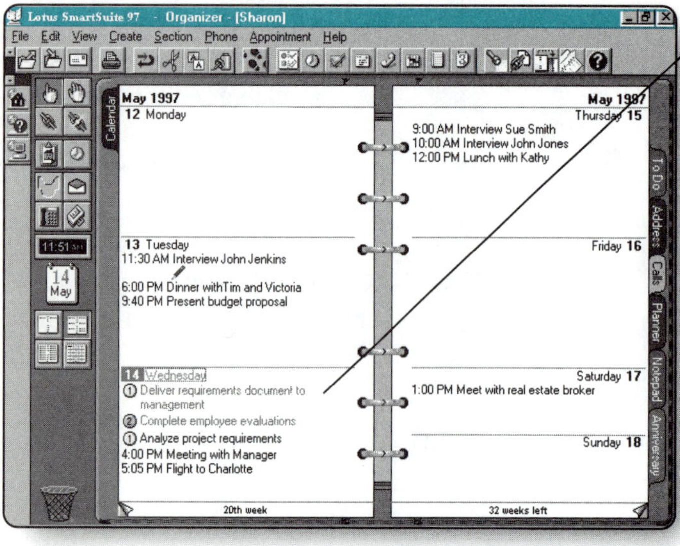

The items will be listed in the section you selected. They integrate with the other items in that section so that you can see them all at the same time.

PRINTING TO DO LIST ITEMS

Organizer provides nine different page layouts for printing your To Do lists.

1. **Click** on the **Print SmartIcon**. The Print dialog box will open.

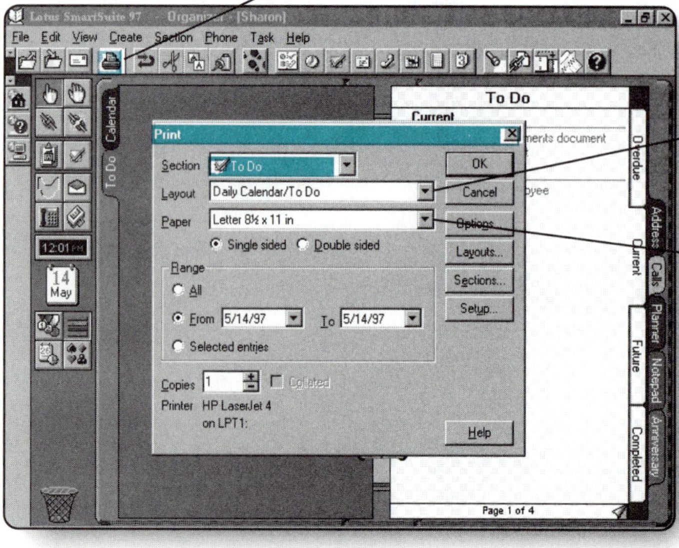

2. **Choose** from the following **options**:

- To choose a different Layout, click on the down arrow (▼) and make your selection.
- If you want to print to a paper size other than the stand letter size, click the down arrow (▼) of the list box next to Paper and click on the paper size you want.

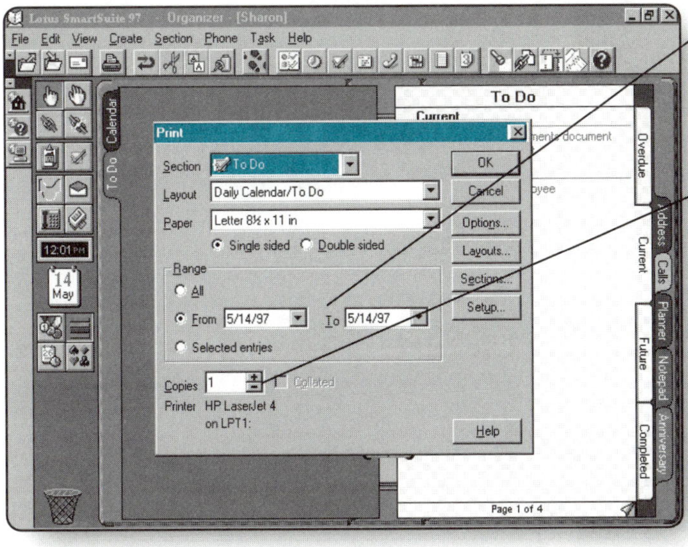

- The preselected range is the current day. You can also print All your appointments or just the Selected entries.
- To print more than one copy, click on the plus and minus buttons.

3. Click on **OK**. The pages will be sent to the printer.

17 Tracking Addresses and Phone Calls

Two of the many advantages of Organizer are its integrated address book and call tracking features. Gone are the days when you had a separate address book and call log. Organizer's Address section lets you track a large variety of information about people, including both business and home information. The Calls section lets you create Calls entries that you can track of your phone calls. In this chapter, you'll learn how to:

- Work with addresses
- Use Organizer's follow-up feature

WORKING WITH ADDRESSES

Organizer's Address section is much more sophisticated than a traditional paper-based address book. Beyond just using it as a repository for information, you can use it to sort and view your Address records by last name, company, category, or ZIP code.

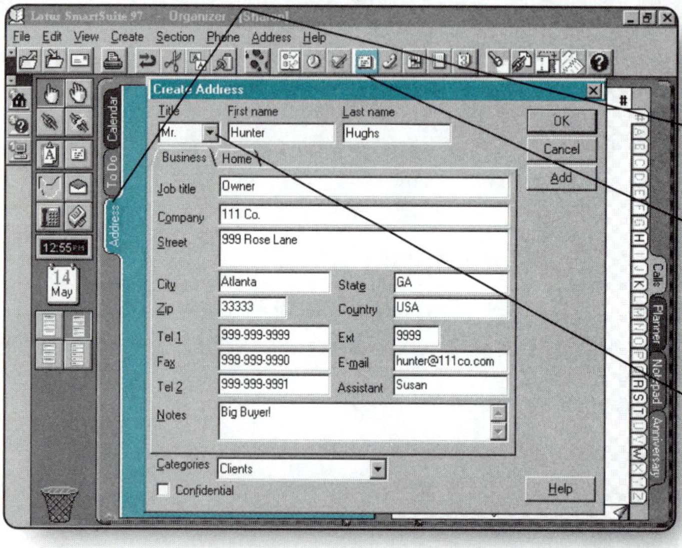

Adding an Address

1. **Click** on the **Address tab**. The Address section will appear.
2. **Click** on the **Create a New Address record SmartIcon**. The Create Address dialog box will appear.
3. **Click** on the **down arrow** (▼) to select a Title. The selected title will be listed in the Title box.
4. **Press** the **Tab key**. The First name text box will be selected.
5. **Type** the **text** for the first name for the entry. The first name will appear in the First name box.
6. **Press** the **Tab key**. The Last name text box will be selected.
7. **Type** the **text** for the last name for the entry. The last name will appear in the Last name box.

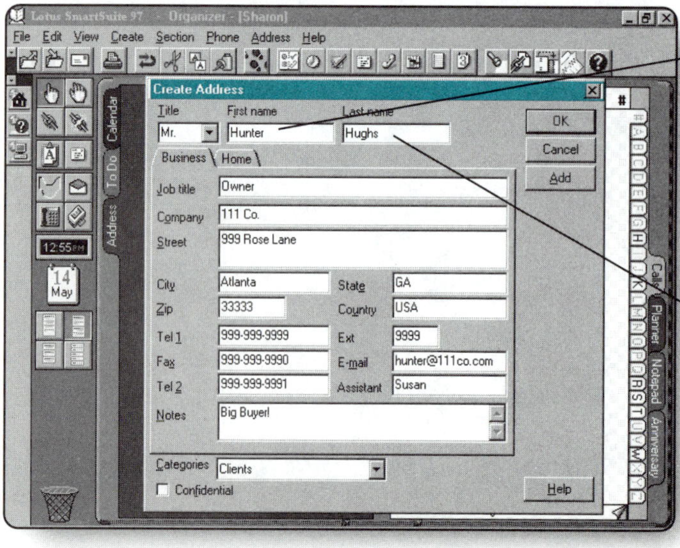

8. Click on the **tab** for the type of Address information you are entering. The selected tab will appear.

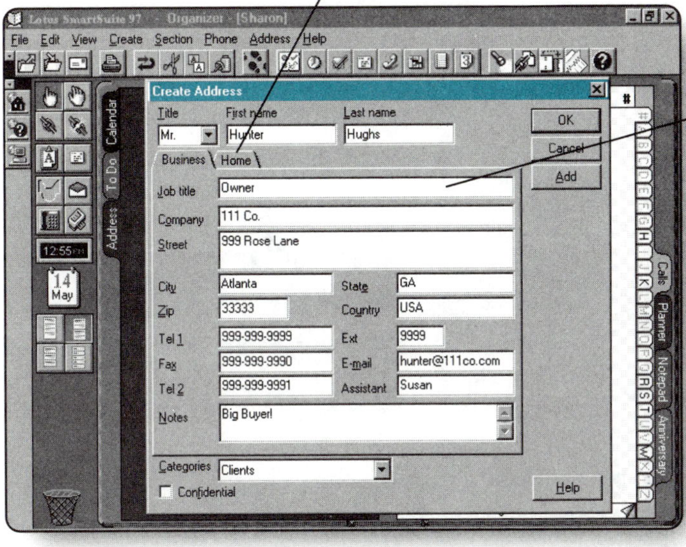

You can either select Business or Home.

9. Click on the **first text box** on the Business or Home tab.

10. Type the **text** for that box. The text will appear in the dialog box.

11. Press the **Tab key**. The next item will be selected.

12. Repeat steps 10 and 11 until you have entered data you want for this entry.

13. Click on **OK**. The Address record will be added.

Modifying an Address

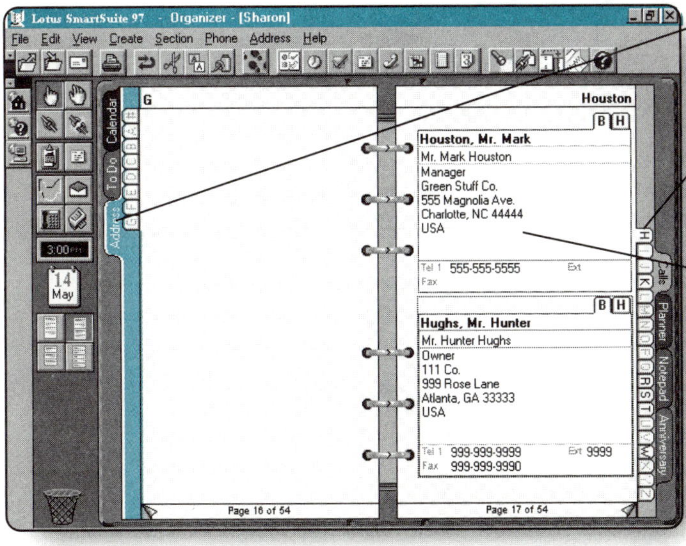

1. Click on the **Address tab**. The Address section will appear.

2. Click on the **tab** where the address record is located. The record's page will appear.

3. Double-click the **record** you want to edit. The Edit Address dialog box will open.

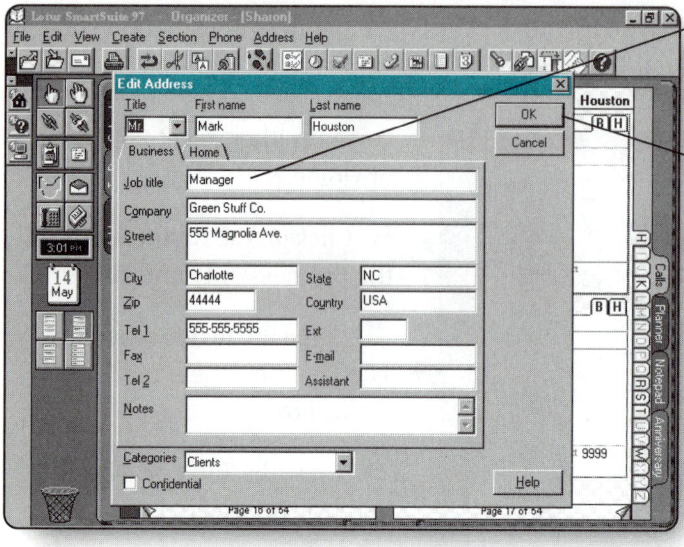

4. Enter the necessary **changes**. The changes will be reflected in the dialog box.

5. Click on **OK**. The record will be updated.

Creating Multiple Address Records for the Same Company

When you create a new address record, Organizer checks to see whether that company has been entered before. If it has, Organizer gives you the option of using the same company information for this record that was entered before. As you can imagine, this is a popular and time-saving feature of Organizer!

1. Click on the **Address tab**. The Address section will appear.

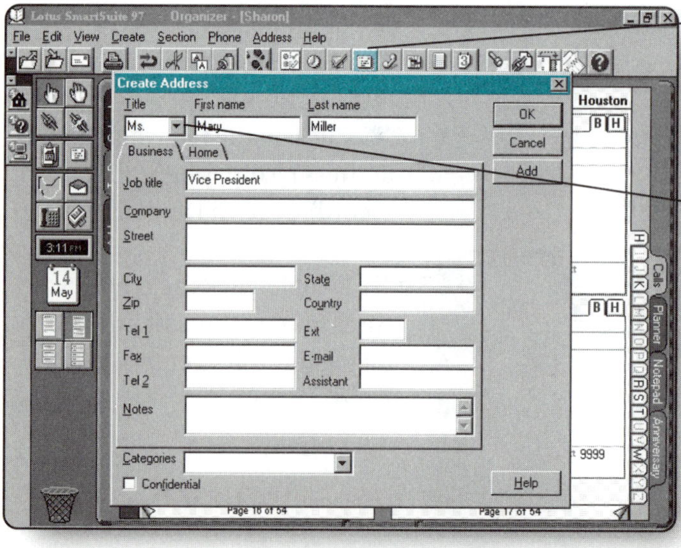

2. Click on the **Create a New Address record SmartIcon**. The Create Address dialog box will appear.

3. Click on the **down arrow** (▼) to select a Title. The selected title will be listed in the Title box.

4. Press the **Tab key**. The First name text box will be selected.

5. Type the **text** for the first name for the entry. The first name will appear in the First name box.

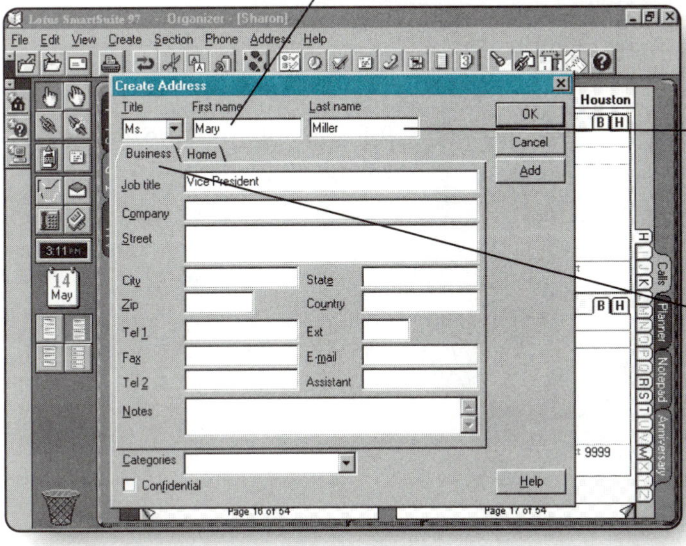

6. Press the **Tab key**. The Last name text box will be selected.

7. Type the **text** for the last name for the entry. The last name will appear in the Last name box.

8. Click on the **Business tab**. The Business tab will appear.

9. Click on the **Job title text box**. The box will be selected.

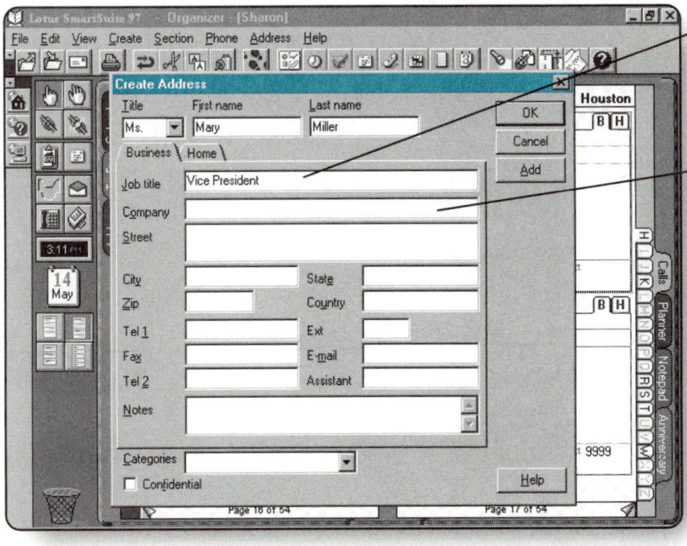

10. Type the **text** for that box. The text will appear in the dialog box.

11. Press the **Tab key**. The Company text box will be selected.

12. Type the **text** for the Company text box. The text will appear in the dialog box.

13. Press the **Tab key**. The Similar Address Found dialog box will appear.

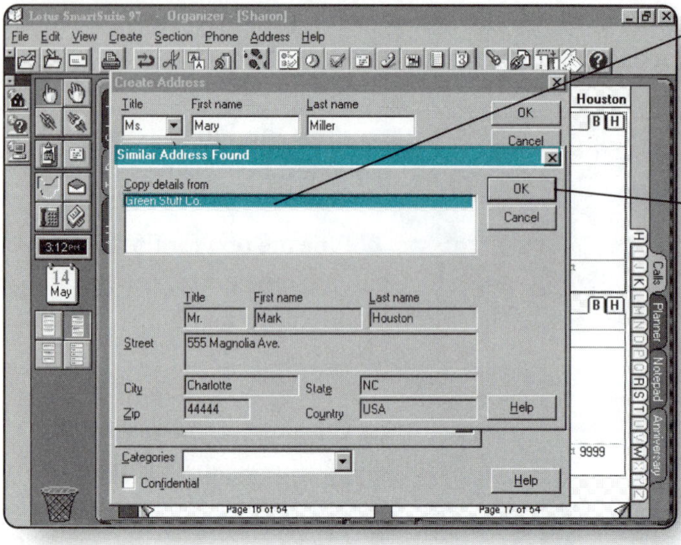

14. **Click** on the **company** you want to use. The address information for that company will appear.

15. **Click** on **OK**. The information from the dialog box will be entered into the Create Address dialog box.

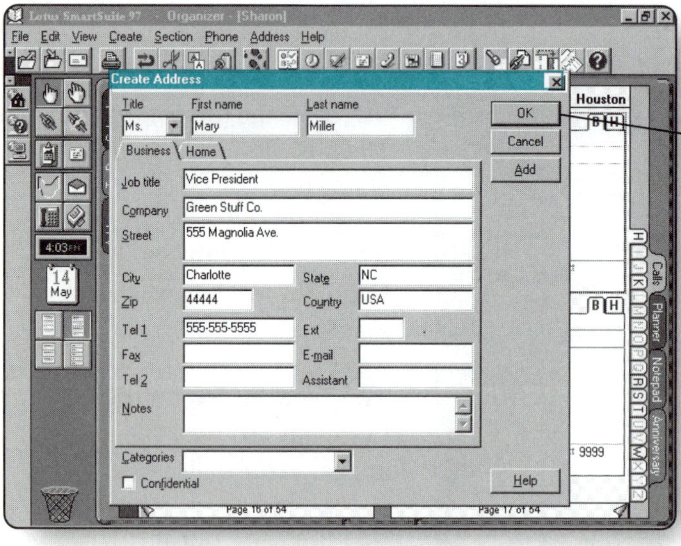

16. **Enter** any **additional information** needed.

17. **Click** on **OK**. The record will be added.

Sorting Addresses

Organizer lets you view your addresses by last name, company name, ZIP code, or category.

1. **Click** on **View**. The View menu will appear.

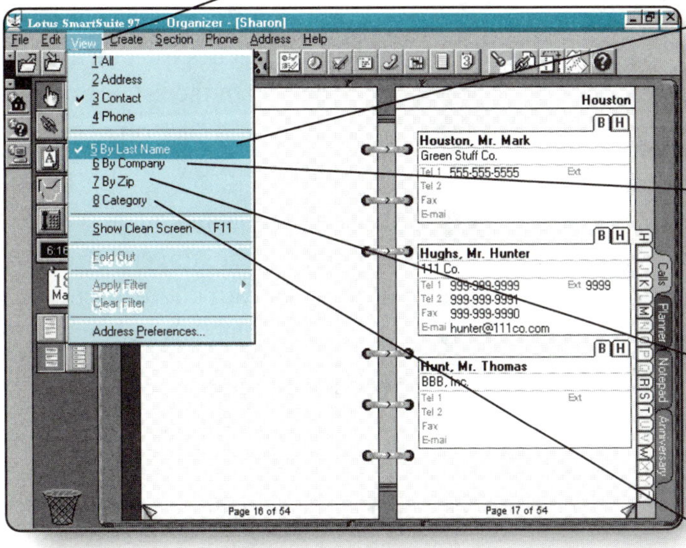

2a. **Click** on **By Last Name**. The addresses will be sorted by last name.

OR

2b. **Click** on **By Company**. The addresses will be sorted by company.

OR

2c. **Click** on **By Zip**. The addresses will be sorted by ZIP code.

OR

2d. **Click** on **Category**. The addresses will be sorted by category.

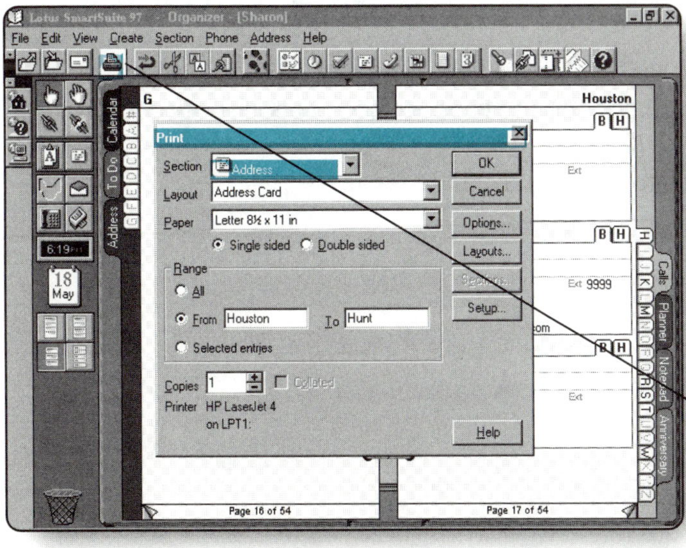

Printing Address Information

You can print your addresses using six different formats including address cards, Rolodex cards, envelopes, and phone lists.

1. **Click** on the **Print SmartIcon**. The Print dialog box will open.

2. Choose from the following **options**:

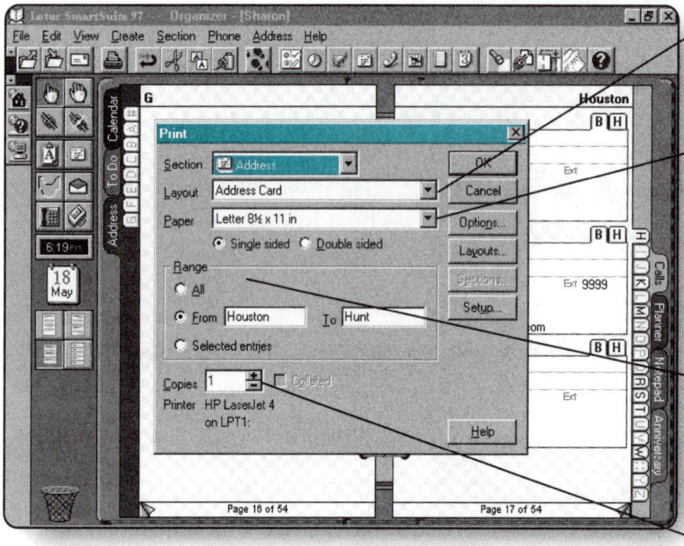

- To choose a different Layout, click on the down arrow (▼) and make your selection.
- If you want to print to a paper size other than the standard letter size, click the down arrow (▼) of the list box next to Paper and click on the paper size you want.
- The preselected range is the current page. You can also print All your addresses or just the Selected entries.
- To print more than one copy, click on the plus and minus buttons.

3. Click on **OK**. The pages will be sent to the printer.

TRACKING PHONE CALLS

A task that many of us are required to do is to keep a call log so that we can track our calls. A call entry is easily tied to the address book because you can select from any of your address book entries when making the call.

Adding a Call Entry

1. Click on the **Calls tab**. The Calls section will appear.

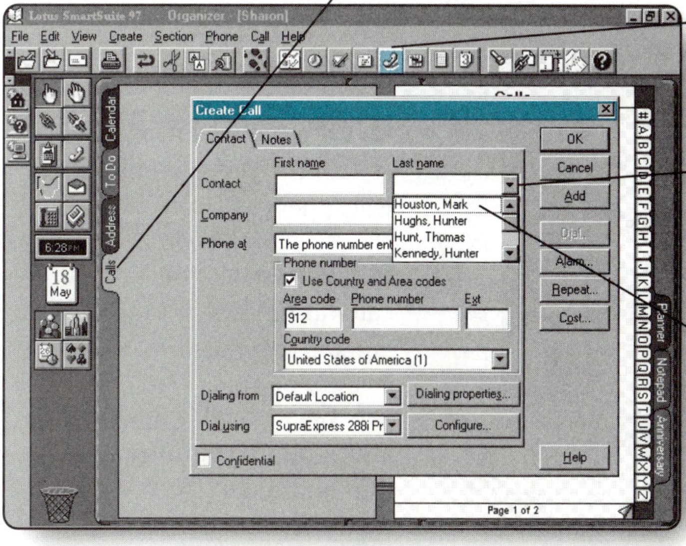

2. Click on the **Create a Calls entry SmartIcon**. The Create Call dialog box will open.

3. Click on the **down arrow** (▼) of the Last name box. A list of names from the address book will appear.

4. Click on the **name** of the person you are calling. The name will be selected.

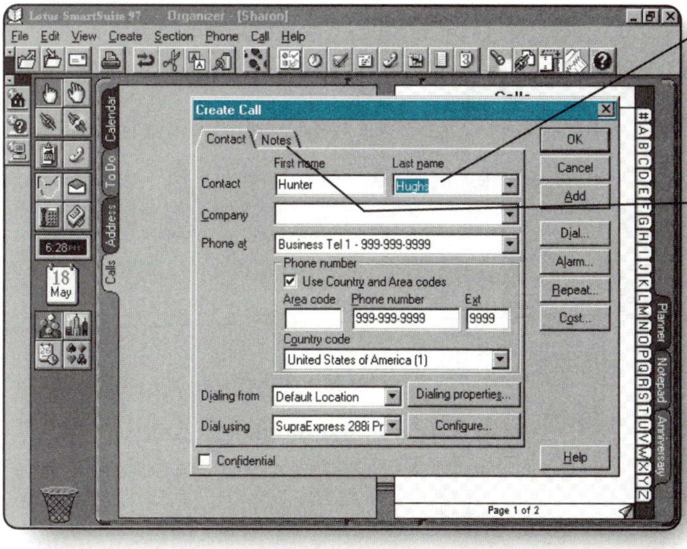

The information entered for that person when you created the address entry will automatically be inserted into the call entry.

5. Click on the **Notes tab**. The Notes tab will appear.

6. Click on the **down arrow** (▼) for the Date. A calendar will appear.

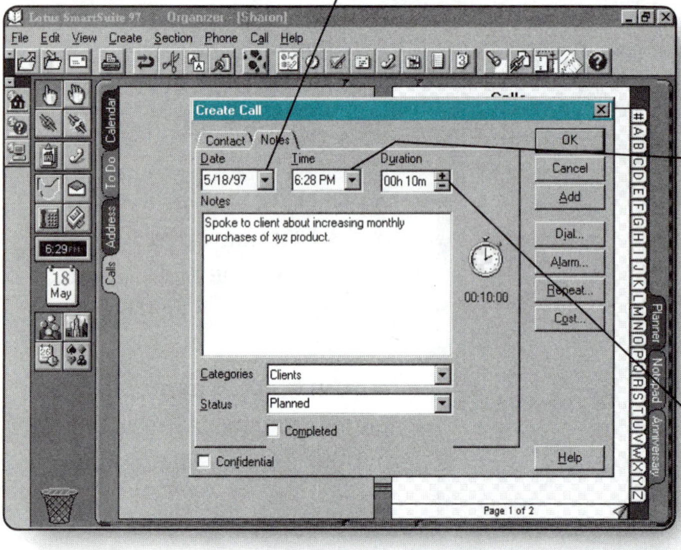

7. Click on the **date** that you made the call. The date will be entered into the form.

8. Click on the **down arrow** (▼) for the Time. A timeline will appear.

9. Click on the **time** that the call was made. The time will be entered into the form.

10. Click on the + (**plus**) and – (**minus**) **buttons** to set the Duration.

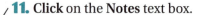

11. Click on the **Notes** text box.

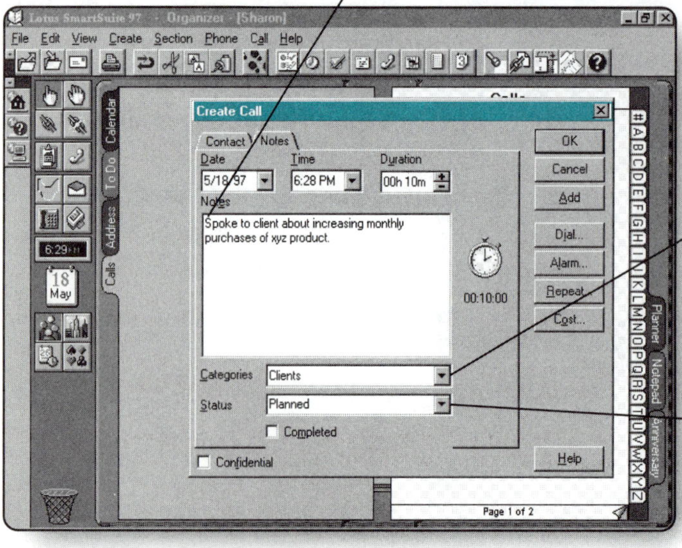

12. Type the **text** of any notes you want to make.

13. Choose from the following **options**:

- ✦ If you want to assign a category to this call, click on the down arrow (▼) next to the Categories box and click on the category you want to use.
- ✦ To change the status of the call, click on the down arrow (▼) beside the Status box and click on the correct status for this call.

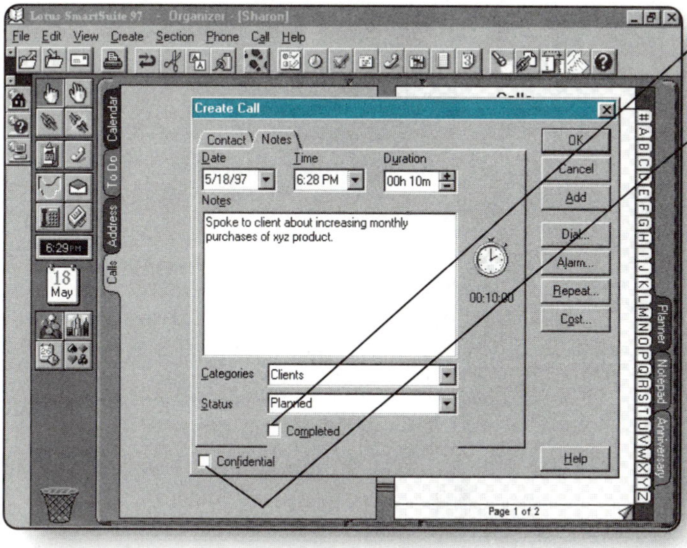

- ✦ If this call topic or series is Completed, ✔ this box.
- ✦ If you want to mark this call as Confidential, ✔ this box.

14. Click on **OK**. The call entry will be created.

Viewing a Listing of Calls

Because you can have multiple calls on a single date, you may have multiple pages to flip through to view the complete listing of calls. Before using the following procedure you may want to change your view to by date by clicking on the View by Date button.

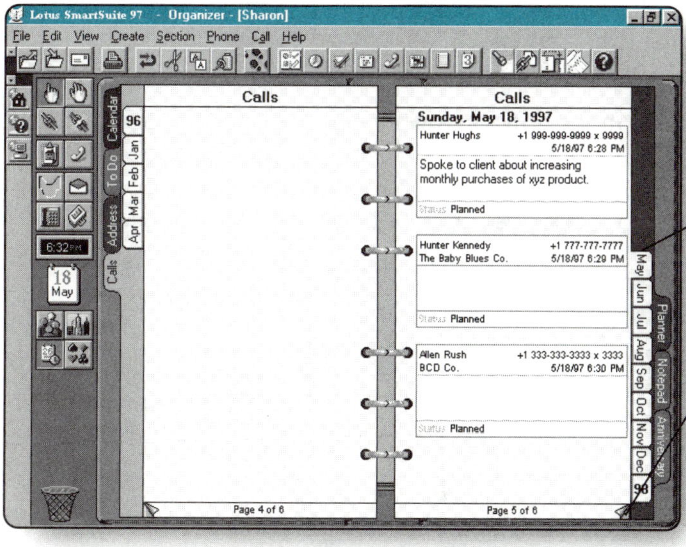

1. Click on the **date tab** for which you want to view calls. The page will turn to that date.

2. Click on the **lower right corner** of the page. The next page in the notebook will appear.

Tracking Follow-up Calls

Often one call leads to another call. This second call is a follow-up call. When you create a follow-up call entry, Organizer links the follow-up call entry to the original call entry.

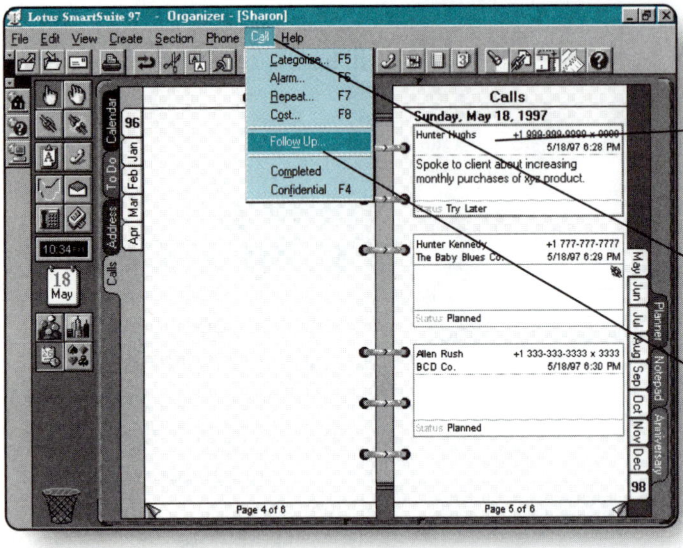

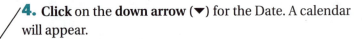

1. **Click** on the **Calls entry** that you are following up on. The entry will be selected.
2. **Click** on **Call**. The Call menu will appear.
3. **Click** on **Follow Up**. The Create Follow up Call dialog box will open.
4. **Click** on the **down arrow** (▼) for the Date. A calendar will appear.

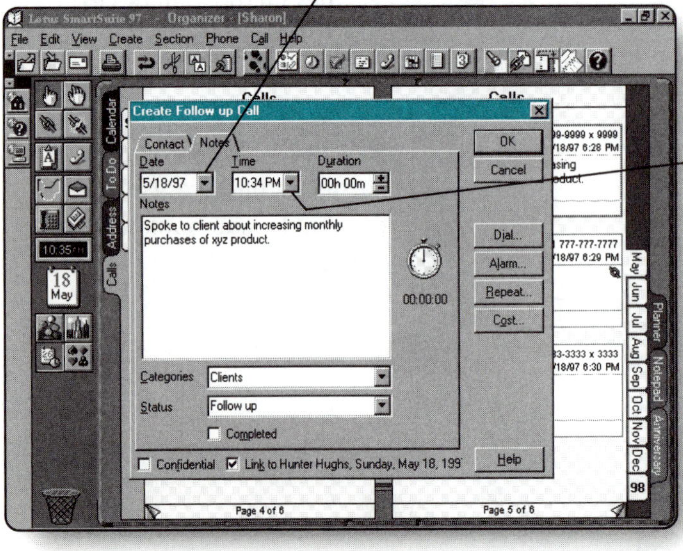

5. **Click** on the **date** that you made the call. The date will be entered into the form.
6. **Click** on the **down arrow** (▼) for the Time. A timeline will appear.
7. **Click** on the **time** that the call was made. The time will be entered into the form.

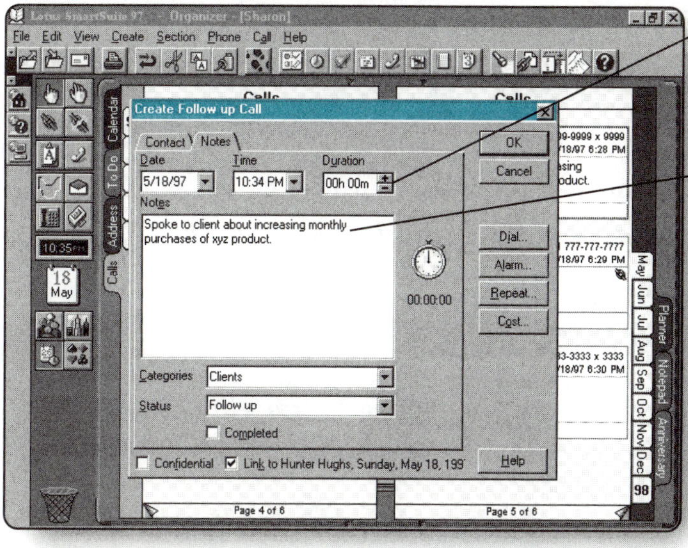

8. **Click** on the + (**plus**) and – (**minus**) **buttons** to set the Duration.

9. **Click** on the **Notes** text box.

10. **Type** the **text** of any notes you want to make.

11. **Click** on **OK**. The follow-up call entry will be created.

PART V REVIEW QUESTIONS

1. **How many different formats are there for printing your calendar?** ***See "Printing Calendar Information" in Chapter 15***
2. **Which SmartIcon do you click to add an appointment?** ***See "Adding an Appointment" in Chapter 15***
3. **How do you reschedule an appointment?** ***See "Modifying an Appointment" in Chapter 15***
4. **What part of Organizer do you use to track tasks?** ***See "Entering To Do Tasks" in Chapter 16***
5. **How does a task differ from an appointment?** ***See "Entering To Do Tasks" in Chapter 16***
6. **How do you view your tasks on your calendar?** ***See "Displaying To Do Tasks in Your Calendar" in Chapter 16***
7. **How do you access the Address section of Organizer?** ***See "Working with Addresses" in Chapter 17***
8. **Is there a fast way to enter a record for someone who works at the same company that another addressee works at?** ***See "Working with Addresses" in Chapter 17***
9. **Do you use a section other than the Address section to track your phone calls?** ***See "Tracking Phone Calls" in Chapter 17***
10. **What is a follow-up call?** ***See "Tracking Follow-up Calls" in Chapter 17***

PART VI

Using Approach

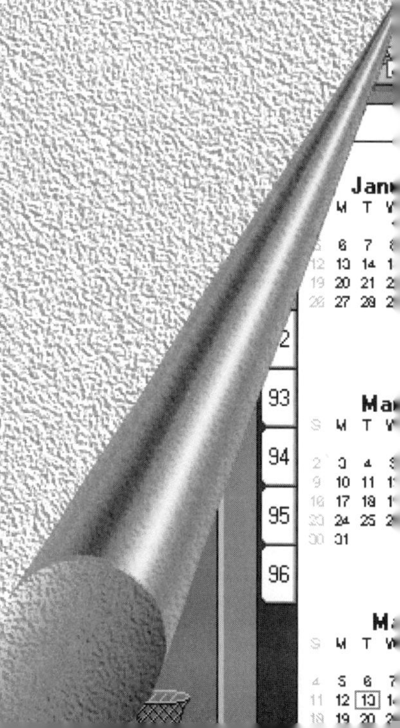

18 Creating a Simple Database

Whether or not you realize it, you use databases every day. Your phone book is a database; your television show listing is a database; even a cookbook is a database. A database in its most simple form is an organized list of information. Lotus SmartSuite provides a database management application called Approach. Approach allows you to create and manage databases. In this chapter, you'll learn how to:

- ✦ Use Approach's SmartMasters
- ✦ Create a simple database
- ✦ Enter data into a database

USING APPROACH'S SMARTMASTERS

There are three basic ways to create a database using Approach. You can use the traditional approach of starting from scratch. You can use a SmartMaster template. Or you can use a SmartMaster Application. Similar to SmartMasters in other Lotus applications, Approach's SmartMasters allow you to quickly create a database with minimum amount of work on your part.

Creating a Database Using a SmartMaster Template

Creating a database using a SmartMaster template saves you time because the template will provide you with a predefined set of field definitions for your database file. The SmartMasters provided by Approach are designed for both business and personal use.

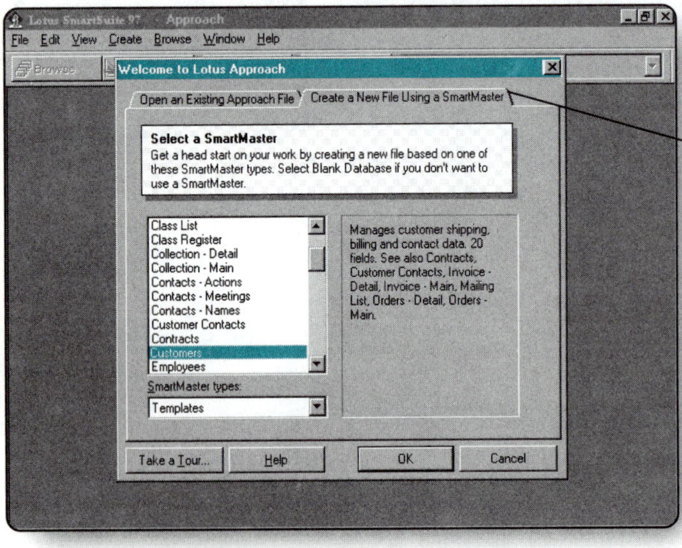

1. **Start Approach**. The Welcome to Lotus Approach dialog box will open.
2. **Click** on the **Create a New File Using a SmartMaster tab**. The Create a New File Using a SmartMaster tab will appear.

NOTE

If you have already started Approach and want to create a new database, click on the Create a new database file SmartIcon. The New dialog box will open. Proceed with the following steps.

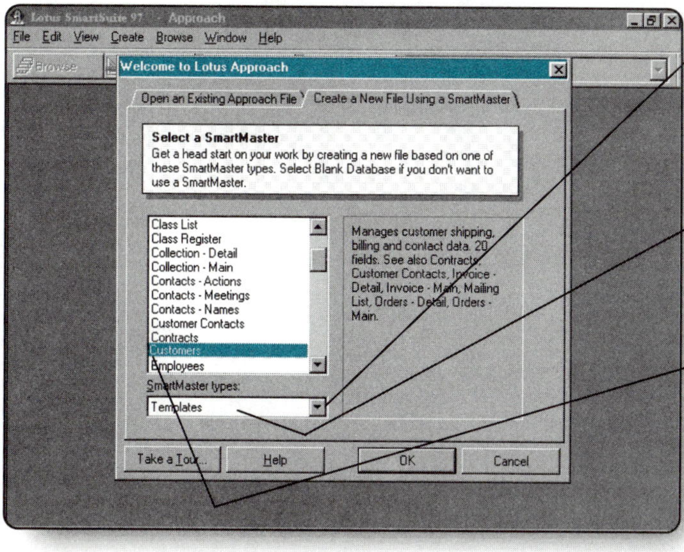

3. Click on the **down arrow** (▼) under SmartMaster types. A list of available SmartMasters types will appear.

4. Click on **Templates**. A list of available templates will appear.

5. Click on the **template** you want.

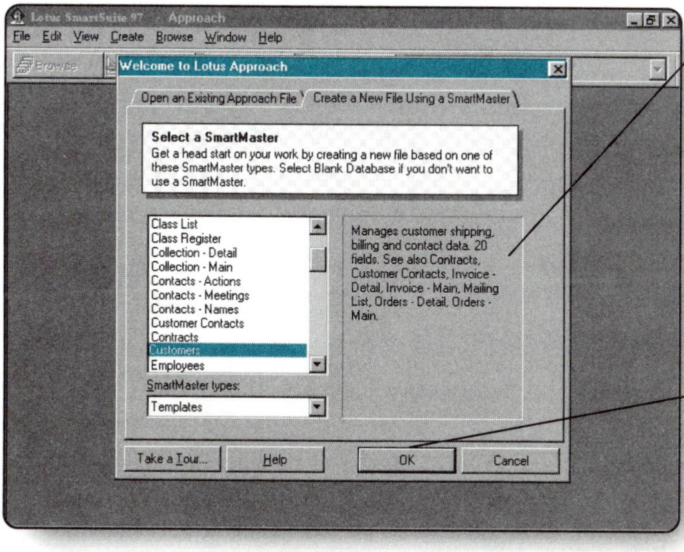

A description of the selected template will appear in the box on the right side of the dialog box. The description provides information about the use of the template, states how many fields are in the database definition, and recommends other templates to examine.

6. Click on **OK**. The New dialog box will open.

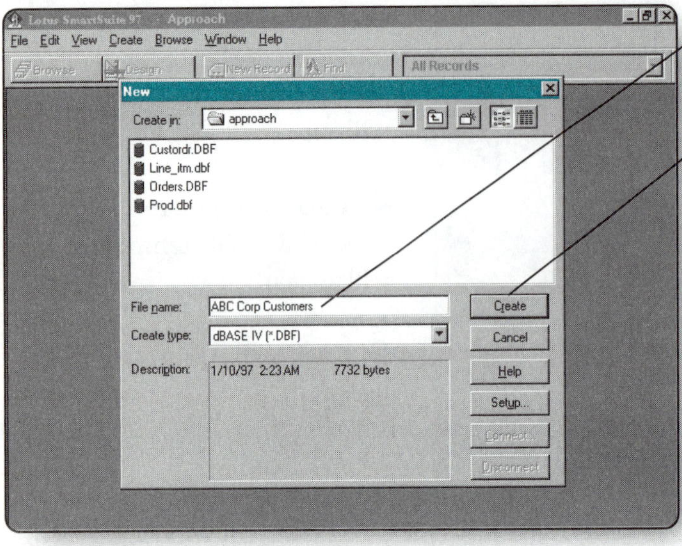

7. Type the **name** of the new file in the File name: box.

8. Click on **Create**. The database will be created.

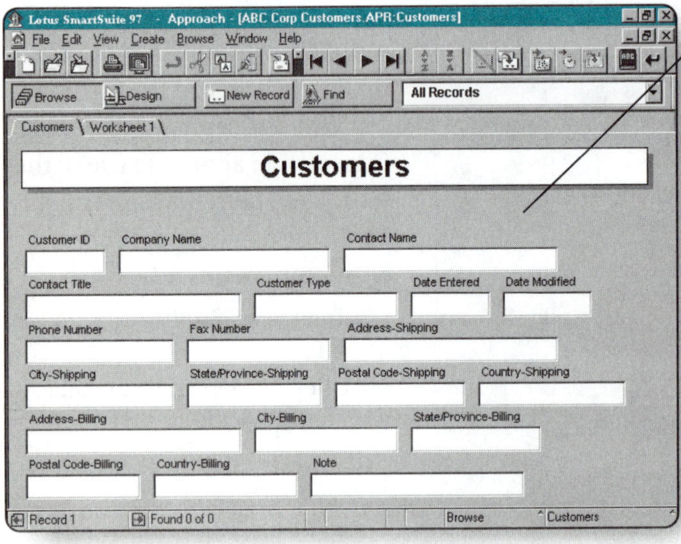

The newly created database appears. You will notice that the fields have already been added for you. You are ready to start entering your data.

Creating a Database Using a SmartMaster Application

To start your database with a more fully developed interface, use a SmartMaster application to create the database.

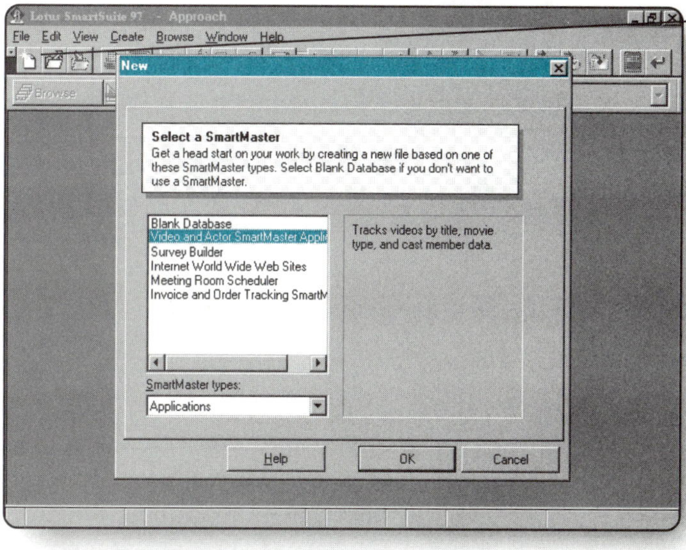

1. Click on the **Create a new database file SmartIcon.** The New dialog box will open.

> **NOTE**
>
> To create a database using a SmartMaster, start Approach, and the Welcome to Lotus Approach dialog box will open. Click on the Create a New File Using a Smart-Master tab. The Create a New File Using a SmartMaster tab will appear. Proceed with the following steps.

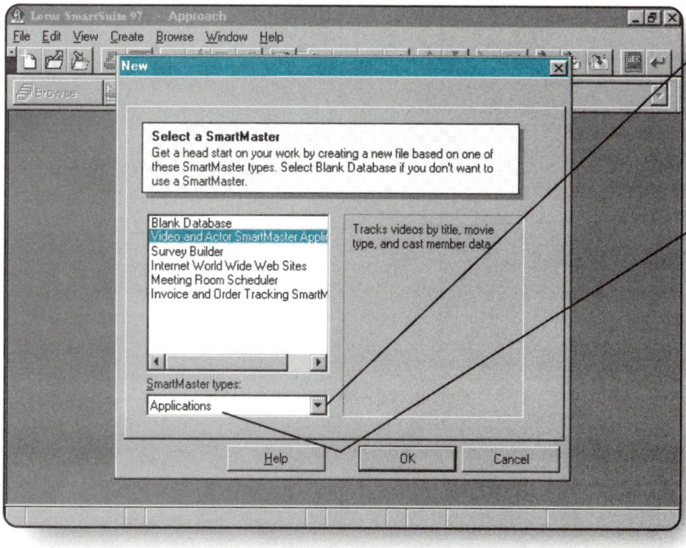

2. Click on the **down arrow** (▼) under SmartMaster types:. A list of available SmartMaster types will appear.

3. Click on **Applications.** A list of available applications will appear.

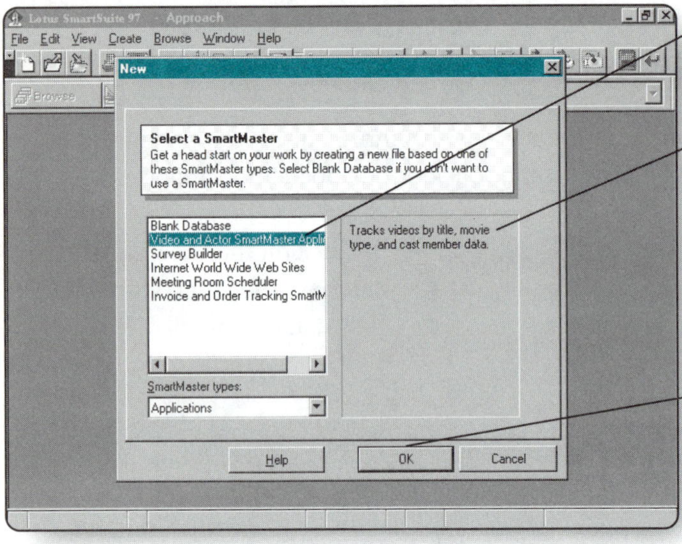

4. Click on the **application** you want.

A description of the selected application will appear in the box on the right side of the dialog box. The description provides information about the use of the application.

5. Click on **OK**. The application will be created.

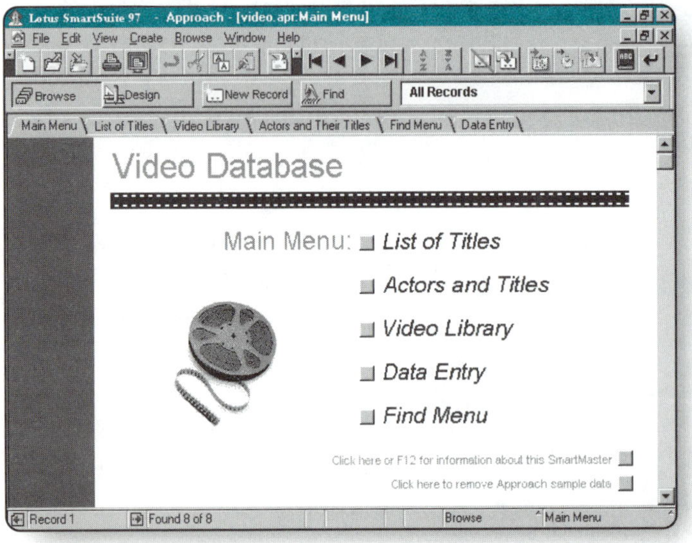

The newly created database application is ready for you to start using. Click on the square gray buttons to perform the various actions supported by the application.

CREATING A DATABASE FROM SCRATCH

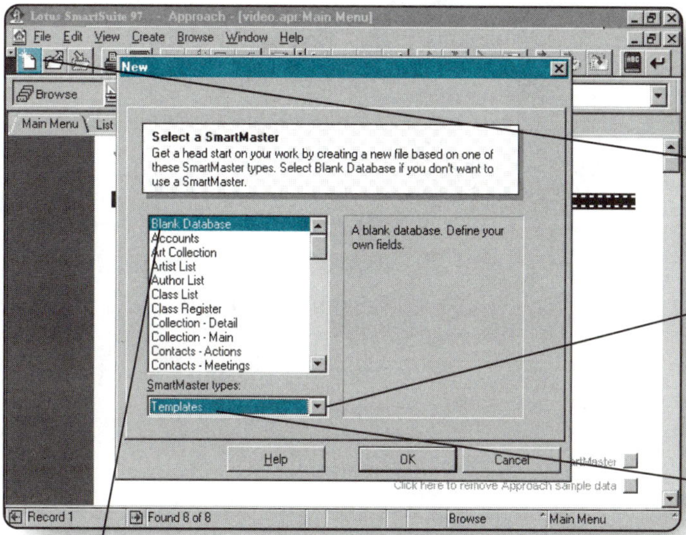

If you do not want to use a SmartMaster, you can create your own database from scratch.

1. **Click** on the **Create a new database file SmartIcon**. The New dialog box will open.

2. **Click** on the **down arrow** (▼) under SmartMaster types:. A list of available SmartMaster types will appear.

3. **Click** on **Templates**. A list of available templates will appear.

4. **Click** on **Blank Database** from the list box.

5. **Click** on **OK**. The New dialog box will appear.

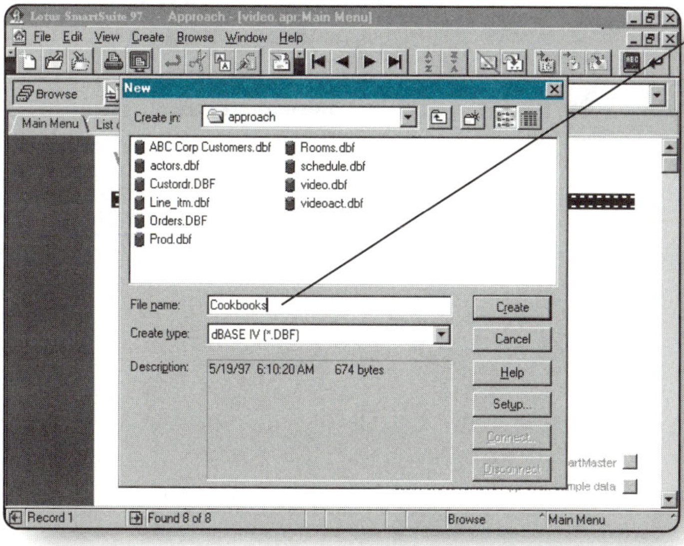

6. **Type** a **File name:** for the database. The name will be assigned to the database.

7. **Click** on **Create**. The Creating New Database dialog box will open.

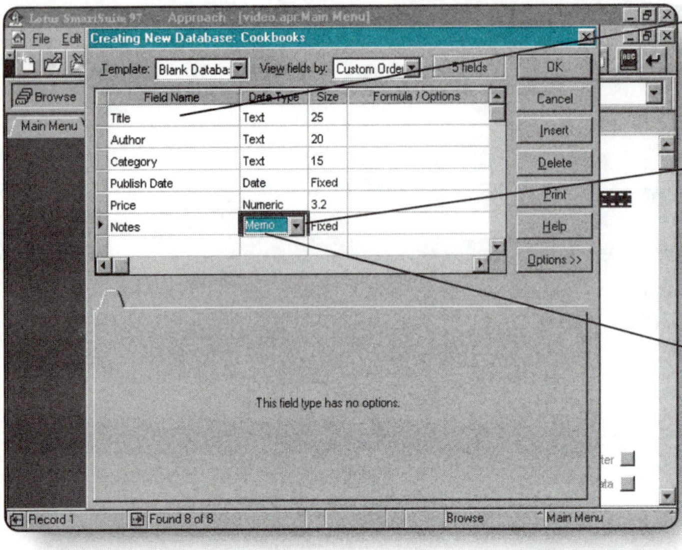

8. **Type** a **name** for the Field. The field will be added to the database.

9. **Click** on the **down arrow** (▼) in the Data Type column. A list of available field types will appear.

10. **Click** on the **field type** for this field. The field type will be assigned to the field.

11. **Press** the **Tab key**. The Size column will be selected.

12. **Type** a **Size** for the field. The field will be made that size.

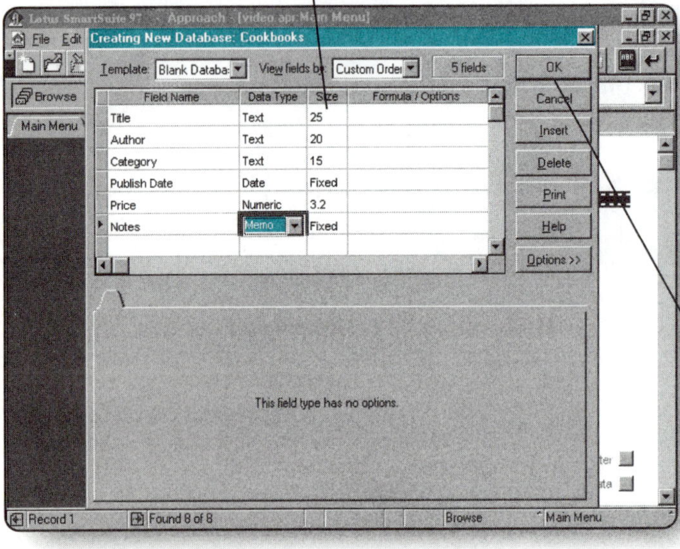

Certain field types, such as Date and Memo, will not allow you to enter a field size.

13. **Press** the **Tab key**. The Field Name column will be selected.

14. **Repeat steps 8** through **13** until all fields have been defined.

15. **Click** on **OK**. The database will be created.

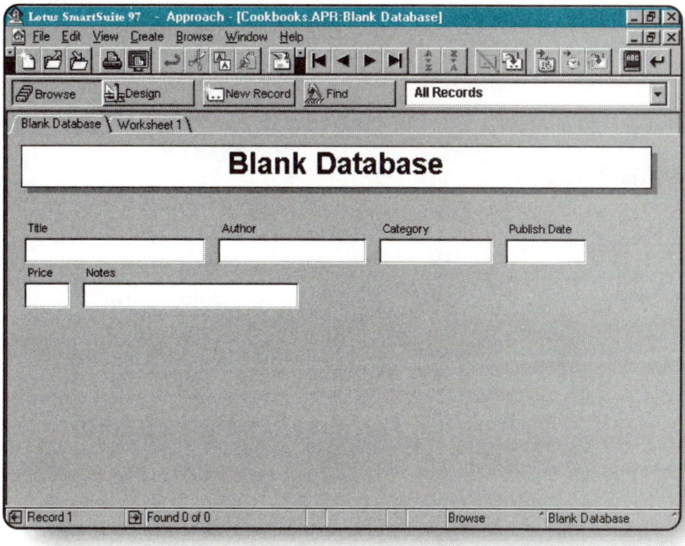

The database is now ready for you to add data to. However, before adding data, you may want to change the form. For example, you may want to change the title displayed on the form.

Modifying the Look of Your Form

When the newly created database appears, it displays the fields on a form. This form is used to input your data. You may want to make changes to your form (and your database), such as changing the title of the form, deleting fields, or adding fields.

Changing the Title on the Form

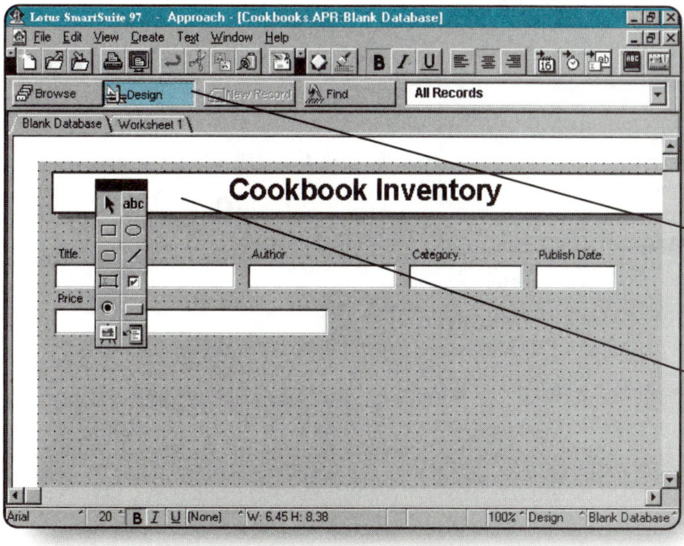

When the form appears, you will notice that it has the less than exciting title of Blank Database. Changing this title requires that you use design mode.

1. Click on the **Design button**. The form will be placed in design mode.

2. Click on the **title box**. The title box will be selected.

3. **Click** on the **title box** again. The title box will be placed in edit mode.

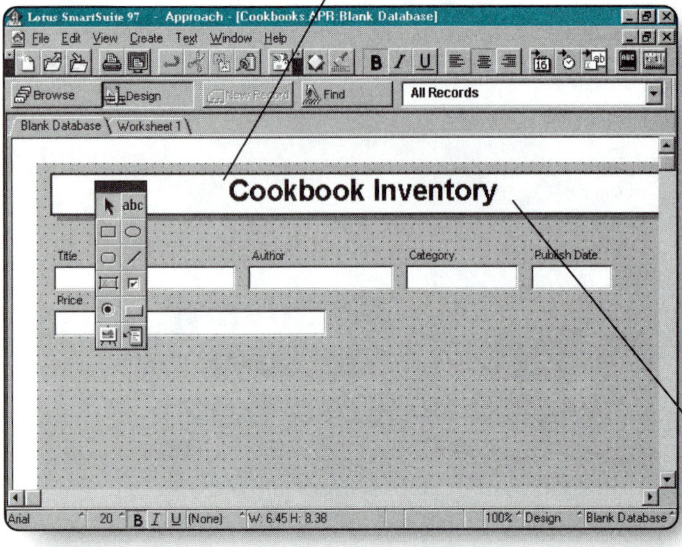

NOTE

If you double-click the title box, the Properties dialog box will appear. To avoid this, perform two single clicks as instructed.

4. **Press** the **Delete key** or the **Backspace key** until the current text is removed.

5. **Type** the new **text** for the title. A new title will be created for display on the form.

Changing the Name of a Form

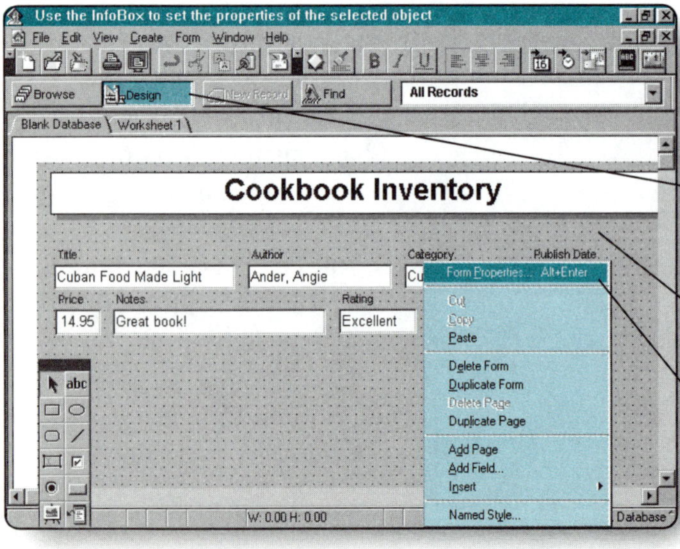

The name of a form appears on its tab. When your database is first created, its form is named Blank Database.

1. **Click** on the **Design button**. The form will be placed in design mode.

2. **Right-click** the **form**. A shortcut menu will appear.

3. **Click** on **Form Properties**. The Properties for Form dialog box will open.

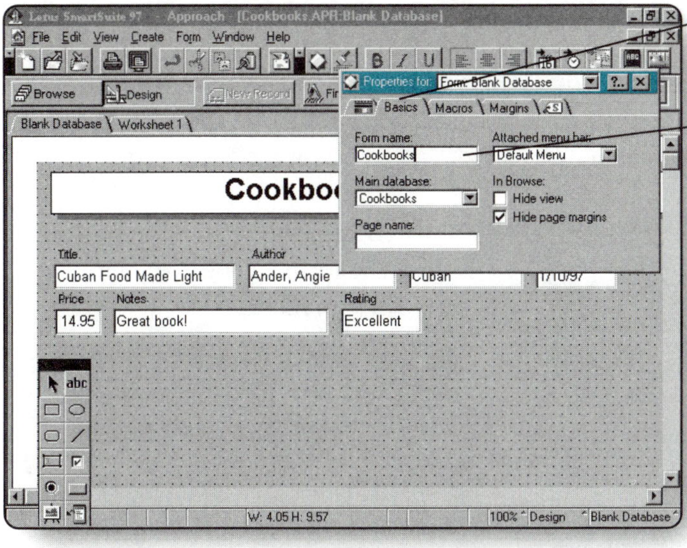

4. **Click** on the **Basics tab**. The Basics tab will appear.

5. **Click** on the **Form Name:** text box. The text box entry will be selected.

6. **Type** the new **name** of the form. The name will be entered in the text box.

7. **Click** on the **Close button** of the Properties for Form dialog box. The dialog box will close, and the form's name will change.

Deleting a Field

If you do not want a field to appear on the field, you can delete it.

1. **Click** on the **Design button**. The form will be placed in design mode.

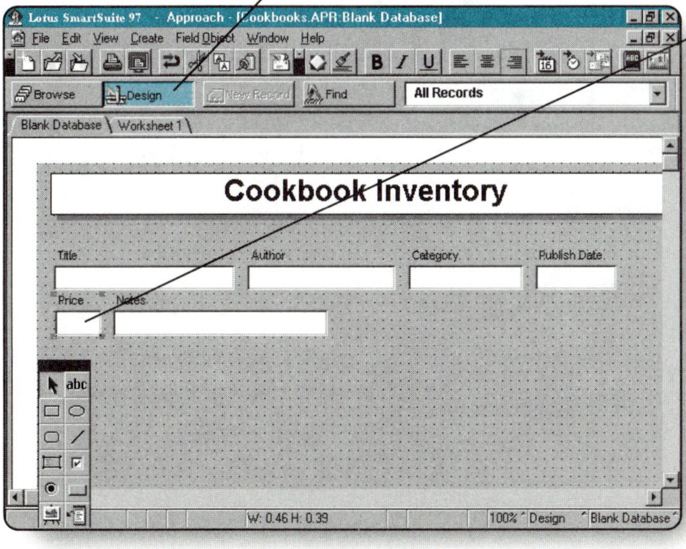

2. **Click** on the **field** to be deleted. The field will be selected.

3. **Press** the **Delete key**. The field will be deleted.

Deleting the field from a form does not delete it from the database. If you have entered data into the field you deleted from the form, you have are not losing that data.

Adding a Field

You may find that you forgot a field when you were creating your database. You can add fields even after the database has been created.

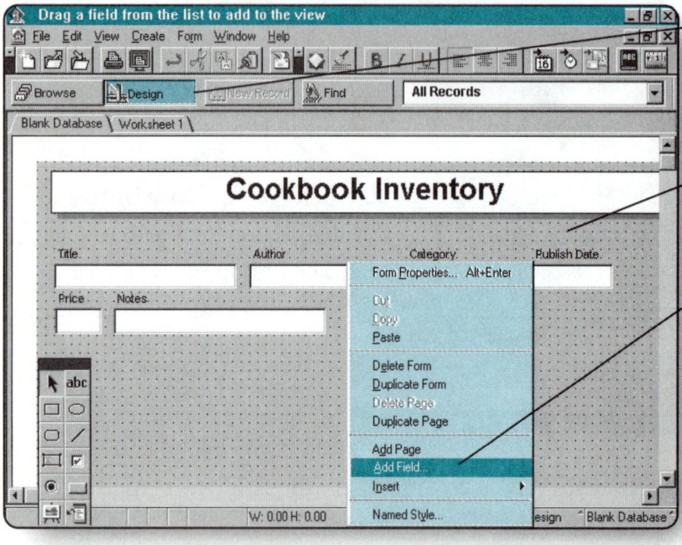

1. Click on the **Design button**. The form will be placed in design mode.

2. **Right-click** on the **form**. A shortcut menu will appear.

3. Click on **Add Field**. The Add Field dialog box will open.

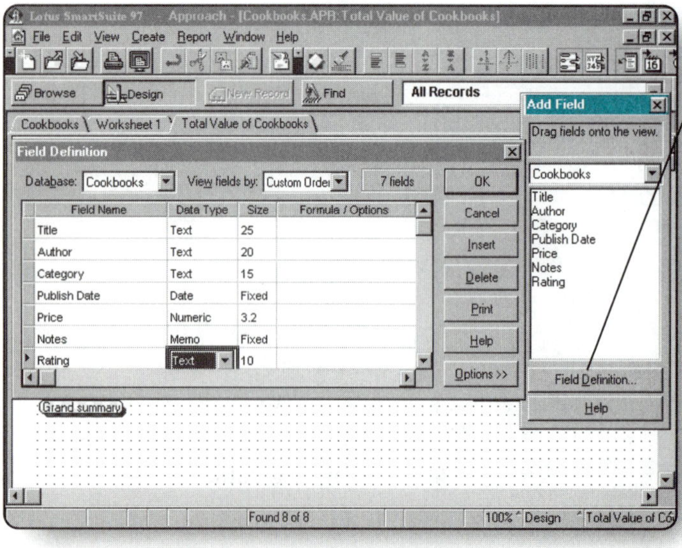

4. Click on **Field Definition**. The Field Definition dialog box will open.

5. Click on a **blank row** in the Field Name column.

6. **Type** a **name** for the new field. The name will appear in the Field Name column.

7. **Click** on the **down arrow** (▼) in the Data Type column. A list of available field types will appear.

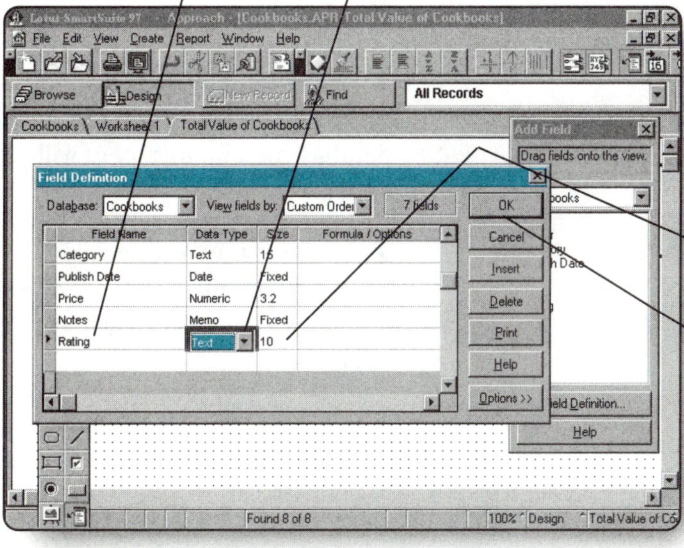

8. **Click** on the **field type** for this field. The field type will be assigned to the field.

9. **Press** the **Tab key**. The Size column will be selected.

10. **Type** a **Size** for the field. The field will be made that size.

11. **Click** on **OK**. The field will be added, and the Field Definition dialog box will close.

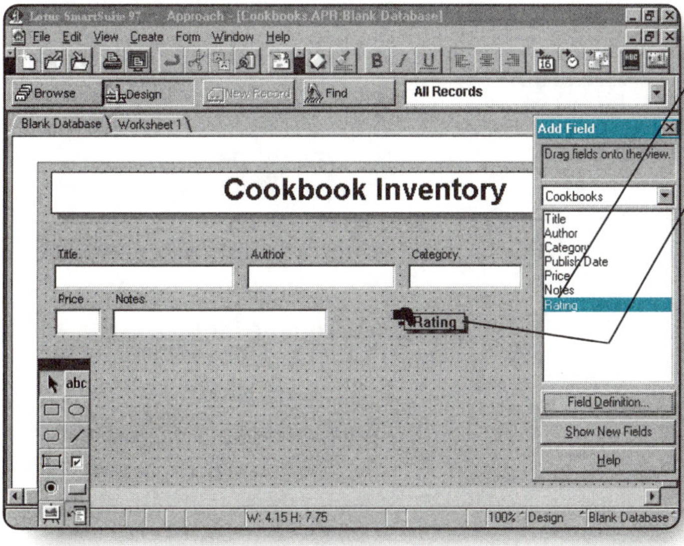

12. **Click** on the added **field** from the list box.

13. **Drag** the **field name** to the location on the form where you want it.

14. **Release** the **mouse button**. The field will be added to the form.

15. **Click** on the **Close button** of the Add Field dialog box. The Add Field dialog box will close.

WORKING WITH DATA

After you have created the database and form, you are ready to add and work with the data for your database.

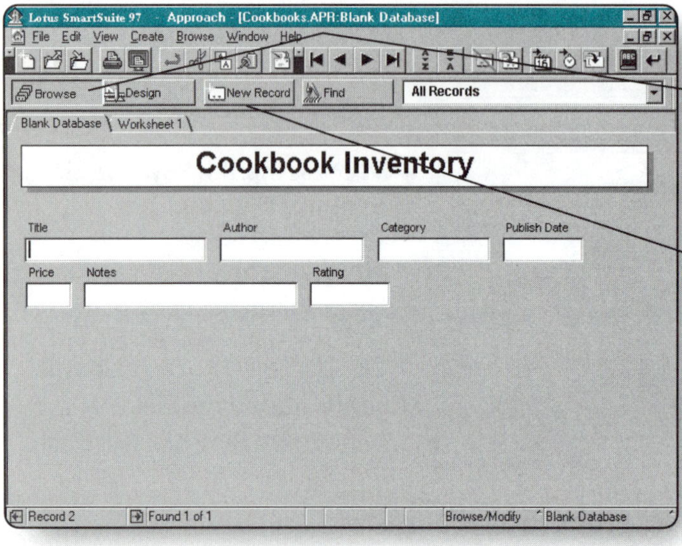

Entering Data

1. Click on the **Browse button**. Either the first record in the database or a blank record will appear.

2. Click on the **New Record button** if a blank record does not appear. A blank record will appear.

If you are working with a new database that does not contain any records, skip step 2.

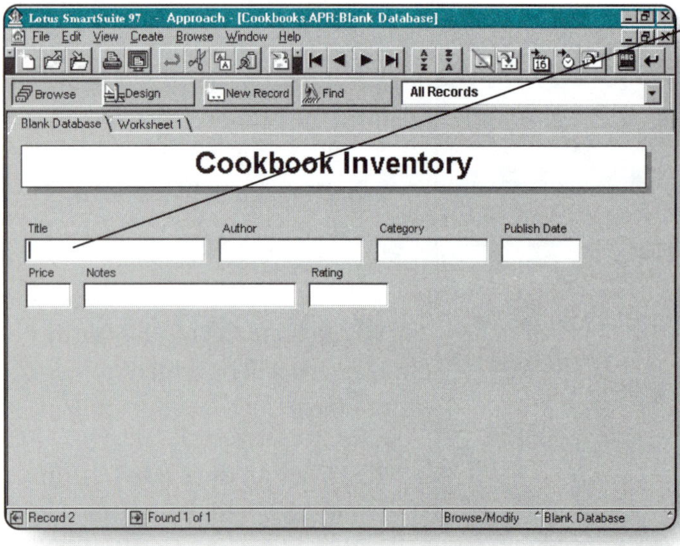

3. Type the **data** for the first field. The data will be entered.

4. Press the **Tab key**. The next field will be selected.

5. Type the **data** for the field. That data will be entered.

6. Repeat steps 4 and **5** until you have entered data for the fields on the form.

If you want to add another record, either press the Tab key when you are finished entering data for the last field or click the New Record button.

Navigating Records

After you have inputted several records, you may need to return to a specific record to review it.

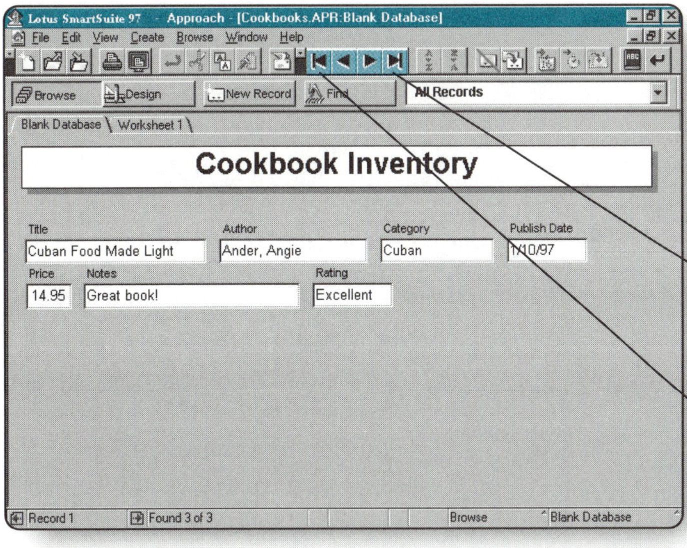

1. **Click** on the **Go to last record SmartIcon button**. The last record will appear.
2. **Click** on the **Go to first record SmartIcon button**. The first record will appear.

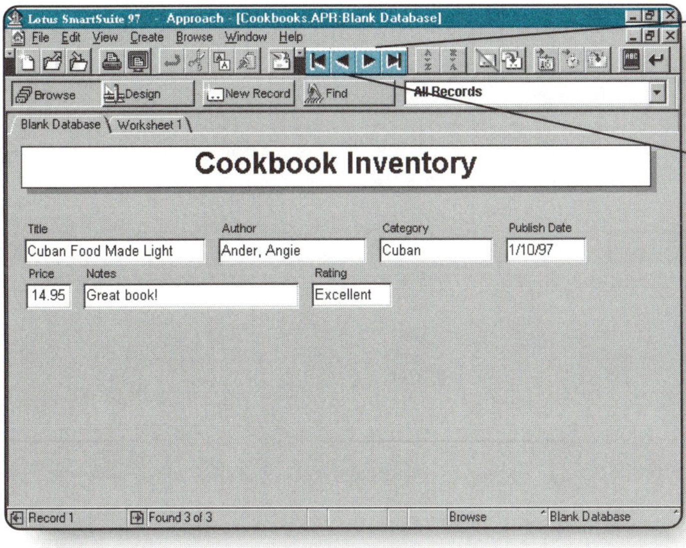

3. **Click** on the **Go to next record SmartIcon button**. The next record will appear.
4. **Click** on the **Go to previous record SmartIcon button**. The previous record will appear.

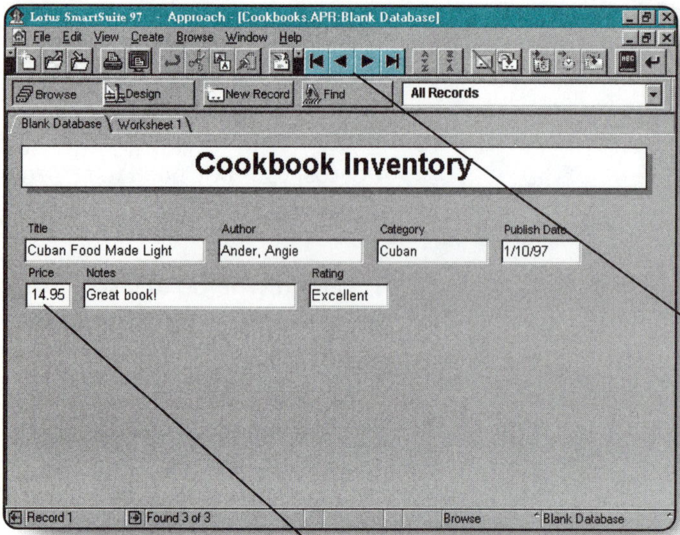

Modifying Data

Data sometimes needs to be changed after it has been entered into your database. You may have typed something in wrong or the data needs to be updated.

1. **Click** on a **Go to SmartIcon**.

By using the Go to SmartIcons, you can move through the records until you locate the one you need to modify.

2. **Click** on the **field** you need to change.

3. **Enter** the **change**.

19 Customizing your Database

Data doesn't do you any good if you can't find it. Approach assists you in this task by letting you find the data. You can also sort the data to make it more meaningful to you. In this chapter, you'll learn how to:

- **Find and sort data in your database**
- **Print your database information**

FINDING AND SORTING DATA

You may need to locate a specific record in your database. Approach makes this easy to do using the Find button. Or you may want to sort your records by a certain field; for example, you may want your database to be listed alphabetically by a field.

Finding Specific Data

To find records, you must create a condition to be matched. Let's say that you want to locate all the records with a price of more than ten dollars. Approach has a feature called the Find Assistant that makes this process easy.

1. **Click** on **Browse**. The Browse menu will appear.

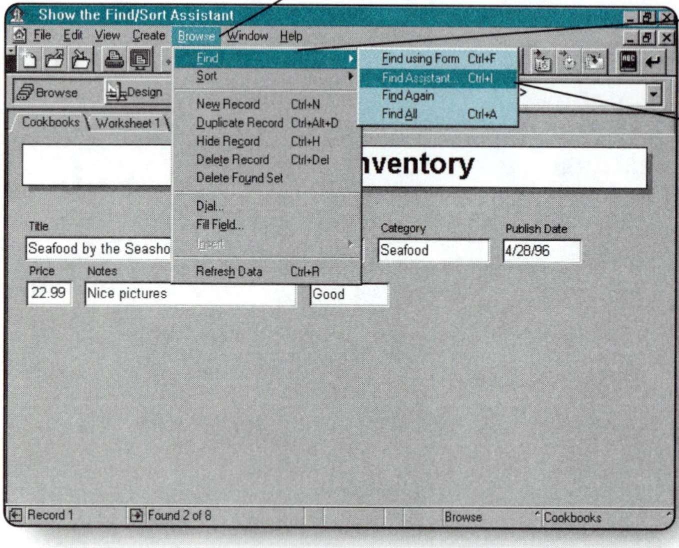

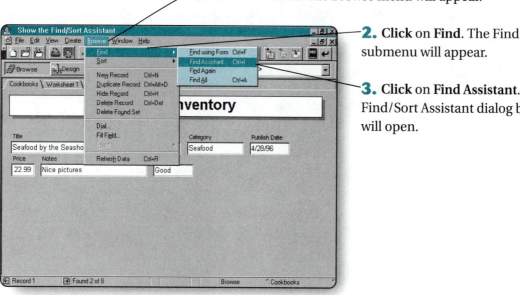

2. **Click** on **Find**. The Find submenu will appear.

3. **Click** on **Find Assistant**. The Find/Sort Assistant dialog box will open.

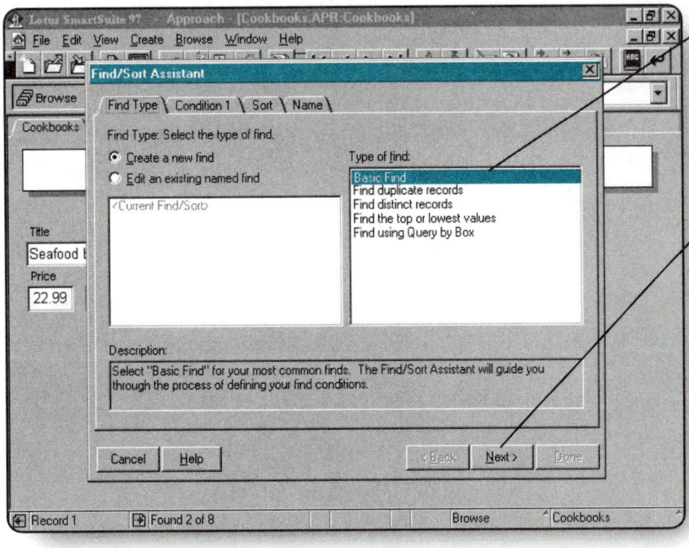

4. Click on the **Type of find:**. A description of that find type will appear in the box at the bottom of the dialog box.

5. Click on **Next**. The Condition page will appear.

6. Click on the **field** for which you want to create a condition from the Fields: list box. The field will be added to the find condition.

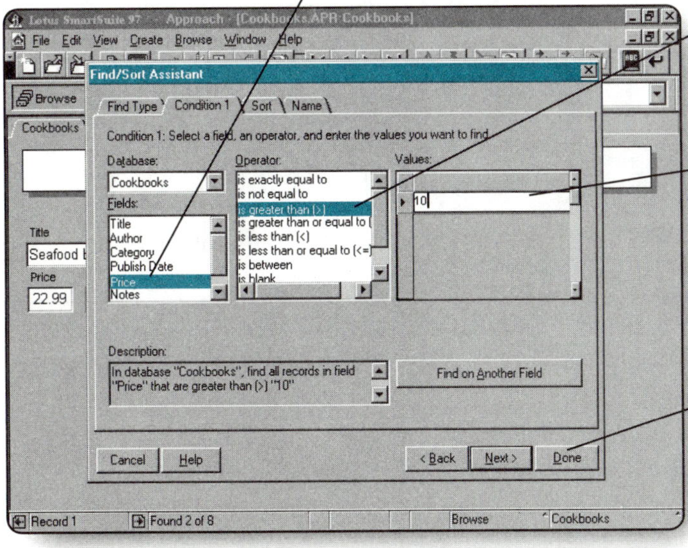

7. Click on the **Operator**: you want. The operator will be added to the find condition.

8. Click on the **Values: box**. The box will be selected.

9. Type a **value**. The value will be added to the find condition.

10. Click on **Done**. The records that match the find condition will be available for you to work with.

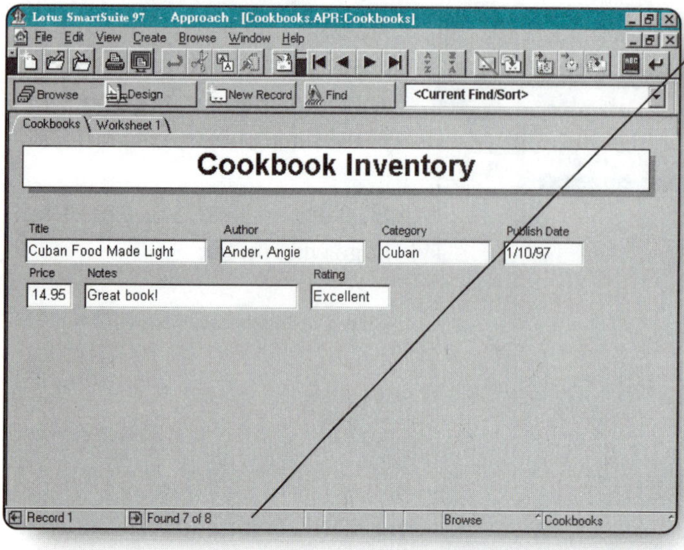

After you find the records, you can look at them and modify them just as you normally would. The status bar lets you know how many of the records in your database match the find condition.

Naming a Find

If you create a find that you want to use in the future, you can name it. Then you can select it from the Find Assistant when you need it.

1. **Click** on **Browse**. The Browse menu will appear.

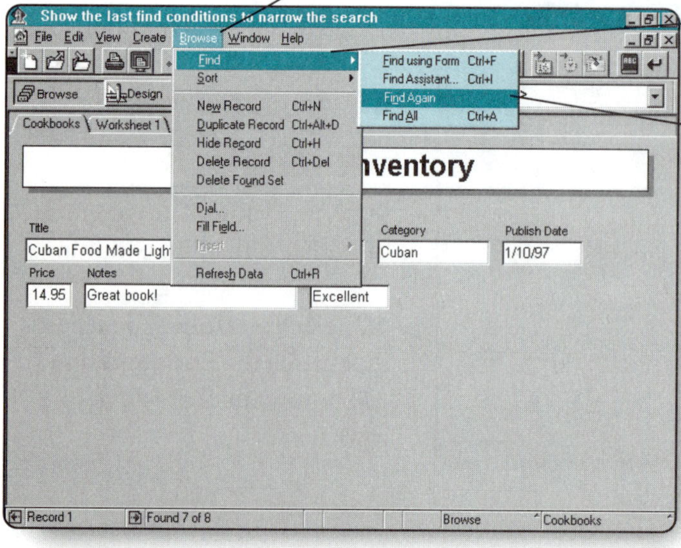

2. **Click** on **Find**. The Find submenu will appear.

3. **Click** on **Find Again**. The Find Assistant dialog box will open.

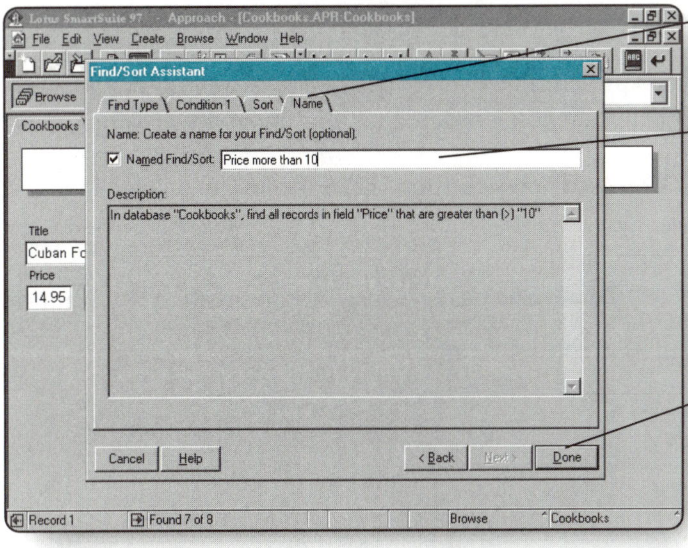

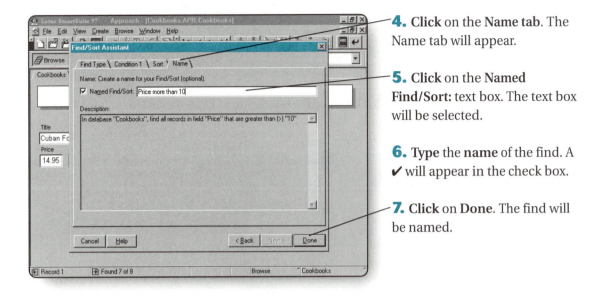

4. Click on the **Name tab**. The Name tab will appear.

5. Click on the **Named Find/Sort:** text box. The text box will be selected.

6. Type the **name** of the find. A ✔ will appear in the check box.

7. Click on **Done**. The find will be named.

Returning to All the Records

1. Click on **Browse**. The Browse menu will appear.

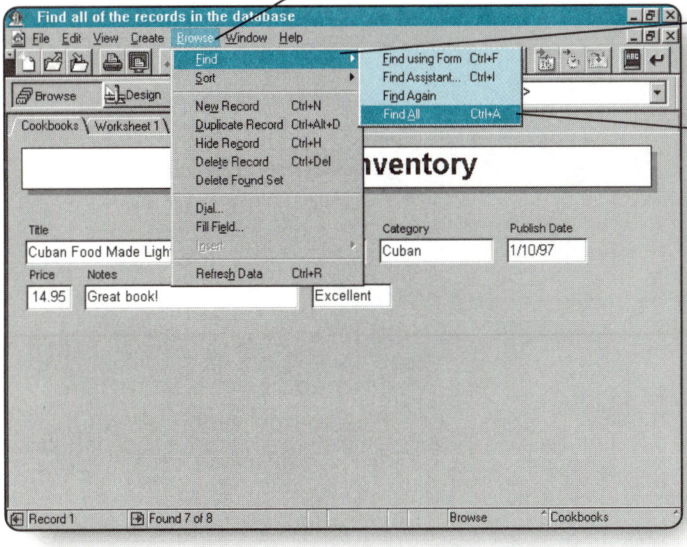

2. Click on **Find**. The Find submenu will appear.

3. Click on **Find All**. All records will appear.

Sorting Your Data

Approach provides two SmartIcons for sorting your records: Sort field in ascending order and Sort field in descending order.

1. **Click** on the **Browse button**. The form will be placed in browse mode.

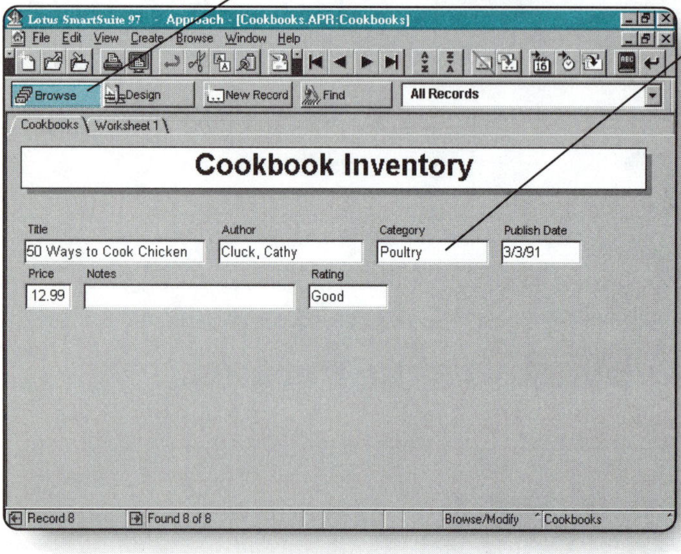

2. **Click** on the **field** you want to sort on. The field will be selected.

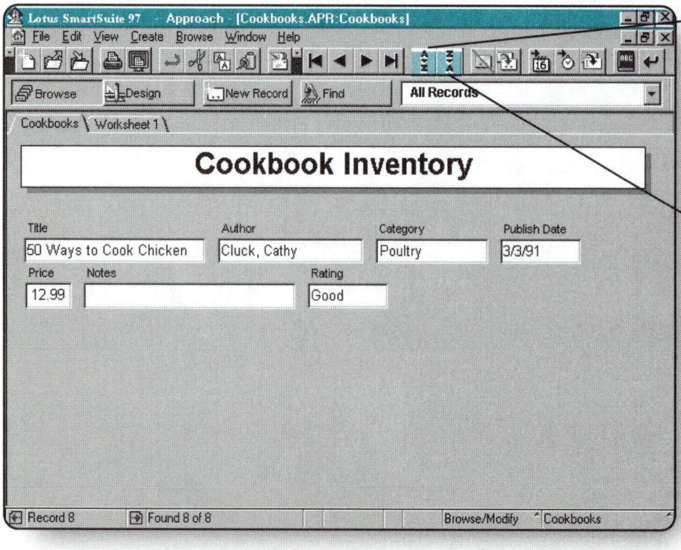

3a. **Click** on the **Sort field in ascending order SmartIcon**. The records will be sorted in ascending order.

OR

3b. **Click** on the **Sort field in descending order SmartIcon**. The records will be sorted in descending order.

PRINTING YOUR DATA

Approach allows you to decide how your printed data should look by letting you create reports. Using reports, you can control the format of the report, which fields are included in the report, and whether you want totals.

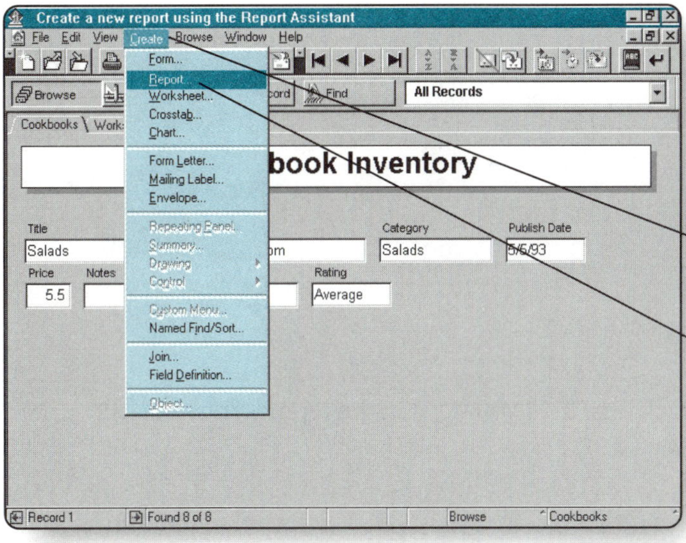

Creating a Report

To create a report, you will use the Report Assistant.

1. **Click** on **Create**. The Create menu will appear.

2. **Click** on **Report**. The Report Assistant will open.

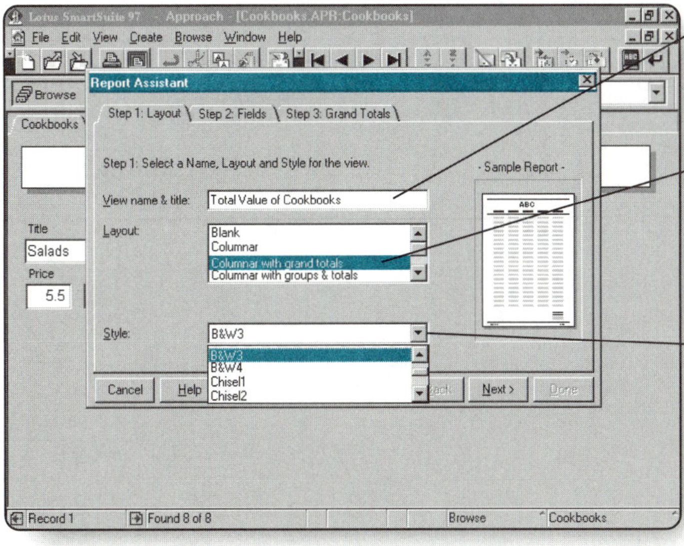

3. **Type** some **text** for the View name & title:. The report will be named.

4. **Click** on a **Layout**: for the report. The layout will be previewed in the Sample Report box.

5. **Click** on the **down arrow** (▼) by the Style: box. A list of available styles will appear.

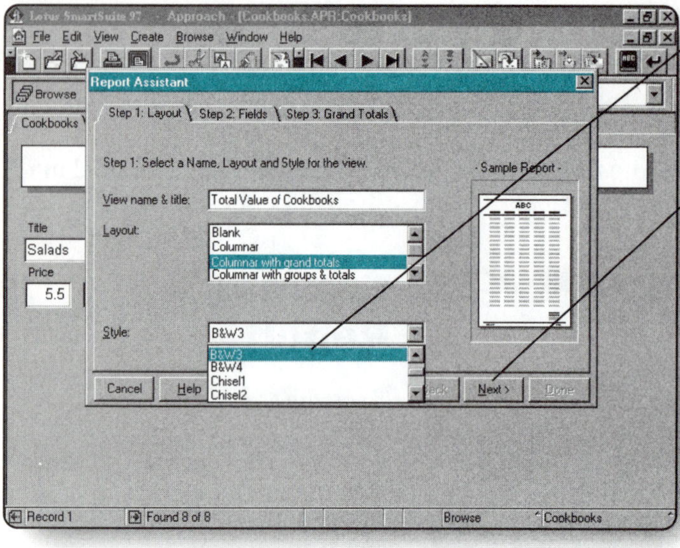

6. Click on the **style** you want. The style will be previewed in the Sample Report box.

7. Click on **Next**. The Step 2 tab will appear.

8. Click on a **field** you want in the report. The field will be selected.

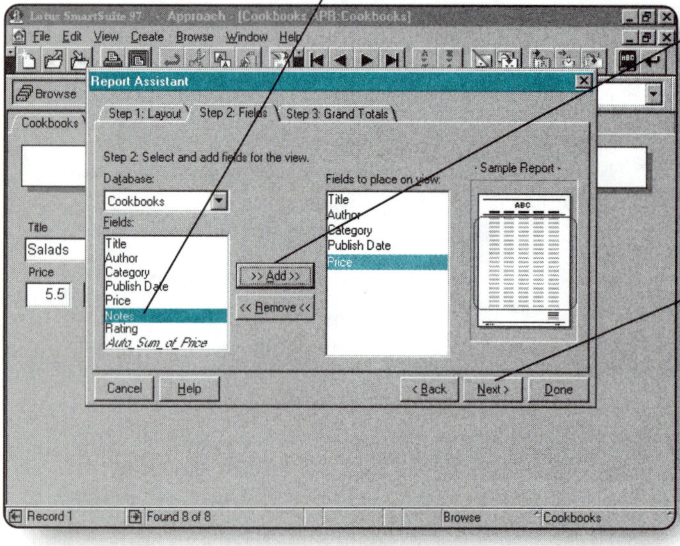

9. Click on the **Add button**. The field will be added to the report.

10. Repeat steps 8 and **9** until all the fields you want in the report are added.

11. Click on **Next**. The Step 3 tab will appear.

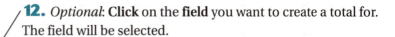

12. *Optional*: **Click** on the **field** you want to create a total for. The field will be selected.

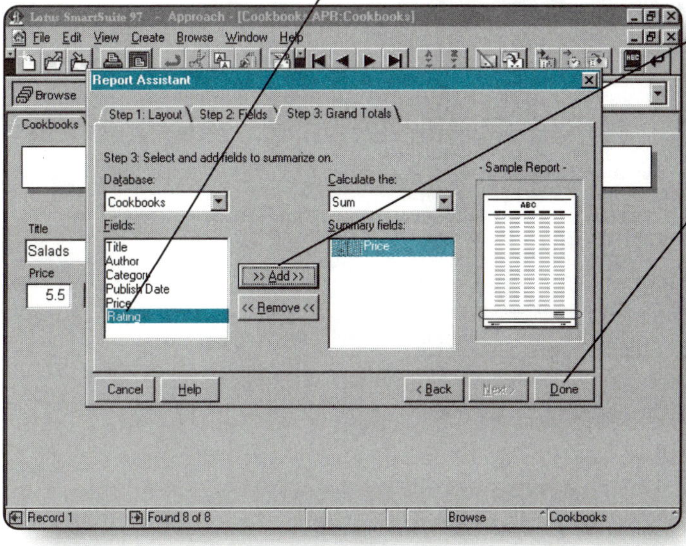

13. *Optional*: **Click** on **Add**. The field will be added as a summary field.

14. **Click** on **Done**. The report will be created.

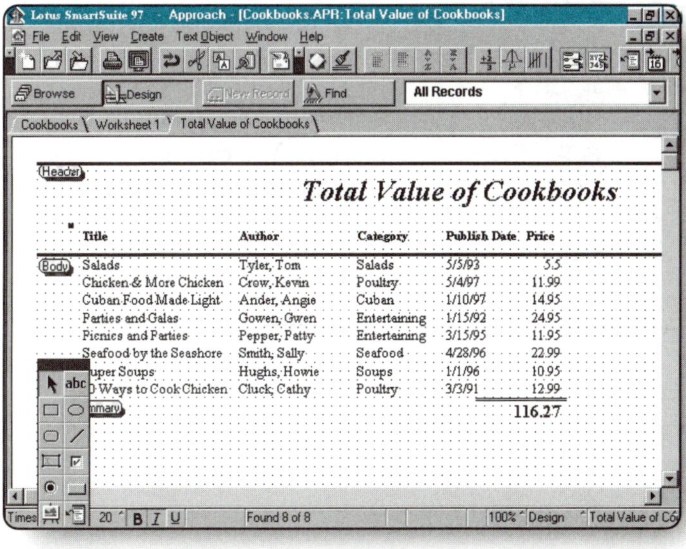

The created report will appear in design mode. You can print the report now.

Printing the Report

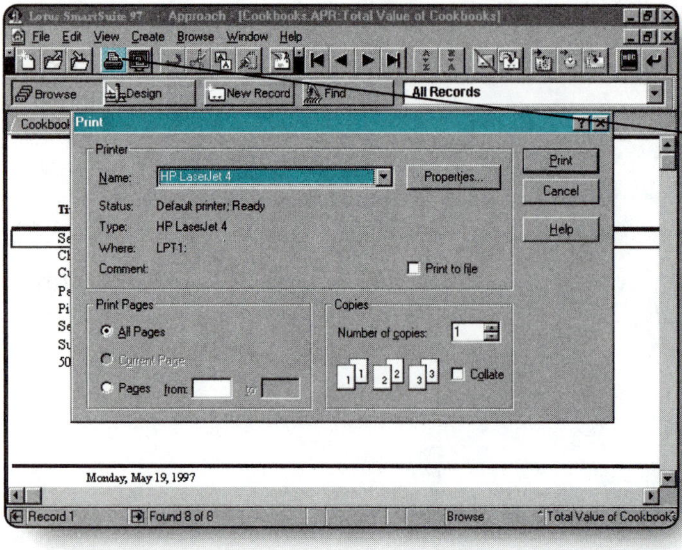

1. **Click** on the **Print SmartIcon**. The Print dialog box will open.

2. **Choose** from the following **options**:

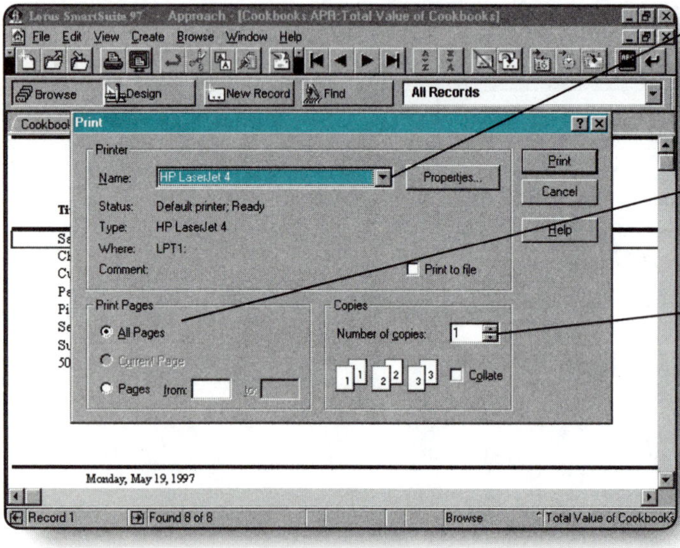

- To choose a different printer, click on the down arrow (▼) by the Name: box and make your selection.
- The preselected range is All Pages. You can also select a different range of pages.
- To print more than one copy, click on the plus and minus buttons.

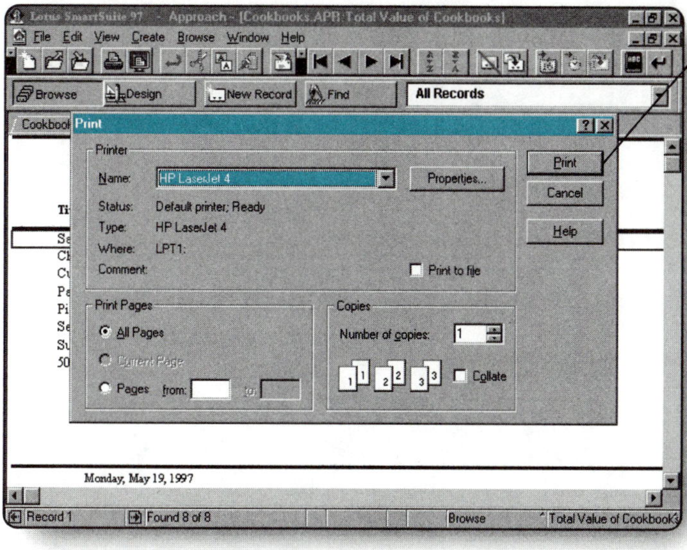

3. Click on **Print**. The report will be sent to the printer.

PART VI REVIEW QUESTIONS

1. **What is the fastest way to create a product inventory database?** ***See "Using Approach's SmartMasters" in Chapter 18***
2. **What is the first step of creating a database?** ***See "Defining Fields" in Chapter 18***
3. **What button do you click to get a blank record?** ***See "Entering Data" in Chapter 18***
4. **How do you get to the next record in your database?** ***See "Navigating Records" in Chapter 18***
5. **How do you change the title on a form?** ***See "Modifying Data " in Chapter 18***
6. **What are the two kinds of sorts available in Approach?** ***See "Sorting Your Data" in Chapter 19***
7. **What is the easiest way to create a find?** ***See "Finding Specific Data" in Chapter 19***
8. **Why would you name a find?** ***See "Naming a Find" in Chapter 19***
9. **What should you do before you print your database?** ***See "Creating a Report" in Chapter 19***
10. **Can you do calculations in reports?** ***See "Creating a Report" in Chapter 19***

PART VII

Using SmartSuite on the Web

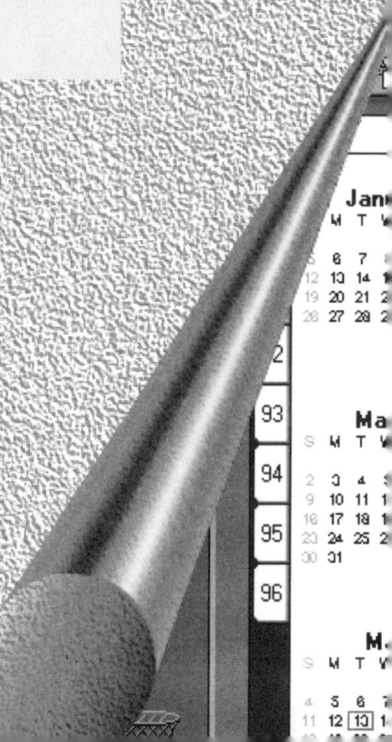

20 Connecting to the Web Using SmartSuite

"Work the Web with SmartSuite" is one of the marketing slogans for SmartSuite. SmartSuite is designed to integrate with the Internet and with your corporate intranet. In this chapter, you'll learn how to:

- Access the Internet from SmartCenter
- Quickly access Lotus's Internet help features
- Use the Internet SmartIcons set

ACCESSING THE INTERNET FROM SMARTCENTER

If you already have defined an Internet connection through Windows 95, SmartCenter automatically prompts you for connection information when it starts.

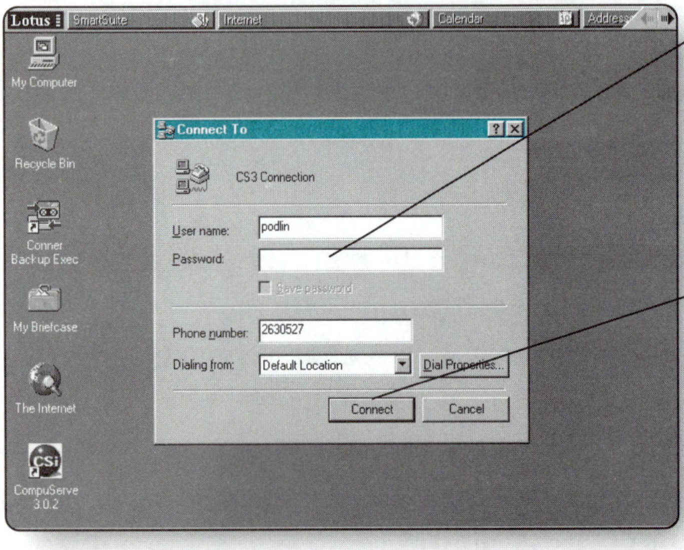

1. **Start SmartCenter**. The Connect To dialog box will appear.

2. **Type** your **password** in the Password: box. Your password will be entered.

3. **Click** on **Connect**. SmartCenter will connect to your service provider.

Using SmartSuite's Web Reference Folder

SmartCenter provides you with the Web Reference folder so that you can search the World Wide Web. Using this folder, you can search for a specific topic, or you can use one of the predefined topics already available in this folder.

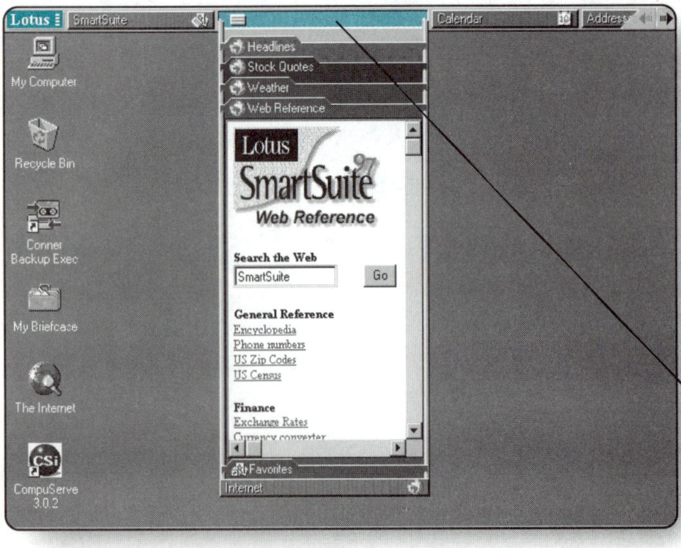

Searching the Web

1. **Click** on the **Internet drawer handle**. The Internet drawer will open.

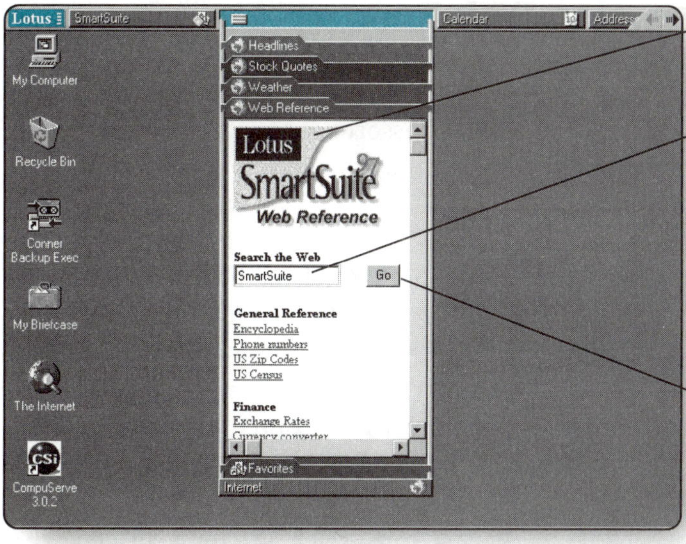

2. **Click** on the **Web Reference folder tab**. The folder will open.

3. **Click** on the **box** under Search the Web. The box will be selected.

4. **Type** the **topic** you want to search for. The topic will be entered.

5. **Click** on **Go**. In a few moments, the results of the search will appear in your Internet Browser.

NOTE

If you have not previously connected to the Internet, the Connect To dialog box will appear at this point. Enter your password and click on Connect.

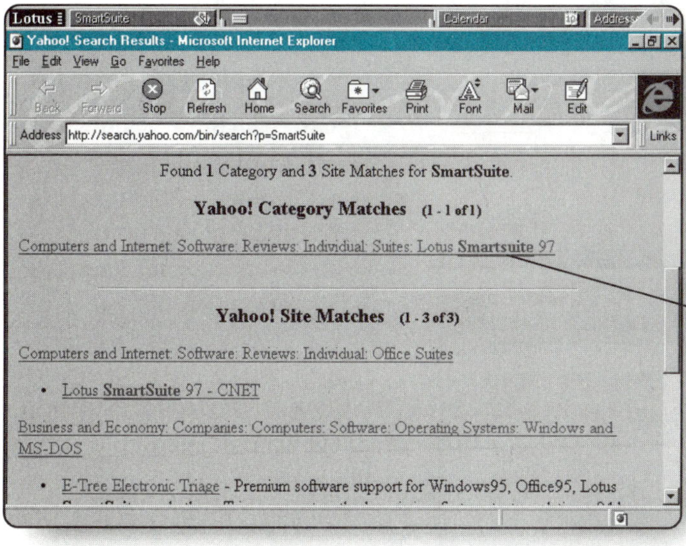

6. **Click** on the **search result** you want to access. The web page will appear.

Accessing Web Reference's Predefined Topics

Web Reference provides an assortment of predefined reference topics including encyclopedias, web artwork, and exchange rates.

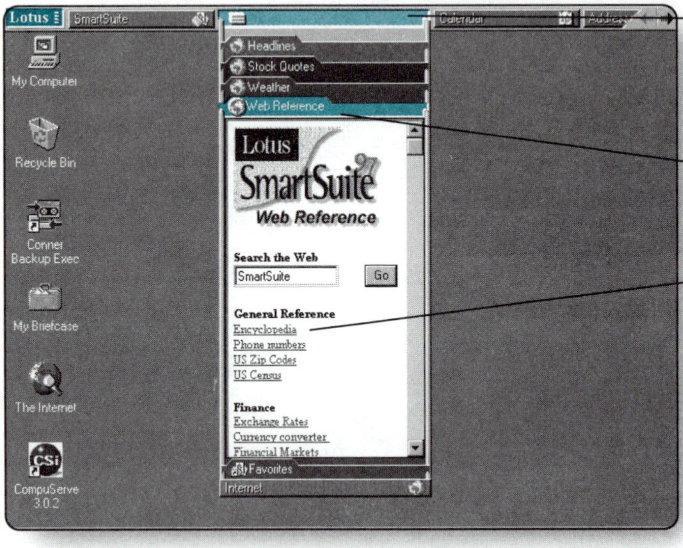

1. Click on the **Internet drawer handle**. The Internet drawer will open.

2. Click on the **Web Reference folder tab**. The folder will open.

3. Click on a **topic**. In a few moments, the matches to that topic will appear in your Internet browser.

> **NOTE**
>
> If you have not previously connected to the Internet, the Connect To dialog box will appear at this point. Enter your password and click on Connect.

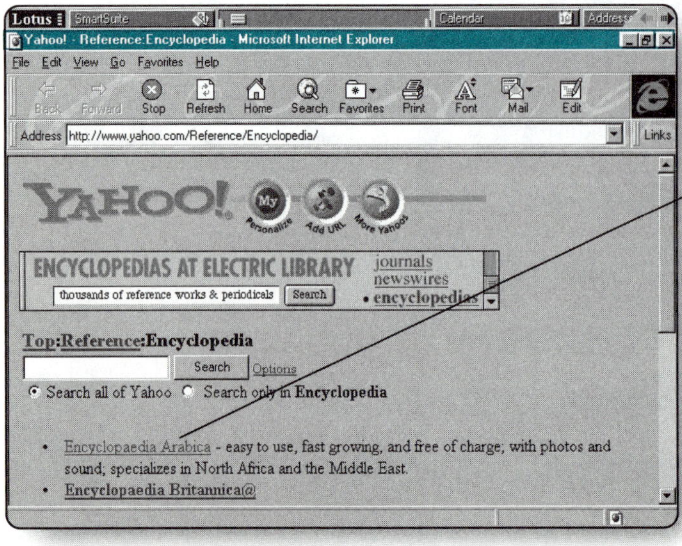

4. Click on the **topic result** you want to access. The web page will appear.

Accessing Your Favorite Sites

SmartCenter is able to read your favorite sites from your Internet browser. Because of this, you can access your favorite sites through the Internet drawer.

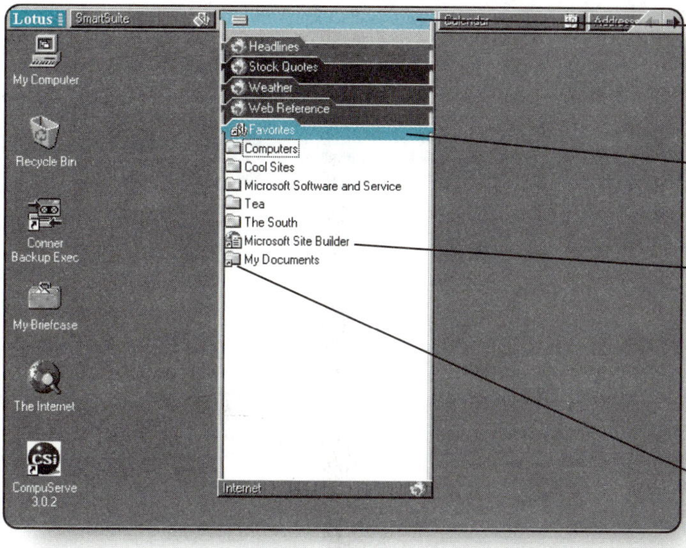

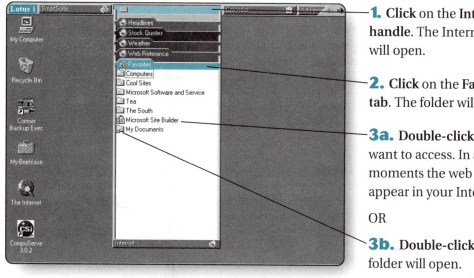

1. **Click** on the **Internet drawer handle**. The Internet drawer will open.
2. **Click** on the **Favorites folder tab**. The folder will open.

3a. Double-click the **site** you want to access. In a few moments the web site will appear in your Internet browser.

OR

3b. Double-click a **folder**. The folder will open.

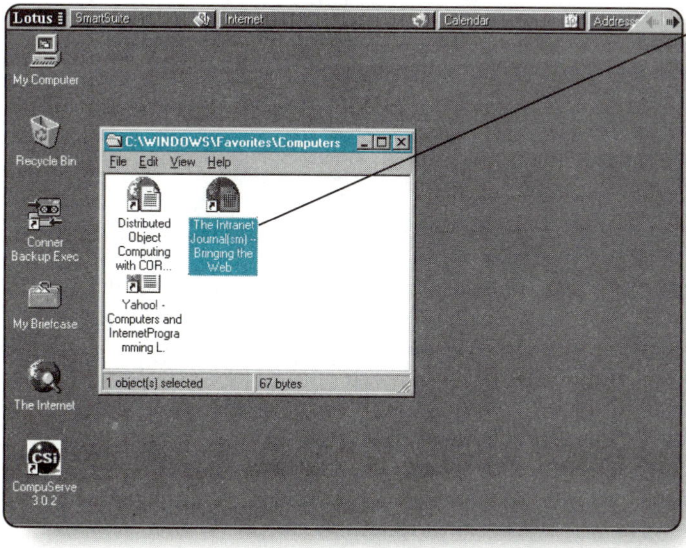

4. **Double-click** the **site** you want to access. In a few moments, the web site will appear in your Internet browser. This step is only required if you performed step 3b.

ACCESS LOTUS'S INTERNET HELP

Lotus SmartSuite's help features are not limited to those that can be accessed from your hard drive or CD-ROM player. SmartSuite is designed to provide additional help via the Internet.

Accessing Lotus's Home Page

If you want general information about Lotus products, access the Lotus home page.

1. **Start** a **SmartSuite application**. The application will open.

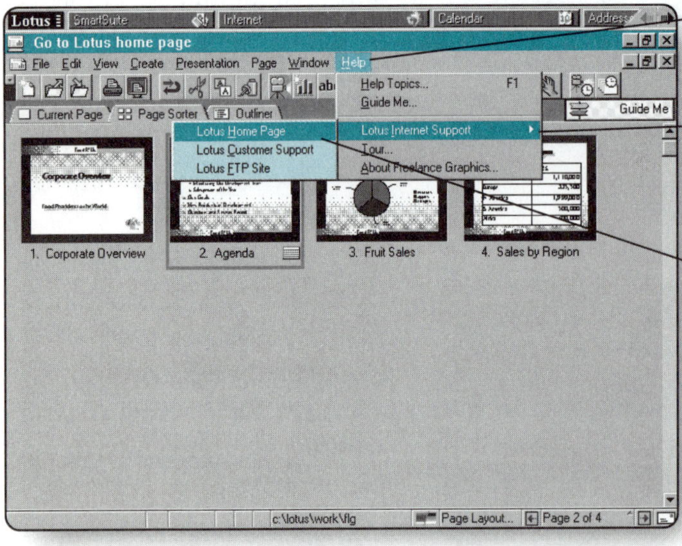

2. **Click** on **Help**. The Help menu will appear.

3. **Click** on **Lotus Internet Support**. The Lotus Internet Support submenu will appear.

4. **Click** on **Lotus Home Page**. In a few moments, the Lotus home page will appear in your Internet browser.

NOTE

If you have not previously connected to the Internet, the Connect To dialog box will appear at this point. Enter your password and click on Connect.

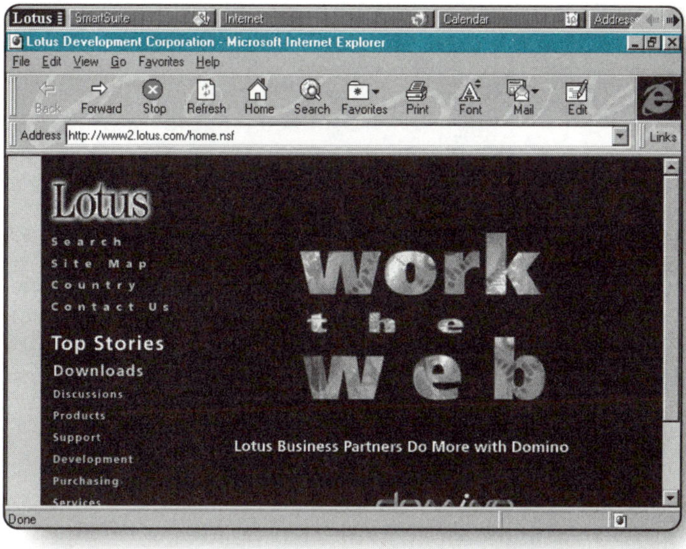

After you have accessed the Lotus home page, you can perform a variety of actions such as get product information and access Lotus support.

Accessing Lotus's Online Customer Support

Lotus's Internet Customer Support site lets you access additional help information.

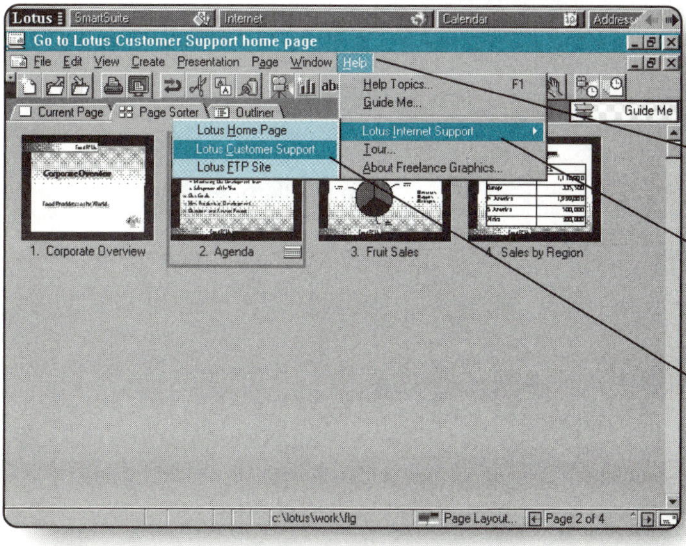

1. **Start** a **SmartSuite application**. The application will open.
2. **Click** on **Help**. The Help menu will appear.
3. **Click** on **Lotus Internet Support**. The Lotus Internet Support submenu will appear.
4. **Click** on **Lotus Customer Support**. In a few moments, the Lotus Customer Support web site will appear.

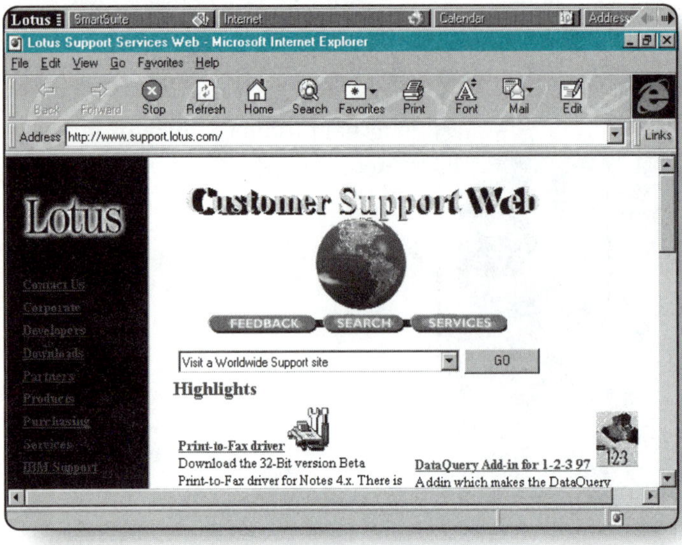

NOTE

If you have not previously connected to the Internet, the Connect To dialog box will appear at this point. Enter your password and click on Connect.

The Lotus Customer Support web site is a great place to get drivers, bug fixes, and add-ins for your Lotus products.

NOTE

If you have not previously connected to the Internet, the Connect To dialog box will appear at this point. Enter your password and click on Connect.

Accessing Lotus's FTP Sites

Lotus's Internet Customer Support site lets you download a variety of documents and other files.

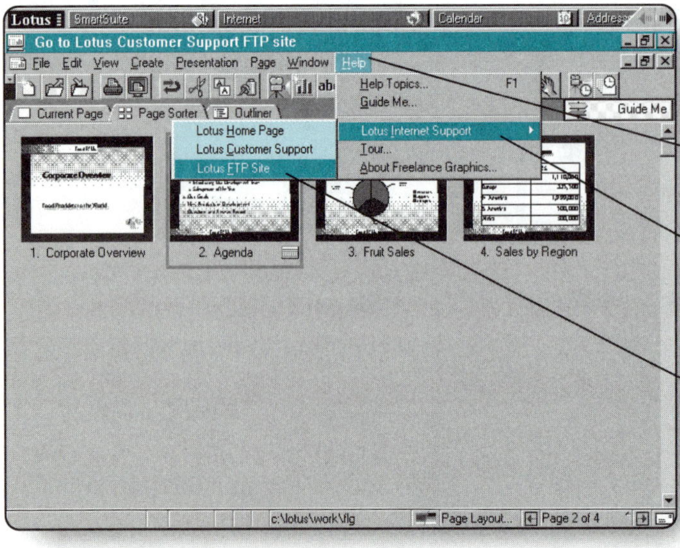

1. **Start a SmartSuite application**. The application will open.
2. **Click** on **Help**. The Help menu will appear.
3. **Click** on **Lotus Internet Support**. The Lotus Internet Support submenu will appear.
4. **Click** on **Lotus FTP Site**. In a few moments, the Lotus FTP site will appear.

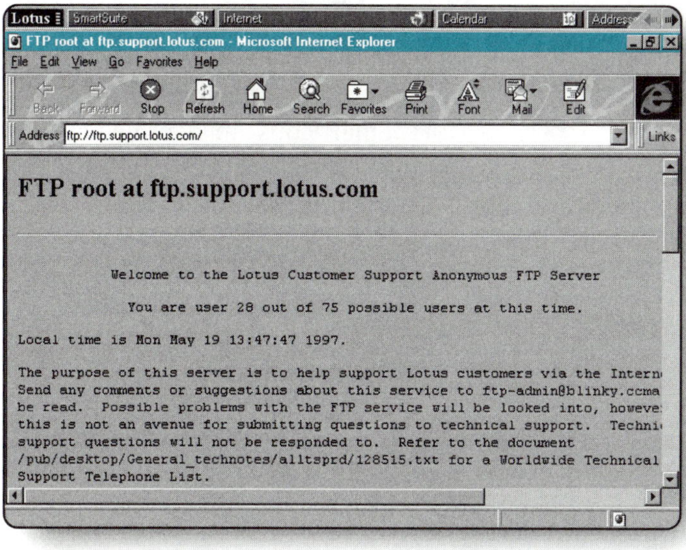

The Lotus FTP site lets you know that it is designed to provide support to Lotus customers. When you scroll through the site's root, you'll find jump points identified by their color and the fact that they are underlined. Click on a jump point to go to that location.

USING THE INTERNET SMARTICONS

If you frequently use SmartSuite's Internet features such as Internet help, you may want to display the Internet SmartIcons set.

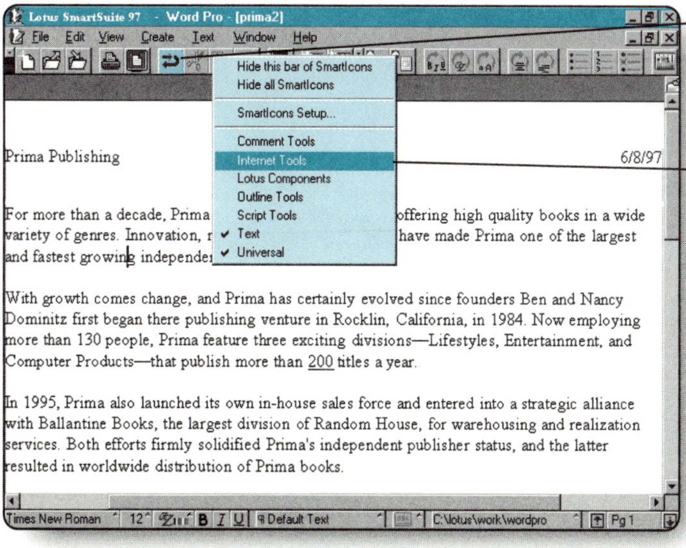

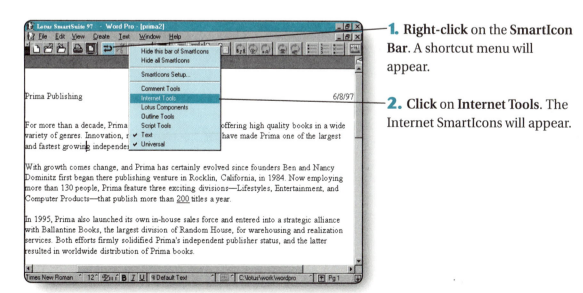

1. **Right-click** on the **SmartIcon Bar**. A shortcut menu will appear.
2. **Click** on **Internet Tools**. The Internet SmartIcons will appear.

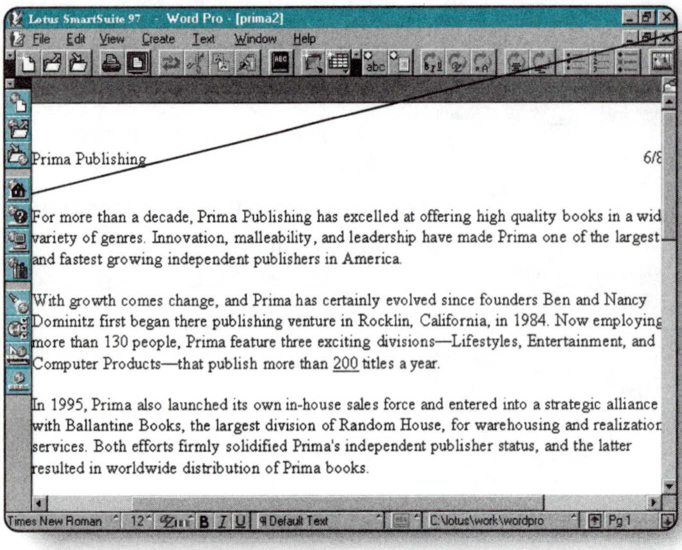

The Internet SmartIcons perform Internet tasks. You'll notice that the Internet SmartIcons are identified by the small world on each of their icons.

21 Using Word Pro to Build a Web Page

The Internet is everywhere you look today. It is becoming difficult to find a book, magazine, printed ad, or even a television ad that doesn't sport an Internet address. If you haven't already, you will probably need to create a personal or corporate web page of your own. Word Pro has the tools to make this task easy. In this chapter, you'll learn how to:

- Build a web page using a Word Pro SmartMaster
- Preview your web page
- Publish your web page

BUILDING A WEB PAGE

Word Pro lets you create a web page without having to know a language such as HTML. Using one of Word Pro's SmartMasters, creating a web page is a process of clicking on predefined areas and optionally adding links.

Selecting an Internet SmartMaster

The first step to creating a web page is selecting the SmartMaster you want to use. You can either select a SmartMaster for creating a corporate or personal web page.

1. Click on the **Create a new document SmartIcon**. The New Document dialog box will open.

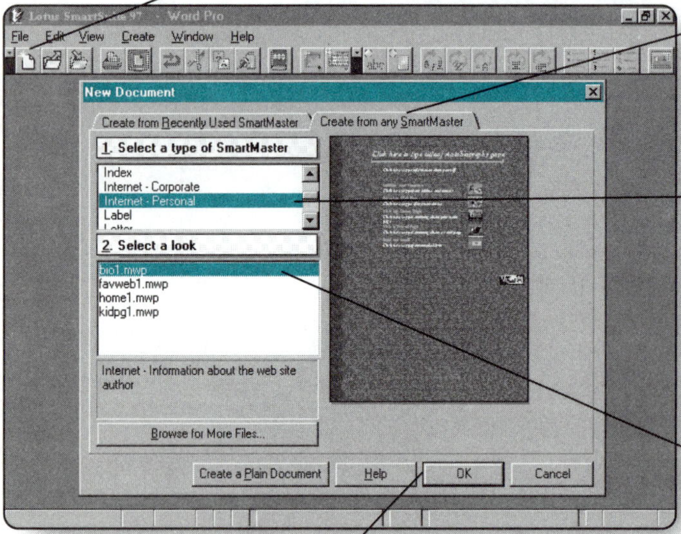

2. Click on the **Create from any SmartMaster tab**. The Create from any SmartMaster tab will appear.

3. Click on the Internet SmartMaster **type** you want. The type will be previewed on the right side of the dialog box.

You can select either Corporate or Personal.

4. Click on a **look**. The look will be previewed on the right side of the dialog box.

5. Click on **OK**. The web page document will be created.

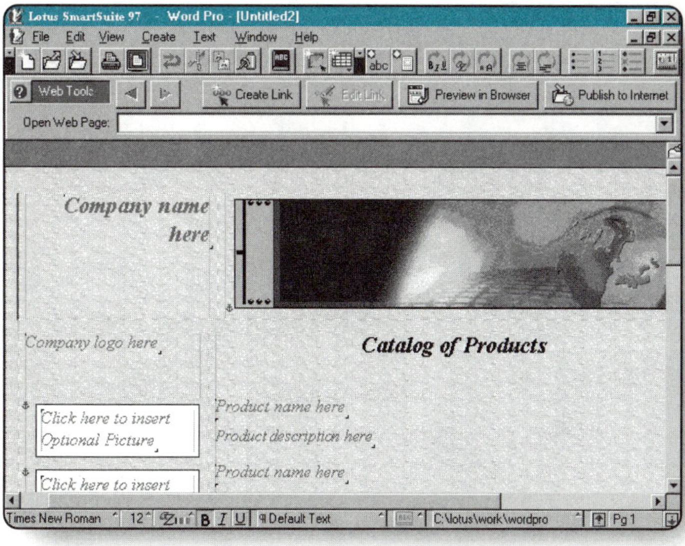

The document that appears has areas for you to customize. You'll see areas that instruct you as to the type of information that should be placed there.

Entering Your Contents

The Internet SmartMasters are designed to assist you in the creation of your web page. These SmartMasters are typically built with Click Here blocks.

Entering the Text of Your Web Page

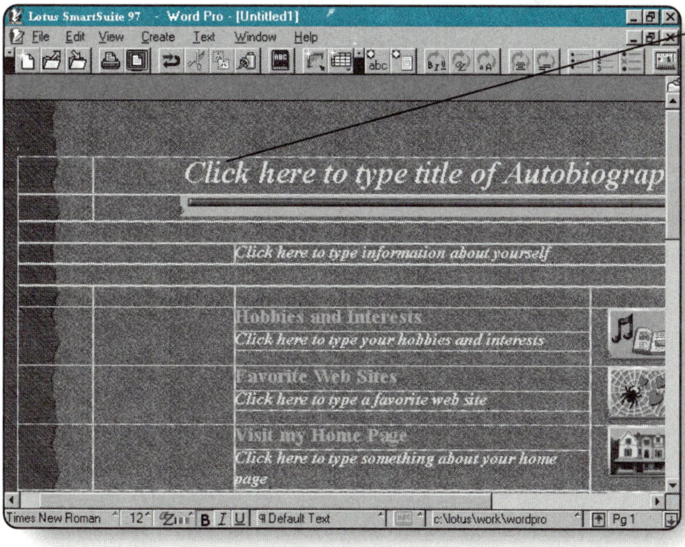

1. **Click** on the word **Click** on a Click here to type block. The area will be placed in edit mode.

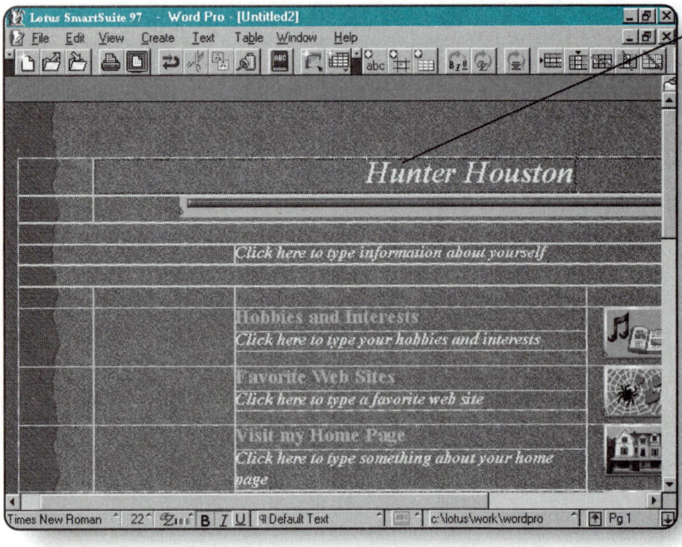

2. Type the **text** for the block. The text will be entered.

3. Repeat steps 1 and **2** until you have entered all the text for your web page.

Don't worry about the Click here blocks you don't use. They will not show up on the final document.

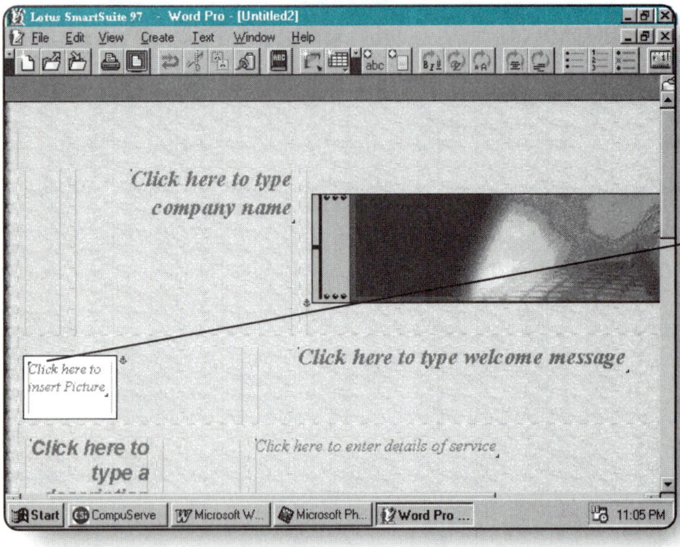

Adding Graphics

Some SmartMasters have graphic Click here blocks defined.

1. Click on the word **Click** of the Click here to insert Picture block. The Import Picture dialog box will open.

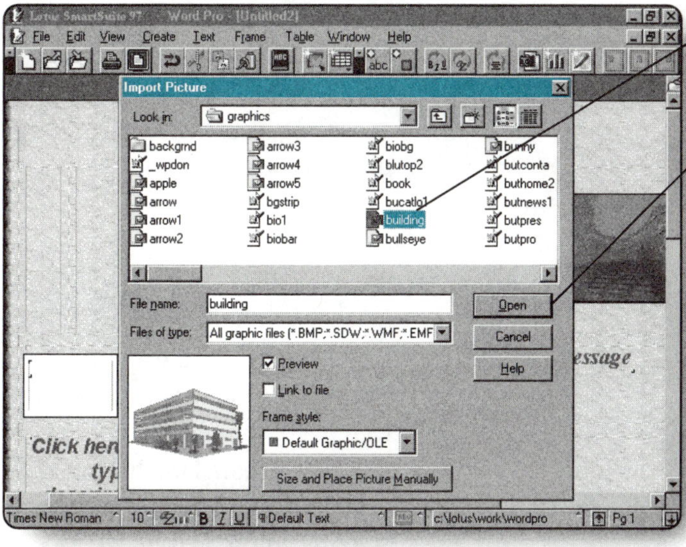

2. **Click** on the **file** you want to use. The file will be selected.

3. **Click** on **Open**. The graphic will be added to your document.

Accessing the Web Authoring Tools

In addition to the Click here blocks found on the Internet SmartMasters, Word Pro provides web authoring tools to make creating a web page easy.

1. **Click** on **File**. The File menu will appear.

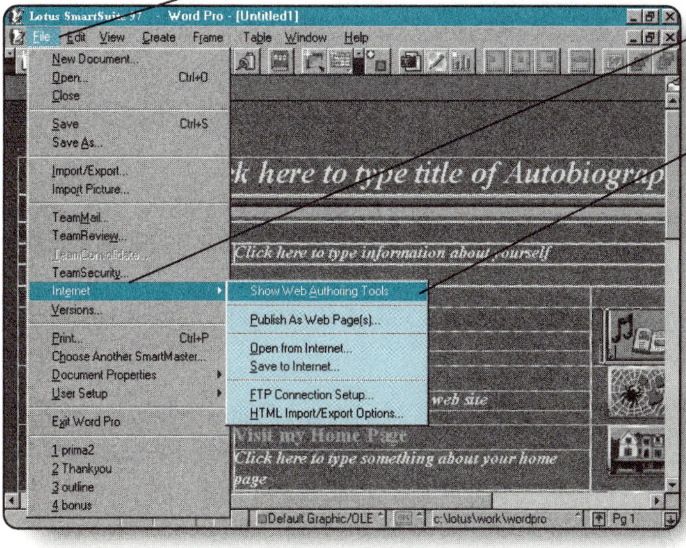

2. **Click** on **Internet**. The Internet submenu will appear.

3. **Click** on **Show Web Authoring Tools**. The Web Tools bar will appear.

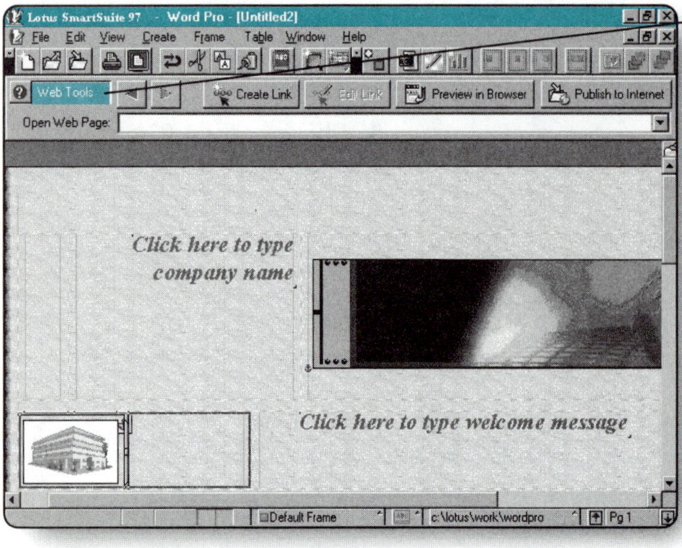

The tools found on the Web Tools bar allow you to perform a variety of tasks including accessing web pages and adding links to your document.

Adding a Link

If you want to create a jump from your web page to another web page, you need to create a link. The Create Link button is available on the Web Tools bar. See preceding section, "Accessing the Web Authoring Tools," to find out how to display the Web Tools bar.

1. **Select** the **item**, either text or graphic, that you want to build the link from.

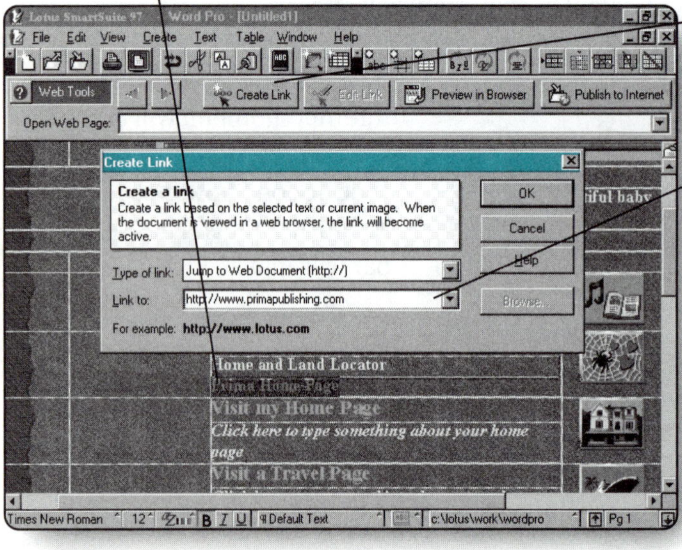

2. **Click** on the **Create Link button**. The Create Link dialog box will appear.

3. **Click** on the **Link to: box**. The box will be selected.

4. **Type** the complete **URL** for the link.

5. **Click** on **OK**. The link will be created.

Don't worry about the color of the text on your page at this point. It will look different on the actual web page.

PREVIEWING YOUR WEB PAGE

> **NOTE**
>
> To preview a web page, you must have Netscape Navigator or Microsoft Internet Explorer installed.

You can preview how your Web page will look before you publish it to the Internet. The page will probably look different than it does in Word Pro. Different browsers will interpret the look of your web page differently.

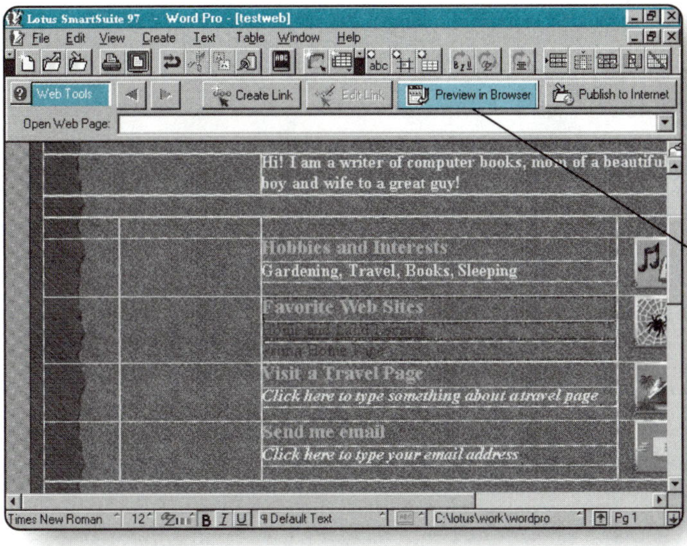

The Create Link button is available on the Web Tools bar. See "Accessing the Web Authoring Tools" earlier in this chapter to find out how to display the Web Tools bar.

1. **Click** on the **Preview in Browser button**. In a few moments, the web page will appear in your web browser.

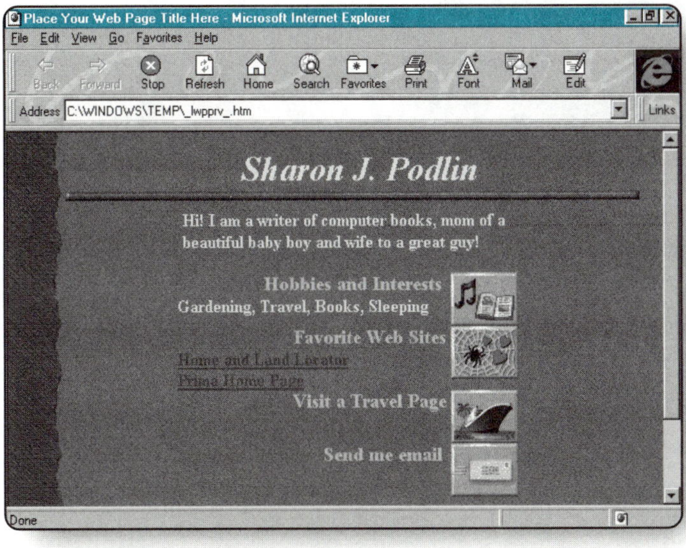

Previewing the web page lets you decide whether you need to change the look of the page or add more text or graphics.

PUBLISHING YOUR WEB PAGE

After your web page is completed, you are ready to publish it. Publishing a web page has several requirements:

- ✦ Your computer and the server where you plan to save your web page must both be connected to the Internet.
- ✦ You must have a WinSock-compatible TCP/IP stack installed on your computer.
- ✦ The server where the page is to be saved must meet one of the following criteria: It must be a public web server; it must support anonymous FTP; or it must support FTP. You must also have an account with permission to access files on the server.

The Publish to Internet button is available on the Web Tools bar. See "Accessing the Web Authoring Tools" earlier in this chapter to find out how to display the Web Tools bar.

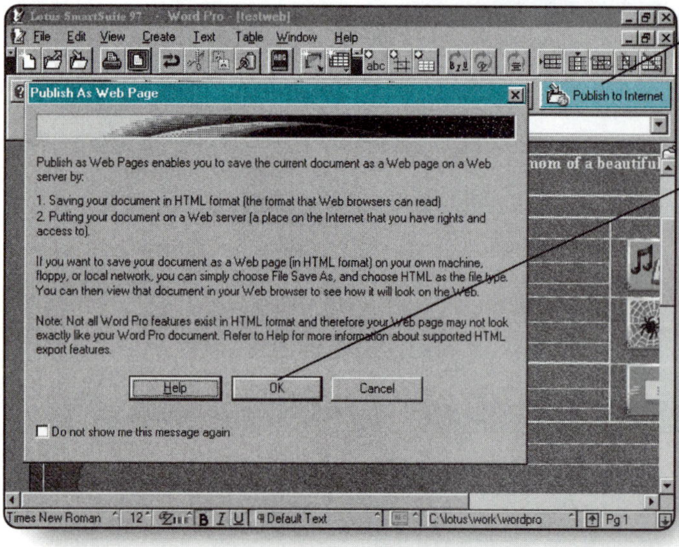

1. **Click** on the **Publish to Internet button**. The Publish as Web Page dialog box will open.
2. **Click** on **OK**. The Save to Internet dialog box will open.

3. Click on a **host domain name or description** from the FTP Servers: box. The server will be selected.

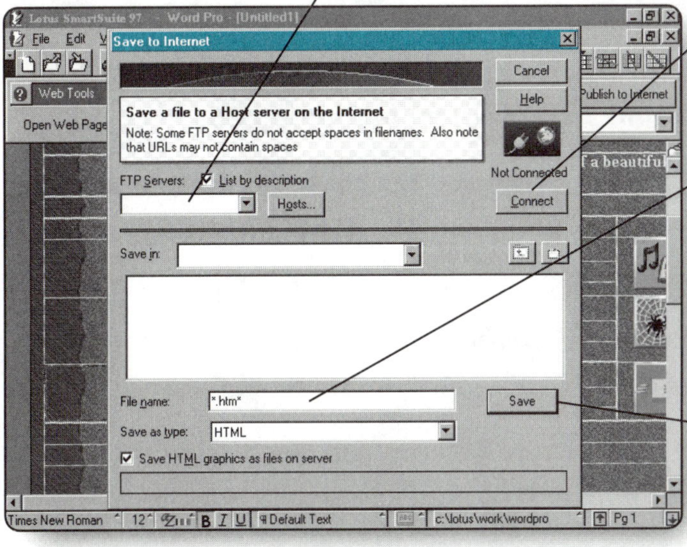

4. Click on **Connect**. A connection to the host will be made.

5. Click on the **File name:** box. The text box will be selected.

6. Type the **name** of the file. The name will be entered into the File name: box.

7. Click on **Save**. The file will be saved to the server.

PART VII REVIEW QUESTIONS

1. **How do you connect to the Internet using SmartCenter?** ***See "Accessing the Internet from SmartCenter" in Chapter 20***
2. **How do you connect to the Lotus home page using a SmartSuite Application?** ***See "Accessing Lotus's Home Page" in Chapter 20***
3. **Where would you find drivers, bug fixes, and add-ins for SmartSuite applications?** ***See "Accessing Lotus's Online Customer Support" in Chapter 20***
4. **How do you display the Internet SmartIcons set?** ***See "Using the Internet SmartIcons" in Chapter 20***
5. **What SmartSuite Application can be used to create a web page?** ***See "Building a Web Page" in Chapter 21***
6. **What two SmartMasters should you select from when you are creating a web page?** ***See "Selecting an Internet SmartMaster" in Chapter 21***
7. **Do you have to know HTML to create a Web page using Word Pro?** ***See "Building a Web Page" in Chapter 21***
8. **How do you add a jump to an Internet address from your web page?** ***See "Adding a Link" in Chapter 21***
9. **What must be displayed before you can create a link?** ***See "Adding a Link" in Chapter 21***
10. **What are the two Internet browsers that you can use to preview your web page?** ***See "Previewing Your Web Page" in Chapter 21***

PART VIII

Appendixes

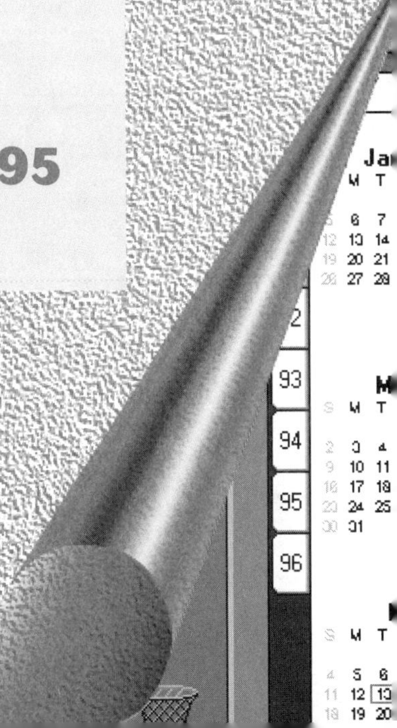

A Creating a Letter Using Word Pro's Letter1 Template

The Letter1 template is a good template to use to create professional letters. This template provides the basic elements needed to create a standard document. It inserts standard text for you and provides areas for you to enter text. In this appendix, you'll learn how to:

- Create a letter using the Letter1 template
- Use Click here blocks
- Print a letter
- Save a letter

CREATING A LETTER USING THE LETTER1 TEMPLATE

1. **Click** on the **Create a new document SmartIcon**. The New Document dialog box will open.

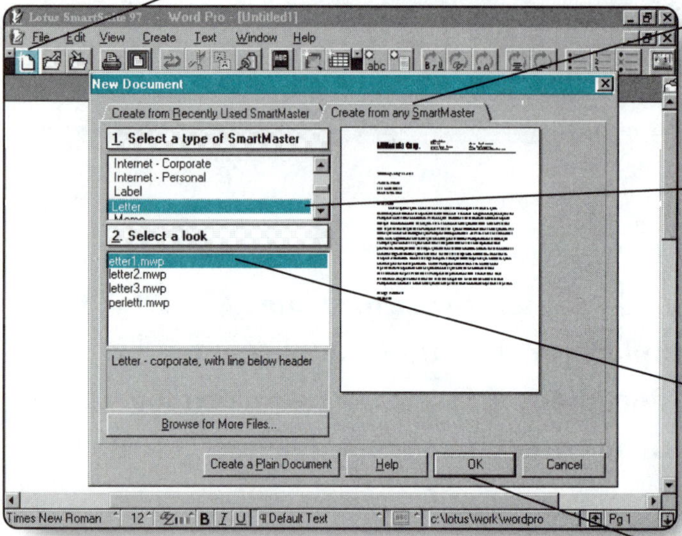

2. **Click** on the **Create from any SmartMaster tab**. The Create from any SmartMaster tab will appear.

3. **Click** on **Letter** from the Select a type of SmartMaster list box. The document will be previewed on the right side of the dialog box.

4. **Click** on **letter1.mwp** from the Select a look box. The look will be previewed on the right side of the dialog box.

5. **Click** on **OK**. The document will be created.

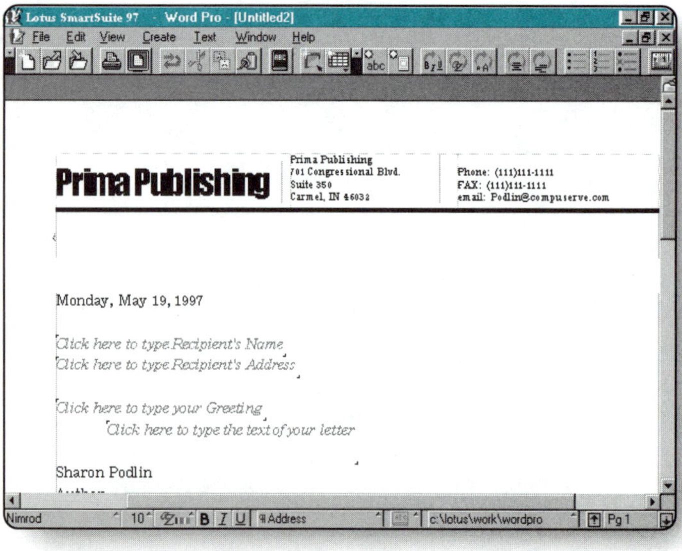

As the letter is created, the SmartMaster automatically inserts your company name, company address, phone numbers, current date, and your name into the letter.

USING CLICK HERE BLOCKS

Click here blocks instruct you where to type text and what kind of text to type.

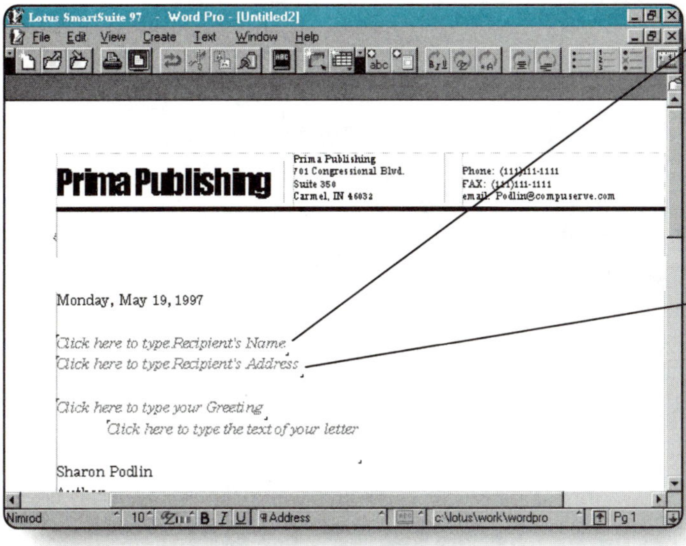

1. **Click** on **Click here to type Recipient's Name**. The block will be selected.
2. **Type** the **recipient's name**. The name will be added to the letter.
3. **Press** the **Tab key**. The Click here to type Recipient's Address block will be selected.
4. **Type** the **recipient's address**. The address will be added to the letter.

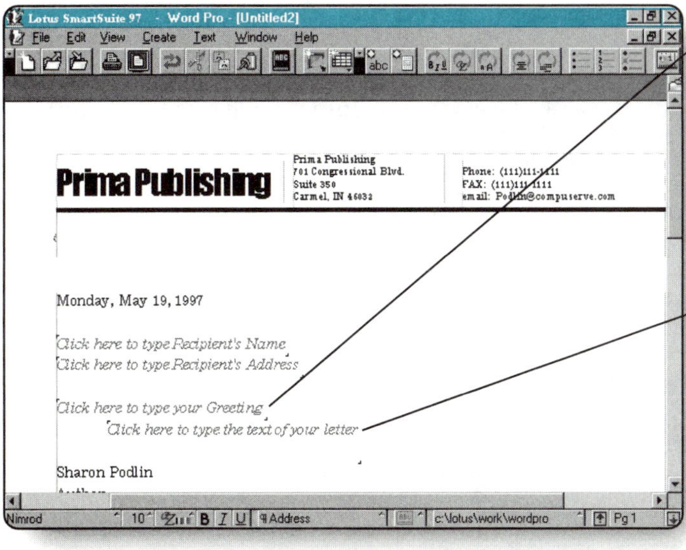

5. **Press** the **Tab key**. The Click here to type your Greeting block will be selected.
6. **Type** your **greeting**. The greeting will be added to the letter.
7. **Press** the **Tab key**. The Click here to type the text of your letter block will be selected.
8. **Type** the **text** of your letter. The text will be added to the letter.

SAVING YOUR LETTER

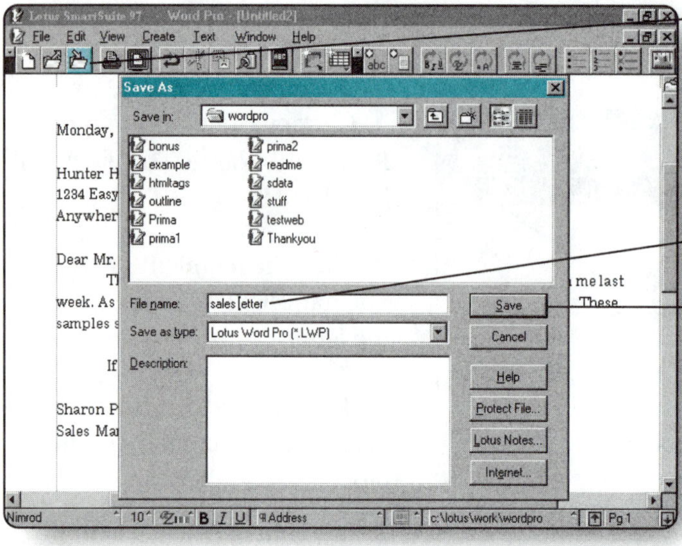

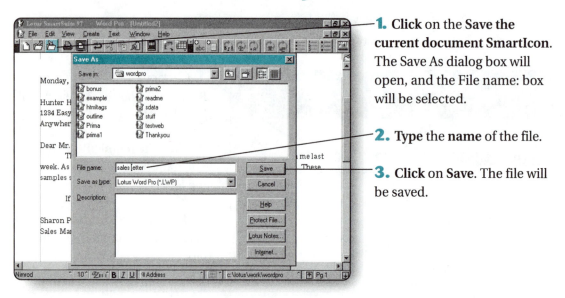

1. **Click** on the **Save the current document SmartIcon.** The Save As dialog box will open, and the File name: box will be selected.
2. **Type** the **name** of the file.
3. **Click** on **Save**. The file will be saved.

PRINTING THE LETTER

1. **Click** on the **Print SmartIcon**. The Print dialog box will open.

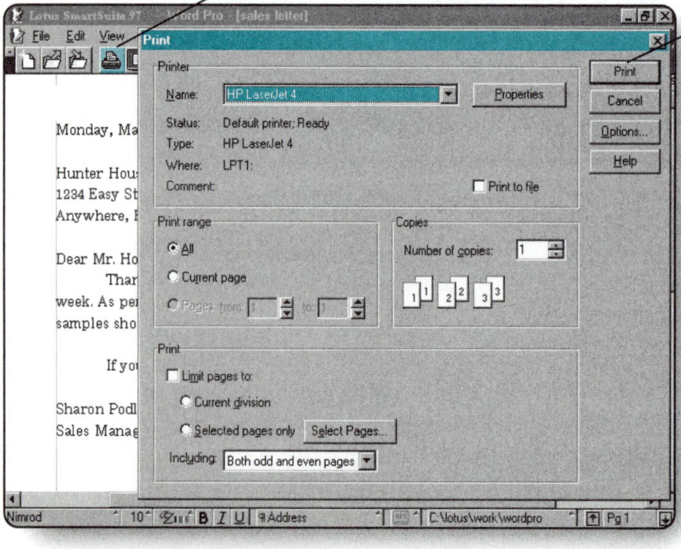

2. **Click** on **Print**. The document will be sent to your printer.

B Creating a Budget Using 1-2-3

1-2-3 has a SmartMaster called personal budget. As you can guess from its name, this SmartMaster is used to create a personal budget. It has sheets for entering the amount you spend on credit cards, utilities, cars, and so on. In this appendix, you'll learn how to:

- Use the personal budget SmartMaster
- Work with multiple sheets
- Print a single sheet of a workbook

USING THE PERSONAL BUDGET SMARTMASTER

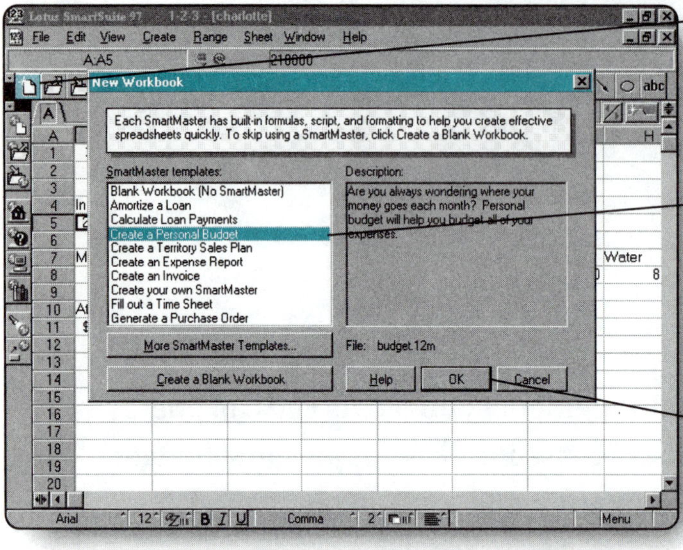

1. **Click** on the **Create a new workbook SmartIcon**. The New Workbook dialog box will appear.
2. **Click** on **Create a Personal Budget** from the SmartMaster templates: list box. A description of the selected SmartMaster will appear in the Description: box.
3. **Click** on **OK**. The new workbook will be created.

Entering Income Information

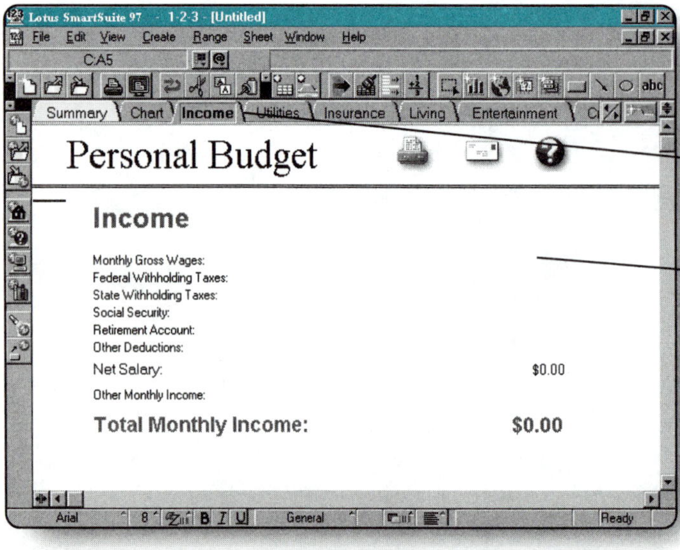

The Income sheet is used to enter your wage and withholding information.

1. **Click** on the **Income tab**. The Income sheet will appear.
2. **Click** on the **yellow cell** next to **Monthly Gross Wages: (G9)**. The cell will be selected.
3. **Type** your **monthly gross wages**. The number will be entered into the cell.

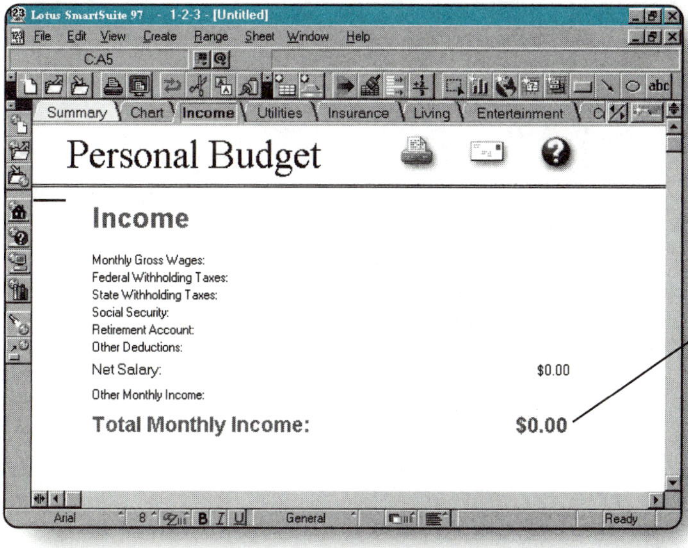

4. **Press** the **down arrow key** on the keyboard. The next cell will be selected.

5. **Type** your **federal withholding taxes**. The number will be entered into the cell.

6. **Continue pressing** the **down arrow key** and entering the requested information. The Total Monthly Income will be calculated automatically.

Entering the Utilities Data

The next sheet you'll want to use is the Utilities sheet. Use this sheet to enter all utility information. Your average monthly utility expenses will be calculated for you.

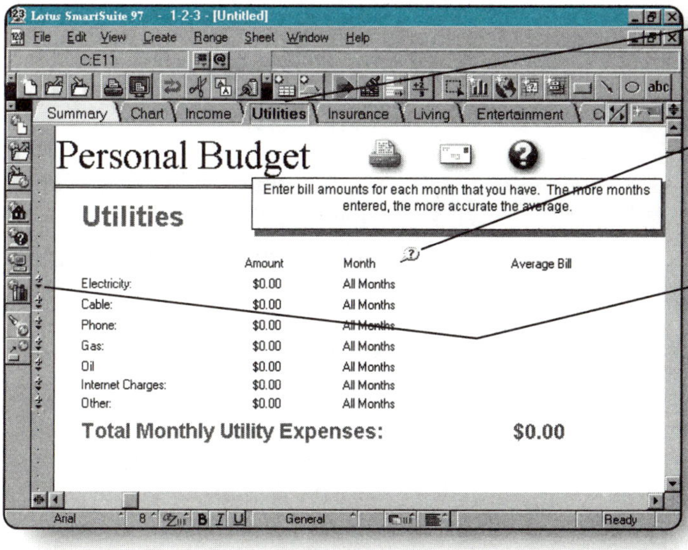

1. **Click** on the **Utilities tab**. The Utilities tab will appear.

2. **Click** on the **question mark icon**. A box will appear with additional explanatory text in it.

3. **Click** on the + next to Electricity. All the months will appear.

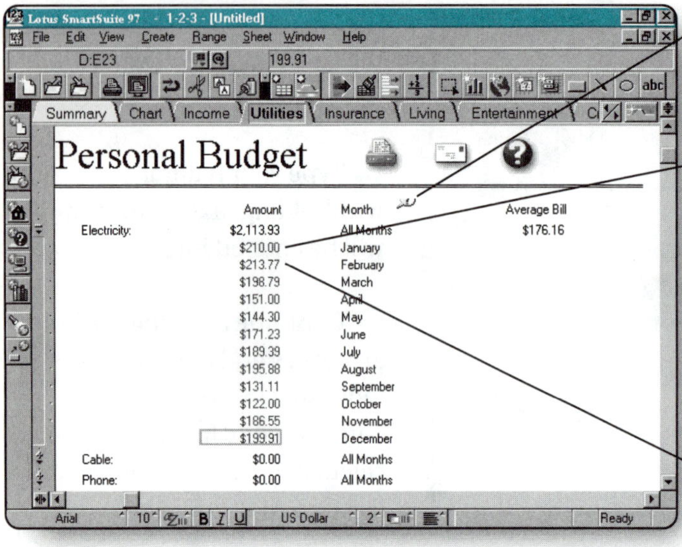

4. **Click** on the **question mark icon**. The explanatory text will disappear.

5. **Click** on the **yellow cell** to the left of January. The cell will be selected.

6. **Type** the **amount for electricity for January**. The number will be entered into the sheet.

7. **Press** the **down arrow key**. The next cell will be selected.

8. **Continue entering amounts** and **pressing the down arrow key** until all the months have been entered.

9. **Continue clicking** the + next to the different utilities and **entering data**. The average monthly utility expense will be calculated for you.

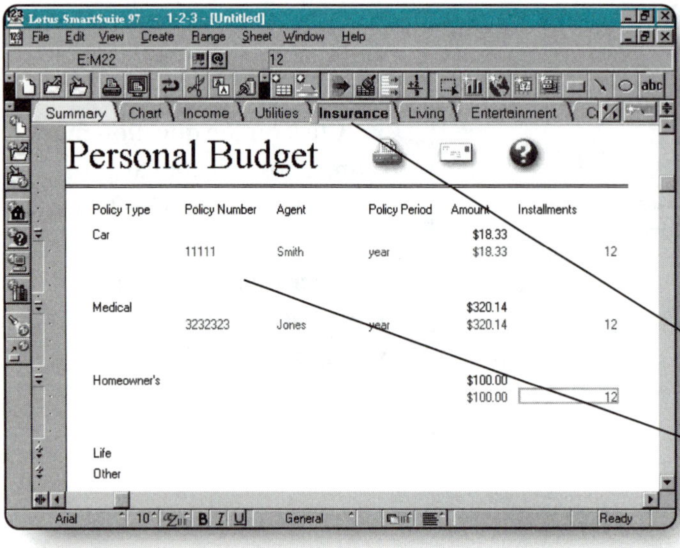

Entering Insurance Expenses

The Insurance sheet is used to enter all your insurance expenses including car, medical, homeowner's, and life.

1. **Click** on the **Insurance tab**. The Insurance tab will appear.

2. **Type** the appropriate **information** in the **yellow cells**. The monthly insurance expense will be calculated for you.

Entering Living Expenses

The next sheet you'll work with is the Living sheet. The Living sheet is used to enter expenses such as rent or mortgage, car payments, groceries, and so on.

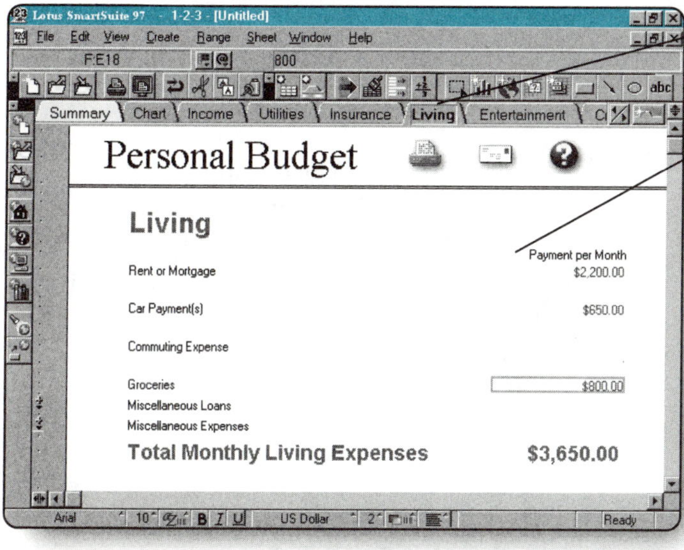

1. **Click** on the **Living tab**. The Living tab will appear.
2. **Type** the appropriate **information** in the **yellow cells**. The monthly living expense will be calculated for you.

Entering Entertainment Expenses

One expense frequently overlooked in a budget is entertainment expense. The Entertainment sheet is used to enter expenses such as dining out, movies, and vacations.

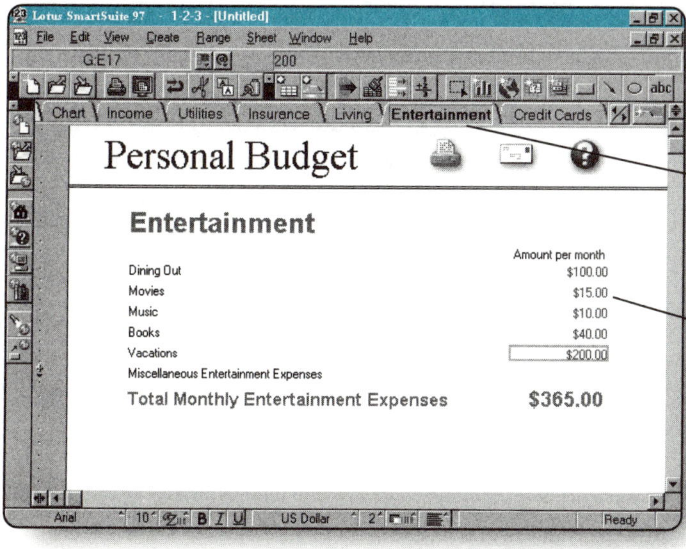

1. **Click** on the **Entertainment tab**. The Entertainment tab will appear.
2. **Type** the appropriate **information** in the **yellow cells**. The entertainment expense will be calculated for you.

Entering Credit Card Payments

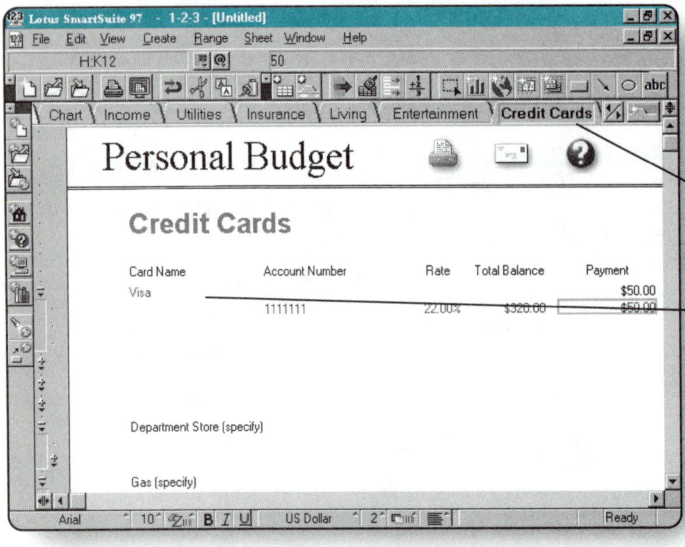

For many of us, credit cards are a way of life. Use the Credit Cards sheet to enter the amount you pay monthly on credit cards.

1. Click on the **Credit Cards tab.** The Credit Cards tab will appear.

2. Type the appropriate **information** in the **yellow cells.** Your monthly credit card payments will be calculated for you.

VIEWING THE BUDGET SUMMARY

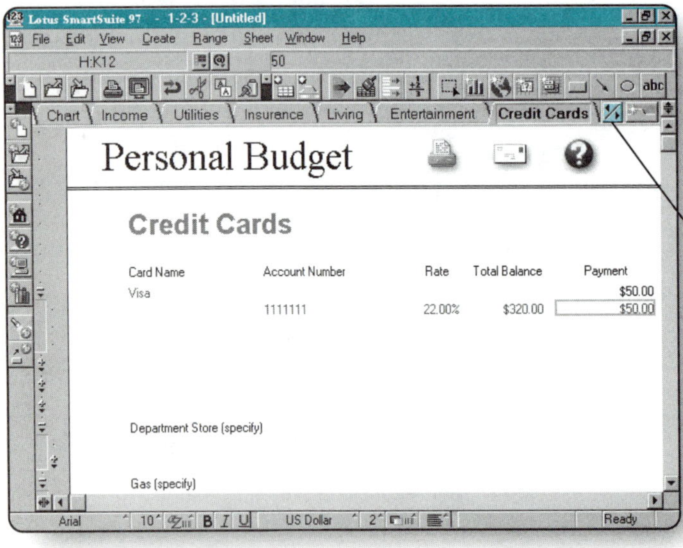

The Summary sheet allows you to view the summary information for your budget. It also allows you to enter variance values so that you can create a best or worst case scenario.

1. Repeatedly click on the **left tab-scroll arrow** until you can see the Summary tab.

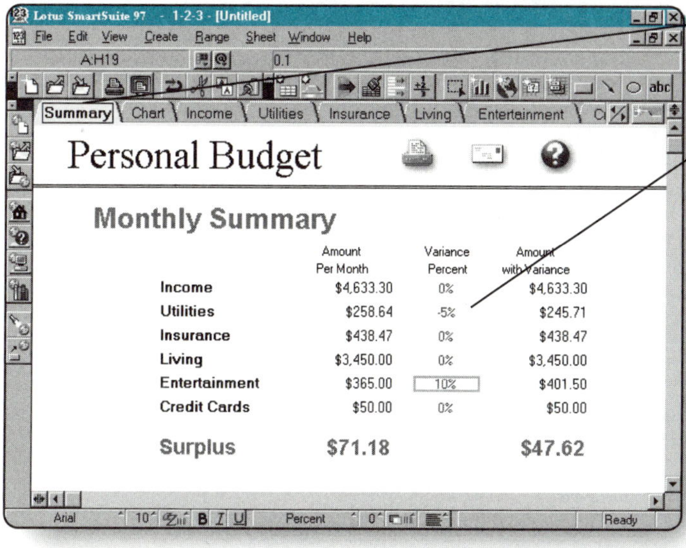

2. **Click** on the **Summary tab**. The Summary tab will appear.

3. *Optional*: **type** variance values in the **yellow cells**. The numbers will be entered in the cells.

The values entered represent a percentage.

PRINTING A SUMMARY SHEET

You may not want to print out all the sheets in this workbook. Instead, you may want to just print the summary sheet.

1. **Click** on the **Print SmartIcon**. The Print dialog box will appear.

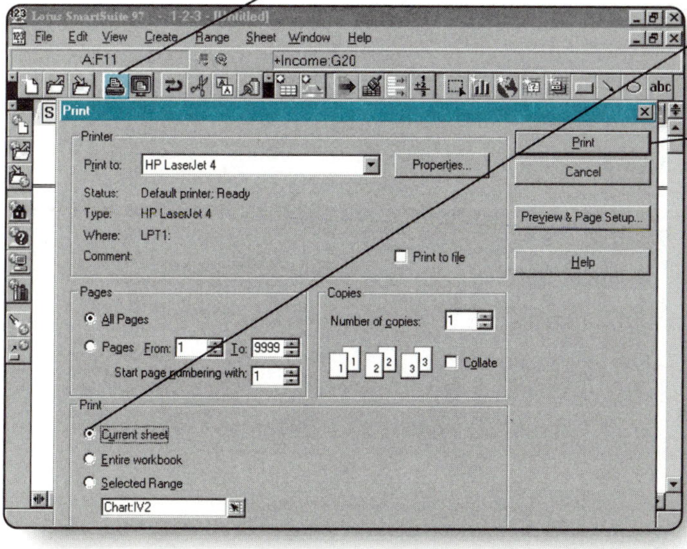

2. **Click** on **Current Sheet**. The current sheet will be selected.

3. **Click** on **Print**. The sheet will be sent to the printer.

C Creating a Meeting Presentation Using Freelance and Content Pages

Using Freelance's Meeting – Standard SmartMaster is a quick way to create a presentation for your next meeting. This SmartMaster has a series of content pages designed to facilitate a standard meeting presentation. In this appendix, you'll learn how to:

- Create a presentation using the Meeting - Standard SmartMaster
- Use content pages
- Add new pages to a presentation

CREATING A PRESENTATION USING THE MEETING – STANDARD SMARTMASTER

1. **Click** on the **Create a new presentation SmartIcon**. The New Presentation dialog box will open.

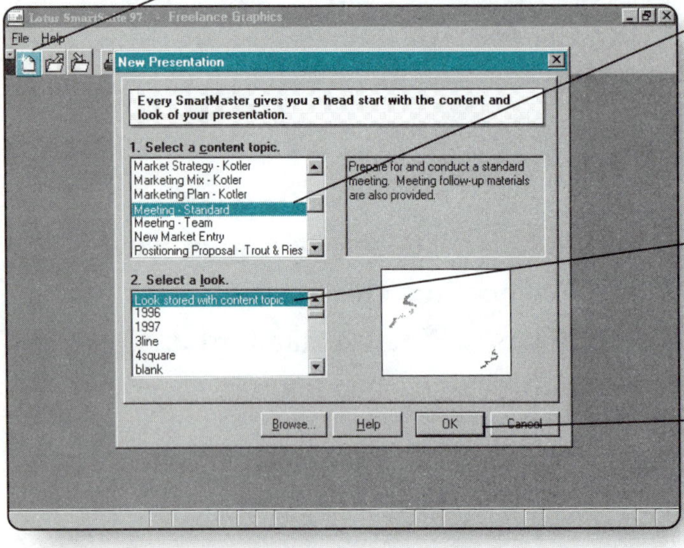

2. **Click** on **Meeting – Standard** from the Select a content topic. list box. The presentation will be previewed in the lower right corner of the dialog box.

3. **Click** on a **look** from the Select a look. list box. The look will be applied to the presentation.

4. **Click** on **OK**. The Welcome! message box will appear.

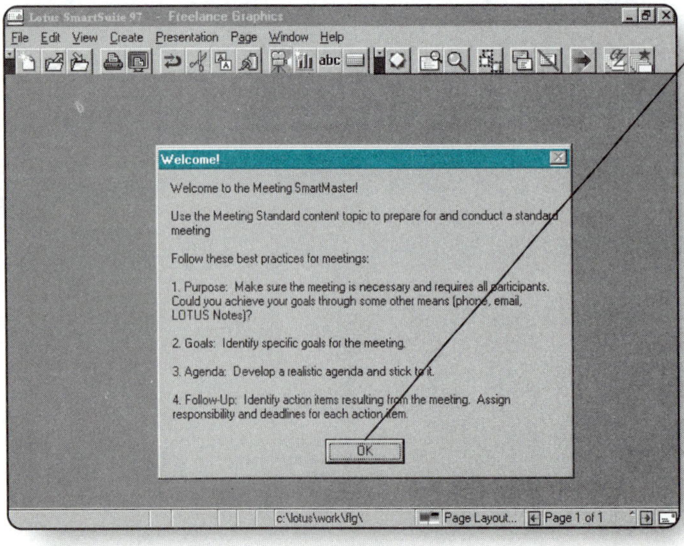

5. **Click** on **OK**. The New Page dialog box will open.

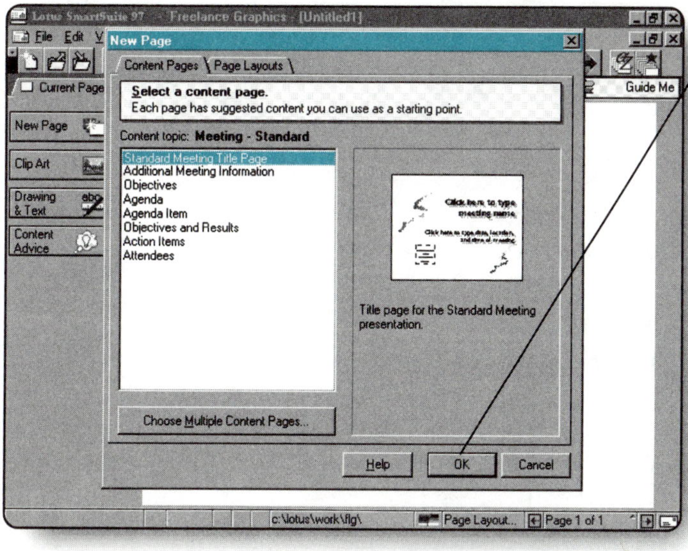

6. Click on **OK**. The Standard Meeting Title page will be added to the presentation.

ADDING TEXT AND GRAPHICS TO A PAGE

The content page will contain Click here blocks on it to guide you in text and graphic placement.

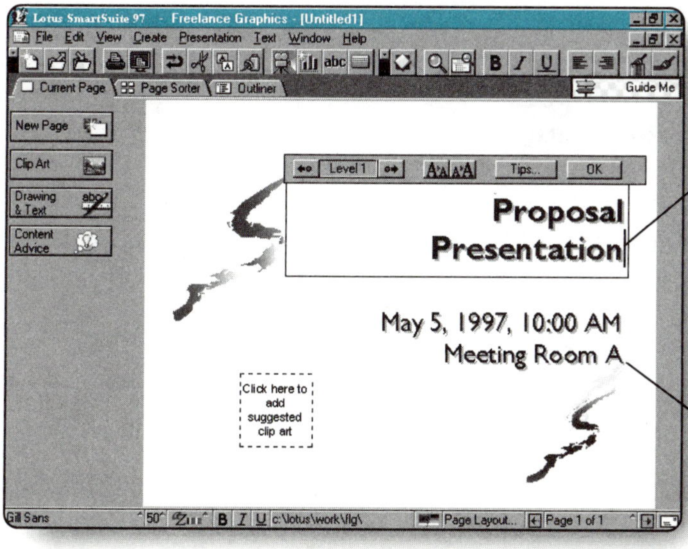

1. Click on the **first Click here block**. The block will be placed in edit mode.

2. Type the **text** for the subject of the meeting. The text will be entered into the block.

3. Click on the **second Click here block**. The block will be placed in Edit mode.

4. Type the **date, time, and location** of the meeting. The text will be entered into the block.

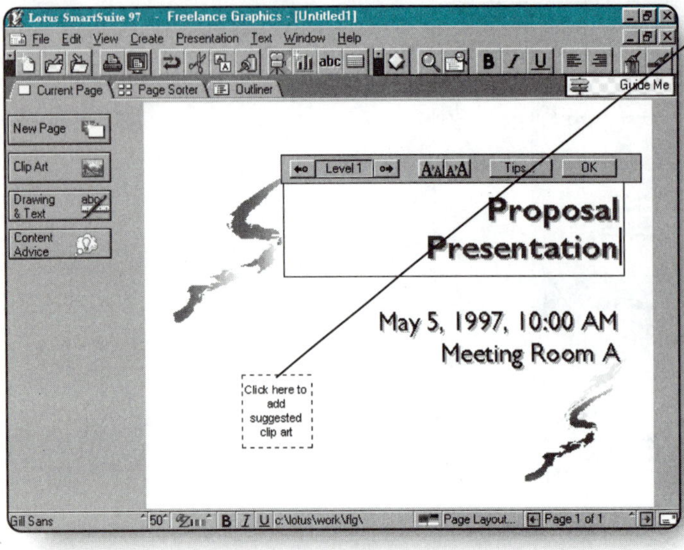

5. Click on the **final Click here block**. The Add Clip Art or Diagram to the Page dialog box will open.

6. Click on the **picture** you want. The picture will be selected.

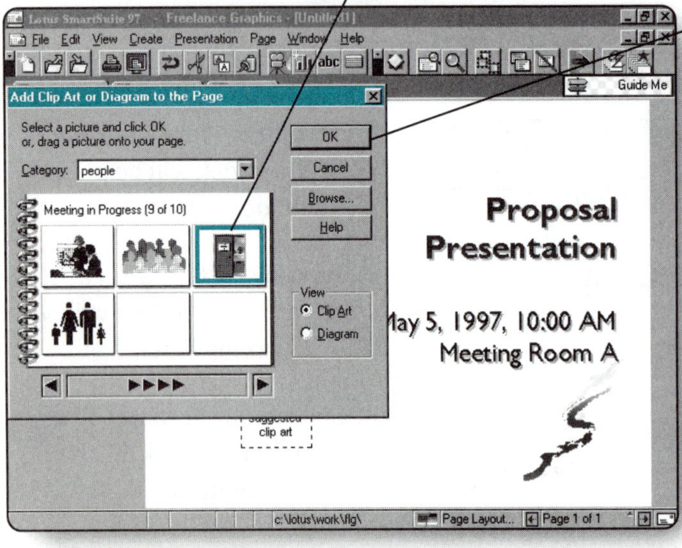

7. Click on **OK**. The page will be completed.

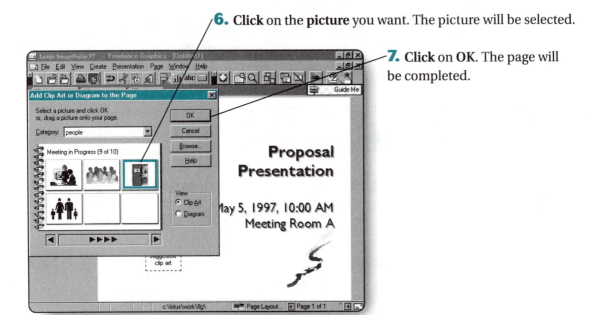

ADDING PAGES TO THE PRESENTATION

1. Click on the **New Page button**. The New Page dialog box will open.

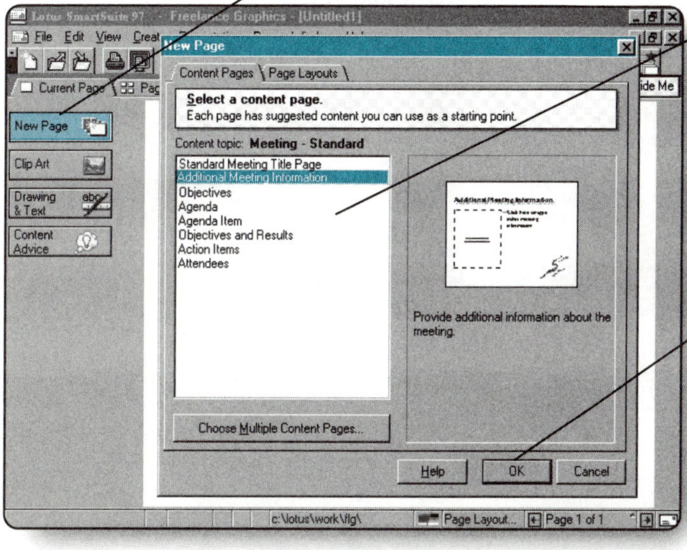

The Additional Meeting Information content topic is automatically selected. This is the next recommended page for your presentation. If you don't want this page, click on another content topic.

2. Click on **OK**. The page will be added to the presentation.

Use the Click here blocks to add text and graphics to the page. When you are ready for the next page, click the New Page button.

GETTING ADDITIONAL INFORMATION ABOUT A CONTENT PAGE

The Content Advice button displays a message box that recommends the use for the current content page. It will give you specific items to include on the page.

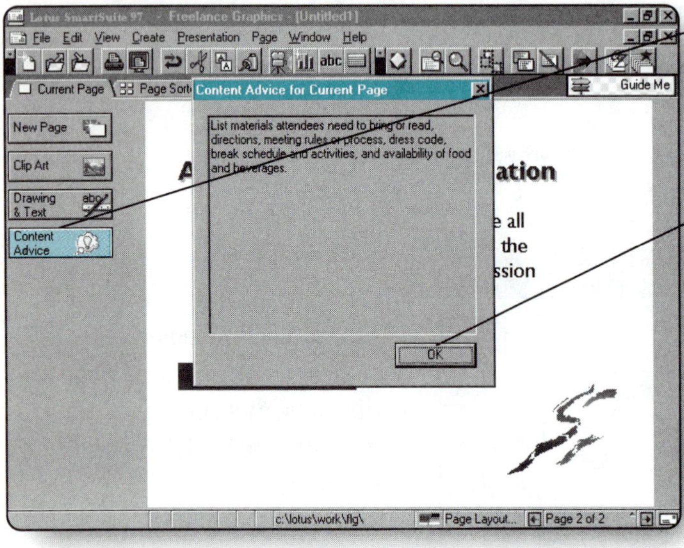

1. Click on the **Content Advice button**. The Content Advice for Current Page message box will appear.

2. Click on **OK**. The message will close.

Glossary

***.** Multiplication operator.

-. Subtraction operator.

/. Division operator.

@Functions Built-in formulas that perform specialized calculations.

+. Addition operator.

<. Less than operator.

<>. Not equal to operator.

=. Initiates all formulas.

>. Greater than operator.

A

Absolute reference. A reference to a cell address that doesn't change based on where a formula is located in a worksheet.

Active cell. The current cell in a worksheet.

Alarm. A reminder of an appointment.

Alignment. The arrangement of text or an object in relation to a document's or cell's margins. Alignment can be left, right, centered, or fully justified.

Appointment. As far as Organizer is concerned, an appointment is anything that requires your time during a specific period.

B

Bar chart. A type of chart that uses bars to represent values.

Bold. When text is bold, its font lines are thicker.

Border. A formatting option that places a line around any or all of the four edges of an object, such as a cell in 1-2-3.

Bullet. A character that precedes an item in a list such as a small circle or a dash.

C

Calendar. The portion of Organizer used to track appointments and meetings.

Cell reference. A cell identification method that uses the cell's row and column intersection.

Cell. The intersection of a row and column in a 1-2-3 worksheet or a Word Pro table.

Chart. Also called a *graph.* A chart is a visual representation of numerical information. Examples of charts are pie charts and bar charts.

Clipboard. The Clipboard is a function of the Windows operating system. It acts as an intermediary area for cut, copy, and paste operations.

Column. A set of cells running vertically down a worksheet or table. Columns are identified by letters such as A, B, C in 1-2-3.

Content topic. Used to create a presentation in Freelance. Content topics facilitate the process of creating a presentation by providing a consistent look for your presentation pages and recommending content.

Cut. Removes the selection from the current document and places it on the Clipboard.

D

Data. Another word for information.

Dialog box. A window that opens during some procedures. This window allows you to choose settings by entering text, selecting items from lists, checking boxes, or clicking on buttons.

Drawers. Containers for folders in SmartCenter.

F

Field. A field contains one part of a record's information.

Find Assistant. Guides you through the process of creating a find and displaying a set of records that meet conditions in the find.

Find. Contains conditions that have been set so that specific records can be found.

Folders: Contained with SmartCenter drawers and used to organize different kinds of work.

Font. The typeface applied to text. The font changes the appearance of the text. Examples of fonts include Courier, Times New Roman, and Arial.

Footer. The area that displays in the bottom margin of a page and typically repeats on each page of the document.

Footnote. Provides references or comments for text in a document.

Form. A view that displays a single record. A form is useful for entering and editing data for a record.

Format. The format of an object controls its appearance. Formatting options include fonts, color, and line style.

Formula. An equation that tells 1-2-3 to perform a calculation.

Found set. The group of records that match a find.

Function. A predefined, named formula.

G

Graph. Also called *Chart.* A graph is a visual representation of numerical data.

H

Header. The area that displays in the top margin of a page and is typically repeated at the top of each page in the document.

Hyperlink. An address to a location, such as a folder on your computer or Web page. When you click on a hyperlink, you jump to the location defined in the hyperlink.

I

Icon. A graphic used to represent the various functions performed when those buttons are clicked with a mouse.

Indent. Indent text is moved away from the right or left margin by a certain amount of space.

Internet SmartIcons. The Internet SmartIcons perform Internet tasks.

Intranet. An internal network patterned after and often connected to the Internet.

Italic. A font style that makes text appear slanted.

J

Justify. An alignment setting that spreads letters on a line or in a cell evenly between the left and right margin or across selected cells.

L

Landscape. A page orientation that prints a document on the horizontal.

Link. A cross-reference or connection to related information in another location such as a page on the Internet.

M

Mail merge. *See* Merge.

Margin. A text-free border that runs around the outside of a document page.

Merge data file. Contains the data to be used to customize your letter in the mail merge process.

Merge. The process of combining variable data in one file with text in another.

N

Named range. 1-2-3 allows you to assign a name to a range of cells so that you can use that name in formulas.

O

Operator. The characters in a formula that define the action to be performed, such as addition (+) or multiplication (*).

Orientation. The way a document prints on a piece of paper.

P

Paste. The act of copying an object such as text or a graphic from the Windows Clipboard to a location in your document. The object is placed on the Clipboard by performing a cut or copy operation.

Pie chart. A round chart type in which each pie wedge represents a value.

Portrait. A page orientation that prints on the vertical. Pages are typically printed using portrait orientation.

Print Preview. A feature that lets you view a document on your screen as it will appear when printed.

R

Range. In 1-2-3, a range is one or more cells.

Record. A collection of information about one subject.

Repeating appointment. An appointment that you tell Organizer to schedule at the same time every day, week, month, and so on.

Right aligned. Text that is lined up with the right side of a tab setting or document margin.

Row. A set of cells running from left to right across a worksheet or table. Rows are identified by numbers such as 1, 27, or 101 in 1-2-3.

Ruler. A special bar in Word Pro that is used to view and set tabs, paragraph indention, and margins.

S

Screen show. If you present your Freelance presentation on a screen, it is called a screen show. The pages of the presentation flow from one to another in a movie-like sequence.

Scroll bar. A control used with a mouse to move up and down or left to right in a document to display various portions of the document on-screen.

Sheet. *See* Worksheet.

Slide. A component of a Freelance Graphics presentation. A slide is equivalent to a page.

SmartIcon. Icons that represent mouse shortcuts for SmartSuite application actions, commands, and scripts.

SmartMaster application. SmartMaster applications allow to start your Approach database with a more fully developed interface.

SmartMaster. When you start a new file in Word Pro, 1-2-3, Approach, or Freelance Graphics, you can use a SmartMaster to provide you with a predefined collection of formatting and style settings on which you can base a new file.

Sort. To arrange data alphanumerically in either ascending (A-Z) or descending (Z-A) order.

Speaker notes. Notes added to a slide presentation concerning comments or points to be made about the associated slide.

Spelling checker. A feature that checks the spelling in your document, making suggestions for corrections as it goes.

Styles. A set of named formatting and appearance properties that you assign to objects.

Symbol. Special characters such as the trademark symbol, the copyright symbol, arrows, smiley faces, and so on that are not found on your keyboard.

T

Table. A collection of rows and columns used to enter text into. Tables are frequently used instead of tabs for the input of columnar text.

Three-dimensional formula. A formula whose elements span multiple sheets.

Transition. A visual effect that occurs when a slide show moves from one slide to another.

U

Uppercase. A capital letter.

V

Value. Another term for a number.

W

Web page. A document that you interact with when you are connected to the World Wide Web.

Web reference folder. A specialized folder that you can use to search the World Wide Web. Using this folder, you can search for a specific topic, or you can use one of the predefined topics already available in this folder.

Workbook. The basic file format of 1-2-3. A workbook is a collection of sheets.

Worksheet. A page in 1-2-3 workbook.

WYSIWYG (What You See Is What You Get). This means that the document on the screen looks like the printed document.

Index

A

B

F

G

H

I

L

M

Q

R

S

T

U

V

W

Send Us YOUR COMMENTS

Dear Reader:

Thank you for buying this book. In order to offer you more quality books on the topics ***you*** would like to see, we need your input. At Prima Publishing, we pride ourselves on timely responsiveness to our readers needs. If you'll complete and return this brief questionnaire, ***we will listen!***

Name: (first) ______ (M.I.) ______ (last) ______

Company: ______ Type of business: ______

Address: ______ City: ______ State: ______ Zip: ______

Phone: ______ Fax: ______ E-mail address: ______

May we contact you for research purposes? ❑ Yes ❑ No

(If you participate in a research project, we will supply you with your choice of a book from Prima CPD)

1 How would you rate this book, overall?

- ❑ Excellent
- ❑ Very Good
- ❑ Good
- ❑ Fair
- ❑ Below Average
- ❑ Poor

2 Why did you buy this book?

- ❑ Price of book
- ❑ Content
- ❑ Author's reputation
- ❑ Prima's reputation
- ❑ CD-ROM/disk included with book
- ❑ Information highlighted on cover
- ❑ Other (Please specify): ______

3 How did you discover this book?

- ❑ Found it on bookstore shelf
- ❑ Saw it in Prima Publishing catalog
- ❑ Recommended by store personnel
- ❑ Recommended by friend or colleague
- ❑ Saw an advertisement in: ______
- ❑ Read book review in: ______
- ❑ Saw it on Web site: ______
- ❑ Other (Please specify): ______

4 Where did you buy this book?

- ❑ Bookstore (name) ______
- ❑ Computer Store (name) ______
- ❑ Electronics Store (name) ______
- ❑ Wholesale Club (name) ______
- ❑ Mail Order (name) ______
- ❑ Direct from Prima Publishing
- ❑ Other (please specify): ______

5 Which computer periodicals do you read regularly? ______

______

______

______

6 Would you like to see your name in print?

May we use your name and quote you in future Prima Publishing books or promotional materials?

❑ Yes ❑ No

7 Comments & Suggestions: ______

______

______

PLEASE
PLACE
STAMP
HERE

PRIMA PUBLISHING
Computer Products Division
3875 Atherton Road
Rocklin, CA 95765

---

8 Where do you use your computer?

Work	❑ 100%	❑ 75%	❑ 50%	❑ 25%
Home	❑ 100%	❑ 75%	❑ 50%	❑ 25%
School	❑ 100%	❑ 75%	❑ 50%	❑ 25%

Other ____________________

9 How do you rate your level of computer skills?

❑ Beginner
❑ Advanced
❑ Intermediate

10 What is your age?

❑ Under 18
❑ 18-24
❑ 25-29
❑ 30-39
❑ 40-49
❑ 50-59
❑ 60-over

11 I would be interested in computer books on these topics

❑ Word Processing
❑ Networking
❑ Desktop Publishing
❑ Database:
❑ Spreadsheets
❑ Web site design

Other ____________________

SAVE A STAMP

Visit our Web Site at: **http://www.primapublishing.com**
and simply fill in one of our online Response Forms

OTHER BOOKS FROM PRIMA PUBLISHING

Computer Products Division

ISBN	Title	Price	Release Date
0-7615-1175-X	Act! 3 Visual Learning Guide	$16.99	Summer '97
0-7615-0680-2	America Online Complete Handbook and Membership Kit	$24.99	Available Now
0-7615-0417-6	CompuServe Complete Handbook and Membership Kit	$24.95	Available Now
0-7615-0692-6	Create Your First Web Page in a Weekend	$29.99	Available Now
0-7615-0743-4	Create FrontPage Web Pages in a Weekend	$29.99	Available Now
0-7615-0428-1	The Essential Excel 97 Book	$27.99	Available Now
0-7615-0733-7	The Essential Netscape Communicator Book	$24.99	Summer '97
0-7615-0969-0	The Essential Office 97 Book	$27.99	Available Now
0-7615-0695-0	The Essential Photoshop Book	$35.00	Available Now
0-7615-1182-2	The Essential PowerPoint 97 Book	$24.99	Available Now
0-7615-1136-9	The Essential Publisher 97 Book	$24.99	Available Now
0-7615-0752-3	The Essential Windows NT 4 Book	$27.99	Available Now
0-7615-0427-3	The Essential Word 97 Book	$27.99	Available Now
0-7615-0425-7	The Essential WordPerfect 8 Book	$24.99	Summer '97
0-7615-1008-7	Excel 97 Visual Learning Guide	$16.99	Available Now
0-7615-1193-8	Lotus 1-2-3 97 Visual Learning Guide	$16.99	Summer '97

ISBN	Title	Price	Release Date
0-7615-0852-X	Netscape Navigator 3 Complete Handbook	$24.99	Available Now
0-7615-1162-8	Office 97 Visual Learning Guide	$16.99	Available Now
0-7615-0759-0	Professional Web Design	$40.00	Available Now
0-7615-0063-4	Researching on the Internet	$29.95	Available Now
0-7615-0686-1	Researching on the World Wide Web	$24.99	Available Now
0-7615-1007-9	Word 97 Visual Learning Guide	$16.99	Available Now
0-7615-1188-1	WordPerfect Suite 8 Visual Learning Guide	$16.99	Summer '97

TO ORDER BOOKS

Please send me the following items:

Quantity	Title	Unit Price	Total
______	______________________	$______	$______
______	______________________	$______	$______
______	______________________	$______	$______
______	______________________	$______	$______
______	______________________	$______	$______

Shipping and Handling depend on Subtotal.

Subtotal	Shipping/Handling
$0.00–$14.99	$3.00
$15.00–29.99	$4.00
$30.00–49.99	$6.00
$50.00–99.99	$10.00
$100.00–199.99	$13.00
$200.00+	call for quote

Foreign and all Priority Request orders:
Call Order Entry department for price quote
at 1-916-632-4400

This chart represents the total retail price of books only (before applicable discounts are taken).

Subtotal	$______
Deduct 10% when ordering 3–5 books	$______
7.25% Sales Tax (CA only)	$______
8.25% Sales Tax (TN only)	$______
5.0% Sales Tax (MD and IN only)	$______
Shipping and Handling*	$______
TOTAL ORDER	$______

By telephone: With Visa or MC, call 1-800-632-8676. Mon.–Fri. 8:30–4:00 PST.

By Internet e-mail: sales@primapub.com

By mail: Just fill out the information below and send with your remittance to:

PRIMA PUBLISHING
P.O. Box 1260BK
Rocklin, CA 95677-1260

http://www.primapublishing.com

Name______________________ Daytime Telephone______________

Address______________________

City______________________ State ______ Zip______________

Visa /MC#______________________ Exp. ______________

Check/Money Order enclosed for $______________ Payable to Prima Publishing

Signature______________________